The YouTube Reader

The YouTube Reader

eds. Pelle Snickars
Patrick Vonderau

Imprint:
National Library of Sweden, P.O. Box 5039, 10241 Stockholm, Sweden

Designed by Ivy Kunze
Copy editor: Steve Wilder
Printed in Lithuania by Logotipas, 2009

ISSN: 1654-6601
ISBN: 978-9-188468-11-6

Table of Contents

Pelle Snickars and Patrick Vonderau

Introduction

On October 9, 2006, an intriguing video was uploaded on YouTube. A little more than a minute and a half long, the clip had a gritty, low-resolution look, marked by jerky camera movements and sloppy framing. Apparently shot near a highly frequented street, the two persons appearing in it had to move into position to address the camera. "Hi YouTube, this is Chad and Steve. We're the co-founders of the site, and we just wanted to say thank you. Today we have some exciting news. We've been acquired by Google."[1]

The short clip, entitled "A Message from Chad and Steve," formed part of YouTube's official statement declaring that the deal with Google finally had been settled, making the two young Web entrepreneurs Chad Hurley and Steve Chen billionaires. In one of the most talked-about Web acquisitions to date, Google paid $1.65 billion in stock for YouTube, a company that had begun as a venture-funded technology startup only a year earlier. As a matter of fact, the Hurley and Chen clip bears some resemblance to the very first video uploaded on YouTube in April 2005—"Me at the Zoo," featuring the third co-founder Jawed Karim—and not only in its seemingly coincidental recording of what would later prove to be a turning point in YouTube's history. In retrospect, Jawed even seems to have had some foreboding about the heavyweight corporation allegedly sucking the YouTube community dry. Speaking in front of two elephants, and partly covering them up, he tersely commented on their "really, really, really long trunks." "And that's pretty much all there is to say," he noted before the camera was turned off.[2]

Posting the clip "A Message from Chad and Steve" in many ways became a performative Web 2.0 act. Since then, more than three million users have watched the video, and almost ten thousand people have left comments. The apparently coincidental recording demonstrated how video could be used as an unobtrusive channel of communication to address the community that had built up YouTube as a proprietary platform in the first place. But it also contributed to the hype around the platform and its many ways of creating business opportunities. For a while YouTube grew at an inconceivable rate of 75 percent a week, and by the summer of 2006 the site had 13 million unique visitors every day that watched more than a hundred million video clips.[3] YouTube quickly outperformed rivals, including previous competitor Google Video, in its ability to attract and distribute content. At the same time, YouTube's management continued to promote the site via Web videos, press releases, interviews and the company blog as being co-created, as a more or less "empty" platform to be filled by the YouTube community with originally produced content of various kinds. In addressing amateurs, advertisers and professional producers alike, YouTube in fact made the term "platform" what it has become: a sales pitch that skips over tensions in services to be sold, as well as a claim that downplays the way YouTube as a cultural intermediary has fundamentally shaped public discourse over the past few years.[4] "A platform enables. It helps others build value," as Jeff Jarvis has stated.[5] It was hardly surprising that Steve Chen made a similar claim in the Google acquisition video: "Thanks to all and everyone of you guys who has been contributing to YouTube and the community. We wouldn't be anywhere close to where we are without the help of this community."

The promotion of YouTube as a community-driven platform certainly strikes one as odd at second glance, not least because of the Google subsidiary's current attempts to increase profits by prompting its users to deliver "better content."[6] After all, monetization is said to be the "no. 1 priority in 2009."[7] Certainly, partnership programs and individual deals with media companies have already allowed YouTube to place ads alongside videos for some time, splitting revenue with its partners. Because of the unpredictable nature of amateur content, however, an estimated less than five percent of the clips on YouTube still carry advertisements, hence the need to find ways "for people to engage in new ways with video," as the YouTube Fact Sheet states.

Turning from an interpersonal video-sharing service into "the world's leading video community on the Internet,"[8] YouTube has transformed not only the very notion of "platform," but also the character of its "community," and will continue to do so in a neat competition for industrializing "usage." As of this writing, Hulu.com has only a sliver of YouTube's traffic volume, but was predicted to bring in the same amount of advertisement revenue, precisely by virtue of providing "better," that is professionally produced, content for advertisers.[9] Hulu and YouTube in fact are "increasingly going after each other's turf, including jockeying for video programming that could generate the most advertising dollars."[10]

But as the fastest-growing site in the history of the Web, YouTube also remains the default site for video and the prototype for all similar sites to come. In March 2009, for example, the site had more than 90 million visitors—in terms of traffic ten times as many users as its closest competitor.[11] And it is YouTube, and none of its rivals, that has been making the news constantly, not least because of the democratizing potential the platform still holds for nations worldwide. Speaking of Hurley and Chen's subtly patronizing address to the community, one therefore should not forget how often YouTube has challenged all forms of outspoken paternalism, especially in the political domain. In our globalized, corporate-controlled mediascape, it is also liberating to see a madly laughing toddler attracting more viewers than *Harry Potter* and *Pirates of the Caribbean* together.[12] YouTube has become the very epitome of digital culture not only by promising endless opportunities for viral marketing or format development, but also by allowing "you" to post a video which might incidentally change the course of history. Establishing a clip culture that outpaces cinema and television, the brand-named video-distribution platform holds the broadest repository of moving-image culture to date.

The peculiarity of YouTube, then, lies in the way the platform has been negotiating and navigating between community and commerce. If YouTube is anything, it is both industry and user driven. Consider music videos, which dominate categories like "most popular" and "most viewed," while still being marginal to the site's overall content in terms of clips uploaded. Then again, the long tail of content generated by amateurs seems almost infinite, and that sort of material often appears to be the "most discussed." "A Message from Chad and Steve" testifies to this very same dialectic. The video promoted YouTube as being community driven, although the company's founders had, prior to the Google buyout, been in talks with media corporations with the intention of increasing their services' value. Arguably, YouTube's management knew that the platform's "community value" derived from the exponentially growing number of videos generated by amateurs, but it also knew that professionally produced entertainment would increase traffic and solidify the binary rule that on the Web, money tends to follow users.

Consequently, it would miss the point to criticize YouTube for employing doublespeak, since the community and the market pair perfectly in its own operational self-conception. Yet it would also be misleading to exempt YouTube's community ideals from criticism. Renowned digital anthropologists like Mike Wesch have analyzed YouTube for its creative and grassroots potentials, but according to the so-called "90-9-1 rule," that 90 percent of online audiences never interact, nine percent interact only occasionally, and one percent do most interacting, ordinary YouTube users hardly see themselves as part of a larger community. The typical "YouTuber" just surfs the site occasionally, watching videos and enjoying it.[13] And most YouTube "stars" never make it outside their own small Web community.[14]

In Lawrence Lessig's view, translating such delimited community spaces into global commercial ventures is a general feature of the Internet's new "hybrid economies."[15] The dialectics of commerce and community, copyrighted material and user-generated content, and the way video is being distributed all relate to economic features of so-called emergent social-network markets.[16] On the one hand, YouTube.com presents and views itself as a platform and not a regular media distributor, especially when copyright issues are involved. At the core of the Viacom lawsuit, for instance, lay an understanding of YouTube as a distributor that does not comply with copyright law, while YouTube stated that it is nothing but a platform, pointing to the rules and regulations for the YouTube community. Videos in fact are constantly taken down—in the first three months of 2009 the site YouTomb recorded nearly three times as many takedowns than in 2008.[17] On the other hand, Google clearly is a vertically integrated corporation operating in distributed ways. Bits of Google are all over the Web, and both the migration of videos to new and old media and the embedding of clips into various sites, blogs and social-networking platforms is undoubtedly crucial for understanding the success of YouTube. Like Google, YouTube has distributed itself constantly. Whereas YouTube.com rapidly established itself as the default site for online video, with average users and dedicated partners using the platform to perform their interests, the public also encountered YouTube videos everywhere on and off the Net. YouTube thus was and is both a node and a network.

YouTube Metaphors

The notion of "platform" is only one of several metaphors widely used to stress YouTube's social, economic and technological importance. When plunging into YouTube discourse, one indeed begins to wonder about the apparent resemblances YouTube bears to a number of established cultural institutions. YouTube is often spoken about as if it were a library, an archive, a laboratory or a medium like television, with the respective metaphor inviting hypothetical exploration of what YouTube's possible, probable and preferred futures might be. This clearly mirrors earlier periods in media history, with early cinema being compared to theater and vaudeville, or television to radio, cinema and theater, in an emergent, that is unforeseeable and uncontrolled process of a new media phenomenon fitting into an existing culture. From a computer-science viewpoint, YouTube is nothing but a database, but in any given cultural context, moving onto the platform and watching a video obviously entails more than that. It is therefore debatable whether "we watch databases" only, as Geert Lovink has stated,[18] even if the pragmatics of viewing moving images have changed in YouTubean times. After all, the functionalities of databases might change too. For instance, up to the 1960s, US cinemas regularly screened movies in a *séance continue*, that is in a continuous showing without a specific starting time, with viewers randomly walking in from the street at the beginning, middle or very end of any given picture. It took a Hitchcock and *Psycho* to enforce more disciplined viewing habits.[19] There is thus no firm ground for making any substantial claims about what YouTube is, despite the institutional pressure to do so.

Suffice it to say that YouTube is not either-or. When changing the metaphor, one faces different horizons of use and enters an open-ended process of experiments and enterprises. Take the archive as a metaphor to designate what "you" might want to do with YouTube. Countless blogs link to YouTube the archival database in order to substantiate an idea or to pass something newly found to others. "Why pay an institution to archive media from around the world when users seem to be doing it for themselves? Open source archiving I suppose it is," as one blogger proclaimed in a post entitled "The Great YouTube Archive."[20] Corporate media has been using the site as an archival outlet for its material, and deals are signed constantly to include older TV series and feature films. In April 2009, YouTube announced a partnership with Sony to expand its library of movies and TV shows. Various treasures from the archive will be promoted at youtube.com/movies and youtube.com/shows, and YouTube has also confirmed rumors about a new advertising model "which allows program makers to place commercials into the ad breaks of television shows being watched online."[21]

Taking advantage of YouTube as an archival platform also entails some sort of media transfer. Within the traditional media archival sector, there are those who mourn the apparent loss of media specificity in the 21st century[22] and others who portray the current archival convergence in a brighter light. For some, the archival mode of online media has become evident with YouTube's collection of perhaps 200 million videos, making the Internet the world's largest vault for moving-image material. Others stress the lack of quality and preservational strategies. Some, like Kristin Thompson, have argued that the celestial multiplex is a myth, and that there will "never come a time when everything is available [online]." And besides, most film "archives are more concerned about getting the money to conserve or restore aging, unique prints than about making them widely available."[23]

Whether or not one likes the distinctiveness of media dissolving into a pulsing stream of bits and bytes, traditional media archives are facing the fact that sites like YouTube and Flickr have become default media-archive interfaces. Every initiative a film archive might launch on the Web will be measured against YouTube's ease of access. The Library of Congress, for example, has already had its own YouTube channel for some years. During spring 2009, the Library announced that it would start uploading millions of clips to YouTube. It already offers most of that moving-image material on its own website, and the expansion to YouTube—and to Apple's iTunes for sound recordings—is part of an effort to make more than 15 million digital items even more widely accessible. The initiative parallels that of Flickr Commons, the "broad strategy" being "to 'fish where the fish are,' " using highly frequented sites that may give content added value.[24] Yet since YouTube actually lacks a centralized "curator of display," as Robert Gehl has noted, large media companies may "step into the curatorial role and decide how each object in YouTube's archives will be presented to users."[25] Mining the vaults of an established media archive remains subject to corporate interests as well.

Interacting with YouTube is reminiscent of using archives or libraries, but is also similar to zapping through television channels, the difference being that tags link content to similar content in YouTube's media flow. If a clip turns out to be uninteresting, there are still millions of other trails to be followed, either by clicking on a linked video or by performing a new search. Since YouTube also contains vast quantities of material that has been broadcast, the platform has often been likened to television. As a medium emerging after the digital turn, YouTube appears to imitate television's specific practices. Arguably, among old 20th century media, television has been the most successful in attuning itself to the new digital environment. Radio is ubiquitous on the Web, but within the visual culture that will allegedly dominate the Internet in the future, digital video has been vital.

"Have you ever wanted to just sit on your couch and watch YouTube on your TV?" YouTube announced on its blog in January 2009. Thanks to a joint project with Apple, www.youtube.com/tv users are now offered "a dynamic, lean-back, 10-foot television viewing experience through a streamlined interface."[26] In an effort to emulate a traditional TV experience using a gaming console, users/viewers are now able to watch YouTube videos on any TV screen. In other words, just as commercial and public broadcasters have been trying to establish themselves on the Web over the last decade—the BBC and its iPlayer probably being the prime example—YouTube's management has also experimented with including the website in an old media environment. Given that new media remediate old media, there is also economic value in "downgrading" to a previous platform in order to stay competitive. In this sense, it seems that YouTube indeed wants to be like your TV. While news media is involved in the introduction of new e-reading devices, YouTube is currently partnering with TV set-top box manufacturers to bring the platform into the living room. At present, few TV sets contain a Web browser. For a site like YouTube, this might prove to be critical, not least since audience ratings in various countries repeatedly show that traditional television remains far more popular than online video. At the same time, two of every three Web surfers who watched video did so on YouTube, so the site has a clear advantage over broadcasting and cable-television networks that are trying to further establish themselves on the Web.

As consumption patterns change, digital screens will arguably become the default interfaces for media access. Providers of Web services, video-recording devices and mobile technology have in any case put great effort into marketing new patterns of media consumption to the younger generation. "YouthTubers" are targeted in both online and offline advertising, and any use of YouTube videos is regularly translated into metadata. Metaphorically speaking, the site thus appears to work not only like an archive or a medium, but like a laboratory registering user behavior also. From this perspective, YouTube appears to be not so much a platform for any individual presenting her- or himself to a community (as in a social-networking system like MySpace or Facebook), but rather as a way of strategically combining video content with numerical data. It can hardly have escaped anyone that YouTube presents videos in conjunction with viewer statistics, not detailed user profiles. As a matter of fact, "users" are by definition reducible to quantified traces of actual usage. With views, clicks, comments and ratings counted, user behavior becomes a byproduct of all the informational transactions taking place on the site, and raw data constantly gets fed back into the YouTube machinery. In this view, YouTube seems to serve as a technology of normalization, as a symptom for a wider social strategy Jürgen Link has called "flexible normalism."[27]

An incident illustrating the laboratory relevance of user-generated data occurred in July 2008, when Google was ordered by federal judge Louis L. Stanton to turn over to Viacom its records of users who had watched Viacom content on YouTube. The range and depth of data available was staggering, and many YouTubers expressed fear that viewing habits might potentially become public. YouTube's management reacted via the company blog, expressing its concern about "the community's privacy." "Of course, we have to follow legal process," the blog stated. "But since IP addresses and usernames aren't necessary to determine general viewing practices, our lawyers have asked their lawyers to let us remove that information before we hand over the data they're seeking."

Interestingly, YouTube not only acknowledged storing user data, the company also felt it was necessary to explain why this information was kept in the first place. "Why do we keep this information? [...] It helps us personalize the YouTube experience, getting you closer to the videos you most want to watch." Viewed from the laboratory perspective, and in light of the fact that Google had been collecting information for years to make its search algorithm more efficient for advertisers, this hardly seems plausible. Exploring YouTube as a laboratory, one might instead point to the uses made of user data, and to the normalizing effect of viewer statistics constantly being presented to viewers. "Broadcast yourself" and be metered—YouTube's display of numbers suggests that communities might relocate to the artificial realities of statistical data fields.

About this Book

When examining YouTube by way of metaphors such as the archive, the medium or the laboratory, one is immediately confronted with a number of inherent (and not easily solvable) conflicts and problems vying for more detailed answers. How does, for instance, the practice of open access relate to traditional archival standards, legal constraints, "old" media distribution and the entrepreneurial interests of the Google subsidiary? To what extent do clip aesthetics challenge traditional notions of, for example, textuality, episodic and serial narrative, documentary forms and also the very basic requirements of teaching and research? And what about the relationships between free-for-download video and mobile devices, between mashup software and patented hardware? How does the promise of empowering the "broadcasters of tomorrow" (YouTube) correspond to the realities of careers in broadcasting and film, to fan participation and management strategies? And finally: if YouTube is to be regarded as the world's largest archive, how do the texts and practices associated with its use work for and against cultural memory?

As the metaphorical explorations above have shown, studying YouTube presupposes a broader theoretical framework and a critical distance vis-à-vis YouTube discourse itself. Consequently, a reader like this one would provide researchers, teachers and students with a programmatic selection of foundational texts, permitting them to mount an intervention. But is there anything to be read about YouTube? So far, media studies have all but ignored the public interest in the YouTube phenomenon. In a marked contrast to anthropologists, educators, IT specialists and scholars of marketing and the creative industries, who have pioneered research on YouTube over the last years, film and media studies have avoided eye contact by lowering their view on random cases of post-television and amateur practice, or by making rather general claims about the nature of "Web 2.0." With the notable exception of Geert Lovink's *Video Vortex Reader*, and the individual research of scholars such as Patricia G. Lange, José van Dijk, Michel Bauwens, Jean Burgess and Joshua Green,[29] no comprehensive work has been done on YouTube as yet. By directly confronting YouTube as an industry, an archive and a cultural form, this book addresses issues hitherto dealt with at the margins of our disciplinary field only. Deviating from what the term "reader" usually implies, our volume consists exclusively of original and actual contributions, thus offering its present readers an update on the frantically changing YouTube sphere, and, for the future present, an historical view of how things looked back then in 2009. As with any selection of readings in a particular academic discipline, this book is also programmatic in its comparison (but not necessarily reconciliation) of conflicting views on the phenomenon at hand. By doing so, it aims at prompting further studies on the cultural and capitalist, social and material, amateur and professional logic of YouTube.

The contributions in this volume analyze various relationships between technology, community and commerce characterizing YouTube practice. The idea was to invite renowned scholars from both the US and Europe to send us short, essayistic articles, employing their own research interests and approaches as a vantage point. As a consequence, the book has been roughly organized into six sections. "Mediality" offers conceptual arguments about YouTube, relating the new phenomenon to prevalent concerns in media theory and history. "Usage" follows those on YouTube in the twisted forms of practice. "Form" examines what was called aesthetics in the days of old media, while "Storage" deals with the archival implications the YouTube platform holds. "Industry" is concerned with the economic relevance of YouTube for society. Finally, "Curatorship" came as an invitation to Giovanna Fossati, curator at the Netherlands Film Museum in Amsterdam, to organize a YouTube exhibition on the Internet. Since it wouldn't make much sense to write a book about YouTube without keeping its moving-image culture alive, we kindly invite all our readers to visit the exhibition at www.youtubereader.com.

In many ways, this book has been developed as a partisan project. In the same way as many clips on YouTube, it was deliberately planned outside the routines of academic presses. "Packaged" like a global Hollywood deal, but produced in less than a year, it involved a Berlin beer garden (research and development) and a major public institution relating to Swedish cultural life (deep pockets), inspired contributions and design (creative talent), and also saw the participation of a Lithuanian printing facility and an industrious UK publisher (distribution). We are grateful to all those who made this book possible, not least our wives and kids who, despite their enthusiasm for YouTube, might sometimes have felt displaced by the uncanny production schedule. We dedicate this book to all our girls—Malin and Lea, Asta, Luka and Ieva.

Endnotes

1 The video "A Message from Chad and Steve" was uploaded on 9 October 2006. See www.youtube.com/watch?v=QCVxQ_3Ejkg [last checked 15 May 2009].

2 See www.youtube.com/watch?v=jNQXAC9IVRw [last checked 15 May 2009].

3 Pete Cashmore, "YouTube is World's Fastest Growing Website," *Mashable*, 22 July 2006 – http://mashable.com/2006/07/22/youtube-is-worlds-fastest-growing-website/ [last checked 15 May 2009].

4 Tarleton Gillespie, "The Politics of 'Platforms'," paper presented at the MiT6 Conference, Cambridge, April 2009, submitted to *New Media & Society* for publication, December 2008. Thanks to Tarleton for pointing the importance of the platform metaphor out to us.

5 Jeff Jarvis, *What Would Google Do?* (New York: HarperCollins, 2009), p. 32.

6 Chad Hurley, quoted by Brian Stelter, "YouTube Videos Pull In Real Money," *The New York Times*, 11 December 2008.

7 See for example Tom Steinert-Threlkeld's blog post "Time for change at YouTube: Monetization 'No. 1 Priority in 2009' " at http://blogs.zdnet.com/BTL/?p=11142 [last checked 15 May 2009].

8 YouTube Fact Sheet at www.youtube.com/t/fact_sheet [last checked 15 May 2009].

9 Frederic Lardinois, "Online Advertising: Hulu Catching Up With YouTube?" *ReadWriteWeb,* 17 November 2008 – www.readwriteweb.com/archives/online_advertising_hulu_youtube.php [last checked 15 May 2009].

10 Jessica E. Vascellaro, Elizabeth Holmes & Sarah McBride, "Video Sites Duke It Out for Content. YouTube, Hulu Race to Sign Deals for Movies, Shows That Draw Advertising," *Wall Street Journal,* 17 April 2009.

11 See the heading "YouTube" at http://topics.nytimes.com/top/news/business/companies/youtube/ [last checked 15 May 2009].

12 As of April 2009, the video "Hahaha," at www.youtube.com/watch?v=5P6UU6m3cqk, had been watched approximately 83 million times. This figure clearly exceeds the attendance numbers for *Harry Potter and the Order of Phoenix* (36,869,485 tickets sold) and *Pirates of the Caribbean: The Curse of the Black Pearl* (29,382,065 tickets sold) in Europe as they were reported on the European Audiovisual Observatory's Lumière database, www.obs.coe.int [last checked 15 May 2009].

13 José van Dijk, "Users Like You? Theorizing Agency in User-generated Content," *Media, Culture & Society* no. 1, 2009, pp. 41–58.

14 In her ongoing research on YouTube celebrities, Alice E. Warwick consequently imported Terri Senft's term "microcelebrity" in order to describe characteristics of YouTube fame. See tiara.org for an overview of Alice's projects.

15 Lawrence Lessig, *Remix. Making Art and Commerce Thrive in the Hybrid Economy* (New York: Penguin Press, 2008).

16 Jason Potts, "Social Network Markets: A New Definition of the Creative Industries," *Journal of Cultural Economy* no. 32, 2008, pp. 167–185.

17 YouTomb.mit.edu is a website—operated by MIT Students for Free Culture—built to track videos removed by YouTube. YouTomb records the title, description, screen shots, etcetera of videos taken down, thus documenting what happened to them.

18 Geert Lovink, "The Art of Watching Databases: Introduction to the *Video Vortex Reader,*" in The Video Vortex Reader: Responses to YouTube (Amsterdam: Institute of Network Cultures, 2008), p. 9.

19 See for example Linda Williams, "Learning to Scream," in *Horror. The Film Reader,* ed., Mark Jancovich (London: Routledge, 1995), pp. 14–17.

20 See www.vi-r-us.com/the-great-youtube-archive/ [last checked 15 May 2009].

21 BBC, "YouTube to stream Hollywood films," 17 April 2009 – http://news.bbc.co.uk/2/hi/entertainment/8003881.stm [last checked 15 May 2009].

22 The film-archive organization FIAT is one example. For a discussion, see Paolo Cherchi Usai et. al, eds., *Film Curatorship. Archives, Museums, and the Digital Marketplace* (Vienna: Synema Publikationen, 2008).

23 Kristin Thompson, "The Celestial Multiplex," blog post, 27 March 2007 – www.davidbordwell.net/blog/?p=595 [last checked 15 May 2009].

24 "Library of Congress Makes More Assets and Information Available Through New-Media Initiatives. YouTube and iTunes Launches Will Follow Groundbreaking Flickr Pact to Bring More Treasures to the Public," press release, 25 March 2009 – www.loc.gov/today/pr/2009/09-055.html [last checked 15 May 2009]. For a discussion, see Grant Gross, "Library of Congress embraces YouTube, iTunes" *NetWorkWorld*," 27 March 2009 – www.networkworld.com/news/2009/032709-library-of-congress-embraces-youtube.html [last checked 15 May 2009].

25 For a discussion, see Robert Gehl, "YouTube as archive," *International Journal of Cultural Studies* no. 1, 2009, pp. 43–60.

26 "Coming Up Next... YouTube on Your TV," blog post, 15 January 2009 – www.youtube.com/blog?month=1&year=2009 [last checked 15 May 2009].

27 See for example Jürgen Link, Mirko M. Hall, "On the Contribution of Normalism to Modernity and Postmodernity," *Cultural Critique* no. 57, pp. 33–46.

28 "The Law and Your Privacy," blog post, 4 July 2008 – www.youtube.com/blog?month=7&year=2008 [last checked 15 May 2009].

29 See the General Bibliography at the end of this volume.

Mediality

William Uricchio

The Future of a Medium Once Known as Television

This article began with an ambition to be a textual mashup, a writerly counterpart to YouTube's aggregation of voices, videos, modes of address, and recycled and repurposed texts. YouTube, after all, stands as an important site of cultural aggregation, whether we consider mashups in the narrow sense (individual videos that make use of disparately sourced sounds and images remixed into a new composite) or the site as a totality, where variously sourced videos, commentaries, tools, tracking devices and logics of hierarchization all combine into a dynamic and seamless whole. A formally recursive article seemed an appropriate way to address and reflect on its textual and metatextual dimensions. And indeed, YouTube contains ample textual material from which to draw, including the Company Blog, Privacy Notice, Terms of Service and of course the rich data generated by YouTube's users in the form of comments. And yet, the more I recombined shards of text, hoping to find a clever way to mashup and repurpose YouTube's words to my analytic ends, the more aware I was of an overarching issue, one that was largely implicit in YouTube's formal organization, that undercut my argument.

YouTube is a creature of the moment. Only four years old as of this writing, it has enjoyed considerable attention, much of it celebratory, emblematizing for some the notion of Web 2.0 and the participatory turn. Its embrace of mashup culture, its openness to textual destabilization and radical recontextualization, and its fundamental reliance on user-generated content all certainly strike a resonant chord. But even more striking is its obsessive pursuit of alchemic chrysopoeia, a binary transmutation of numbers into gold. Google's massive investment in YouTube and its hope of transforming user-generated content into money seems as fraught as the pursuits of the alchemists of old. The tensions between these two approaches, one deriving from a reconfigured notion of text, property and agency and the other rooted in the old logics of ownership and profit, have for the moment resulted in something that is neither fish nor fowl, at least given the simple conceptual categories that we continue to work with. While YouTube's economic model is indeed predicated on participation, it fails the "2.0 test" since users may only upload—and not download—its videos. Add to this YouTube's EULA, the intrusive logics of its filtering software, its processes for takedowns, its capitalization of user behaviors, and its status as an emblem of Web 2.0 seems more wishful thinking than anything else.

Within four short years, YouTube has found a large participating public, attracted an astounding level of financial investment, and been the subject of mythmaking and hyperbolic celebration. And yet its definitional contours are both contradictory and fast changing. This is attributable in part to its environmental setting. The digital turn has accelerated the challenges to the ontological distinctions among established media, offering both new definitional conceits and new media forms with wide-ranging implications for traditional media. It has informed our understanding of media history, shaping our historical agenda and the questions we put to the past. The digital turn has enhanced our sense of rupture with that past, magnifying our impression of inhabiting a privileged historical moment and our status as witnesses of the new. In the case of YouTube, it has enabled us to look upon a steadily morphing set of technological, social and business practices—some radically innovative and others hopelessly compromised—finding there an emblem of the new.

And so the recursive tale of a radical mashup slowly smothered under too many qualifiers, while the story of YouTube as an experimental practice loomed ever larger. In this article I would like to reflect on YouTube as a set of practices—both corporate and popular—that interrogate our ideas of media and particularly the process of media change. Specifically, I would like to explore YouTube's implications as an experimental laboratory that may have its greatest relevance for the future of the medium currently known as television, and a medium—together with film—that is experiencing its own crisis.

The Case for Television

"We Won a Peabody! (No Joke)" read the headline on YouTube's April 1, 2009 blog.[1] But even if the date had been different, YouTube might have been genuinely surprised to be included within the domain of the Peabody Award, which has until now focused on terrestrial and cable television and radio. In making its selection, Peabody's award committee noted that YouTube's Speaker's Corner, a "video-sharing Web site [...] where Internet users can upload, view and share clips, is an ever-expanding archive-cum-bulletin board that both embodies and promotes democracy."[2] The worthy cause of promoting democracy, however, neither masks Peabody's struggles with television as a shifting set of technologies and practices (and therefore its own shifting institutional relevance) any more than it does YouTube's relevance for the television medium's future. Peabody may be expanding their remit, moving beyond television and radio in much the same way that Nielsen expanded their audience-metrics service to include the Web, or they may finally be accepting some of YouTube's own rhetorical positioning. Consider the discursive resonance of the "Tube" in YouTube, the trademarked claim to "broadcast yourself," the structuring of content into "channels" and a core business that turns on the distribution of videos.

YouTube is not alone in thinking about television in terms flexible enough to include the Internet. The major American terrestrial and cable-television networks all have their own online operations, in many cases positioned under the umbrella of their transmedia parent companies. CBS Interactive, Fox Interactive Media, Turner (CNN, TNT, TBS, Cartoon Network) and Viacom Digital (MTV, BET, Paramount), plus industry-backed portals such as Hulu (NBC Universal and News Corp.), offer a spectrum of services from providing scheduling information, to channeling fan activities, to providing various levels of access to television shows, films and music. Other portals such as Joost provide an international assortment of television, film and music, and sites such as Mysoju take a more nation- and genre-specific approach, offering access to unlicensed Japanese, Korean and Taiwanese soaps. Although the interfaces and services provided by these various sites differ widely, two things stand out. First, the online presence of television content has been normalized and is growing steadily; second, virtually all mainstream American television programs have been spoken for by their parent companies, and at a moment of aggressive intellectual property protection, this leaves very little for outside players such as YouTube and Joost.

And yet, according to comScore Video Metrix, more than two of every three Internet users who watched video used YouTube. During the month of January 2009, 100.9 million viewers watched 6.3 billion videos on YouTube.com (62.6 videos per viewer) for a 43 percent market share. Fox Interactive Media ranked a distant second in terms of videos viewed, with 552 million videos (3.7 percent), followed by Viacom Digital with 288 million (1.9 percent) for the month respectively.[3] Viewed more globally, nearly 77 percent of the total US Internet audience watched online video for an average of six hours in January 2009. And although average online video duration is getting longer—from 3.2 minutes in December to 3.5 minutes in January—Megavideo, a portal whose motto is "Your content, your money. We just charge a little fee for bandwidth and coffee," has an average video duration of 24.9 minutes, which is growing quickly. As of January 2009, Megavideo entered the ranks of the top 10 most-viewed sites with 15 percent growth over the previous month.

These data from the start of 2009 can be interpreted in several ways. On one hand, they point to a mismatch between viewer activity and the sites of traditional television content that is easy to dismiss as a sign that television audiences are doing their viewing the old-fashioned way—on television (or the new-fashioned way, through their DVRs), not on YouTube. And indeed, coincident with these Internet metrics, Nielson announced "TV Viewing Hits All-time High" (Nielsen's numbers include broadcast, cable, DVR time shifts, mobile and Internet). The average American now watches more than 151 hours of television per month.[4] On the other hand, we can also interpret this and other data as showing steady growth of the Internet market, steady growth of the numbers of videos viewed online, and steady growth in the length of those videos. In this regard, it is also interesting to note that cellphone video use has been growing, particularly in the 12- to 17-year-old market, where usage is nearly double that of any other age cohort (and where short form, "casual" viewing is the norm). YouTube's enormous advantage over the nearest television company Internet site may speak to an interest in elements that the competition is not providing—elements, I will argue, that are central to the future of the television medium.

If the networks are largely monopolizing their own television content, then what kind of television is on YouTube? YouTube of course has licensing deals with CBS, BBC, Universal Music Group, Sony Music Group, Warner Music Group and many others, but its content skews towards music from its American partners, as can be seen from the corporate subdivisions that do the actual partnering. CBS, for example, allows access to promotional television material (interviews, previews, program headers), ephemeral material (logos, advertisements), and some historical shows, news and local affiliate coverage. YouTube has responded to the constraints in the entertainment sector by launching what it calls "short-form content": clips of popular prime-time shows like *Lost*, *Desperate Housewives* and *Grey's Anatomy*, as well as behind-the-scenes footage, celebrity interviews, online-only specials. Considering these constraints, YouTube would not be a destination for the viewer seeking standard television fare or formats. But for the trans-brand or trans-network fan, the synoptic viewer and the growing cohort of young cellphone viewers, it is fast providing an array of alternatives from new textual forms to annotation systems, to community-building strategies, all consistent with its user-driven profile.

Ontological Ambivalence

A look at YouTube's channels recalls Borges' description in his short essay "The Analytical Language of John Wilkins" about the Chinese emperor's encyclopedia.[5] Functions, topics and media forms are jumbled together with "comedy, education, entertainment, film and animation, gaming, music, people and blogs, and sports," vying with one another for attention. Thanks to the just mentioned deals struck with media conglomerates, it serves as a significant cross-media outlet, and a site where content familiar from other media forms is repackaged. YouTube offers a rich set of provocations into larger questions regarding continuity and change in media and specifically interrogates the intermedial mix available in networked computing environments. One could argue that this interrogation process is inadvertent, largely reflecting the uncertainties of a new medium as it struggles to find its own expressive capacities, whether we conceptually frame this uncertainty as remediation or the backward-looking, precedent-bound "horseless carriage" syndrome.

But the confusion evident in today's transmedia industries over where, precisely, a medium begins and ends, seems not unlike that in many media-studies programs. The film-production pipeline, for example, moves between digital and analog, between computer-based and photochemically based, with final release still generally occurring on celluloid, but more often than not with revenue streaming in through DVDs and television exhibition rather than theatrical box office. How then should we think of the film medium—through its technological genealogy? Its participation in legitimizing rituals such as film festivals? The site of its greatest exposure, even if that is television or Internet or the iPhone? Through some circumscribed set of physical parameters or signifying practices—celluloid or a particular length, format or genre? Its discursive claims? Or the conceptual framework that it is afforded by its various publics? The choice is determining, and we know of course that different constituencies may make different selections with different results.

It is this ambiguity, or better, this definitional ambivalence that provides such fertile ground for YouTube. At a moment when the full implications of the digital turn have yet to transform our ways of thinking about moving-image content and our categories of analysis, when the relations between producers and consumers characteristic of the industrial era are slowly being eroded, and when convergent media industries are themselves spreading content across as many platforms as possible, YouTube offers a site of aggregation that exacerbates—and capitalizes upon—that uncertainty.

Along with many of the portals backed by transmedia companies, YouTube continues to rely upon traditional media distinctions as a navigational aid to its users and as a means of appealing to existing communities of interest, while in fact all but flattening the media distinctions in practice. Let's consider the case of film. A best-case scenario appears in the form of the "YouTube Screening Room," where the case for *film* is legitimized by site design—a screen framed by curtains, for instance—holding to a theatrical-style release schedule (two-week runs complete with shorts) and foregrounding where possible the cinematic legacy of its films with evidence that they have played at international film festivals. The "YouTube Screening Room" declares itself to be the "world's largest theater" and part of a new generation of filmmaking and distribution. Other groups, such as aficionados of Super 8mm films (the Straight 8 team), organize festivals of their favorite films. As they explain it, the "granddaddy of all low-budget formats was popular in the 1960s and 70s for making home movies and is still used in amateur and professional films because of its unique and beautiful characteristics, as well as its extreme affordability."[6] Despite this historical framing, Super 8's affinity to YouTube's project is underscored when grouped together with "analog video, digital video, HD video, Photoshop, computer animation, multimedia formats [...] the list is long enough to keep any enterprising auteur busy for a lifetime." Nostalgia and aesthetics combine to legitimize YouTube as part of a much longer amateur trajectory. From the echoes of cinema-style theatrical release, to format-specific appeals to the amateur movement, to festivals, the development teams at YouTube work through familiar categories while in fact offering far more than simply the film artifact itself—or in many cases, without even offering the artifact itself! Consider for example YouTube's promotional blurb for The Sundance Film Festival:

> The Sundance Film Festival recently launched a YouTube channel that allows all of you movie enthusiasts to get a glimpse of what took place during the 25th anniversary year of the influential festival. For those of you interested in the filmmakers behind the films, there's the "Meet the Artists" playlist, featuring interviews with filmmakers from around the world and clips of the films that brought them to Sundance. If you're looking for coverage on the ground—from premieres to parties and more—you can check out the Live@Sundance segments. And to hear what some of the film industry's leading thinkers had to say about the state of the business today...[7]

Although in most cases we are only given access to "clips of the films that brought them to Sundance," the trappings of the festival constitute the main event and are covered in their full glory. Just as in the example of its "short-form" approach to mainstream television, YouTube has seized the periphery, providing access to the scene even more consistently than to the films (or television shows) themselves.

The game channels operate in similar fashion. Games, by definition interactive, are watchable rather than playable in the YouTube context. The various channels provide walkthroughs, commentaries, trailers, previews, sneak peeks, cheats, highlights and event coverage across the various gaming platforms. These elements are the topic of much commentary, effectively reinforcing the community-building strategies that seem to lurk behind the event coverage "peripheral" to television shows and films. The music channels by contrast are able to deliver both music and videos, providing something like MTV-on-demand with a few bonuses. The curatorial act is embodied in algorithmic correlations of user interest patterns as well as in community recommendations, both serving to address taste formations in quite a different way than mere alignment with a VJ's profile. And the act of commodification, of transforming listening and viewing pleasure into a purchase, is prompted by on-screen reminders to "click here" if we want to pay for and own the music. Unlike television and games, where the core artifacts are largely absent and peripheral activities are provided in abundance, in the case of music, playback is permitted and a broader array of affordances addresses both the scene (interviews, reviews, behind-the-scenes peeks and so on) as well as the industry's interests in the pinpoint targeting of potential customers and sales.

But Is It Television?

At a moment when, in the wake of Janet Jackson's 2004 "wardrobe malfunction," live television broadcasts have been ended in the United States, when most viewers perceive television as something coming through a cable rather than the ether, and when increasing numbers of people are using DVRs and DVDs to pursue their own viewing habits, the medium's definition is in a state of contestation. Much as was the case with the discussion of film, definition turns on the parameters that we privilege as essential and distinguishing. Television, more than film—which has enjoyed a relatively stable century—has been through a series of definitional crises over its long history. Indeed, how we even date the medium and where we chose to locate its start reveals much about how we have chosen to define it.[8] But there is no escaping the slippery slope on which we tread today.

One of the oldest elements in television's definition was its potential for liveness. It defined television conceptually in the 19th century, distinguished it from film for much of the 20th, and although it has largely been supplanted by video in order to enhance the medium's economic efficiencies, liveness (even in the era of the seven-second delay) nevertheless remains a much touted capacity. Even slightly delayed, televised sports events, breaking news and special events attest to the medium's conceptual distinction from film, which was, for the duration of its photochemical history, emphatically not live.

YouTube, like film, misses the capacity for televisual liveness. This is not to say that it doesn't at times seek to simulate it. For example, as I write this, YouTube has been auditioning interested musicians for the YouTube Symphony Orchestra by having them submit video introductions and performances of a new piece written by Chinese composer Tan Dun. The videos were posted and voted upon over the period of a week, and the winners invited to travel to New York to play at Carnegie Hall under the direction of Michael Tilson Thomas, complete with a mashup video of the submissions as a backdrop. The selection process played out with a few days of "real" time, and the recursive mashup did its best to keep the time frame tight. While a useful experiment in using YouTube to create a real-life event, televisual liveness was almost never an issue.[9] In fact, if one searches on YouTube for live television, one is prompted with subcategories such as "bloopers, mistakes, accidents, gone wrong, and fights"—indications that liveness is understood by YouTube's minions as an excess of signification that cannot be cleaned up, edited away or reshot.

Flow constitutes another key concept in television, first articulated by Raymond Williams in 1974 and reiterated ever since by the medium's theorists.[10] As with liveness, it can certainly be circumvented through the use of videotape, DVRs and video-on-demand, but by and large it remains present as a potential. Television adheres to the same notions of flow that characterized the earliest days of broadcasting: a temporally sequenced stream of program units constantly issues forth from the programmer, and audiences may dip in and out as they choose. YouTube, like film in the time-based domain—but also like libraries—lacks flow in this sense, offering instead a set of equivalently accessible alternatives at any given moment. Underlying this distinction is a key conceptual difference between television as heterochronic and YouTube as heterotopic. The term heterochronia traditionally refers to certain medical pathologies characterized by irregular or intermittent times (the pulse), or erratic developmental sequence (organ growth). This notion of displacements in time or the vitiating of sequence was picked up by Foucault as something of a temporal extension of his notion of *heterotopia*. The latter term denotes for Foucault sites with a multiplicity of meanings, defined by uncertainty, paradox, incongruity and ambivalence; sites best exemplified by long-term accumulation projects such as libraries and museums; sites for which he suggested a temporal corollary: *heterochronia.*[11] An evocative term as much for its weak definitional status as for its promise, heterochronia is a term I would like to define between its diagnostic roots (the vitiating of sequence, displacements in time) and Foucault's institutional setting. Like museums and libraries, television is a space of accumulated artifacts that are endlessly recombinatory.[12] Unlike them, however, and this is a crucial distinction from Foucault's meaning, television's recombinatory process plays out as flow, as a structured linear sequence over *time*. YouTube's place in this is somewhat ambivalent.

Like the difference between collage and montage, a similar principle (the compositing of differently sourced artifacts) works to a very different effect along a durational axis. Collage, in which visual elements from various provenances and with different histories are uprooted and combined in a new composition, is certainly a radical recombinatory act. The resulting whole is greater than the sum of its parts, and many collages exploit the dissonance of source, materiality and referenced temporality to great effect. But montage, the *durational* assemblage of divergent materials, relies upon sequence and ever-changing context for its effect. While it is certainly the case that users of YouTube experience their texts over time, often viewing multiple videos and therefore generating sequential context for individual videos, there is a significant shift in agency (producer-controlled flow as distinct from user-generated flow), and a shift from flow as default to flow as a condition that requires active selection. In this, YouTube looks very much like the DVR-mediated television experience.

Another recurrent element in the definition of television regards its ability to aggregate dispersed publics. Although this vision can be traced back to the medium's postwar institutionalization and reflects its inheritance from broadcast radio, it has roots in the late 19th century. In its earliest manifestations, television was imagined as a point-to-point, person-to-person medium akin to the telephone, but bolstered by a number of public functions such as news and entertainment.[13] In a certain sense, we have come full circle: from the broadcast era where large publics were the norm, through a period of deregulation at which point cable, satellite and VCR helped audiences to sliver into ever smaller niches. While not yet individualized (our webcams have shouldered that burden), we inhabit a moment where the steady erosion of the mass viewing public has created anxiety in political terms regarding the future of television as a collective mode of address.

YouTube and the emergent practices referred to as IPTV, Internet-protocol television, might be seen as the final straw, fragmenting the cable era's slivers into atomic particles and pushing our expectations and definitional conceits regarding television to the breaking point. YouTube, however, has launched a number of initiatives that seek to restore notions of collectivity. The comments feature enables users to respond to videos and interact with one another by exchanging reactions and links. Videos can be easily shared and recommended to friends, constructing objects of common interest. Interest groups and sub-channels draw together communities of participation and shared enthusiasms. YouTube's collaborative annotation system enables users to invite people to create speech bubbles, notes and spotlights on their videos, providing a site of interaction and collaboration. And as in the case of the YouTube Symphony Orchestra and the New York-based collective Improve Everywhere's videos such as "No Pants Subway Ride" and "Frozen Grand Central Station," YouTube even serves as a catalyst for gatherings and community activity in the physical world.

1 "No Pants Subway Ride" - January 2009

Liveness, flow and aggregated publics, while long-term concerns and even definitional components of television, have also modulated in response to social needs and available technologies. Over the past 130 years, television has been imagined and deployed as a set of practices that make use of a shifting technological base, including the telephone, radio, film and, most recently, the networked computer. Each of these *dispositifs* brought certain affordances to light, and each inflected these concepts in distinctive ways. YouTube emblematizes a set of inflections and modulations that address the role of the most recent transformation of television's *dispositif*—the shift to networked computer technologies. Its notion of liveness is one of simulation and "on demand"; its embrace of flow is selective and user-generated; and its sense of community and connection is networked and drawn together through recommendation, annotation and prompts.

YouTube as Next-generation Television?

From what we have already seen, YouTube's focus on the "periphery" of what has long been held as the center of attention—the television show or the film—positions it to play a key role in helping to construct meaning, communities of interest, and the frameworks of evaluation so important to the cultural experience. Especially as our creative economies shift to more user-generated content, destabilizing the long monopoly of media industries as the exclusive producers of texts and authorized conduits of interpretation, YouTube seems to have adroitly taken on the broader space where social meaning and cultural value take form. This choice may well have been inadvertent, since the film and television industries have been reluctant to let go of their products, leaving YouTube hollow where it might otherwise have been filled with traditional texts. The established industries have instead chosen to develop their own online portals. But those portals resemble a robust DVR more than anything else, with archives of program episodes surrounded by strategic appropriations from YouTube. The latter, by contrast, has emerged as a dynamic experimental forum built around shared information—some of it promotional, some of it synoptic texts, some of it fan commentaries, parodies and mashups.

To be clear, I do not want to suggest that the text, and particularly the professionally produced media text, is dead. The content industry will certainly continue to survive and change, just as questions about culture and ownership will continue to be asked. Nor do I want to stuff YouTube with all of its radical potential into an old media category. The point is rather that the industrial era of television, with us since the early 1950s, is fast changing under pressure from the disaggregation of content from media platforms characteristic of today's cross-media industries, and as a response to bottom-up appropriations of the affordances of networked computers and various mobile devices. This doesn't pose a threat to the concept of "seeing at a distance" that has long characterized television so much as to the institutional logics that have held it in a vice grip over the past few decades. If anything, the television industry has stuffed itself into an unnecessarily small conceptual space, and YouTube is providing a set of radical alternatives. YouTube has successfully (again, if inadvertently) sidestepped the industrial-era artifacts of the 30- and 60-minute program formats; it offers relatively transparent usage metrics; it provides a mix of voices including corporate, governmental, NGO and public; and it seems particularly persistent about targeting community engagements. In each case, YouTube is making use of network affordances, unlike its industrial counterparts who are using the network as little more than a data dump and alternate channel.

Initiatives such as YouTube Senator/Representative of the Week, offering officials an opportunity to weigh in on "important issues facing Congress right now," are designed to elicit debate and participation. So too "one of the coolest, unintended outcomes of the site's existence," YouTube EDU provides "campus tours, news about cutting-edge research, and lectures by professors and world-renowned thought leaders [...] from some of the world's most prestigious universities, including IIT/IISc, MIT, Stanford, UC Berkeley, UCLA, and Yale."[14] New alliances and natural affiliations are given voice with user channels such as Survival Of The Fastest, an initiative from the London Business School, The Daily Telegraph and Google, designed to showcase "insights and inspirational ideas from some of the best business brains in the UK." The *Today in History* series invites exploration of the archive, contested notions of public memory, and debates over the meaning of the past. In these sectors and many more like them, YouTube can be seen experimenting with existing social processes (education, politics, the construction of history), institutions and visions, offering new outlets, enhancing its own centrality as an all-purpose portal, and learning as it does so.

Epilogue: "YouTube on Your TV"

Regarding the future of television, let's step back and take a long view of the medium: one stretching back to the interactive, point-to-point television envisioned in the late 19th century (like the telephone); one reconfigured as a ubiquitous domestic appliance (like radio); one functioning as an event-driven, visually rich spectacle (like cinema); and today, one taking advantage of the affordances of networked computers. Framed within this perspective, YouTube's limits as an exemplar of mashup culture and Web 2.0 may be precisely its strengths as a transitional model to next generation television.

On January 15, 2009, YouTube's company blog announced a beta version of YouTube for Television: "a dynamic, lean-back, 10-foot television viewing experience through a streamlined interface that enables you to discover, watch and share YouTube videos on any TV screen with just a few quick clicks of your remote control. [...] Optional auto-play capability enables users to view related videos sequentially, emulating a traditional television experience. The TV website is available internationally across 22 geographies and in over 12 languages." The beta version relies on Sony PS3 and Nintendo Wii game consoles, but YouTube has thrown down the gauntlet, and announced that it plans to expand its platform interfaces. Emulation as a strategy may yet come full circle.

Endnotes

1 Unless otherwise noted, all quotes are from the YouTube Company Blog for the date noted.

2 See the Peabody Award website – www.peabody.uga.edu/news/event.php?id=59 [last checked 15 April 2009].

3 *MarketingVOX*, "YouTube Tops 100M Viewers, Fuels 15% Online Video Jump," 6 March 2009 – www.marketingvox.com.

4 For a discussion, see Nielsen-Online, *Television, Internet and Mobile Usage in the US: A2/M2 Three Screen Report* (3rd quarter, 2008); as well as Alana Semuels, "Television Viewing at All-Time High," *Los Angeles Times*, 4 February 2009.

5 Jorge Luis Borges, *The Analytical Language of John Wilkins* (Austin: University of Texas Press, 1993). Borges refers to a Chinese emperor's encyclopedia in which animals are divided into: (a) those that belong to the emperor, (b) embalmed ones, (c) those that are trained, (d) sucking pigs, (e) mermaids, (f) fabulous ones, (g) stray dogs, (h) included in the present classification, (i) those that tremble as if they were mad, (j) innumerable ones, (k) those drawn with a very fine camelhair brush, (l) others, (m) those that have just broken a flower vase, (n) those that resemble flies from a distance. See also the preface to Michel Foucault, *The Order of Things, An Archaeology of the Human Sciences* (New York: Vintage Books, 1970).

6 See www.youtube.com/blog, 20 February 2009.

7 Ibid.

8 William Uricchio, "Contextualizing the broadcast era: nation, commerce and constraint," in *Annals of the American Academy of Political and Social Science* (forthcoming in 2009).

9 An important exception in this regard is the YouTube Live Channel – youtube.com/live. Despite the discursive claim, the channel only simulated liveness in order to promote YouTube (and YouTube celebrities). All clips originated with "YouTube's first ever live streamed event—November 22, 2008."

10 Raymond Williams, *Television: Technology and Cultural Form* (London: Fontana, 1974); see also William Uricchio, "Television's next generation: technology / interface culture / flow," in *Television After TV: Essays on a Medium in Transition*, eds. Lynn Spigel & Jan Olsson (Durham, NC: Duke University Press, 2004), pp. 232–261.

11 See Foucault 1970, and Foucault's article "Different Spaces," in Michel Foucault, *Essential Works of Foucault 1954–1984* (London: Penguin, 1998), pp. 175–189.

12 "Museums and libraries are heterotopias in which time never ceases to pile up and perch on its own summit, whereas in the seventeenth century, and up to the end of the seventeenth century still, museums were the expression of an individual choice. By contrast, the idea of accumulating every-thing, the idea of constituting a sort of general archive, the desire to contain all times, all ages, all forms, all tastes in one place, the idea of constituting a place of all times that is itself outside time and protected from its erosion, the project of thus organizing a kind of perpetual and indefinite accumulation of time in a place that will not move—well, in fact, all of this belongs to our modernity." Foucault 1998, p. 182.

13 See for example Albert Robida, *La vingtième Siècle* (1883) and his vision of the telephonoscope as a means of transmitting public news and entertainment.

14 See www.youtube.com/blog, 27 March 2009.

Bernard Stiegler

The Carnival of the New Screen: From Hegemony to Isonomy

For Hidetaka Ishida

In 1985, I proposed to the Collège international de philosophie a seminar that would also have been an audiovisual program, and which would have the title "Can One Philosophize about Television?" The "audiovisual" was then at the very beginning of a period of intense transformations. Besides the appearance of cable broadcasting (which made way for a "cable plan" in France), the possibility to see—and to see again—audiovisual objects was still quite new. It was primarily the consequences of this, at the time, new possibility that I wanted to study, or to which I wanted to devote a seminar organized as a television program—whose principle would have been repetition. I ascribed a philosophical virtue to the power of repetition.[1]

Beside cable broadcasting, the 1980s were of course also marked by the video recorder becoming common in the homes of industrial countries. Put to commercial use for the first time in 1954 by the Radio Corporation of America, this device would remain a professional tool until the end of the 1970s. It then became one of the main products exported by Japan, making for example JVC famous and wealthy, to the extent that the French government tried to hinder its entrance onto the market. Until the appearance of the home video, it was more or less impossible for a cineaste to see a work that was not chosen by a film distributor or a television programmer. Thus, the immense popular success of the video recorder relied on choice at an *individual* level.

Twenty years later, the appearance of YouTube, Dailymotion and video servers has ended the hegemony of the "hertzian broadcast" and represents an irreversible break with the model of the cultural industries whose domination marked the 20th century. It is again primarily the organization of broadcasting that transforms video servers today—but on a collective level. "Broadcast yourself": such is the slogan of YouTube. Video servers and databases have replaced the television transmitter, and there is also an industrial revolution taking place in the domain of what one should no longer call the cultural *industries*, but rather the cultural *technologies*.

Broadcast yourself, but also, first look for yourself *(push media)*, and of course again, produce yourself: what this *yourself*, this *self*, this *auto* presupposes is the existence of navigation functions. They are indispensable for accessing the servers and typical for the digital cultural technologies. They create a rupture in the producer/consumer model of the cultural industries, and also develop and structure what home video makes accessible in a partial and embryonic way.

In fact, home video allows the public to access for the first time the functions of freezing the image, of slow motion and of rewinding the film—even if not true navigation—and this is what gave me the hope that this tool would begin a transformation that would continue and get stronger with the development of digital audiovisual technology, whose arrival was announced (there was already talk of the DVD) and which would, I believed, deeply modify relations to the *audiovisual temporal flux*,[2] allowing one to imagine the appearance of a more reflective and less consumerist gaze. This seemed all the more reasonable as JVC and other Japanese companies—especially Sony[3]—flooded the market with cameras connected to portable video recorders, and worked actively on the development of video cameras, later to become DV cameras. Their functions were later to be found on mobile phones and on PDAs, making the recording of animated pictures common and generalizing the practices of self-production, including those of post-production.

What was called analog "light video" in France in the 1980s—an expression connoting the image of a "light brigade/cavalry" at the service of a freedom fight, just as what happened with the 16mm camera during the Nouvelle Vague that "liberated" cinema from a strangling industrial dependence—has since then become "ultralight digital video," in which most portable computers are equipped with webcams. It thus constitutes a terminal of input inscription just like the alphanumeric keyboard and the microphone that permits audio-visual exchanges on Skype, where one can see how "the audiovisual" changes its function and becomes truly useful and functional—at the same time as the *new form of "heavy video"* is generalized and constitutes networks of video surveillance.

Anyway, when I proposed the seminar on how to philosophize about television—which was never realized because it was refused by the professionals of the profession—I believed that the possibility of duplicating temporal audiovisual objects, together with the access to the tools of production, could produce new forms of knowledge, new philosophical questions and a completely novel relationship to animated images. Most of all, I believed that this new relationship to images could in the long run create profound changes in psychosocial individuation. Perhaps these were even comparable to what happened when writing enabled the duplication of the spoken, when its comparative consideration and discretization of each individual one, and its *auto-production* (which is also *isoproduction* as we will see) through a *literate collectivity* becoming *precisely in this way* a *polis* and forming a *critical time and space*, thus a true *politeia*, an *individuation of citizens* that could be qualified according to their ability to judge, in other words to criticize—the Greek work for "to judge" is *krinein*.

My thesis was that alphabetic writing of the spoken, *la parole*, and of discourses and the audiovisual recordings of perceptions and modes of life were part of the same process, which I have since, by using and broadening a concept devised by Sylvain Arnoux, called grammatization. Grammatization is what allows the discretization and reproduction of the flux by which both individuals and groups individuate themselves (that is, become what they are) through *expression*, primarily through their utterances, but also through their gestures, perceptions and transmissions of signs as well as their actions—which are also, secondarily, an output of signs and information.

Grammatization allows for the spatialization of the temporal fluxes that produce an existence through the writing of the spoken as well as the mechanical reproduction of workers' gestures, then through the recording of the sensually audiovisual (the flux of sonorous and luminous frequencies), and through it, representations of the real past (their memory) and representations of possible futures (their imagination). Since the 19th century, the grammatization processes have operated increasingly as a functional relation to networks: objects of intuition are first distributed through wired networks like the telephone for the voice—and then, starting in the early 20th century, through hertzian networks for radio and then television. Then this happened by way of multidirectional, hyper-reticulated numerical networks connecting mobile objects in Wi-Fi and soon after that in WiMAX for all grammatized objects, including gestures crystallized in the automated machines of teleaction. In the meantime, Radio Frequency Identification systems and the technologies of recording and geolocalized traceability as well are also forming grammatized networks that short-circuit the subjects whose objects they are.[4]

However, the process of grammatization in fact began in the Neolithic Age with the earliest forms of notation, first numeration systems, then ideograms. As this makes the engramming of linguistic flux possible, it forms the basis of the psychic and collective individuation processes that constitute citizenship. The space and time of the *cité*, its geography and its history, or its geopolitics, are critical *avant la lettre*, in other words *through* the letter. As Al Gore has underscored this diacriticity, which has spread all over the world—particularly in America thanks to the printing press—and which has opened a new era of the diachronic as well as of the synchronic. It is all based on knowledge which is, in essence, distributed through reading and writing. Henri-Irénée Marrou has for example shown how this partition was the condition for both Greek and Roman citizenship. I myself have also repeatedly emphasized this techno-logical dimension of noetic and political judgment, especially in *La Désorientation*, and more recently in a commentary I have proposed in relation to Kant's *Was ist Aufklärung?*[5] Gore also underlines—as I myself have done[6]—that audiovisual media have short-circuited and left in ruins both this diacriticity and the knowledge it is based on—thus fundamentally threatening democracy, in America as in the entire world.[7]

Discretization in Ancient Greece

Since I did not succeed in convincing the professionals of my profession of the great intentions of my televisual seminar project, I made a script in which television in transition constituted the very platform of a new psychic and collective process individuation. This was in fact one of the arguments of the exhibition "Mémoires du futur" that I presented at

Centre Pompidou in 1987. The general thesis of this exhibition was that the 21st century would see the development of numerical networks as well as new storage platforms and new *dispositifs* for reading and writing, a kind of *dispositif* of computer-assisted reading and writing—what Alain Giffard now calls "industrial reading"[8]—where a sound file and an image file are "read" simultaneously. The thesis argued further that this made wide dissemination of a new kind of knowledge through the development of instrumental practices based on integrated digital machines necessary. This knowledge and these practices were directed by the studios, which were the main objects of the exhibition, in which the members of the audience could educate themselves—and in this way they and their productions were put at the center of the "show."[9]

However, between the 1980s and today a complete elimination of reflection and an ever-increasing populism of the audiovisual media subordinated to market research seem to have characterized the cultural industries' evolution. The VCR has for example not developed any alternative to what constitutes the law of the cultural industry: the production of the "time of available brains"[10] as the psychological condition organizing the consumption of industrial production. Secondarily, as a psychopower exploiting for itself the psychotechnologies from the final stages of grammatization, the cultural industries create a cultural and political consumerism that destroys all forms of culture and knowledge as well as the *politeia* as such, and not only democracy—without even mentioning the general toxicity resulting from consumerism in itself.

If it is true that the condition for the constitution of individuation as a *diacritic* is alphabetic writing—which analyzes, synthesizes and mnemonically reproduces the spoken, just as the audiovisual analyzes, synthesizes and techno-logically reproduces perceptions and sensual fantasies[11]—there are also primary practices of non-reflexive, disindividuating writing: in its first stages of development, writing doesn't produce any reflexivity. It has at this time essentially an instrumental and controlling accounting function and is reserved for a class of writers who monopolize the knowledge of it—the professionals of the profession at the time were ancestors to the Mandarins, as an inevitable consequence, considering the complexity of writing in ideograms.

With technical evolution leading to the alphabetic grammatization of the spoken, the regime of psychic and collective individuation that makes the appearance of the law as such possible installs itself. This is the precondition for the political forms of the *cité* as well as for all forms of literalized and literary knowledge, which transforms poetry and makes tragedy emerge, and which constitutes together with geometry the context for the appearance of pre-Socratic thought, leading to historiographic narrative and to philosophy in its proper sense, to the analysis of parts of discourses and to what was later called logic, and finally to the form of the intellect as we know it today and which Aristotle describes as the noetic soul—an intellectual structure that has been exported all over the world with literalization. And by the way, the globalization of these intellectual techniques was to a large extent secured by the Jesuits from the 17th century and onwards.

At least in certain ways, it could be said that alphabetic writing, which opened up the possibility of the *politeai*, of positive law and of *isonomy*, was during the age of hieroglyphic writing what the new digital media are to the production and reproduction of analog audiovisual temporal objects. Collaborative techniques and auto-broadcasting seem to set up the conditions for a sort of *technocultural isonomy*, where hegemonic subjective relations imposed by the cultural industries seem reversed and which make an auto-production based on isoproduction possible. Hieroglyphic writing, which was fully independent of language in Egypt, began its phono-logical development in Mesopotamia with the advent of cuneiform, but it did not then constitute a process of critical collective and psychic individuation: it remained the hieratic-administrative medium of an imperial power. Alphabetic writing with consonants, which appeared with the Phoenicians, is itself the foundation and the vector of an essentially commercial practice.

Within Greek society the transformation of the capture of language's flux through alphabetic writing was born. This created a general reflexivity, inducing a crisis and a criticality of all modes of life, but also the opening of a critical space and time by means of the discretization of language, forming in turn a political space and time and opening the book of history in its proper sense—ideograms and cuneiform writings characterize the *proto*-historical age, an object of archaeology—and tracing the first maps of conquering travelers. However, the diacritical situation that is the foundation of the *politeia* reached a crisis, where the *cité* entered into a conflict with itself because of what had been achieved during the three first centuries of this critique. The passage from a warlike struggle between individuals to a logical, linguistic noetic opposition between parties on the *agora* resulted in citizens rather than combatants. But this transformation also lead to a crisis of the written and its credit, since sophisticated minds appropriated it as a force that can control minds.

As is well known, the Sophists were accused of exploiting psychopower—the power over young souls, constituted by writing—for manipulating the minds of young Athenians. In a way, philosophy then accuses the Sophists of exploiting the "time of available brains" that can be harnessed and converted into a material good thanks to writing (the Sophist appears primarily as a merchant of illusions in Plato).[12] Sophistico-literal psychopower is artisanal: its foundation is a *psychotechnique*, which means that the reader is also a writer. In the industrial analog psychopower based on *psychotechnologies*, the functions of broadcasting and reception are separated just like those of production and consumption, and the constitution of networks allows for massification, the exploitation and the commercialization of the time of consciousness, thereby becoming the time of the available brains *without* consciousness. The analysis of the Sophist period in Greek history, which is also the origin of philosophy—itself born in its combat against the misuse of writing—is key to the understanding of what is happening in the current discretization of analog media. For if there is a possible analogy between the inception of alphabetic writing as a discretization of the flux of utterances and that of digital media as the discretization of audiovisual temporal objects, it is to the extent that the audiovisual object, just like alphabetic writing, is a *pharmakon*.

Writing is a poison in the hands of the Sophists, as Socrates declares in *Phaedrus*. However, this poison is also a cure. Reading this famous dialogue, which Jacques Derrida suggested will show that the *anamnesis*—which for Plato constitutes the beginning of the noetic act par excellence, through which the dialog, as dialectic time and space, is *by this very fact* diacritic—is always *already inscribed* in *hypomnesic* time and space. In short, the writing that records the dialog is the means by which it is grammatized and discretized. Consequently, the *anamnesis* should essentially be apprehended as a therapeutically and curative practice of the *hypomnesis*—such is *for me* the meaning of what Derrida calls grammatology, and also deconstruction, which is always the deconstruction of metaphysics as an illusion of thought that believes it can purify itself of any *pharmakon*-like scapegoat. In fact, this is exactly what has happened with consumerism, and exactly what should change a *politics* of cultural and cognitive technologies that are neither more nor less "pharmacological" than writing, and that shape the technologies of the mind (and of its autonomy) as well as the technologies of stupidity (of the heteronomy that hinders thinking). That which shapes a *psychopower* should become a privileged object; i.e. where video servers concretize the discretization of images, they inscribe an activity of perception analytically and reflexively in memory and in imagination.

So the techno-logical being that can be affected by grammatization—which is to be precise exactly a techno-logization of all signifying fluxes through which this being makes signs, and thus individuates itself through symbolization—is intrinsically and ineluctably pharmacological. It follows that what is true for writing is true for all mnemonic productions stemming from grammatization. Put differently, every epoch of grammatization—of which YouTube is one of the later cases, as it is contemporary with nanotechnologies and synthetic biology—constitutes a major turn in the cultural hegemony and the *poisonous* heteronomy imposed by the consumerist industrialization of culture. Thus, a pharmacological analysis is required to elaborate a therapeutic prescription—a system of care, i.e. a social and economic organization deriving from a political decision. But to the contrary, as anticipated by Antonio Gramsci, the *cultural hegemony of consumerism* consists of *imposing heteronomy*, while making believe that political decisions are no longer possible—"there is no alternative"—because politics has been absorbed by the market and the economy. This happens precisely through psychopower subordinating the time of available brains to the pure law of merchandise. But Gramsci's concept is not sufficient for imagining either grammatization or its pharmacological dimension, or the therapeutics of which a new politics should consist.

YouTube is, then, the entrepreneurial instantiation of a mutation in grammatization that calls for a political battle. The issue is not about fighting for or against YouTube, but for a therapy and a politics, and against a poisoning at an age where techno-economical systems such as YouTube and Dailymotion are made possible by a level of grammatization that makes a new *pharmakon* scapegoat appear—a digital audiovisual pharmakon that links to the analog audiovisual pharmakon which has manifestly become toxic—which constitutes the base of consumerist society and which disgusts young generations more and more, and which will perhaps crumble like its system partner, the automobile industry, as Adorno claimed in the 1940s. But the new pharmakon cannot become either a cure or a poison if it doesn't constitute a diacritic space and time based on the digital discretization of images. Like any pharmakon, it can put this characteristic at the service of a new age that is extremely poisonous. The therapeutic question is then to know how the discretization can be curative—i.e. constituting an isonomy supporting autonomy—and which the political, cultural and industrial conditions of such a care are.

Digital Discretization of Analog Images

To understand how the process of grammatization modifies the process of psychic and collective individuation characterizing and founding civilizations according to concrete technical conditions, one should study the different stages of this process of literalization and literarization of society, that is, the foundation of the development of the West in all its aspects, and how it leads to a planetary and de-Westernized industrialization—something which I can of course only sketch out here. Alphabetic grammatization makes the historio-graphic narrative the principle of collective individuation[13] at the same time as it develops a judiciary isonomy on the writing of the law that constitutes a noetic autonomy, which led to the constitution of proper citizenship with the Greeks. It led to monotheism with the Hebrews, then, with the printing press, the constitution of a new form of religious individuation, the Reformation, the condition for the forming of capitalism according to Max Weber, then the Republic of Letters and Enlightenment, i.e. the French Revolution, and finally, the generalization of mandatory public education, inaugurating the literalization and liberalization of everyone in industrial and democratic society.

These facts must be studied to understand what the advent of video servers that self-broadcasting combined with auto-production and auto-indexing make possible. Partly because these four elements, typical of what arrives with YouTube and Dailymotion, depend on the digitization of the audiovisual, which is a recent stage in the process of grammatization, and partly because the audiovisual in general recognizes different stages of grammatization just like there are layers and strata in the history of writing. This inscription in an industrial economy is evidently not the case for writing, which on the contrary opens the space for calm living (*otium*), the privilege of citizens as far as they escape the limitations of an economy of living in ancient Greece and Rome, who may then fully cultivate the economy of their existence, i.e. their libidinal, and for this reason sublimated, economy. It is only with consumerism that this sort of pastime, like the cultural industry, becomes an essential function of the economy of living.

The Industrial Revolution and the development of the bourgeoisie's power put an end to the division between the *otium* and the *negotium*. The cultural industries can be of use for economic development in this context, and with them, sensibility and intuition just like science can become a techno-science, and with it, understanding and reason can be of use for economic warfare. This is how the consumerist cultural hegemony was formed—up until its contemporary crisis. The grammatization beyond writing that took place in the 19th century allowed for this economic functioning of noetic activities, and the pharmacological questions here present themselves in a configuration that reaches its limits at the moment when the consumerist industrial model *as a whole* enters into crisis.

However, the audiovisual apparatus, which appeared in the 19th century, spread widely with the hertzian networks in the 20th century—there were a billion television sets in 1997—by imposing on the entire world a globalized kind of relation that in some ways is comparable to the ones characterizing the hieratic societies controlled by the Egyptian and Mesopotamian scribes, the digital networks do indeed transform this organization. Such is the context of YouTube—and of Google, which means that one can no longer distinguish between the destiny of digitized writing or the digitized image—or that, evidently, of digitized sound—and reciprocally: digitization depends on metadata, which is captions of images and sounds as well as of texts themselves.

The metadata remains the fundamental issue: it is through it that the discretization is concretized for the "practitioners" of video servers. The cultural and economic hegemony imposed with the audiovisual media—something which Adorno described as the industry of cultural goods, and which is the key to the consumerist society serving primarily to control the behavior of individuals through marketing—began a transformation process throughout the 1980s, less through the appearance of light video and the VCR than through research conducted on signal treatment in the telecommunications sector in order to define algorithms and norms for the compression of images. This research, which lead to the different standards of the MPEG norm[14] as well as the MP3 standard, on which basis P2P systems are developed, wasn't concretized in the public sphere until the end of the 1990s, and even more at the beginning of the 21st century, with the arrival of animated images on mobile networks at the same time as the generalization of the production of metadata and navigation functions that make it all possible.

However, the real ruptures take place through technologies of digital analysis of analog images—and not through the synthesis of images created digitally, as many researchers of the 1980s believed. Digital analysis of images attracts a process of discretization, and introduces—in a most discreet fashion and for a long time not considered[15]—a diacritic function that doesn't exist in analog technology. Not only is this state of fact not often considered, it is even less valorized—not for reasons of technological limitations, but because the economic and political worlds still haven't understood the stakes. An analog recording of course also demands a discretization: it defines a grain (or a gram) that discretizes and quantifies the luminous or sonorous signal. But in the analog, this discretization is only functional at the level of the apparatus. It is masked and "transparent to the user," as computer scientists say: the listener or spectator only deals with the continuity of the signal, which thus constitutes precisely an analogon of the sensual. The apparatus simultaneously dispenses with the necessity of acquiring any knowledge, as well as of accomplishing any action. This delegation of knowledge to the machine is what makes a process of proletarization of consumers possible—the discretization is here so discreet that it is transferred to the machine entirely and escapes the receiver completely. This is why analog media permit a perfect realization of the opposition between producer and consumer—which is the reign of the *scribes of the audiovisual*, typical for the 20th century.

We live in the 21st century, though, a century of digital technologies. Contrary to the analog stage of grammatization, these allow discrete elements to be produced in full functionality for the users—particularly because they become elements of navigation, something that happens when recording practices are generalized, but also because they are elements of montage and thus of operational discretization and expertise selection. In digital networks, the spectator is active on a motor level: he must learn how to make functions work and is no longer only in the position of the consumer. In addition, the economy of the Internet clearly rests on the activity of the totality of its users—they constitute, as a whole and as a process of psychosocial individuation, the production system of the network.

The New Screen

Back in the mid-1980s, when I planned the seminar "Can One Philosophize about Television?," I still had not clearly and correctly integrated the question of discretization—even though I already knew that repetition, as iterability, presupposes such discretization (as Derrida has shown). In fact, I only understood these stakes when I began working on the script for the exhibition "Mémoires du futur," which eventually lead me to the question of the given conditions of navigation in one of the exhibition's CD-ROMs.[16] Here, navigation, and the functions linked to it—the indexing and what began to be called metadata from 1994 (which then mainly consisted of markers formalized by descriptive languages like SGML)—still primarily concerned text.

The compression of the image is, however, going to play a multifaceted role in the sense that Gilbert Simondon speaks of a process of technical concretization when he addresses the process of functional integration. Alongside the work of the MPEG group, it was in this way that compression of the image and, more generally, the analysis of data led to semantic Web projects initiated by Tim Berners-Lee—i.e. the development of an algorithm for automated discretization of spatial (through decomposition of discretized objects in the space of an image), temporal (whose most elementary function is the recognition of ruptures between planes) and spatiotemporal continuities (for instance as camera movements), and the automated comparison of such isolated, discrete elements, allowing for signatures of images and searches in a body of diverse occurrences of the same type of iconic or sound information (an object, a voice, a face).[17] In addition, the compression of digital images, together with the appearance of ADSL technology (installed in France from 1999), then with Wi-Fi, will make full broadcasting on the mobile net possible—which means the concretization of the YouTube slogan "Broadcast Yourself"—as well as on mobile objects, which will become sender-receivers of sound moving images. Furthermore, when digitization has made evident the need for information describing digital objects (the metadata), the social Web will extend the rule that makes this *new screen* a space for psychosocial individuation where receivers are also receivers of the metadata.

Internet users are invited to produce tags, keywords, indexations and annotations of all kinds for this "new screen," which becomes a collaborative effort, what one calls Web 2.0 and which constitutes the participative architecture of an infrastructure itself based on cloud computing.[18] This has led to an age of the *bottom-up* production of metadata, which in turn constitutes a radical novelty in the history of humanity. Up to this moment, the production of metadata, whose digital concept was formulated in 1994, but whose practice goes back to Mesopotamia, had always been executed in a *top-down* way, by the official institutions of various forms of symbolic power. Produced automatically for the semantic Web, or produced by Internet users' analytic and synthetic capacities of judgment for the social Web, this new type of metadata opens up the possibility of delinearizing audiovisual works to include editorial markers, to inscribe pathways and personal annotations, to make signed reading,[19] signed listening and signed vision accessible by all users.

Though there was no navigation function in the consumerist model of the cultural industries, there was a calendar organization for program access—i.e. audiovisual temporal objects were aired at a given time on a given day: a social synchronization organized by calendar. But this calendar organization is shattered by YouTube and video servers, which offer access to *stocks* of traces called data and metadata, and no longer to the *flow* of programs that constitute radio and television channels. The standardized calendar organization and the *top down* are thus substituted by a cardinal principle based precisely on discretization and the *bottom-up* production of metadata. This new mode of cardinal access to what no longer presents itself as the archi-flow of a channel linking a programmed audiovisual flux,[20] but as stocks of audiovisual temporal objects whose broadcasting can also be produced by calendar flows of a new kind, *RSS*, soon leads to podcasting and what is called *catch-up TV*. As video servers destined for a global public (since they are supported by global infrastructures) appear, new mass social practices of protocol-based video will spread with enormous speed compared to the strictly consumerist industrial modality of the cultural industries, thus opposing functions of production to functions of consumption.[21]

Top-down calendar organization has given way to cardinality where the *bottom up* based on metadata is combined with *bottom-up* production, which is also auto-production. An apparatus of video capture has become a terminal function of the Net through webcams, apparatuses for audio and video capture on PDAs and cellphones, dictaphones, DV cameras with USB keys, and iPod recorders. This abundance of images is neither more nor less widespread than the ability to read and write among citizens, which political life was based on. As images are primarily an industry in contemporary societies, the market self-evidently appropriates this situation and amateur press-photo agencies appear quickly—while the political world, lobotomized and fascinated by the "porno-politicians," leaves for others the question of the conditions for constitution of a common knowledge, requested and made possible by the established fact that concretizes the last stage of grammatization—even if Tony Blair chooses to congratulate Nicolas Sarkozy on his election as president of the French Republic on YouTube!

Auto-Production and Indexation in the Networked Society

Let us call *networked* a society in which individuals are mainly and constantly connected to all others through power, and to some others in actions, in a bi-directional net that allows everyone to be senders as well as receivers, and where the receivers receive only to the extent that they send[22]—which is to say that they make their reception public, which thus becomes their production: their *individuation*. A networked society thus breeds a "hyper-networkedness" in the sense that not all human societies, which are always constituted by nets, are necessarily networked. The networked society, to put it differently, is a society that has more or less systematically grammatized its social nets, and that by this fact organizes technologies of transindividuation in an industrial context.

Networked society and the hyper-networked relation that it makes possible and installs as its social norm structurally and simultaneously opens up two pharmacological possibilities, on the one hand, that of a generalized control and traceability that would lead through the systematization of short circuits and the absence of counterforce to an extreme disindividuation. The short circuits in the transindividuation, the psycho-epistemic effects of which the Platonic critique describes are here transformed to the level of collective individuation by all sorts of effects. On the other hand, there is also the possibility of a highly contributive society, where the reindividuation of dissociated individuals is the social novelty; based on processes of collective, collaborative and associative individuation; built upon critical apparatuses supporting counterforces; producing long circles; supported by institutions forming contributive, analytical knowledge; by a politics of research and of investment in a public priority in this field, and by political institutions with regulations appropriated to this new stage of grammatization.

The networked society is the one that links together the places of psychosocial diachronic individuation: the processes of collective, collaborative and associative individuation are formed around these centers of common interest, drawing circles where the practices of auto-production are developed and protocols of indexation are established from individual initiatives by amateurs and more generally of contributive actors—from the militant to the hacker, and from the hobbyist to the scientist. The grammatization of relations induces a grammatization of the conditions for the passage from psychic to collective individual, i.e. a formalization of nets through which collective individuals emerge. This is also a formalization and discretization of micropolitical relations that call for a new critical theory as well as new political practices at all levels, perhaps nothing less than a new political technology, in the sense that Foucault spoke of technologies of power. But here, the stakes are no longer only biopower, but psychopower also. In this context a fundamental reversal takes place, where the production of metadata is rising *(bottom up)*, which was always the opposite in the past *(top down)*, and the development of techniques of auto-production creates new, empirically acquired knowledge, through which the public is qualified. This breeds a reidiomatization of the audiovisual languages: styles grow from all parts, while a gloss of images develops from images, and new kinds of graphisms, of annotations, of categories, i.e. discretizations that are interiorized by those who perform them. Naturally, there is also the industrial, political and commercial control of these processes—in which the technology of the social Web is inextricably linked to the production of metadata in general.

The social Web formed around video servers is based on the auto-broadcasting, auto-production and auto-indexation performed by the authors or the broadcasters of temporal objects as well as their audience. This is what constitutes the effective reality of this new stage of grammatization, where indexation makes the production accessible. The combination of auto-broadcasting, auto-production and auto-indexation can create processes of transindividuation that short-circuit the short circuits engendered by the *top-down* system of the cultural industries through a *bottom-up* movement—where one is tempted to believe that minus plus minus equals plus.

Conclusion: Toward a Textualization of Images

In late 2008, at the Web 2.0 Summit in San Francisco, YouTube proved itself to be *the* major player of the young generation in the field of auto-broadcast, auto-produced and auto-indexed images on video servers—perhaps to the point where one can legitimately talk of a new reference of the process of transindividuation, based on videogram *hypomnemata*. This constitutes the basis for a process of psychic and collective individuation, which is also, in the strongest imaginable sense, a process of collective imagination, if one believes that the imagination is the movement through which mental images and object images forge transindividual relations. Or as one of the speakers put it: "The easy access to online video, shown by the video sharing platform YouTube, profoundly changes society. [...] Not only does almost the whole world see video online, but every conversation, important or unimportant, is shot—and all these films are accessible on YouTube."

The question is then if the image practice is going to compete with that of texts—and with them, if the *deep attention* produced in reading will be replaced, according to the analyses by N. Katherine Hayles, with what she calls "hyper attention." Younger people have a tendency, according to Hayles, "to use YouTube as a search engine, i.e. to view the content of the web only from the video angle, as if the textual contents no longer existed. For them, a large part of their experience of the web ends with the videos they find." [23]

One must both rejoice and worry about such a state of affairs—in the sense that worrying is what makes one think, which consists in fighting against the reactivity that it can also set off. One should also rejoice because the image practices creating this new attractiveness transform the calamitous state of affairs to that of dissociation. One should, however, worry because this new pharmacology—completely ignored by political thought except when it tries to instrumentalize it "pornopolitically"—which calls for a politics of industrial development on a grand scale, based on new educational, cultural and scientific politics, as well as on the audiovisual media completely at their mercy, can lead to either the destruction of attention and the individuation resulting from this deep attention, which has been cultivated through the text since the beginning of the great civilizations—or to the production of a *new kind of deep attention*, closely connected to new attentional forms created by the development of hypomnemata resulting from the last stages of grammatization.

A new form of tele-vision is hence developed, which for instance makes Skype possible (recently named Visiophony in France), which also leads to new kinds of gatherings as online conferences—and consequently to the formation of new processes of collective individuation. Simultaneously and elsewhere, the age of the utilitarian video is massively shaped in the most varied fields (small trade, education, institutional communication), parallel to a spectacular growth of the vision culture where GPS navigators and video surveillance cameras, installed in the streets of London or on geostationary satellites, are the elements. At this moment, a collective intelligence of transindividuation through images is indispensable for the renaissance of political as well as economic life.

The new isonomy of equal distribution of rights and privileges produced by the grammatization of animated sonorous images is thus a primordial element in the economy of contribution that should replace the worn-out Fordist consumerist model. The two new platforms, YouTube and Google, are the industrial infrastructure of this new isonomy. It is up to us to fight—through the development of machines and circles of critical transindividuation—to create from it the space and time of the new autonomies.

Endnotes

1 I also proposed a project based on repetition to the Centre Pompidou in 2004, an exhibition named "The Repetition. On the Cavern." It was turned down also.
2 I analyzed the transformations of the audiovisual temporal object by the digital in *La technique et le temps 3. Le temps du cinéma et la question du mal-être* (Paris: Galilée, 2001) and in "Les enjeux de la numérisation des objets temporels," in *Cinéma et dernières technologies*, eds. Gérard Leblanc & Franck Beaud (Paris: INA/De Boeck University, 1998); as well as in a postscript, "De quelques nouvelles possibilités historiographiques," to Sylvie Lindeperg, *Clio de 5 à 7* (Paris: CNRS Éditions, 2000).
3 Whose campaign at the time was "I dreamed it, Sony did it."
4 I outlined this development at the time of the project "Can One Philosophize about Television?" in "Technologies de la mémoire et de l'imagination," *Réseaux*, April 1986. Later, I developed the concept of hypermatter to show how the question of a grammatization at a structural level of what one can no longer simply call matter—but hypermatter—that makes the hypermaterial formed by "the internet of objects" possible.
5 Bernard Stiegler, *Prendre soin. De la jeunesse et des générations* (Paris: Flammarion, 2008; forthcoming in English, Stanford University Press.).
6 Ibid.
7 "As the proverbial fish ignores that it lives in the water, during its first century the US has only known the written. [...] But for the last forty years, Americans don't receive their information in written form any longer," i.e. since the appearance of television. Al Gore, *The Assault on Reason* (New York: Bloomsbury Publishing, 2008), pp. 13–14.
8 Cristian Fauré, Alain Giffard & Bernard Stiegler, *Pour en finir avec la mécroissance* (Paris: Flammarion, 2009).
9 One of these studios, organized with the cooperation of l'Institut national de l'audiovisuel (INA) thanks to Francis Denel, was moderated, most importantly, by Serge Daney and some other non-professionals of the profession, among others Jean-Pierre Mabille, who was later made responsible for the studio for hypermedia production that we created at the INA in 1997. Alain Giffard also contributed his support for two studios dedicated to new reading and writing machines.

10 The expression by which Patrick Le Lay—then president of TF1, the prime TV channel in France—made himself famous, where he explained that his job consisted of selling the attention of television viewers to its advertisers.

11 The reproduction of audiovisual perception is what allows for the recording of movement, i.e. life itself. This is why McLuhan described cinema as the recording of life itself.

12 I have already quoted and commented on the following passage in my *La technique et le temps 3, Le temps du cinéma* (Paris: Flammarion, 2001): "A Sophist, Hippocrates, isn't he a bargainer or a merchant who debited the goods that the soul lives on? [...] The risk is [...] all the greater when one buys science rather than groceries. What can be eaten or drunk can be carried in a specific container when one buys it from the seller or the dealer, and can be placed at home before one devours it. [...] When it comes to science, one doesn't carry it in a container: one must absolutely, when the price is paid, receive it in oneself, put it in one's soul, and when one leaves, the good or the bad is already there."

13 See my postscript in Lindeberg 2000.

14 Defined by the Motion Picture Standards Group installed by the International Organization for Standardization, which was formed in Ottawa in 1988.

15 I raised the question in the last chapter of *Echographies of Television: Filmed Interviews* (with Jacques Derrida) (New York: Polity Press, 2002).

16 The exhibition "Mémoires du futur" presented one of the first CD-ROMs to the French public, produced by the Canadian newspaper *Globe and Mail*, together with the catalogue of the Bibliothèque publique d'information du Centre Pompidou, which at the time had just been stored on the new CD-ROM format.

17 I have myself initiated research in these diverse fields since 1996, when I was appointed General Co-director of the INA, in charge of the department for innovation, which entailed the direction of research, production, education and the service for studies and publications.

18 On this topic, see Fauré, Giffard & Stiegler 2009.

19 The concept was developed together with the group for the conception of computer-assisted reading that I developed and presided over at the request of Alain Giffard and the Bibliothèque nationale de France in 1990.

20 I have developed the matter in detail, that is the concepts of cardinality, calendarity, flux, archi-flux and audiovisual temporal object in *La technique et le temps 3. Le temps du cinéma et la question du mal-être*, 2001.

21 The creation of the site ina.fr is typical for putting a function previously reserved for the professionals of the cultural industries at the public's disposal—the function of archiving and documentation.

22 I have maintained in my book *De la misère symbolique 2* (Paris: Éditions Galiliée, 2005) that perception that is not a semiotic production of the perceived is not a perception in action. It is a perception in force that may, however, actualize itself afterwards. That is what the Proustian anamnesis signifies.

23 N. Katherine Hayles, "Hyper and Deep Attention: The Generational Divide in Cognitive Modes," *Profession* no. 13, 2007, pp. 187–199.

Richard Grusin

YouTube at the End of New Media

I am not a big YouTube fan. It's not that I never visit the site, but that I rarely—if ever—spend time there without a specific purpose, either searching for a video I have heard about, or hoping to discover a video I would like to have seen. YouTube is promiscuous, however; any video can easily be embedded within virtually any digital medium. Thus when I learn about a video I should watch, the video is almost always embedded in another medium—the e-mail, text message, blog, Facebook page or other media form where I learned of the clip in the first place.

In the few times that I have looked around on the site, then, the most rewarding experiences I have had have been historical, or more exactly archival. For example, I have been delighted to find some old, black-and-white Hamms Beer commercials that I remember from watching televised coverage of Chicago Cubs baseball games when growing up in the 1960s. I have also been interested to find older videos of the Mutants, Tuxedomoon, or the Residents, obscure or lesser-known post-punk bands I followed in my graduate school days at Berkeley in the late seventies and early eighties. I have sometimes searched and found video clips of old television shows. During the 2008 presidential campaign, I was happy to find will.i.am's mashup of Barack Obama's "Yes We Can" stump speech. And before Google purchased YouTube, I was excited to find non-US videos of suicide bombings and improvised explosive devices posted to dramatize and glorify resistance to the unjust US invasion of Iraq.

Browsing YouTube produces something like the experience of what I would characterize as the YouTube sublime. The number of videos on YouTube is almost too large to comprehend. Especially in print, televisual and networked news media, this sublimity is expressed in various permutations of the following sentence: "The video of X attracted more than Y million views on YouTube." When I googled "more than", "million views" and "YouTube" on January 26, 2009, I got over 100,000 results on the Web. "Million views" and "YouTube" produced 729,000 hits. "More than," "views" and "YouTube" gave me 159,000,000 hits. The rhetorical force of such numbers is to produce something like the feeling of what Kant characterized as the "mathematical sublime." Experiencing the YouTube sublime, the mind is unable to conceive the immensity of the YouTube universe even while it is empowered by the experience of an affective awe in the face of such immensity.

Is YouTube a Medium?

In *Remediation* Jay Bolter and I defined a medium as that which remediates. According to this definition, then, YouTube would appear to be a medium insofar as it remediates TV. Or is it simply an immense archival database which has successfully integrated the media practices of social networking? From the governing metaphor of its trademarked motto "Broadcast Yourself," to the implicit equation with (or more accurately difference from) the "boob tube," YouTube sets out to remediate TV not merely as a neutral intermediary but as an active mediatior.[1]

Remediation entails the translation of media forms and practices, the extension and complexification of media networks. In our book we saw television at the end of the 20th century as participating in the double logic of remediation via the simultaneous immediacy of televisual monitoring and the hypermediacy of proliferating mediation, not only in its windowed interface but also in its connection with the World Wide Web. YouTube similarly participates in this double televisual logic both through the immediacy of its extensive, seemingly global monitoring and through the hypermediacy of its multiple networks of YouTube users, bloggers, news media, social networkers and so forth. Marshall McLuhan famously defines media as "extensions of man," technical devices to extend the nervous system throughout the universe. In McLuhan's sense, then, YouTube would also seem to be a medium. It archives and distributes audiovisual media, which allows us to extend our senses beyond the range of our body's geographic environment, introducing us to people and places, sights and sounds that we would not otherwise have the opportunity to perceive. But it cannot be emphasized strongly enough that McLuhan does not mean the "nervous system" to be a metaphor for technology or perception or even culture. Rather he means to insist on the physical agency of media to alter not only what he calls "the ratio of the senses" but also our physiology, our embodied nervous systems. In *Understanding Media*, for example, McLuhan repeatedly cites texts like Hans Selye's *Stress of Life* to emphasize the point made explicit in the title of his collaborative graphic book, *The Medium is the Massage*— that our media impact us physiologically.

Too often McLuhan's talk about the neurological and physiological effect or impact of media is dismissed as a kind of mystical `60s pseudoscience. But as neurologists, psychologists, social scientists and increasingly humanists are coming to recognize, the affective or physiological impact of literature and other media is not incidental, but instrumental to their cultural power and meaning. Kazys Varnelis, for example, notes that YouTube participates in the global social changes that "mass media" like TV have undergone. "Ours is a world of networked publics, in which consumers comment on and remix what they consume. Composed entirely of clips uploaded by individuals, YouTube threatens television networks. Snarky commentary on media is now the norm, much to the broadcasters' chagrin. Individuals often create their own media—posting on blogs and on-line venues set up to display their creations, such as photo-sharing sites."[2]

YouTube functions as a remediation of television in the "world of networked publics" that we inhabit in the 21st century. For Varnelis and enthusiasts like Lev Manovich, YouTube is an element of a more interactive, creative public than that produced by television for much of the second half of the 20th century. Manovich understands this public in terms of "the dynamics of Web 2.0 culture—its constant innovation, its energy and its unpredictability."[3] Paolo Virno, however—along with Michael Hardt and Antonio Negri—characterizes this public more critically as the "multitude," whose contributions to YouTube and other socially networked media participate in the 21st century manifestation of Marx's "general intellect," providing the affective labor of mediation in the service of infomedia capitalism.[4]

Remediation and Premediation

When Jay Bolter and I created the concept of remediation in the 1990s, we argued that its double logic took a particular form in the IT boom of the last decade of the 20th century, when new media sought simultaneously to erase and proliferate mediation. Since 9/11 I have been tracing the emergence of a media logic that I call "premediation," which names one of the predominant media formations deployed by the "general intellect." YouTube participates most extensively in one key aspect of premediation, the intensification and multiplication of technical and social media networks to the point that all future events would always be pre-mediated. Premediation, I argue, intensified after 9/11 as a form of medial preemption, one aim of which was to prevent the multitude, as citizens of the global media-sphere, from receiving the kind of systemic or traumatic shock produced by the events of 9/11—or later of 7/7 in England or of 11/26-29 in Mumbai.[5] Premediation does not displace remediation but deploys it in different aesthetic, sociotechnical, or political formations. The double logic of remediation still obtains within our mobile, socially networked culture, but its conflicting media logics are formally different.

In the 1990s the ultimate in immediacy was conceived of along the lines of virtual realities free from the gloves and headpieces of early VR technology, and artists, academics and activists envisioned and pursued projects that explored and advanced military, commercial and cultural applications and implications of these new media technologies. After the events of 9/11 immediacy is epitomized in the form of media like YouTube, or projects like the Open Web, which aims to make seamless one's multiple interactions with commercial and social networking, with health and medical records, juridical and educational records, shopping and entertainment preferences. Immediacy after 9/11 materializes itself as an unconstrained connectivity so that one can access with no restrictions one's networked mediated life at any time or anywhere through any of one's social-media devices.

Hypermediacy in the 1990s was marked by fragmentation and multiplicity, by the graphic design of *Wired* or the windowed desktop or TV screen, or by the audiovisual style of MTV videos and TV commercials. In the IT boom of the late 1990s, the proliferation of new media forms and technologies and an increasingly hypermediated screen space was enthusiastically celebrated along with IPOs (initial public offerings), venture capitalist funds and Silicon Valley start-ups. After 9/11 the logic of hypermediacy is marked by the multiplication of mediation among sociotechnical, commercial and political networks like YouTube. This is less the 1990s hypermediacy of formal features or technologies of mediation and representation than the hypermediacy of network connectivities, of affective participation in and distribution across multiple sociotechnical and medial networks. In the 21st century hypermediacy operates within a paradigm of securitization, which entails the registration of every commercial, communicational, or juridical transaction by a networked media security infrastructure, the complexity and scope of which proliferate in direct relation to the seamlessness of circulation through an increasingly open Web.

Towards the End of New Media

So, does the advent of YouTube mark the end of "new media"? I do not mean to ask if the creation of YouTube has brought about the end of new digital media—but if it signals the end of the usefulness of "new media" as a category of analysis or classification to make sense of our current media environment (what I have been thinking of as our "media everyday").

Are we, I want to ask, coming to the end of new media, both as a conceptual or analytic category and as a certain kind of media practice that intensified in the 1990s and has begun to be supplemented by or remediated into other forms of mediation that entail the logics and desires of mobile social networking rather than virtual reality or hypermediacy? The question is, thus, whether "new media" within the current media regime of premediation has become too limiting a concept.

The product of certain late 1990s global post-capitalist economic and sociotechnical formations, new media may turn out to be a problematic analytical concept to make sense of our media everyday, particularly insofar as it continues to emphasize the "newness" of digital media rather than their "mediality." The key to the creation of the field of new media studies was not its "newness," but its intensification of mediation at the end of the 20th century. When Jay Bolter and I invented the concept of remediation, the first general theoretical framework to identify and analyze the formation of "new media," we sought precisely to distinguish what was most interesting about digital media at the end of the 20th century from the limited corporate concept of "repurposing." Unlike repurposing, remediation emphasized the intensification and proliferation of forms and practices of mediation, not simply new media commodities. Remediation argued explicitly that what was new about new media was its incessant remediation of other, mostly earlier, forms of mediation; but it was also the case that remediation operated through "older" media forms as well, which remediated newer ones according to the same double logic of immediacy and hypermediacy. Thus remediation describes a logic of mediation that can be identified in many different historical media formations and the project of remediation was to insist on the significance of mediation itself.

As at the end of the 20th century, there is still of course a rhetoric of newness surrounding our culture's embrace of the latest social-networking platforms like YouTube, MySpace, Facebook and Twitter—particularly in the mainstream media. This newness participates in the "info-media-capitalist" need to sell more technical media devices by making them faster, more powerful, more interactive and more immediate. But in our current era of wireless social networking the emphasis is not on radical new forms of mediation but on seamless connectivity, ubiquity, mobility and affectivity. YouTube provides perhaps the paradigmatic instance of this new media formation, insofar as its popularity is less a result of having provided users with new and better forms of media than of making available more mediation events, more easily shared and distributed through e-mail, texting, social networks, blogs or news sites. YouTube is also part and parcel of the proliferation of still and video cameras as standard features of mobile phones and the multiplication and mobilization of social networking, so that 3G phones now routinely carry both cameras and social networks.

At the current historical moment, the double logic of remediation marks immediacy both in terms of uninterrupted flow and in opposition to mainstream media. What Jay Bolter and I explained in terms of remediation, Henry Jenkins for example understands as "convergence culture," the collision of old and new media. Jenkins proclaims YouTube as the fullest embodiment of convergence culture, which exemplifies a completely networked media environment in which different cultural forms of production converge to provide alternatives to the forms and practices furnished by consumer culture. Such convergence, Jenkins argues, is economic and technical as well, furnishing the material conditions for an ideal of a seamlessly interconnected network of data, media forms and things.[6] By making this seamless interconnection easy and affectively pleasurable, the socially networked immediacy enables and promotes the proliferation of many different media forms for interacting with the network—different appliances (iPhones, iPods, Blackberry, home and portable networked game consoles, mobile personal computers) as well as different media interfaces (YouTube, Facebook, MySpace, Twitter, RSS, blogs, discussion boards and so forth). Hypermediacy is encouraged through the proliferation of different mobile, socially networked media forms. Leaving as many traces of yourself on as many media becomes a culturally desirable goal—made pleasurable in part because leaving such traces works to produce positive affective relations with our media devices, setting up affective feedback loops that make one want to perpetuate through the proliferation of media transactions.

Henry Jenkins's commitment to convergence culture, however, prevents him from recognizing that the hypermediacy of YouTube also produces a *divergence culture* that is fragmented, niche-oriented, fluid and individuated—or perhaps "dividuated," as Gilles Deleuze says of control societies.[7] Jenkins thus runs the risk of seeing only the immediacy of convergence culture, one half of the double logic of remediation in the 21st century. Remediation and premediation call our attention to divergence culture as well, which YouTube serves to exemplify with its ability to be embedded in other media formats, its thousands of channels, its recommendation system and other features of what has come to be called networked media's "long tail." Unlike the network television of the 1950s through the 1970s (whether private or government sponsored), which aimed at producing a convergence of a mass audience of sufficient scale at a particular place and a particular time, YouTube produces a divergence of audience and message, temporally and territorially, fostering multiple points of view rather than the small number of viewpoints represented by broadcast television. YouTube not only functions as a 24/7, global archive of mainly user-created video content, but it also serves as an archive of affective moments or formations, much as television has done for decades.

Endnotes

1 Bruno Latour, *We Have Never Been Modern* (Cambridge, MA: Harvard University Press, 1993).

2 Kazys Varnelis, "Simultaneous environments – social connection and new media," *receiver magazine* no. 21, 2009 – www.receiver.vodafone.com/simultaneous-environments [last checked 15 February 2009].

3 Lev Manovich, "The Practice of Everyday (Media) Life: From Mass Consumption to Mass Cultural Production?" *Critical Inquiry* no. 2, 2009, pp. 319–331.

4 See Paolo Virno, *A Grammar of the Multitude* (New York: Semiotexte, 2004); as well as Michael Hardt & Antonio Negri, *Multitude: War and Democracy in the Age of Empire* (New York: Penguin Press, 2004).

5 Richard Grusin, "Premediation," *Criticism* no. 1, 2004, pp. 17–39.

6 Henry Jenkins, *Convergence Culture*: *Where Old and New Media Collide* (New York: New York University Press, 2006).

7 For a discussion, see Gilles Deleuze, *Negotiations* (New York: Columbia University Press, 1995).

Usage

Patricia G. Lange

Videos of Affinity on YouTube

Years ago I watched a documentary about a mutual-support group for terminally ill people. The facilitator told the participants, "One of the greatest gifts you can give another person is your attention."[1] I was moved by this remark. Even though it was uttered under extreme circumstances, I believe it is widely applicable and relevant. Indeed, it may be beneficial in social contexts to consider human attention as a gift rather than an economic manifestation of capitalist value. Somewhere between highly charged support groups and YouTube videos—some of which contain the voices of ill people, and some which do not—lies a social negotiation that determines who merits our attention, and under what circumstances.

Informing this decision is a moral calculus based on maximizing a limited resource: time. People who post biographical updates are often generically diagnosed as narcissistic.[2] Critics and some so-called "haters" on YouTube may express moral outrage that a poorly crafted video wasted limited moments of their lives. The outrage is exacerbated by, or emerges from the fact that, the perceived time/life violation was unexpected, and therefore a deception concerning the video's attentional merit. Evaluations of YouTube videos often consider only whether a video is monetizable and thus "valuable." Trapped in a binary categorization, professional videos are portrayed as easily monetized, in contrast to uneven amateur content.[3] This binary effaces the spectrum of professional video quality, and the relational value that individuals in specific social networks may place on certain amateur or "user-created" videos.[4] Social networks are defined as connections between people who deem other members important to them in some way.[5] Across different social networks, people may find a video personally meaningful in ways that merit attention, despite its seeming lack of normatively valued "content." Negative assessments of certain videos often ignore supportive viewers' responses. Yet, what does it mean for a video to have hundreds of views or text comments?

Based on a two-year ethnographic study, this article explores a category of YouTube videos that I propose to call "videos of affiliation."[6] Affiliation might be defined in several ways. It can include feelings of membership in a social network, or feelings of attraction to people, things or ideas. On a broad level, people might have affiliations to many types of things such as hobbies, institutions or ideologies that form the overt content of a video's subject matter. YouTube offers many opportunities to stay attuned to favorite topics. However, this article focuses on the type of affiliation that refers to "feelings of connections between people,"[7] some of whom may already be a member of or wish to join a videomaker's social network. Of particular interest is exploring the characteristics of videos of affinity. How do they compare to other home-mode media? How do they establish a "labile field of connection"[8] between video creators and viewers, and how do such videos create and maintain dispersed social networks?

Videos of affinity try to establish communicative connections to people, often members of a social network. Some people might equate videos of affinity to amateur video blogs[9] because they are both assumed to focus on home-based forms of videomaking. Although videos of affinity appear in some video blogs, not all video bloggers make home-mode, diary or confessional videos. In addition, numerous people casually share videos of private moments online, but they would not consider themselves video bloggers who have a social or personal obligation to post videos regularly. Videos of affinity can facilitate large, business-oriented social networks, or small personal ones. They vary in levels of sincerity. They can be the main focus of a creator's body of work; more commonly, they lie in the intercies of other work. Videos of affinity attempt to maintain feelings of connection with potential others who identify or interpellate themselves as intended viewers of the video.[10] The interpellative process is important because attention, at a basic interactional level, is a managed achievement that requires work. Videos of affinity are, in short, useful objects of study because they inform explorations of how social networks are negotiated through video.

Attention as a Managed Achievement

Scholarship on computer-mediated communication has yielded important insights. Yet, one unfortunate legacy of its historically comparative focus is that some studies assume a binary opposition between so-called "face-to-face" and mediated interaction. The widely adopted and rather unquestioned adjective "face-to-face"—which actually applies to only a subset of a much wider field of in-person interaction—connotes warm, concentrated attentiveness. In the popular imagination, mediated encounters are cold and require work. Yet, linguistic studies convincingly demonstrate that securing someone's attention in person is an ongoing, managed process that easily and frequently breaks down.[11] In his highly detailed analysis of in-person conversation, Charles Goodwin showed that some conversational breakdowns and subsequent repairs resulted from a speaker's attempt to secure a listener's attention.[12] Remarks were repeated or co-constructed until "precise eye gaze coordination" was achieved.[13] Such an ongoing effort challenges the assumption that in person, interlocutors' attention is automatic.

Securing attention requires negotiation, a process exhaustively discussed in the literature on turn taking and interruption.[14] Knowing who will speak next is not pre-determined prior to an interaction; in fact, ongoing negotiations about who *deserves* to speak show that attention is not guaranteed in any interaction. The interruption literature states that participants may display anger when someone speaks out of turn, thus not meriting attention *at that moment.*[15] Some researchers argue that interactive processes break down the moment attention is lost. In experimental studies, researchers have compared storytellers' abilities when responses were attentive versus distracted, where "speakers with distracted and unresponsive listeners could not seem to finish their stories effectively."[16] This occurred even when the speaker had a dramatic finish. Everyday interactions are filled with constant micro-negotiations for attention.

Some scholars claim that attention takes on a much greater salience in intensely mediated environments. According to this view "everyone has always lived with some degree of an attention economy, but through most of human history it hasn't been primary."[17] Yet, linguists have shown that securing attention is basic to interaction and requires ongoing work, even in person. In economic models scholars suggest that originality is the best way to secure attention amid a competitive, mediated field.[18] Yet, videos of affinity are not particularly original from the perspective of people who are not part of a creator's social network. Even creators may feel that a video of affinity is not necessarily original or interesting; instead, such videos are often communicative attempts to negotiate attention from other people to maintain ongoing connections or relationships. From the perspective of a viewer to whom the video is not "addressed," the video's seeming lack of content appears to draw undeserved attention.[19] Yet viewers to whom the video is addressed may respond and help maintain a field of connection between creator and viewer.

Videos of Affinity

Anthropologist Bonnie Nardi defines affinity as "feelings of connection between people." A feeling of connection is often "an openness to interacting with another person.[20] Affinity is achieved through activities of social bonding in which people come to feel connected with one another, readying them for further communication."[21] In her study of instant messaging in the workplace, Nardi notes that even highly paid telecommunications executives often exchanged short messages such as saying "hi" or nothing in particular. Participants reported that these messages did not necessarily have a purpose. Yet, they were part of what Nardi calls the "work of connection," and were crucial for keeping a "labile" field of communication open in ways that later facilitated exchange of substantive business information.[22] The affinity framework illustrates the instability of continued interaction, social networks and attention.

Videos of affinity are not targeted nor read as necessarily containing material for general audiences. They typically interest delineated groups of people who wish to participate and remain connected socially in some way to the videomaker. The content of such a video is often not original or interesting, although it certainly can be. Often the content is stereotypical, spontaneous and contains numerous in-jokes and references that many general viewers would not understand in the way creators intended. Videos of personal celebrations such as birthdays and weddings—and other types of what Richard Chalfen has called "home-mode" mediated communication—are potential examples of videos of affinity in that they interest specific individuals or social networks of individuals.[23]

According to previous scholarship, home-mode films, or analogue "home movies" in the United States, were often recorded by fathers and focused on specific kinds of rituals such as Christmases, birthdays and weddings.[24] The proliferation of less expensive video has facilitated an ability to capture more personal ephemera, such as spontaneous and small moments in life that are not necessarily part of large-scale or highly momentous life celebrations and rites of passage.[25] The availability of less expensive and lightweight video equipment, it is argued, also enables a broader range of family members with varying amounts of expertise to more freely capture a wider array of spontaneous moments that they may enjoy sharing with friends and family.[26] The rise of the Internet and YouTube have changed distribution options from that of small-scale home-mode viewing to global sharing and exchange.

A primary characteristic of "home-mode communication" is its "selection of audience." People sharing home-mode media "know each other in personal ways."[27] Photographers and subjects know each other; subjects can identify other subjects. Today as in Chalfen's day, however, it is important to remember that many people wield cameras at large, public social events. Applying the term "home-mode" to events like weddings and anniversaries risks ignoring the large number of people that may record and appear in various kinds of personal footage. People may not know well or even be able to identify all persons at their wedding. Then as now, images of a number of people outside the social network of the immediate celebrants could be collected. The difference today is that the Internet and YouTube facilitate distribution of personal media to wide, dispersed groups of people.

Chalfen argues that previously, people who engaged in "home-mode" media-making described photographs and videos primarily as memory aids. They were useful to help them "remember how [they] were then." In contrast, videos of affinity have a present focus and communicative orientation. Although they are technically records of past events (when compared to live video chats, for instance), many videos of affinity nevertheless aim to transmit a feeling of sharing a particular moment, large or small, or a certain state of affairs in the creator's life.

One video of affinity that I give the pseudonym "Ninjas and Knights" is a five-minute video in which two college students wrestle each other in a dormitory. Between its initial posting on September 30, 2006, and July 28, 2007, it received 2,779 views. One student is dressed in military gear; the other is wearing a suit of medieval armor. The video is a spontaneous recording that captures their humorously awkward moves. They are laughing as they charge at each other, often using kicks, broad lunges and knees. The amusing sight of the youth in their gear prompted several people to emerge from their dorm rooms and watch. Surmising that this would be appropriate for YouTube, some people recorded the hallway tussle. Later they edited this footage and added music. The lyrics of the first song, which plays as they are wrestling and laughing, are apropos. Metaphorically, the lyrics emphasize that the content is not novel, but is part of collective personal histories that the youth wish to share. As the boys wrestle in front of camera-wielding onlookers, a voice (which sounds like Shirley Bassey's) belts out the following lyrics: "The word is about, there's something evolving/Whatever may come, the world keeps revolving/They say the next big thing is here,/That the revolution's near/But to me it seems quite clear/That it's all just a little bit of history repeating."

The song is well chosen, considering that one of the participants was a history major who had a ready-to-wear suit of armor. The song is appropriate, given that the video's content—two youths wrestling in a college dorm room—is not novel or well choreographed; it has happened before and will happen again. For some 30-odd seconds, as the song plays, they spar. Just after the "history repeating" reference, the video uses a transition. The music continues and we are still in the hallway. This time, the video is speeded up. This use of fast-motion is interesting to contemplate. By this time, the viewer has watched 30 seconds of tussling, and the next sequence offers similar fare. Fast motion often provides a comic effect or marks the passage of time. It can also suggest that what is happening is not worth watching in real time. Speeding up the video enables the viewer to see a general sequence of events, without requiring too much viewing time. In the video culture of YouTube, such a technique resembles a "fast forward" button. The creators could have edited this footage out. Yet, its faster pace is cool, matches the tempo of the lyrics, and its comedic connotations amplify the effect of youth having fun.

The video records a moment in time that acquired increased interest when recorded by onlookers in order to share it on YouTube. The participants expressed gratitude to the people who took the time to record their spontaneous fun. The youth said they thought of YouTube partly because of its reputation as a site with amusing videos with similar subject matter. They also posted the video on YouTube because they knew that it would be a convenient distribution method for sharing their experience with friends. As Brian1 put it, "We know a lot of other people watch [YouTube] like our friends, and it's—if we wanted to tell our friends, 'Hey, come and watch this,' it'd be a lot easier if we just put it on YouTube instead of sticking it in an e-mail and waiting for the e-mail to get there and waiting for them to open it which would take forever 'cause the file was so big. So we just put it on YouTube and got the link, sent the link to everyone, and they watched it."

Many critiques of contemporary, personal forms of online video fail to consider the material constraints that people face with regard to sharing media to wide social networks. Many study participants said their friends watch YouTube, and it was far more convenient to share high-bandwidth media on an easy-to-use site. Current alternatives for sharing videos such as copying them onto multiple disks (assuming the disks accommodated the videos) and mailing them to numerous, dispersed, transitory college students is not practical. Nor is sending high-bandwidth videos via e-mail. Instead, they sent the link to the video to specific individuals within their network whom they believed would be interested in seeing them have fun. Brian1 uses the term "everyone" in a way that does not indicate the world population, or even all YouTube viewers. Rather, it connotes all members of a group of individuals to whom the youth were close enough to have an e-mail address and who might enjoy seeing the video.

Of course, not every individual who receives the link will watch or enjoy the video. People not in their network may also find it and watch. The boys listed their university in the video tag (or keyword) list, so that current students and alumni searching for videos about their university would see it. Alumni of the university might be interested in the video, as an example of what is "currently" happening on campus. In this sense, the video may provide feelings of affinity to a large social network of people from the same university (as well as to the university itself). Posting a video targeted for a social network does not imply that non-members will automatically eschew it. The experience of watching a video of affinity, although often targeted and read as meant for specific social networks of people, does not preclude others' enjoyment of it. But the people who receive links or who interpret the inside jokes and references in a way similar to the videomakers comprise a much smaller population of people than the general public, or even regular YouTube viewers. For those who receive the link in a personal e-mail from a known friend, or who appreciate seeing the experiences of their friends or relatives, the video may encourage feelings of connectedness, closeness or friendship.

A video of affinity attempts to keep the lines of communication open to certain social networks, large or small, by sharing informal experiences. These videos may or may not contain much "content" or artistic aesthetics defined in traditional ways. These videos, often made by and distributed to one's peers, tend to disrupt past ideologies of father-driven home-media creation, yet researchers and members of the general public may not value them. Past scholarship on home media argues that camera manufacturer's exhortations for non-professionals to be attentive to standardized modes of content and style enforced rather than eased divisions between professional and amateur filmmakers. Patricia Zimmerman argues that the "emphasis on Hollywood-continuity style dominated and restricted amateur-film aesthetic discourse; it naturalized its own codes and reined in the flexibility and spontaneity inherent in lightweight equipment."[28] She argues that in the decades after World War II, home movies in the United States were often made by fathers and reproduced a certain kind of domestic ideology rooted in the ideals of a patriarchal, middle-class, nuclear family.[29] She notes that the technical affordances of video might promote more democratic uptake of mediated self-expression, so that future amateur filmmaking "may liberate it as a more accessible and meaningful form of personal expression and social and political intervention."[30] What a sad betrayal it is that next-generation youth who are using video in ways not dominated by standardized ideological, political, educational and aesthetic discourses in filmmaking are criticized for sharing seemingly private ephemera.

Habeas Corpus

Feelings of affinity are normally promoted by communal eating and drinking, sharing an experience in a common space, conducting an informal conversation.[31] Nardi uses the term "habeas corpus" to stress the importance of the body in promoting affinity. Two videos, "I'm Not Dead" and "Just an update guys," provide important material with which to understand how creators involve the body to establish affinity. Even the videos' titles frame them as not oriented around content but rather around human connections. "I'm Not Dead," a roughly five-minute video which was posted on March 2, 2008, had 824 views and 86 text comments as of March 25, 2009. In the video, a young woman who refers to herself as "panda" assures her viewers that she is alive and will be posting more videos. She states: "Um, just want to let you guys all know that I'm alive. Yes, I wasn't kidnapped in San Fran, unfortunately. But um, I've got a couple of videos coming up. And yes I know I still have to put up my gathering videos. I'm going to do an LA to San Fran video, kill two birds with one stone."

2 Panda drinking tea in "I'm Not Dead"

This video arguably lies in between her other work, as panda states an intention to post future videos, having not posted videos in a while. Intimacy of a close encounter is facilitated by the setting and camera work. She is seated and appears to be holding the camera in her left hand while she directly addresses it. The image is jittery as if the camera is not stationary, which is a common index of more spontaneous, personal, human interaction. The video breaks down into several parts that can be characterized as: telling a story about making sweet tea; promising to post future videos; taking issue with rumors circulating about her, and previewing an upcoming gathering. These parts are not well delineated, and interweave throughout the video. In the first minute and a half, panda talks about how she was thirsty in the middle of the night. Eschewing water, she went to the kitchen to make sweet tea. As she says the words "sweet tea," she brings the cup she's been holding closer to the camera. She looks into the cup several times as she tells her story. Making the tea did not go as she anticipated; she had to chop a block of frozen ice with a butcher knife. She puts down the cup and simulates the motion of wielding the knife. She drinks from the cup, says, "mm" and slightly tips the cup in the viewer's direction. She says that the tea "actually turned out really good," at which point she once again points the cup at the camera, almost long enough for the viewer to see inside.

The vignette contains characteristics that one would expect in an encounter that tries to provide social affinity. Not only does it engage in informal conversation (by relating an ephemeral story about making sweet tea for the first time), it does so in a way that enables her to "have a cup of tea" with the viewer. The lack of stationary camera, the motions of the cup toward the camera, and her consuming of the tea all provide a means to establish a personal, communicative effect. The title "I'm Not Dead" indexes her live body and reassures her viewers that she is still alive and making videos even if she has not posted in several weeks. Evaluating content is culturally and aesthetically relative; people may enjoy her story about making sweet tea. Yet panda mentions her intent to make other videos several times, which gives the video a feeling of existing in the intercies of her other work with more defined content. Videos of affinity often provide a preview of something that is about to happen such as a promise to release a new video. Such previews index a present-focused perspective. "I've got a couple of videos coming up," she states in the middle of the video. "And yes I know I still have to put up my gathering videos. I'm going to do an LA to San Fran video, kill two birds with one stone." She acknowledges that she "knows" she has to put up gathering videos, which implies that a common practice in her social network of YouTube creators and viewers is sharing YouTube gathering videos. She also mentions that she is "bored," which young people often cite as a motivator for making videos. Panda's explanation of being "stuck" and "lazy" index her current state at the moment, and socially account for her lack of recent videos.

Panda acknowledges that certain themes in her forthcoming videos might not be widely appreciated. For example, in mentioning plans to post "meet-up" footage from a YouTube gathering (a popular genre on YouTube and one that merits additional study), she speculates that only some viewers will find this subject interesting. "I'm stupid I didn't take any footage so it's just going to be um photos, so [I] guess it's only for the people who were actually there they'd probably enjoy it. But probably for you other guys it'd probably be boring." She also refers to people circulating "rumors" about her: "It's not a gathering without rumors about panda. Panda did this and panda did that. And I'm actually kind of surprised because half of the rumors are coming from people who weren't even at the gathering. So if you've got something to say just ask. I'm not going to get offended. I just find it hilarious." She exhorts the gossipers to ask her questions instead of spreading rumors. She furthermore addresses "little birdies talking" who used private messages to gossip about her—"I know who you are; I know what's going on it's okay I still love you guys."

Even within a video of affinity that appeals to certain members of social networks, elements within the video may target even smaller sub-portions of a creator's social network. Viewers may interpellate their identities as the subjects of different themes within panda's video. In the interpellation metaphor, a policeman calls, "Hey you there!" down a crowded street. A successful completion of this hail is one in which a person turns around and answers, thus recognizing him- or herself as the actual subject of the hail.[32] Those viewers who know they have been circulating rumors are able to interpellate themselves as the subjects of her admonition and her request that they pose their questions directly. One viewer joked, "I don't know enough YouTubers to talk about you. lol:P." This substantive comment resists interpellation as the subject of panda's admonishing hail. Other remarks, such as "Woot!" are "comments of affinity" that indicate affective support for panda.[33] Thus, in panda's video of affinity different groups of people are hailed as potentially interested parties, such as regular viewers, participants at meet-ups, and people who spread rumors about her. The video's messages are interpellative communications of social interest targeted toward different groups of people. She also uses other techniques such as drinking, sharing an experience, and engaging in informal conversation to indicate affinity to those who are able and willing to interpellate themselves as subjects of her social hails. She keeps her communication channel open, by showing her live (recorded) body, by encouraging gossipers to ask her questions directly, and by promising forthcoming videos.[34]

Phatic Signals

The video "Just an update guys" similarly codes it as something that lies between other postings. This roughly two-minute video was posted on April 4, 2008. As of March 25, 2009, it had accumulated 366 views and 27 text comments. The title word "just" frames it as relatively modest in importance. The text description posted to the video says, "This is my new room all pink and purple this is just an update" which the creator Ryan made partly because he "just wanted to see what it looked like." He says he wanted to make a "quick" update to let people know what was happening with him. The word "quick" indexes it as something not well crafted or labored over. The scene is intimate; he sits in a bedroom. He admits that the image is "terrible" due to the light duplicating in the mirror in the background. Although he has made many other informational and entertainment videos, in this video Ryan talks a lot about his communication problems. He mentions being "officially" moved in to his "new room" but he does not have "Internet access." He does not use his "normal mic" because he left the stand at home and plans to retrieve it later. He holds a mic up to the camera, looks at it, and shakes it while speaking.

3 Ryan discussing his connection problems and showing his new hairstyle

The frequent references to his technical communication problems resemble what Roman Jakobson called the "contact" function, or what Bronisław Malinowski called the "phatic" function of language.[35] In the case of a primarily phatic message, its focus is on "serving to establish, to prolong, or to discontinue communication, to check whether the channel works [...] to attract the attention of the interlocutor, or to confirm his continued attention."[36] Jakobson argues that some phatic exchanges focus entirely on prolonging communication. Messages can purport to continue communication although they do not necessarily communicate crucial information.

The image cuts away and seconds later he reappears and sings, "I have run to the mountains. I have run through the sea. Only to be with you. Only to be with you. And I'm still hanging on to what I'm looking for." The small fragment of song, appearing between segments of dialogue about his access issues, evokes affective images of "being" with "you." On one level, it is just a nice song to sing. But it appears between shots in which he speaks about the difficulty he is having making Internet connections. One metaphorical reading is that it reaffirms his wish to "be" with viewers and members of his social network who watch him on YouTube. Later, he reports that he has Internet access. He turns the camera to show another computer that has Internet connectivity. The second computer is his "little laptop" on which he can get the Internet. But he cannot put the Internet on his Macintosh computer. He shrugs and says that if "anyone could help me with that that would be great. So for now I'm just going to use my laptop I don't want to but I will." Ryan ends the video by mentioning an upcoming YouTube gathering, and asks attendees to contact him. "Also if you're [going] to the YouTube gathering, tell me I'll compile a list and then I will put it online." Just as messages have different functions, videos of affinity may contain multiple functions. By inviting forthcoming meet-up participants to contact him, he uses the video as a bulletin board in ways that enable interested parties to interpellate themselves as members of a social network interested in attending a forthcoming meet up.

Ryan's video also produces the body, shares an experience, and informally discusses his quotidian network problems. He indexes his body by running his hands through his hair and talking about his haircut. He talks about ephemera such as the color of his room, his haircut and his Internet difficulties. The video's multiple functions include asking for help, requesting meet-up attendees to contact him, and dealing with his patchy Internet connection. Notably, he takes the time to record these thoughts in a way that demonstrates a social willingness to communicate even when a physical connection is uncertain.

Conclusion

Analyses of YouTube videos often orient around a broad-scale division between amateur or so-called "user-created" versus professional content. While useful for many types of scholarship, these labels also tend to generate a cascading binary of assumptions about a video's attentional merit. But such categories efface potentially interesting interactional dynamics that are appearing within and across these categories in contemporary online video. One such dynamic is the use of videos of affinity to establish communicative connections with other people.

Videos of affinity can appear in both user-created and professional contexts—an analytical division which is increasingly understood to be less strictly delineated. Videos of affinity are not necessarily always warm, personal, amateur videos that contrast to cynical professional content. Many so-called amateur video creators can use characteristics found in videos of affinity to gain support and viewership for work that they would happily commercialize. In addition, videomakers who are professional media makers have used videos of affinity to make more personalized contacts with like-minded individuals. They enable an interaction that gives viewers a feeling of being connected not to a video, but to a person who shares mutual beliefs or interests. Videos of affinity can exhibit varying degrees of sincerity, personalization and realistic expectations for interactivity, depending on who they are targeting and how the videos are received. Whatever their origin, videos of affinity have observable characteristics such as a presentist focus that aims to transit feelings of connection and maintain an open, active communication channel. They often contain ephemeral content that the videomakers themselves label as existing in the intercies of their other work.

Seen not as a cinematic end point, but rather as a mediated moment in an ongoing social relationship, the videos help maintain connections between individuals and groups of people in a social network, large or small. These types of videos resemble communicative exchanges in other media such as particular instant messages that are used for "checking in" rather than "exchanging data." In videos of affinity, people often produce evidence of their live body and provide a spontaneous, present-status update. People often engage in these types of exchanges to prepare a social channel for the eventual arrival of new, important content.

Further research might investigate the differences between the content and structure of videos of affinity in comparison to affinity messages in other media. For instance, how does the contextual structure of a video of affinity differ from instant messages or text updates on sites such as Facebook or Twitter? In addition, the effects of time should receive scholarly attention when analyzing these interactions. Videos are sometimes viewed long after they have been posted. How do future viewings affect the perception of the message? Do videos of affinity retain their presentist impact across time? How do they function in cultural, social and communicative terms when viewed just after they have been posted compared to when viewed many weeks or months later? Scholarly descriptions and categorizations often take a synchronic view of a video's creation, content and reception although videos may be perceived differently at various points in time.

Critics of videomakers who broadcast ephemera often ignore social, cultural and material circumstances that influence how individuals use video to communicate. Sending video messages to wide, dispersed social networks is far easier to accomplish on a free, public and oft-watched site such as YouTube. Moral judgments about who deserves our attention based on idiosyncratic ideals about normative content ignore the value of connections that videos of affinity attempt to achieve. Videos of affinity defy the logic of economically driven models of attention that would predict a glut of spectacular and novel content in an era of more intense attentional competition. Videos of affinity are made by various types of creators, including popular YouTubers who, judging by their view counts on YouTube, have demonstrated an ability to make well-crafted or at least interesting videos. Economic models do not take into account the fact that basic forms of interaction—whether offline or online—require work and may include multiple methods, such as making videos of affinity, to secure attention.

Videos of affinity can broaden one's social network by inviting self-interpellated viewers to participate in a video-mediated exchange. Amid labile, dispersed social networks, videos of affinity facilitate the possibility of further communication. Elements within the videos may target different individuals who may or may not ultimately attend to or socially connect with the video's creator. Issuing an invitation does not guarantee its acceptance. Returning to the vignette that began this essay, it is a painfully poignant reminder that even terminally ill people with severely limited time were being encouraged to give someone *else* their attention, in the hopes that they too would reciprocally benefit from one of humankind's most important gifts.

Endnotes

1 David Grubin's documentary *Healing and the Mind: Wounded Healers* was made in 1993.

2 The objection here is to generic diagnoses of popular interpretations of narcissism. Generic diagnoses are based on broad characteristics such as age or type of media use, such as making videos. People who make videos are assumed to be more narcissistic than people who make other forms of media.

3 Yi-Wyn Yen, "YouTube Looks for the Money Clip," *Fortune*, 15 October 2008 – http://techland.blogs.fortune.cnn.com/2008/03/25/youtube-looks-for-the-money-clip/ [last checked 15 February 2008].

4 Patricia G. Lange, "Publicly Private and Privately Public: Social Networking on YouTube," *Journal of Computer-Mediated Communication* no. 1, 2007 – http://jcmc.indiana.edu/vol13/issue1/lange.html [last checked 15 February 2008].

5 Barry Wellman, "Are Personal Communities Local? A Dumptarian Reconsideration," *Social Networks* no. 18, 1996, pp. 347–354.

6 The study focused on YouTube and video blogging by children and youth in the United States. It included two years worth of observations on YouTube, analyses of videos, over 150 interviews with media makers and attendance at meet-ups across the United States. The researcher also directly participated on YouTube through the video blog called "AnthroVlog." The study was part of the larger Digital Youth and Informal Learning project, which was funded by the MacArthur Foundation. The goal of the project was to understand informal learning practices of children and youth in digital environments, such as online media cultures. For more information see http://digitalyouth.ischool.berkeley.edu/report [last checked 15 February 2008].

7 Bonnie A. Nardi, "Beyond Bandwidth: Dimensions of Connection in Interpersonal Communication," *Computer-Supported Cooperative Work* no. 14, 2005, pp. 347–354.

8 Ibid.

9 A video blog or vlog is similar to a blog, in that videos are posted in reverse chronological order so that the viewer encounters the most recent video first. Although video blogs may contain text graphics and photographs, video bloggers often prefer to privilege video as the central mode of communication.

10 Louis Althusser, *Lenin and Philosophy and Other Essays* (New York: Monthly Review Press, 1971), pp. 173–177.

11 Charles Goodwin, *Conversational Organization: Interaction Between Speakers and Hearers* (New York: Academic Press, 1981).

12 Alessandro Duranti, *Linguistic Anthropology* (Cambridge, MA: Cambridge University Press, 1997).

13 Ibid., p. 273.

14 Starkey Duncan & Donald W. Fiske, *Face-to-Face Interaction: Research, Methods, and Theory* (New York/Toronto: John Wiley & Sons, 1977); Lynn Cherny, *Conversation and Community: Chat in a Virtual World* (Stanford: CLSI Publications, 1999); Deborah James & Sandra Clarke, "Women, Men, and Interruptions: A Critical Review," in *Gender and Conversational Interaction*, ed. Deborah Tannen (Oxford: Oxford University Press, 1993), pp. 231–280.

15 James & Clarke 1993, pp. 231–280.

16 Janet Beavin Bavelas, Linda Coates & Trudy Johnson, "Listener Responses as a Collaborative Process: The Role of Gaze," *Journal of Communication*, September 2002, pp. 566–580.

17 Michael H. Goldhaber, "The Attention Economy and the Net," *First Monday* no. 2, 1997 – www.firstmonday.org/issues/issue2_4/goldhaber/ [last checked 15 February 2008].

18 Ibid.

19 Video creators often express puzzlement that people select or continue to watch a video that they did not initially enjoy.

20 Nardi 2005.

21 Ibid.

22 Ibid.

23 Richard Chalfen, *Snapshots Versions of Life* (Bowling Green, OH: Bowling Green State University Popular Press, 1987). Chalfen studied white, middle-class Americans in the northeastern United States, and examined photographs taken between 1940 and 1980.

24 Chalfen 1987 and Patricia Zimmerman, *Reel Families: A Social History of Amateur Film* (Bloomington: Indiana University Press, 1995). Zimmerman studied the history of nonprofessional film from the late 19th century to the early 1990s.

25 However, much more historical, empirical research is needed to understand the precise content of past decades of home movies in comparison to contemporary video. Today's digital video contains many instances of celebratory ritual as well as more spontaneous ephemera. In addition, it is unclear from past scholarship to what extent amateur filmmaking was devoted to recording a variety of events, large and small. For instance, in her analysis, Zimmerman relies heavily on written rhetoric and home-movie discourses in documents such as camera manufacturing brochures and popular magazines, as opposed to close empirical readings of a sample of home-movies over time.

26 See for instance, James Moran, *There's No Place Like Home Video* (Minneapolis: University of Minnesota Press, 2002). However, as Moran also implies, deterministic arguments about cultural use based on medium specificity cannot be taken too far. Studies have also shown that a number of factors other than medium specificity play a role in who operates a camera and when. See for instance, Patricia G. Lange and Mizuko Ito, "Creative Production," in Ito et al., *Hanging Out, Messing Around, and Geeking Out: Living and Learning with New Media* (Cambridge, MA: MIT Press, forthcoming in 2009).

27 Chalfen 1987, p. 8.

28 Zimmerman 1995, p. 126.

29 Zimmerman 1995.

30 Ibid., p. 157.

31 Nardi 2005.

32 Althusser 1971, pp. 173–177.

33 Viewers may interpellate themselves as intended targets of different remarks within the same video. For example, I attended several YouTube gatherings. When she mentions posting meet-up videos, I am interested in this theme, and thus arguably a viewer being "hailed" to view them. However, when she speaks of "little birdies" who circulate rumors, I do

not know who these individuals are, nor am I familiar with the rumors. This portion of the video is targeted toward those who have circulated rumors (or are interested in this topic).

34 Although coded by her as existing between other videos, it received similar orders of magnitude in terms of views. "I'm Not Dead" received 824 views and 86 text comments between its posting on March 2, 2008, and March 25, 2009. Views here are not actual viewings that are retrospectively unknowable (as when several people stand around a computer to watch, for instance), but are rather view counts as recorded when a video is accessed on YouTube. Her prior video involving answering a call to see how many grapes she could put in her mouth received 1,055 views between February 13, 2008, and March 25, 2009. Her subsequent video about a YouTube cruise received 1,032 views between its posting on March 14, 2008, and March 25, 2009.

35 Roman Jakobson, "The Speech Event and the Functions of Language," in *On Language*, eds. Linda R. Waugh & Monique Monville-Burston (London: Harvard University Press, 1990), pp. 69-79.

36 Ibid., p. 75.

Jean Burgess and Joshua Green

The Entrepreneurial Vlogger: Participatory Culture Beyond the Professional-Amateur Divide

YouTube's status as the dominant website for online video is a regular topic for discussion in technology, popular and academic presses. The site is often characterized as a significant challenger to the dominance of traditional broadcasting and television services—celebrated in hyperbolic fashion when *Time* magazine declared "You" the 2006 Person of the Year. Unsurprisingly, YouTube was included in the range of sites where, from "rumpled bedrooms and toy-strewn basement rec rooms," "ordinary" citizens were "seizing the reins of the global media [...] founding and framing the new digital democracy [...] working for nothing and beating the pros at their own game."[1] Infamously branded as a place to "Broadcast Yourself," YouTube is a key site where the discourses of participatory culture and the emergence of the creative, empowered consumer have been played out.

Certainly, YouTube appears to be exemplary of the disruptive effect that new networks of content production and distribution are having on existing media business models. The website has been directly in the firing line of the most powerful traditional media companies. Some have developed official streaming sites in direct response, such as NBC Universal and News Corp.'s Hulu. Others have pursued legal action, claiming the site (more than tacitly) supports copyright infringement.[2] Alternatively, some media companies have approached the service as a site offering substantial reach and potential viral distribution—providing exposure through word-of-mouth networks that might cut through the clutter of the advertising space. Some commentators (including many members of the YouTube community itself) have interpreted the entry of commercial media players into YouTube as a corporate takeover of what had been a "grassroots" media platform (despite the obvious fact that YouTube has always been a commercial enterprise, although one without a clear business model).[3] The notion that professionally produced videos (be they music videos or viral content) signals a period of corporate appropriation assumes that the "real," original YouTube was driven primarily by purely social or non-market motivations, an idea underlying some of the most significant academic work on the nature and potential of participatory media.[4] This discourse encourages us to imagine as an ideal a specific type of participant—an ordinary, amateur individual, motivated by a desire for personal expression or community, whose original content either expresses the mundane or everyday—represented by the ubiquitous and much-maligned "cat video"—or demonstrates a high level of creativity and playfulness through the production of fan videos and mashups. There is no doubt that there is a recognizable mode of production and a particular aesthetic style associated with the culture of user-created content on YouTube, and that amateur and everyday content creation is an essential driver of this. However, upon taking a closer look at how YouTube actually works, it becomes clear that amateur and professional media content, identities and motivations are not so easily separated.

While much has been made of the newly empowered, creative audience-turned-producer, in this article we argue that some of YouTube's most significant cultural and economic implications lie elsewhere. YouTube *is* symptomatic of a changing media environment, but it is one where the practices and identities associated with cultural production and consumption, commercial and non-commercial enterprise, and professionalism and amateurism interact and converge in new ways. YouTube is disruptive not only because it unsettles the producer-consumer divide, but also because it is the site of dynamic and emergent relations between market and non-market, social and economic activity. Arguing along with Banks, and Potts, et al., that social networks are fundamental as sites of innovation and activity within the creative industries,[5] we frame YouTube as an example of "co-creative" culture—whatever YouTube is, it is produced dynamically (that is, as an ongoing process, over time) as a result of many interconnected instances of participation, by many different people. In order to understand these co-creative relationships, it is important not to focus exclusively on how the "ordinary consumer" or "amateur producer" are participating in YouTube; rather, we argue it is necessary to include the activities of "traditional media" companies and media professionals, and more importantly the new models of media entrepreneurialism that are grounded in YouTube's "grassroots" culture. Hence, this article focuses the role that "YouTube stars"—highly visible and successful "home-grown" performers and producers—play in modeling and negotiating these co-creative relationships within the context of YouTube's social network and the new models of entrepreneurship within participatory culture that they represent.

Making Sense of YouTube

This article draws on the results of our recent study of YouTube's most popular content.[6] The study aimed to develop an understanding of the forms and practices associated with the dominant or most popular uses of YouTube, which will be referred to as YouTube's "common culture." The study relied in the first instance on a large-scale content survey, drawing on a sample of 4,320 videos from four of YouTube's categories of popularity—Most Viewed, Most Favorited, Most Responded, Most Discussed—gathered in the second half of 2007.[7] The study made YouTube's popular culture the central object of investigation, rather than exploring the practices and cultural participation of a particular group (say "amateurs," "young people" or "independent producers") by examining their use of the site. The coding scheme used in this survey began with two primary categories: the first was the apparent industrial origin of the video (whether it was "user-created"[8] or the product of a traditional media company—material taken from another source with minimal adaptation and posted to YouTube); the second was the apparent identity of the uploader, initially divided into four groups: traditional media companies, small-to-medium enterprises or independent producers, government organizations, cultural institutions or the like, and "amateur users." We concentrated on four categories of popularity—Most Viewed, Most Favorited, Most Responded, Most Discussed—based on the hypothesis that comparing across them would give us a sense of the way different kinds of video content are made popular by audiences in different ways. Finally, the videos were sorted into a large number of broad categories based on formal and generic characteristics, allowing us to observe patterns of media production and use in relation to particular measures of popularity and therefore modes of engagement within YouTube itself.

Approximately half of the content in the sample was coded as "traditional media content," and approximately half as "user-created content." However, around two-thirds of the total number of videos in the sample were contributed by uploaders coded as "users"—uploaders represented as individuals not associated with media companies, production companies or organizations of any kind. On closer examination, however, it becomes clear that YouTube's popular videos are contributed by a range of professional, semi-professional, amateur and pro-amateur participants, some of whom produce content that is an uncomfortable fit with the available categories of either "traditional" media content or the vernacular forms generally associated with the concept of "amateur" content. For the purpose of thinking through the relations between "professional" and "amateur" participation on YouTube, and based on their locations within or alongside the formally constituted creative industries, there are three immediately identifiable groups of participants in YouTube. First, there are the "big media" companies, established players within mainstream broadcast, music and cinema industries, some of whom are especially successful inside YouTube. Universal Music Group (UMG), for instance, ranks among the top subscribed channels on the site—a measure YouTube is increasingly using as a meaningful measure of success across their platform. UMG uploads music videos and content featuring their artists, reaping the rewards of revenue-sharing deals with YouTube.[9] Along with these "big media" companies, large rights holders such as the National Basketball Association (NBA) similarly capitalize on the wide reach of YouTube for promotional purposes. The NBA regularly uploads clips of their games, post-game discussions and weekly highlight packages in order to promote telecasts of their games, official copies of which are not uploaded to YouTube. Like UMG, the NBA's channel is significant within the YouTube ecology, ranking within the top 100 subscribed channels on the service. It represents a significant effort by a large rights holder to make sense of the YouTube space.

The second group concerned are Web-TV companies, such as JumpTV Sports, who put together sports packages and deliver content to a range of sports sites around the world, and NoGoodTV, who produce vaguely risqué, male-targeted content. Many of these companies ape traditional television producers but make use of the Internet to distribute niche programming or specialized content without needing to negotiate cable or television distribution deals. Content from NoGoodTV, for instance, resembles the "laddish" programming regularly seen on US cable channels such as Spike and the video-game-oriented G4TV. It is a mixture of music videos, celebrity interviews, sketches, informational programming and miscellanea, wrapped in on-screen graphics. Its resemblance to television content points to the way digital delivery options such as YouTube and the increasing move of material online are destabilizing medium-dependent definitions of media forms.

Third, one might consider the "ordinary user"—contributors who at first glance appear to be individual, amateur participants, because they are not obviously representatives of mainstream media companies or other large institutions. Patricia Lange's study[10] of these casual users demonstrates that this category is more complex than it may first appear. Lange's ethnographic investigation of YouTube develops a typology that breaks down the notion of a singular "ordinary" or "casual user," looking at YouTube participants who might be considered: "1) former participants; 2) casual users; 3) active participants; 4) YouTubers or 'Tubers'; and 5) YouTube celebrities." Lange's approach helpfully problematizes how we can understand participation in YouTube by distinguishing between different types of non-corporate, individual users. While content produced within both the mainstream and alternative media industries regularly features among YouTube's most popular videos, it is on the cultural activity that occurs within this third group—the "users"—that we will focus much of our attention for the purposes of this article. It is within this group that the assumed divisions between amateur and professional, market and non-market practices and motivations are most disrupted, and it is this group that is most actively and reflexively engaged in experimenting with and negotiating the specificities of YouTube's culture. For the remainder of this article we will focus in particular on the convergence of a peculiarly YouTube form often associated with "amateur" video production—the videoblog, or vlog—and the emergence of new models for building audiences and brands, both of which are exemplified by a number of the most popular uploaders in our sample: participants that can be understood as "YouTube stars," whom we characterize as entrepreneurial vloggers.

The YouTube-ness of Vlogs

Videoblogging, or "vlogging," is a dominant form of user-created content, and it is fundamental to YouTube's sense of community. Typically structured primarily around a monologue delivered directly to camera, vlogs are characteristically produced with little more than a webcam and some witty editing. The subject matter ranges from reasoned political debate to the mundane details of everyday life and impassioned rants about YouTube itself. Vlogging itself is not necessarily new or unique to YouTube, but it is an emblematic form of YouTube participation. The form has antecedents in webcam culture, personal blogging and the more widespread "confessional culture"[11] that characterizes television talk shows and reality television focused on the observation of everyday life. In our study, vlog entries dominated the sample, making up nearly 40 percent of the videos coded Most Discussed and just over a quarter of the videos coded Most Responded.

Not only is the vlog technically easy to produce, generally requiring little more than a webcam and basic editing skills, it is a form whose persistent direct address to the viewer inherently invites feedback. While television content—news, sketch comedy, clips from soap operas—may draw people to YouTube for a catch-up, traditional media content doesn't appear to attract high levels of conversational and intercreative[12] participation, as measured by the numbers of comments and video responses. By contrast, more than any other form in the sample, the vlog as a genre of communication invites critique, debate and discussion. Direct response, through comment and via video, is central to this mode of engagement. Particular vlog entries frequently respond to other vlogs, carrying out discussion across YouTube and directly addressing comments left on previous entries. Given all this, it is not surprising that some of the most effective entrepreneurial uses of YouTube have been built around vlogging. Indeed, vlogging is a prototypical example of "situated creativity"[13]—that is, creativity as a social process, rather than a static individual attribute, embedded within and co-evolving with

YouTube as a dynamic cultural environment, not an inert publishing mechanism.

In 2006, high-profile video blogger LonelyGirl15, apparently a teenage girl called Bree posting personal diary entries from her bedroom, was revealed as the creation of independent filmmakers Mesh Flinders and Miles Beckett. Bree's profile as a vlogger bore many of the markers of authentic amateur participation: her posts featured a talking head speaking straight-to-camera, and covered the domestic, personal topics then considered characteristic of the videoblog form. Some of her videos seemed a little too slickly edited, and a suspiciously coherent narrative began to develop across her posts, but Bree and fellow characters seemed to participate in YouTube's affective economy as many "legitimate" users do—they followed each other's videos, communicated through the network, and maintained profiles on other sites such as MySpace.

4 "Really excited": Bree, the manufactured vlogger

The unveiling of Bree as a "manufactured" vlogger by the YouTube community and some members of the press[14] brought mainstream media attention to what might be YouTube's emblematic form, as well as to the murkiness between professional and amateur production practices on YouTube. The possibilities of inauthentic authenticity are now a part of the cultural repertoire of YouTube; subsequent vloggers have built identities around a similar ambiguity about their authenticity and trying to figure out how much of a given YouTuber's act is real (notable in the discussion around the highly popular vlogger daxflame), or how big their production team is (a topic of debate in discussion around the comedic YouTuber LisaNova), is now something of a "game" for participants within YouTube`s social network.

In fact, vlogs make up almost half of the top thirty Most Subscribed channels on YouTube. Of the thirty with the most subscriptions of all time, thirteen are channels predominantly built around vlogging. These vloggers range from sxephil, a 23-year-old American who provides daily commentary and critique about news and current affairs; to ItsChrisCrocker, a personal vlog commenting on celebrity culture and everyday life by 20-year-old Chris Crocker, who gained some notoriety in 2007 when he posted an impassioned plea imploring both the mainstream press and the blogosphere to "leave Britney [Spears] alone!"; and, mileymandy, a vlog run for a short time by young US stars Miley Cyrus and Mandy Jiroux. This latter channel is a good example of the wide range of content styles and genres that the vlog as a form can include. Like other top channels such as Nigahiga, kevjumba, davedays and AtheneWins, mileymandy features a range of content: conversational pieces to the camera, concert footage from their performances, and short comedic sketches. Indeed, a number of the top channels mix musical performances with "traditional" vlogging, amateur or professional performances accompanied by personal discussion or journaling.

Entrepreneurial Vloggers

The channels in the Most Subscribed list reveal that, although the vlog form is grounded in ordinary, domestic creative practice, not all vlogs are purely amateur productions, created in bedrooms for the purposes of self-expression alone. Indeed, a number of prominent vloggers, or performers using the videoblog form, are quite clearly using YouTube in an entrepreneurial way. Exploiting a buxom figure and coquettish presentation, Marina Orlova's highly popular *Hot For Words* videos are a series of philological discussions that explore the etymology of common words and common expressions. According to her bio, Russian-born Orlova possesses degrees in "Teaching of Russian Language and World Literature Specializing in Philology and the Teaching of English Language Specializing in Philology from State University of Nizhni Novgorod Region in Russian Federation" and taught English for two years. Often appearing in pigtails and outfits with plunging necklines, her videos are presented as simultaneously tongue-in-cheek titillation and education. Her videos, user page, website and press materials feature the slogan "Intelligence is Sexy," and her chosen topics for presentation highlight the marriage of the two. Her discussion of the etymology of "booby" starts with the Spanish word *bobo* from the late 1500s ("meaning, a stupid person"), works its way through the "booby bird" ("a very slow and stupid bird") and the Oxford English dictionary ("a dull stupid person...the last boy in the class, the dunce"), before arriving at the possible German root *bubbi* (for "teat"), all while Orlova affects coy confusion about why viewers might request such an etymological excursion.

Orlova's videos capitalize on the dialogic opportunities of YouTube. Addressing her viewers as "my dear students," Orlova petitions the audience to leave queries and suggestions in the comments to her videos, often setting them "homework" tasks such as guessing the correct definition of a word. Words are regularly submitted by viewers, and episodes often commence not only with an announcement of the word to be featured but also with an acknowledgement of each of the commenters who have requested discussion of that particular word. Orlova directly responds to particular queries, corrections and comments left for her in response to her videos, invites her viewers to join her next time, and ends her videos with the now common prompt to viewers to subscribe. Her blend of sexuality and smarts has made Orlova a YouTube success: her channel ranks among the highest subscribed of all time, especially within YouTube's "Gurus" and "Partners" categories. She has been granted access to the company's revenue-sharing program, which extends a cut of the revenue from page views to prominent producers who create their own content—a system that includes not only prominent YouTubers (such as LisaNova, renetto and smosh) but also "traditional media" producers like television stations and large rights holders. The significance of this is not lost on Orlova herself, whose bio mentions that her channel is one of the most viewed of all time—"just ahead of Universal Music Group and the NBA."

But the attention Orlova garners is only partly due to her visual appeal. Orlova not only navigates YouTube's attention economy through regular engagement with her viewers and commenters, she has collaborated with a number of both prominent and less prominent YouTubers. These collaborations not only increase her visibility within the community, they constitute "shout-outs" to the YouTube community. Orlova is also sure to mention the YouTube profiles of users from whom she gets music for her vlogs, and maintains a list of these and her collaborations on her website hotforwords.com (where she also offers 2009 calendars and "hot cards" featuring lingerie shots of herself). Orlova's success has resulted in a move into "mainstream" attention. Readers of *Wired* voted her the "sexiest geek" of 2007, US tech television channel G4 has included her in its top-ten list of "Hottest Women on the Net" on more than one occasion, and Orlova has been subject of a number of profiles across the blogosphere (including men's magazine AskMen.com). Her prominence online led to repeated appearances on Fox New Channel's *The O'Reilly Factor* during the US election campaign to explain the origin of political terms, where the high numbers of views her YouTube videos had received were regularly mentioned to establish her expertise as a commentator.

5 *Hot for Words* – "Sarcasm in HD"

With rapid-fire delivery and acrid commentary, Michael Buckley's *What the Buck?!* program has similarly brought the vlogger to the attention of the media industry outside of YouTube. *What the Buck?!*—which delivers regular celebrity news and pop-culture commentary with a decidedly camp affect—is regularly among the top-subscribed channels of all time. Buckley's YouTube success has brought him to the attention of executives at HBO, who in 2008 signed the comedian to a development deal with the network, purportedly to work on a project unlike his YouTube show. Aping the style of a news update, and following in the tradition of long-running US cable program *Talk Soup* (now known as *The Soup*) and the footsteps of prominent blogger and pop-culture commentator Perez Hilton, who came to the attention of the mainstream press in 2005, Buckley's show provides celebrity news and decidedly bitchy commentary on popular culture.

Like Orlova, Buckley's success on YouTube stems in part from his engagement with the YouTube community. His program regularly responds to reader comments in program descriptions, and he includes discussion of some of the controversies and disputes that take place across the YouTube community, blurring the divide between notoriety in the YouTube community and in the wider popular culture. Buckley rewards his viewers with regular celebrations of milestones in subscription; he celebrated 30,000 subscribers in August 2007 with a video reflecting on the evolution of the style of his show, and on attaining 100,000 subscribers he produced a show editing together the good wishes of other YouTubers.

Not just representative of innovation on YouTube, both Orlova and Buckley have been recognized as representatives for YouTube itself. Both were engaged as backstage correspondents during *YouTube Live*, with Buckley fulfilling some front-of-stage MC duties. The event, a variety-concert-cum-awards-night in late November 2008, featured a combination of homegrown YouTube "stars" and what the company referred to as "real world personalities"—performers and celebrities whose basis of fame lay in the traditional media or music industries, but who were also highly popular within YouTube itself. Drawing together "all that YouTube has to offer including bedroom vloggers, budding creatives, underground athletes, world-famous musicians, gut-busting comedians and more,"[15] the event was streamed live from San Francisco, in a stunt designed to promote the introduction of live-streaming functionality to the website. At its peak, it drew 700,000 simultaneous viewers, and YouTube reported that videos edited from the original footage received 2,500,000 views in the 24 hours immediately following the live show.

Because of its "liveness," in the mainstream press the event inevitably drew comparisons with broadcast television.[16] Peter Kafka pointed out that while these viewership figures might have been momentous for an online event, they were insignificant in the broader context of US broadcast television, where "a poorly performing show on network TV, by comparison, draws millions of viewers."[17] Even moderately performing Saturday night programming, Kafka noted, can draw five million viewers. The issue Kafka suggested was that the "real world" personalities YouTube assembled just weren't enough of a draw, and that YouTube personalities appeal best when forwarded through YouTube's viral channels.

But looking at the number of views alone may only tell half the story when considering what success on YouTube looks like. As we have argued elsewhere,[18] it is the extensive "spreadability" of the ideas, styles and materials associated with YouTube's homegrown stars that make them important within the YouTube ecology. And the means of this "spreadability" can just as easily include parody as it does praise. For example, in her video "LisaNova does sxephil and HotForWords" fellow YouTube star LisaNova enlisted the help of fellow YouTuber Danny "The Diamond Factory" to parody both sxephil (vlogger Philip DeFranco) and Orlova. LisaNova's parody focuses on both shots of plunging necklines and Russian diction. It is introduced as a parody of "two of our favorite YouTubers" and included as part of a series of collaborations collected under the banner of "LisaNovaLive." LisaNova, in turn, is also the subject of the many parodic representations of YouTube "stars" produced by other members of the YouTube community—and so on it goes. Indeed, we might view YouTube stars not only as moderately successful cultural entrepreneurs and performers, but also as a shared cultural resource for other YouTube participants; this is why the numbers of subscribers and video responses are so important in understanding how popularity works in YouTube. The "stars" provide markers for a sense of "YouTube-ness"—through their participation and ways in which other YouTubers engage with them, a sense of YouTube's "common culture" is created. It is above all this embeddedness within and permeability to the activities of the distributed YouTube community that marks out the difference between the practices of the "entrepreneurial vloggers" and most mainstream media uses of YouTube.

Oprah Comes to YouTube

The launch of Oprah Winfrey's YouTube channel in early November 2007 provides a particularly stark example of the potential misfit between corporate promotional strategies and organic participation in YouTube. The launch was cross-promoted via a "YouTube special" episode on the Oprah television show in which a number of the subjects and creators of YouTube's most viewed videos were featured as guest stars. There was an intense and immediate flurry of protest videos, spawning discussion about the implications of this event, and the incursion of such a major corporate media player into YouTube's attention economy. One point made by several YouTube commenters was that Oprah was importing the convergence of celebrity and control associated with "big media" into the social media space (by disallowing external embedding of videos moderating comments on videos in her channel) and therefore ignoring the cultural norms that have developed over the life of the network. Late-arriving corporate partners were seen as exploiting the attention that had been produced by earlier, more "authentic," participants, a situation only exacerbated by YouTube's practice of proactively promoting their partnerships with mainstream media companies and celebrities who hadn't done the "hard yards" in the subculture.

The blog devoted to YouTube, YouTubeStars,[19] summed up the themes of the debates that occurred around this event, noting widespread objections to the Oprah channel's "one-way conversation" approach and concerns that the incursions of the mainstream media into YouTube meant an inevitable and ongoing process of corporate colonization, making "authentic" YouTube participation less visible and less valued: "With the corporate accounts racking up lots of viewers, its hard to get on the most discussed or most viewed lists without resorting to histrionics and sensationalism. YouTube seemed more like a community of videomakers before 'partners' came on to advertise to us." At the same time, the website acknowledges YouTube Inc.'s need to find a way to draw revenue from the site, if only to offset its massive bandwidth costs. However, although the launch of Oprah's YouTube channel provided an opportunity for the YouTube community to perform their own knowledge of how YouTube works, and to make claims about how it should be run, once the dust had settled it became clear that Oprah would not be as disruptive to YouTube's internal attention economy as many of the participants in these debates feared: as of November 2008, a year later, the Oprah channel had only 47,909 subscribers—a significant number, but still only just over a tenth of the number of subscribers to Michael Buckley's program, *What the Buck?!*. Given Oprah's immense media power and cultural influence, especially in comparison to Michael Buckley's, how can this apparent failure to engage the YouTube audience be explained?

6 "I am Oprah, of course!" – Oprah's "Message To YouTube"

The Oprah brand's faltering steps into the world of participatory media are all the more interesting given that the Oprah show is ostensibly built around, or claims to try and harness, a conversational form and a democratic ethos that could have been eminently *compatible* with YouTube as a participatory media platform. As well as adopting a more conversational, improvisatory and intimate mode of address than the talk-show hosts who had come before her on American television, Oprah "staged an immediate and embodied relationship with her audience" by offering them "tears and hugs."[20] She was an early innovator in the talk-show format, emphasizing the dialogic possibilities of television through her apparently unscripted performances and the placement of conversation on center stage. She addresses the audience "directly at home, in an ordinary conversational manner, thereby creating a relationship based on trust and care."[21] But on television, the Oprah franchise controls, directs and stage-manages these conversations; the Oprah YouTube channel for a time did not allow unmoderated comments, and Oprah's appearances within it were an extension of her television persona, never directly engaging with the specificity of YouTube or any of the people who represent themselves as members of a YouTube "community." As of November 2008, the Oprah YouTube channel is focused around making available "highlight" clips from the television show, which occasionally feature YouTube stars as guests; and cross-promoting the Oprah.com website—but there is very little sense of the same direct address and conversational intimacy in the ways in which Oprah herself engages with the YouTube community. YouTube is not treated as a participatory space, but as a brand-extension platform.

Conclusion

In most mainstream discourse, YouTube is by turns understood as a space driven by the social interactions of "amateur" participants, and the site of possibility or conflict for the promotional desires of large media companies. However, the examples discussed in this article show that amateur and entrepreneurial uses of YouTube are not separate, but coexistent and coevolving, so that the distinction between market and non-market culture is unhelpful to a meaningful or detailed analysis of YouTube as a site of participatory culture. In broadcast media like television, access to visible participation is restricted by the politics of scarcity and institutionalized professionalism. In contrast, YouTube is an open and underdetermined platform with low barriers to entry. YouTube's culture—the media forms and practices that combine to constitute the "YouTube-ness" of YouTube—is determined through the interaction of YouTube Inc., which provides the framework, infrastructure and architecture of the service; the various users who upload content to the website; and the diverse audiences who engage with that content and each other. The contributors to the site are diverse—from large media producers and rights-owners such as television stations, sports companies and major advertisers to small-to-medium enterprises looking for cheap distribution or alternatives to mainstream broadcast systems, cultural institutions, artists, activists, media-literate fans, non-professional and amateur media producers. In particular, the professional-amateur divide is disrupted by entrepreneurial vloggers—quasi-professional producers who are also at the same time authentic participants in the YouTube "community."

Entrepreneurial vloggers participate in YouTube's advertising sharing scheme and draw revenue from their presence on YouTube. But unlike digital media companies such as NoGoodTV, who seem to bring to YouTube the same one-way model of participation we know from broadcasting, these producers are active and authentic participants in the YouTube community as well as entrepreneurs, and they use communicative and aesthetic conventions that are continuous with the practices of the YouTube community. Their online success is as much due to their grounded knowledge of and effective participation within YouTube's communicative ecology as it is the savvy with which they produce content, and they are virtuosic in their mastery of YouTube's homegrown forms and practices. As this article has shown, the performers and producers who are understood as YouTubeStars, because of their large subscriber base, and the strong brands they have built within YouTube, can be associated with commercial enterprises, or they can be strictly amateurs. Hence, the distinction between professional and amateur, or market and non-market activity, is not the key difference between, say, *Hot For Words* and the Oprah channel. The key analytical distinction, rather, hinges on the extent to which content producers understand YouTube as a participatory medium, and work responsively and proactively within it, rather than attempting to import models of content and experiences from somewhere else.

The examples discussed in this article show that it is difficult to make sharp distinctions between professional and "user-created" content, or between "producerly" and audience practices in YouTube. These distinctions are based in industrial logics more at home in the context of the broadcast media rather than an understanding of how people use media in their everyday lives, or a knowledge of how YouTube actually works as a cultural system. It is more helpful to shift from thinking about media production, distribution and consumption to thinking about YouTube in terms of a continuum of cultural participation.

In this context, what the "entrepreneurial vloggers" can teach us is not so much how to make money from YouTube, but how to build a meaningful presence and an engaged audience in a participatory media space. However charming, distasteful or silly the content of their videos might be, what all the entrepreneurial YouTube stars have in common is the fit between their creative practice and the dynamics of YouTube as a platform for participatory culture. These dynamics rely on reciprocal activity: the vlogging YouTube stars are also subscribers to other channels, participants in discussions occurring within the YouTube community, and audiences for other YouTube videos; their audiences act as interlocutors, co-creators and critics by making related videos drawing on the YouTube stars' characters and material, leaving comments, or simply watching. Garnering this type of success requires more than knowledge of how YouTube's culture works; it also requires direct, ongoing participation within it. This can be a challenge for those organizations, whether market-based or publicly funded, that have built strong brands elsewhere, and who rely on those brands to generate attention within YouTube—with varying degrees of success. Media organizations, cultural institutions and educators with a remit to innovate in social media can learn much from the entrepreneurial vloggers. They may not provide models of aesthetic innovation or of an elevated cultural vision, but they do provide models of how to create attention and engagement in ways that are appropriate to and sustained by YouTube's participatory culture.

Endnotes

1 Lev Grossman, "Time's Person of the Year: You," *Time,* 13 December 2006 – www.time.com/time/magazine/article/0,9171,1569514,00.html [last checked 15 February 2009].

2 Telegraph Online, "Premier League to take action against YouTube," 23 May 2007 – www.telegraph.co.uk/sport/football/2312532/Premier-League-to-take-action-against-YouTube.html [last checked 15 February 2009]. See also Anne Becker, "YouTube to Viacom: We Will Pull Your Clips," *Broadcasting and Cable,* 2 February 2007, as well as Rhys Blakely, "YouTube fails to satisfy critics over copyright," *The Times,* 17 October 2007.

3 Ben Walters, for instance, writing for *The Guardian*'s film blog, proposed that the high degree of corporate-produced content in the top 20 YouTube videos of all time suggests that the dream of YouTube as a home for immensely popular user-created content is coming to an end. See www.guardian.co.uk/film/filmblog/2008/nov/20/mark-ravenhill-youtube-competition [last checked 15 February 2009].

4 Yochai Benkler, *The Wealth of Networks: How Social Production Transforms Markets and Freedom* (New Haven, CT: Yale University Press, 2006), pp. 299–300.

5 John Banks & Sal Humphreys, "The Labour of User Co-Creators: Emergent Social Network Markets?" *Convergence: The International Journal of Research into New Media Technologies* no. 4, 2008, pp. 401–418; Jason Potts, John Hartley, John Banks, Jean Burgess, Rachel Cobcroft, Stuart Cunningham & Lucy Montgomery, "Consumer Co-Creation and Situated Creativity," *Industry & Innovation* no. 5, 2008, pp. 459–474.

6 The study was a collaboration between the Comparative Media Studies Program and Convergence Culture Consortium, MIT, and the ARC Centre of Excellence for Creative Industries and Innovation, Queensland University of Technology. Our forthcoming book is entitled *YouTube: Online Video and Participatory Culture* (Cambridge: Polity Press, 2009).

7 The 4,320 videos were gathered by sampling from six days over two weeks in each of three months of 2007.

8 This category recognized the significant transformation of professionally produced materials as resulting in "user-created" content. Rather than counting every instance of the use of copyrighted material as an appearance of "traditional media, " which would, for instance, note instances of copyrighted content in Anime Music Videos, mashups and sports-highlight packages, we factored in the degree of transformation—the extent to which "traditional media" , were used in the creation of new content.

9 See "Universal Music Group and YouTube Forge Strategic Partnership," 9 October 2006 – www.youtube.com/press_room_entry?entry=JrYdNx45e-0 [last checked 15 February 2009].

10 Patricia Lange, "Commenting on Comments: Investigating Responses to Antagonism on YouTube," unpublished paper. See also Lange's article "Publicly private and privately public: Social networking on YouTube," *Journal of Computer-Mediated Communication* no. 1, 2007, pp. 361–380.

11 Nicole Matthews, "Confessions to a New Public: Video Nation Shorts," *Media, Culture & Society* no. 3, 2007, pp. 435–448.

12 Christina Spurgeon, *Advertising and New Media* (London: Routledge, 2008); Graham Meikle, *Future Active: Media Activism and the Internet* (Sydney: Pluto Press, 2002).

13 Jason Potts et al. 2008.

14 See especially *New York Times* journalist and blogger Virginia Heffernan, "Well, It Turns Out That Lonelygirl Really Wasn't," *The New York Times,* 13 September 2006.

15 According to the company's press release "Celebrities and YouTube Users Come Together at YouTube Live," 24 November 2008 – www.marketwatch.com/news/story/Celebrities-YouTube-Users-Come-Together/story.aspx?guid [last checked 15 February 2009].

16 Matthew Ingrahm, "Was YouTube Live a Success? That Depends, " *NewTeeVeeLive* 24 November 2008 – http://newteevee.com/2008/11/24/was-youtube-live-a-success-that-depends [last checked 15 February 2009]. See also Paul Glazowski, "YouTube Live! (But Dead on Arrival)," *Mashable,* 22 November 2008 – http://mashable.com/2008/11/22/youtube-live-dead/ [last checked 15 February 2009].

17 Peter Kafka, "YouTube's Big Live Debut: Pretty Small," *MediaMemo,* 23 November 2008 – http://mediamemo.allthingsd.com/20081123/youtubes-big-live-debut-pretty-small/ [last checked 15 February 2009].

18 Jean Burgess, " 'All Your Chocolate Rain Are Belong to Us?' Viral Video, YouTube, and the Dynamics of Participatory Culture," in *The Video Vortex Reader: Responses to YouTube*, eds. Geert Lovink & Sabine Niederer (Amsterdam: Institute of Network Cultures, 2008), pp. 101 – 110.

19 The YouTubeStars blog post discussing Oprah's arrival on YouTube is available at http://youtubestars.blogspot.com/2007/11/oprah-is-on-youtube.html [last checked 15 February 2009].

20 Eva Illouz, *Oprah and the Glamour of Misery: An Essay on Popular Culture* (New York: Columbia University Press, 2003), p. 54.

21 Ibid., p. 131.

Patrick Vonderau

Writers Becoming Users: YouTube Hype and the Writer's Strike

In November 2007, former Disney chairman and CEO Michael Eisner took a risky bet on the future. Speaking at the Dow Jones/Nielsen Media and Money conference in New York, Eisner declared that any expectations for revenues flowing from digital distribution platforms such as YouTube were premature. Indicating that studios had talked up the potential of digital revenues over the last years, Eisner said that attempts to satisfy claims on such "nonexistent [revenue] flows" would be "insane."[1] Eisner's remarks came on the occasion of the 2007–2008 Writers Guild of America (WGA) strike, which made new-media content a central issue of debate. More than 12,000 writers picketed between November 5, 2007, and February 12, 2008, in a battle with the Alliance of Motion Picture and Television Producers (AMPTP) over how to determine compensation for content that is reused or created for new-media outlets, and how revenue from digital services should be divided up. Eisner seemingly had no doubts about the desirable outcome of the writers' strike: "For a writer to give up today's money for a nonexistent piece of the future—they should do it in three years, shouldn't be doing it now—they are misguided they should not have gone on the strike. I've seen stupid strikes, I've seen less stupid strikes, and this is just a stupid strike."[2]

Only one year later, *The New York Times* reported that Michael Buckley, a former administrative assistant for a music promotion company, was earning a six-figure income from YouTube for his thrice-a-week show, *What the Buck?!* Having generated millions of clicks with his celebrity chatter streaming from "the second bedroom of his home,"[3] Buckley became a member of YouTube's partner program early on, with YouTube ending up paying him over $100,000 as his share of the site's advertisement revenue.[4] Certainly, Buckley had, as many of his fellow "most popular" YouTubers, no proven writing credentials and no Hollywood track record when he started his show at about the time of Eisner's anti-strike rant. His online career as a host/writer/producer seems to demonstrate, however, that the concerns voiced by the WGA were not stupid at all. Given that there was indeed future potential for revenues flowing from original, derivative and experimental new-media content produced for exhibition on the Internet back in 2007, it made perfect sense that the writers fought and won the battle for a new WGA Minimum Basic Agreement covering these issues.[5] And although Eisner was apparently right in pointing out the lack of waterproof business models, this ironically occurred at the very moment when Google's YouTube began competing with Hulu, co-owned by NBC Universal, News Corp. and Providence Equity Partners, for the best solution on how to "monetize" creative content online.[6] In 2008, Hulu's model of repurposing TV shows and movies for advertising revenue turned out to be more promising than YouTube's, recently prompting YouTube to include both movies and TV shows[7] and to arrange new partnerships with premium content providers such as Disney and MGM.

In retrospect, then, it might seem obvious to state that Eisner had been wrong (possibly deliberately so), but this is not the point. The point is that for those involved in the creative economy at that time, YouTube markedly contributed to a situation in which *nobody could know*. It is debatable whether YouTube had an overall disruptive effect on old-media production, but the platform certainly undermined a long-held consensus on the value of entertainment.[8] YouTube constantly provides information on the marketability of forms and formats, challenging shared beliefs in the price structure and the organization of media work. At a time of perceived major industry turmoil, with disintegrating ancillary markets, sinking advertising revenues and Hollywood's agglomeration of capital and labor endangered by runaway productions and global media conglomerates, YouTube thus served, and still serves, as a sort of media laboratory—a laboratory producing data which is not only inconclusive, but downright confusing for those involved.[9]

This article investigates YouTube's capacity as a testing ground for old and new models of creative work during and after the writer's strike. By taking the writer's cause as a case in point, I would like to make some suggestions regarding the analysis of agency and power under conditions of uncertainty. Uncertainty of course has always been a key feature of the creative economy,[10] but YouTube made this economic problem a widely debated issue of practice. With a large number of accomplished writers turning to the Internet and reports on successful YouTube celebrities circulating widely, the generation of content by users gained new importance. In this article, I will outline how the dynamics of expectations funneled by YouTube relate to new role models for creative workers hyped in 2007–2008. Based on research conducted in Los Angeles during and after the strike, and inspired by Andrew Pickering's work in the field of science studies, my article also holds some implications for the present scholarly interest in "production culture."[11] My main point is that in trying to understand the intentionality of production practice, it is important to pay attention to time. I take it that human agency is temporally emergent in practice and that analyzing production in realtime makes a number of things look entirely different.

Commonists vs. Subservient Chickens

For industry observers at the time of the writer's strike, YouTube not only offered evidence of innovative formats and potential revenue streams, it also presented new role models for media workers. The successful convergence of executive and creative authority, apparently realized by Brooke "Brookers" Brodack, Michael Buckley and other famous one-person media enterprises, was heralded as a prospect for writers in the fragmented and slowly recombining television industry.[12] TV director-producer Doug Liman remarked in January 2008 that if the last strike was remembered for the studios attempting to show they could create programming without writers, this would be "the strike where the writers show they can do it without the studios. We are at a moment of opportunity in television where we have gone from three networks to six and from a handful of channels to a thousand and YouTube. In that environment, what matters is compelling programming—and compelling programming starts with the writer."[13] This surely did not come without precedent, as writers combining their artistic and entrepreneurial roles had already demonstrated their success in managing the institutional environment of Hollywood with the advent of flexible specialization.[14] Famed prime-time television "hyphenates"[15] like Steven Bochco had been associated with the end of the classic network system, and during the strike, writer-producers like Seth MacFarlane, J.J. Abrams and John Wells were seen as a dominant force. A *Los Angeles Times* columnist even claimed that with the television business tilting its way toward the Internet, writer-producers were gaining more bargaining power than the traditional holders of that power—trade unions, studio bosses, network executives and agents.[16]

Yet studies on the writer's strike and established Hollywood talent crossing over to the Internet are still missing.[17] In general, YouTube discourse has focused on non-professional and even unintentional media workers, relating the story of their online activity in either of two ways, depending on the respective notion of "youser" agency.[18] One way to render the story is to point out opportunities for new-media entrepreneurs opening up as a consequence of YouTube's disruptive effect on old media. "You" may now participate in the economy as an equal, co-creating value with your peers, with your hobby incidentally becoming new markets, and with prominent user-creators like Buckley acting as exemplary "innovation agencies," navigating and shaping social network markets.[19] Contrary to this story of digital "commonism"[20] runs another, in which the Internet is already embedded in the logic of post-industrial capitalism. Ever since Burger King launched its effective "Subservient Chicken" online campaign back in 2004, the story might go, the Internet has been exploited for marketing opportunities, and both YouTube and "You" form an important part of a larger cultural project of engaging (if not identifying) consumers with advertising.[21] From this point of view, consumers are more or less willingly supplying unpaid labor to a new industry founded on old modes of production.

The Commonist and the Subservient Chicken plots differ in conceptual and political terms, but both tend to speculate about the future, grounding their arguments on retrospect assessments of human agency. And although both depart from neoclassic economics (albeit for different reasons), both versions of the story imply that yousers and media institutions act rationally and know what they are doing, not least because of YouTube's apparent technical feature of making choice and preference for creative content directly observable.[22] However, YouTube's role in the writer's strike, and the writers' role on YouTube, seem to call for a more complex narrative about agency which balances the material and the social. If the social world of production has indeed changed because of YouTube during the strike, this has not been a purely social event, and certainly not one organized into any clear-cut causality.[23]

In order to briefly lay out my argument, allow me to introduce Jim O'Doherty.[24] Jim has been known mostly for his work on the NBC sitcom *3rd Rock from the Sun* (1996-2001). He joined *3rd Rock* as an executive story editor in 1997 and soon became a supervising writer-producer for the NBC show. His work earned him an Emmy nomination and Jim continued to work for *The Tracy Morgan Show* and *Grounded for Life* before signing a three-year overall development deal with NBC Universal in 2005. At NBC, he did three TV pilots, half-hour comedies, and was in the last year of his deal when the writer's strike occurred. In November 2007, Jim was fired, sharing this fate with many high-profile colleagues. So how did Jim position himself in relation to the expectations of writer-producers becoming the dominant force in the YouTube age?

> What I am doing right now is I am regrouping, you know, I am trying to be very creative, and think of things I want to work on because I really want to work on them. It is a scary time for a guy like me who is kicked out of his deal with a steady pay check, but sometimes those scary times in life force you to reinvent yourself. [...] If you go on the strike and you are fired, one of the things is, if you are a survivor, you start to think very entrepreneurial. [...] So it forces you to kind of reinvent yourself and the Internet is a place where you can be very creative, very independent, you can get out of bed in the morning, get an idea, go shoot it, come back to your home, edit it on your laptop and get it out onto a variety of different platforms.[25]

When I interviewed him in March 2008, Jim stated that he had to "reinvent himself" after the strike. He clearly expressed the necessity of strengthening his entrepreneurial role, while at the same time confining his creative role to the Web 2.0 approach of amateur participation. Given that Jim had a considerable track record and reputation as an NBC showrunner, one might of course wonder why he would redefine his role outside professional routines. In a seminal paper on the changing roles of above the line workers, for example, Wayne Baker and Robert Faulkner described how roles were used as resources when the blockbuster strategy "disrupted" Hollywood production in the 1970s and 1980s.[26] In this tumultuous industrial context, claiming the role of a producer or writer-director allegedly provided the institutional and cultural means for adapting to the environment. With the blockbuster as a new rationale, workers used roles as resources to obtain social positions, to negotiate funding or to attract talent, thus both changing the rules of the game and being changed by the rules of the game.[27] At that time, industry hype set a trend for a separation between entrepreneurial roles (producer) and creative hyphenates (writer-director) respectively.

7 Turning to YouTube: Jim O'Doherty, March 2008

In what sense, then, if any, was Jim using roles as resources? Having been an accomplished writer-producer, in what ways would YouTube make him strive to become a "producer," and to what ends? From a Commonist perspective, one might argue that Jim simply realized his new entrepreneurial role in a market characterized by the adoption of novel ideas within social networks for production and consumption,[28] while supporters of the Chicken version of youser agency might argue that he very obviously felt "forced" into his own, degrading "reinvention" as a YouTube volunteer. I am afraid, however, that things turn out to be a little more complicated. Let's have a closer look at Jim's aims and plans and then explore the routes of agency in the construction of his then present future.

The Entrepreneurial I

The main idea of Jim's renewed self-conception in the post-strike-era was "to turn the viewers into your workforce."[29] What did he mean by that?

> What I am trying to find out right now is: What is the concern to corporations? What is the message that they want to get out? If I can find that out then I can generate content that's funny and potentially viral but also speaks to a specific need. Starbucks Coffee is in trouble. [...] As a matter of fact in a lot of McDonalds now they have espresso machines. And they want the world to know McDonalds has good coffee. So with that piece of knowledge, I can create a piece of content that is not told to me by an advertising agency, it's not told to me by McDonalds, it's something that I come up with. [...] I call it grout advertising, I actually registered that name, because grout is what goes between the tiles. And if one tile is the advertising agency, they don't have a business model to set up to do what I can do in terms of calling in actors, doing stuff very cheaply, getting a small crew together and creating a piece of content that they don't have to run past the client, they don't have to get all those layers of permission and approval. So that's one tile. The other tile is the corporation. [...] Well, the grout in the middle, the guy in the middle can create a piece of content that makes McDonalds go "Oh, my god! Five million people just hit on that! That's great!" And the advertising agency, as the other tile, is going: "Ha?!"[30]

Jim thus reinvented himself as a "microfirm,"[31] supplying work in several related markets and performing various occupational roles within his artworld. He planned to use his experience and reputation as a writer-producer in the analog world for reinventing himself as an advertising director-writer-producer-amateur in the digital sphere, somehow squeezed in between national brands and the ad agencies. More precisely, he aimed at becoming an entrepreneur in the literal sense of the word, "a person who generates profit from being between others."[32] Being an entrepreneur means precisely entering the structural hole between two players in order to broker the relationship between them.[33] If media culture can be described as a network in which information (i.e. projects and products) circulates, Jim obviously attempted to channel the flow of information by taking advantage of an observed state of the industry.[34] That is, by using YouTube as a "brokerage system"[35] through which institutionalized intermediaries can be bypassed, Jim planned to become an intermediary all by himself, reconnecting parties which arguably were just being "disrupted." It was however already clear back then that YouTube's usability as a trading platform in the information economy was grounded on a merger between old and new media.

As talent agencies and other intermediaries before him, Jim the microfirm would try to benefit from the paradox of a permanent industry made of and sustained by temporary organizations. His plans demonstrate the mutual interdependence of the immaterial and material spheres of production and the rather complex interplay between peer production and capitalism that make it difficult to interpret his statements by either a Commonist or Chicken version of agency.[36] Although Jim's idea of becoming the "guy in the middle" is consistent with observations on the individualized, informal, contingent context of media work, reinventing himself as a "grout" entrepreneur would not necessarily mean a loss of status, as creative roles never develop in a straightforward fashion.[37] And even if one might maintain that YouTube rather served and serves as a machine for managing structural oversupply, there is no doubt that at the time of the interview, the potential of YouTube to create, promote and perform talent was emerging. Still, all this only concerns Jim's goals and plans. How did he put them into practice?

Jim's aim to reinvent himself as an amateur-entrepreneur soon took the form of a YouTube webisode entitled *Wicked Pissers*.[38] His idea to develop his own short-form comedy format resonated with a number of writers turning to the Internet for home-produced content, and with a surge of new websites for comedy such as My Damn Channel and Funny or Die being credited with the potential of becoming "a part of life" after the strike.[39] *Wicked Pissers* adapts to the guerilla look of user-produced content and builds its formal strategy, as some of the most successful videos on YouTube before it, on the spontaneous feel of improvised comedy. At the same time, its characters and jokes cater to an audience defined in clearly demographic terms. The show is about a guy (played by stand-up comic Bob Marley) trapped in a job servicing vending machines for a company called Vieking Vending and is set in the backwoods of Maine. Jim claimed to have shot the show more or less single-handedly, working with a local cast and a budget of "five dollars":

> We took four jokes that Bob tells in his act and expanded them into a three minute joke told with a narrative and fleshed out characters. We knew full well that this would not be for everyone but really wanted to experiment with this kind of storytelling. What was crazy fun was that there was no script. We would get into a huddle and talk about what the intention of the scene was then we would shoot it. It was important for me to not let the actors think too much about it. I didn't want them writing a script in their head. So we acted quickly and didn't really stop between takes. I did have the same objective as I had when I would be doing a show for network which was how do I make this as funny as I could. It was the same pressure to deliver good comedy, it didn't matter if I was in a sound stage in LA or a frozen lake in Maine, I needed it to be funny.[40]

8 Brand casting as short-form comedy: *Wicked Pissers*

According to Jim, the creative work on this webisode relied on similar routines and standards as in network television, while at the same time opening up possibilities for breaking with conventions. The show furnished new opportunities for stand-up comedy, but it also served as a video pitch for advertisers, promoting Jim's abilities to sell a potential audience of "17 to 34 year old men"[41] to Madison Avenue. *Wicked Pissers* is brand casting in comedy format. It attempts to prove its own potential for plot placements, for weaving products directly into the narrative. For example, in all of the four episodes distributed over YouTube, Bob and his friend Jake are traveling the back roads of Maine in a white van full of cardboard boxes supposedly containing candy, cookies and chips for the vending machines. In the first episode, "The Birthday Present," framing and editing repeatedly draw attention to the van and its boxes, implying the possibility of replacing the "Vieking Vending" lettering with any given brand's name and logo. According to Jim, this was an attempt to accommodate potential corporate sponsors who would insist on unobtrusive advertising. "You have something in your hand that you can show to people," he said. "When it comes to the Internet I used to ask a lot of questions. And I stopped asking questions. Because what I found was—nobody got this figured out. So there is no one real business model you can look at and go 'that's how you make money.' So when I stopped asking questions I just followed my own instincts."[42]

Your Tube in Practice

Still, the question is how youser agency manifested itself in the production of this YouTube webisode? To begin with, there is obviously more to agency than just production. As José van Dijk has pointed out, any YouTuber's agency comprises content production, consumer behavior and data generation, and Jim reportedly had been active in all of these fields.[43] But there is also more to agency manifesting itself in the making of the *Wicked Pissers* episodes than Jim. So far, my narrative has focused on Jim and his intentionality, following the still widespread approach of identifying authorship with issues of personality, causation and control.[44] It should have become clear, however, that we would fall short explaining agency simply by referring to Jim's plans or goals and to his "instincts" concerning how to put them into practice.

The story of online distribution platforms changing the social world of production during the strike began in fact with the discovery of an emergent phenomenon which was both material and immaterial—YouTube registered that content produced by amateurs for non-commercial purposes attracted large numbers of viewers. No one in particular, that is no single agent, no network and no community, *caused* this phenomenon, as nobody could have foreseen or steered a computational dynamic in which an individual's payoff turned out to be an explicit function of the choices of others.[45] More to the point, it doesn't even make sense to call this phenomenon "social," as it was emerging through a complex interplay of human and non-human, material and non-material factors. For example, since video content is the main vehicle of communication and social connection on YouTube,[46] the video replaces any human actor as a medium of agency, becoming the very agent of brokerage. And on YouTube, any video is subject to the platform's "coded mechanisms,"[47] following a logic unrelated to any creator's artworld. YouTube in fact represents a Web 2.0 model of the sharing economy and not a true commons project; groups or individuals may share their creative content, but they have to rely on a proprietary platform which, again, bundles and computes without making its own operations evident.[48]

Only after the new recipe for generating attention had been discovered in the YouTube laboratory were attempts made to translate it into Hollywood industry practice. The goal of industrializing the YouTube phenomenon was clearly socially structured. By translating the laboratory findings into industry practice, models came into play based on considerations of production and capital. Although the lack of efficient business models was widely lamented, they were constantly discussed, the most obvious being cultural, namely the idea that success in the entertainment industry somehow rests on personality.[49] As I have shown, Jim related the "reinvention" of himself both to institutionalized role models (i.e. the hyphenate) and to role models just emerging as part of a new institution (YouTube entrepreneurs). With Jim aligning his plans to those models, agency was situated in a cultural field of existing ideas. In this process of "tuning into the social" of the original recipe,[50] something happened to Jim as an agent. In order to translate the recipe into his own practice, Jim the microactor turned into "Jim," the macroactor, that is into a group of collaborators henceforth representing his practice.

During our conversations, Jim didn't talk much about the social dimension of his practice, presenting himself as the lone wolf trying to survive "in a world where your job is to get 'clicks' forgetting about the subjective or the creative."[51] In fact, Jim not only relied on widely debated models, he also partnered with professionals in both the analog and the digital worlds. On the one hand, he collaborated with his long-time writing partner David M. Israel with whom he had been working since *The Pursuit of Happiness*.[52] On the other hand, he found a new partner in Brent Weinstein, of 60Frames, a new syndication company engaged in financing, selling ads for and syndication of professionally produced online content, distributing shows like *Wicked Pissers* over a syndication network including YouTube, Veoh, Joost, Blip.TV and Bebo, and also to iTunes, peer-to-peer networks and mobile phone operators. 60Frames is actually in the "grout" business as well.[53]

If we follow this trajectory of agency as it evolved over time, it becomes obvious that there is more to agency then just intentions emerging in a cultural field. Jim could not have foreseen the actual grouping of "Jim" (and its consequences, to which we will return), but more to the point, he also could not have foreseen what would happen when Jim/"Jim" turned into the "grout" between the "tiles." The social dimension of the *Wicked Pissers* production unfolded in relation to maneuvers in a field of material agency. So far, studies on youser agency have downplayed this relation between the social and the material. Although they tend to base their argument on notions of distributed or networked agency, most of them still center their notion of agency firmly on human (rational) agents.[54]

Yet in the digital world, everything social seems to turn into something technical. This certainly is not to advocate technical determinism, or to claim that YouTube acts as some sort of electronic lottery with careers as a coincidental output. From a decentered, post-humanist perspective, however, one might explain the emergent aspects of youser agency by referring to a process during which human and material agency mutually transform each other. This, again, is nothing specific to YouTube, but YouTube certainly makes the emergence of agency very easily observable. Only part of what we may attribute to Jim and other agents' goals and plans, then, is of importance for an understanding of youser agency. Youser agency also is partly, at least metaphorically speaking, a transit of matter. Jim had a plan that emerged in a cultural field through an adoption of prevalent models, but in realizing this plan, he also distributed agency among non-human agents—a video, a Web platform, etc. At this very intersection of the social and the material, "clicks" emerged over time. However, as the video and the platform didn't generate enough "clicks," that is results translatable into the model of Hollywood's attention economy, Jim's ideas were confronted with a sequence of resistances, and at the end Jim had to change his plans.[55] But that is another story.

Conclusion

So, of what importance is all this, anyhow? The Commonist and the Chicken plots at least had the advantage of providing us with clear-cut answers, and this article will certainly not make these two versions of the story obsolete. Nor does it attempt to do so. One aim of this article has been to prevent the current discussion on youser agency becoming overly reductive, as it often rests on a flat notion of agency. In YouTube discourse, agency appears to be flat where it is described as being without precedent—without history or context, and more or less functional for the workings of the creative economy. Such a flat notion of agency cuts out important layers of analysis—differences between agents and users, models and individual plans, plans and resistances, the social and the material, and finally also the very dynamic of expectation within which agency emerges in the first place. Yet agency is indeed irreducible to any form of rational human action, especially in a technoscientific environment such as YouTube's.

Another aim of this article has been to explain how the expectations prompted by YouTube related to new role models for writers during their strike. Like the blockbuster in Baker and Faulkner's account, YouTube served as a rationale providing new role models, with a clear strengthening of the entrepreneurial side of creative work. In retrospect, this model seems to have promoted a new class of cost-efficient (if not to say easily disposable) creative workers ready to perform their personality in an intermediary role, brokering all kinds of deals between the analog and the digital. It also resulted in very different forms of practice. For example, after being hailed as YouTube's "first crossover viral video star," Brooke "Brookers" Brodack signed a talent/development deal with Carson Daly. Not much came of this deal, which was supposed to provide content for TV, Internet and mobile outlets.[56] Lisa Donovan, aka LisaNova, signed a contract for the Fox comedy series *Mad TV* and was characterized as a "rare crossover from the ranks of amateur Internet production to professional television"[57] before disappearing after only four episodes. She currently advertises the Sanyio Xacti HD camera in a video pretending to be a comedy sketch.[58] Caitlin Hill, who attracted millions of hits with her YouTube vlog, became Chief Creative Officer of Hitviews, a company that promises to connect Web celebrities with corporate patrons. For someone exploring YouTube in 2007-2008, however, all these and other YouTube personalities formed part of a promising, if yet unknown future. Agency might be networked or distributed, but it is in some way structured by time. As YouTube's role during the strike has demonstrated, it is the nature of hype that it comes first, modeling the future from the practices of the present. If plans and goals are imaginatively transformed versions of its present, it is indeed interesting to see how they are constructed from existing culture in a process of modeling (existing culture, to use Foucault's phrase, is literally the surface of emergence for the intentional structure of human agency).[59]

In the long run, the *Wicked Pissers* experiment didn't affect Jim's career—he sold a script to one of the Hollywood majors while producing the webisode.[60] Still, there is some lasting irony about his story as it unfolded. Jim O'Doherty lost his job due to a strike that promised writers a higher share of Internet revenue. Having been fired, Jim at first not only *had* to work in the digital sphere in order to substitute the loss of work in the analog world, he also had to share his revenues from the YouTube experiment with a company like 60Frames, which—and I wonder how surprising this is—was actually funded by a major Hollywood talent agency, UTA (United Talent Agency), in conjunction with an advertising company. Nobody has yet analyzed these connections between the writer's strike, the talent agencies and Google. Who knows—perhaps Michael Eisner was right after all?

Endnotes

1 Mimi Turner, "Eisner calls writers strike 'insanity,' " *The Hollywood Reporter,* 8 November 2007.

2 Ibid.

3 As Buckley himself claimed; see the channel of "YouTube's #1 entertainment show": www.youtube.com/user/whatthebuckshow?blend=1&ob=4 [last checked 15 April 2009].

4 Brian Stelter, "YouTube Videos Pull In Real Money," *The New York Times,* 11 December 2008.

5 See "Sideletter on literary material written for programs made for new media," 26 February 2008, retrieved from the WGA homepage – www.wga.org/contract_07/NewMediaSideletter.pdf [last checked 15 February 2009].

6 Michael Learmonth, "NBC, News Corp. unveil Hulu.com," *Variety,* 29 October 2007.

7 See youtube.com/movies and youtube.com/shows [last checked 23 April 2009].

8 Patrick Goldstein, "Big Picture: What is entertainment worth?" *Los Angeles Times,* 4 December 2007.

9 Bruno Latour, Steve Wolgar, *Laboratory Life. The Construction of Scientific Facts* (Princeton, NJ: Princeton University Press, 1986), p. 68.

10 See for example Arthur De Vany, *Hollywood Economics. How Extreme Uncertainty Shapes the Film Industry* (London, New York: Routledge, 2004).

11 See John Caldwell, *Production Culture. Industrial Reflexivity in Film and Television Practice* (Durham, London: Duke University Press, 2008); and Vicki Mayer, Miranda Banks & John Caldwell, eds., *Production Studies. Cultural Studies of Media Industries* (London, New York: Routledge, 2009).

12 See for example Denise Martin, "Carson Daly bonkers for Brookers. YouTube leads to development deal," *Variety*, 12 June 2006.

13 Carl DiOrio, "Liman offers Jackson Bites for WGA deal," *Hollywood Reporter*, 18 January 2008.

14 Cf. William T. Bielby and Denise D. Bielby, "Organizational Mediation of Project-based Labor Markets: Talent Agencies and the Careers of Screenwriters," *American Sociological Review* no. 1, 1999, pp. 64–85; Keith Acheson and Christopher J. Maule, "Understanding Hollywood's Organisation and Continuing Success," in *An Economic History of Film*, eds. John Sedgwick & Michael Pokorny (London, New York: Routledge, 2005), especially pp. 317–320; see also Michael Storper and Susan Christopherson, "Flexible Specialization and Regional Industrial Agglomerations: The Case of the U.S. Motion Picture Industry," *Annals of the Association of American Geographers* no. 1, 1987, pp. 104–117.

15 "Hyphenate" is *Variety*-speak for a person who is active in more than one occupational role.

16 Scott Collins, "Showrunners run the show," *Los Angeles Times*, 23 November 2007.

17 See for example Susan Faulkner and Jay Melican, "Getting Noticed, Showing-Off, Being Overheard: Amateurs, Authors and Artists Inventing and Reinventing Themselves in Online Communities," *Ethnographic Praxis in Industry Conference Proceedings* no. 1, 2007, pp. 51–65; and also Mark Deuze, *Media Work* (Cambridge, MA: Polity Press, 2007).

18 José van Dijk coined the term "youser" in order to denote "the intricate intertwining of viewing and consuming behaviour with activities involving the generation and exchange of content." See José van Dijk, "Television 2.0: YouTube and the Emergence of Homecasting," paper presented to the Creativity, Ownership and Collaboration in the Digital Age conference, Cambridge, Massachusetts Institute of Technology, 27–29 April 2007–2008

http://web.mit.edu/comm-forum/mit5/papers/vanDijck_Television2.0.article.MiT5.pdf [last checked 15 February 2009].

19 See John Banks and Sal Humphreys, "The Labour of User Co-Creators. Emergent Social Network Markets?" *Convergence* no 4, 2008, pp. 401–418; Don Tapscott and Anthony D. Williams, *Wikinomics: How Mass Collaboration Changes Everything* (New York: Penguin, 2006), p. 150; for a more critically balanced account, see Jean Burgess and Joshua Green's contribution to this book and Deuze 2007, pp. 171–200.

20 Michel Bauwens, "Class and capital in peer production," *Capital & Class* no 97, 2009, p. 124.

21 As part of an advertisement portfolio for Burger King's TenderCrisp chicken sandwich, Crispin Porter + Bogusky's campaign contained a viral marketing website with a man in a chicken costume performing a range of actions based on the user's input (www.subservientchicken.com, last checked 15 February 2009). The site received 20 million hits in a week. In 2004, streaming media became popular too, and marketers realized that consumers were in control of content in the Internet. See Susan B. Barnes and Neil F. Hair, "From Banners to YouTube: Using the Rear-View Mirror to Look at the Future of Internet Advertising," paper presented at the Eighth Annual Convention of the Media Ecology Association conference – http://en.scientificcommons.org/39077240 [last checked 15 February 2009]. See also Bauwens 2009, pp. 122–124.

22 On the importance of consumer choice for new economic models of the creative industry, see for example Jason Potts, "Social Network Markets: A New Definition of the Creative Industries," *Journal of Cultural Economy* no. 32, 2008, pp. 167–185.

23 Cf. Andrew Pickering, "Decentering Sociology: Synthetic Dyes and Social Theory," *Perspectives on Science* no. 3, 2005, pp. 352–405.

24 I am extremely grateful to Jim O'Doherty for his openness and for allowing me to use the interview without anonymizing my source—which indeed would have made the whole argument pointless. The interview took place on March 7, 2008, in Los Angeles, with follow-up questions via e-mail until June, 2008. Thanks also to Michael Renov (USC), Evelyn Seubert, Robert Rigamonti, the German Research Foundation (DFG) and Vinzenz Hediger for having made my research stay in LA possible.

25 Interview, March 7, 2008.

26 See Wayne E. Baker and Robert R. Faulkner, "Role as Resource in the Hollywood Film Industry," *The American Journal of Sociology* no. 2, 1991, pp. 279–309.

27 Baker and Faulkner 1991, p. 290.

28 Cf. Potts 2008, p. 171.

29 Interview, March 7, 2008.

30 Ibid.

31 Pierre-Michel Menger, "Artists as Workers: Theoretical and Methodological Challenges," *Poetics* no. 28, 2001, p. 248.

32 Ronald S. Burt, *Structural Holes. The Social Structure of Competition* (Cambridge, MA: Harvard University Press, 1992), p. 34.

33 Ibid.

34 Alexander Böhnke, "Beziehungsmakler in Hollywood. Logik der Zirkulation und Unterbrechung in Netzwerken," paper presented at the conference Verteilt. Vertauscht. Verhandelt. Entstehung ungeplanter Strukturen durch Tausch und Zirkulation in Kultur und Medien, Paderborn, 2009.

35 Cf. José van Dijk, "Users Like You? Theorizing Agency in User-generated Content," *Media, Culture & Society* no. 1, 2009, p. 52.

36 See Bauwens 2009, p. 130.

37 Deuze 2007, p. 87; and Jeremy Tanner, ed., *The Sociology of Art. A Reader* (London, New York: Routledge, 2003), p. 110.

38 See www.youtube.com/watch?v=Bk8g3pOvTTQ for the first episode and the YouTube channel www.youtube.com/user/wickedpissers [last checked 15 February 2009]. The website wickedpissers.com originally accompanying the clips is no longer available.

39 Steven Zeitchik, "Web entertainment could bloom," *The Hollywood Reporter*, 2 November 2007.

40 E-mail to author, 29 April, 2008.

41 E-mail to author, 1 June, 2008.

42 Interview, 7 March, 2008.

43 van Dijk 2009, p. 45.

44 Janet Staiger, "Authorship approaches," in *Authorship and Film*, eds., David A. Gerstner & Janet Staiger (London, New York: Routledge, 2003), pp. 27–60; see also Caldwell 2008, pp. 198–199.

45 Potts 2008, p. 169.

46 Jean Burgess and Joshua Green, "Agency and Controversy in the YouTube Community," paper presented at the Internet Research 9.0 conference, Copenhagen, 2008, p. 3 – http://eprints.qut.edu.au/15383/ [last checked 15 February 2009].

47 van Dijk 2009, p. 46.

48 Bauwens 2009, 126.

49 Cf. Warren I. Susman, *Culture as History. The Transformation of American Society in the Twentieth Century* (New York: Pantheon Books, 1984), pp. 271–286.

50 Pickering 2005, p. 367.

51 E-mail to author, 24 April, 2008. Cf. Caldwell 2008, p. 203, on the lone wolf as a "recurrent cultural motif of the showrunner."

52 Josef Adalian, "O'Doherty, Israel grounded at C-W," *Variety,* 18 January 2001.

53 See for example Steven Zeitchik, "Brent Weinstein to run 60frames," *Variety,* 10 July 2007 and the press releases on the 60frames.com website.

54 For example, Burgess and Green 2008 speak about collective agency, relating agency to the idea of a communicative space, while Dijk 2009 problematizes the notion with regard to different human users and agents (p. 46).

55 Pickering aptly called this dialectic of practical resistances and adaptations the "mangle of practice," and my argument on agency obviously relies on his findings. See Andrew Pickering, *The Mangle of Practice. Time, Agency and Science* (Chicago: Chicago University Press, 1995).

56 Martin 2006.

57 Andrew Wallenstein, "How YouTube Helped LisaNova Start Her Career," *The New York Times*, 29 April 2007.

58 Brian Morrissey, "Sanyo Enlists YouTube Stars," *AdWeek.Com*, 20 March 2009.

59 Hype is also something different than "industrial self-reflexivity" as understood by Caldwell. Cf. Caldwell 2008 and Nik Brown's work on the sociology of expectations, e.g. "Hope Against Hype: Accountability in Biopasts, Presents and Futures," *Science Studies* no. 2, 2003, pp. 3–21.

60 E-mail to author, 11 April, 2008.

Eggo Müller

Where Quality Matters: Discourses on the Art of Making a YouTube Video

Like many other digital achievements, YouTube's and other video-sharing sites' accessibility have provoked visions of a total democratization of the audiovisual space, where there are no more barriers between producers and the audience, or between professionals and amateurs. For example, *Wired* magazine announced in May 2006: "Any amateur can record a clip. Follow these steps to look like a pro."[1] Producers of digital photo cameras and video equipment, indeed, provide users with the most accessible technology and software to record and share clips on the go. Casio, for instance, has introduced with one of its new models a "YouTube capture mode" which supports optimized recordings according to YouTube's standard. And as a convenient extra, these cameras automatically record any 15 seconds before the record button is pushed.[2] Thus, if a user realizes with some delay that a situation turns out to be a typical "YouTube moment" worth recording and sharing online, it is (almost) never too late to push the button: the camera has already captured 15 seconds of the immediate past.

As a matter of fact, many of the countless video clips on YouTube give evidence of its low barriers for anybody who has access to technological means of recording and uploading a video clip. Many of these clips seem at first sight to demonstrate that most of these "anybodies" have no skills in videomaking at all, or have no ambitions and just don't care about the quality of their clips.[3] As the website's self-promotion goes and as commentators repeatedly affirm, YouTube is first and foremost a cultural space of community building and shared experiences. Many critics therefore lament the poor aesthetic quality and moral shiftiness of many of the self-made clips on YouTube, often recorded on the spot with facilities like mobile phones, webcams or digital photo cameras and then uploaded without "wasting time" on postproduction. YouTube is—at least for "contributing users" as opposed to "lurking users"[4]—all about sharing moments online with a potentially worldwide audience, but actually a limited number of viewers.

Against this background, enthusiast advocators of participatory media discuss the new possibilities of Web 2.0 as a challenge for critics, educators and policymakers, since, as Henry Jenkins states in his White Paper on *Media Education for the 21st Century*, one cannot subsume that users would acquire the necessary skills and competencies "on their own by interacting with popular culture." As a consequence, Jenkins claims "the need for policy and pedagogical interventions." He identifies three main concerns, namely the "participation gap," the "transparency problem" and "the ethics challenge." In addition to the problem of unequal access to digital media—the participation gap—and in addition to the problem of participants not being aware of the conventions and protocols defining conditions of digitally enabled participation—the transparency problem—Jenkins also points at the "ethical problem of participants" lacking skills in and knowledge about the use of digital media. This derives, as Jenkins puts it, from "the breakdown of traditional forms of professional training and socialization that might prepare young people for their increasingly public roles as media makers and community participants."[5]

This critical perspective on the challenges of participatory cultures differs fundamentally from the enthusiastic perspective on users' activities Jenkins develops in *Convergence Culture*, in which he praises the participatory achievements of digital media.[6] What Jenkins performs with these two different takes on participatory media I would call the "participation dilemma" that is inherent to a lot of theorizing about digital media and participation. On the one hand, critics embrace new possibilities of participation as a democratization of our media culture: untrained non-professionals can now gain access to the formerly exclusive world of professional media and start redefining the tacit norms and standards of the established media culture. On the other hand, this is identified as a problem, since the new, "uneducated" participants neglect professional standards of craftsmanship, aesthetic quality or ethic norms. As a reaction, professionals, critics and educators identify the need to train the new participants in order to guarantee the "state of the art," or, as Jenkins argues in his White Paper, to prevent inexperienced participants from being exploited, abused or mocked. The dilemma then is that the new participants have to achieve some skills that enable them to contribute to online cultures in meaningful ways, but whenever a cultural elite starts to train and thus to "professionalize" new "ordinary" users, those traditional cultural barriers and hierarchies that have been questioned by the emerging participatory cultures are rebuilt.

Jenkins points to the dilemma above by developing two contradictory perspectives on digital participation. However, I would argue that this dilemma derives from a "theorization" caught up in 20th century media theories' binary thinking in oppositions of top-down versus bottom-up forces; the industry versus the audience, producers versus consumers, the power block versus the people, etcetera. These traditional oppositions tend to romanticize the "user" as an authentic, self-conscious subject, as well as condemn "the industry" and educational institutions as manipulative exploiters by definition. Therefore, academic research trying to understand the forces that shape the YouTube as a "space of participation" has to go beyond such traditional oppositions.[7]

One of these shaping forces, for instance, is the popular discourse about YouTube where participants discuss questions of knowledge, skills and video quality—if still on a basic level. That is to say that beyond the world of suspect academics, conservative cultural elitists or "the industry," there is a discourse on YouTube engaging in teaching skills of videomaking for YouTube. This discourse cannot be identified as either top-down or bottom-up; rather, it is a discourse in, on and about YouTube negotiating the site as a specific space of expression, exchange and community building.

In this article, I will take a closer look at this discourse and the ways in which it has emerged on YouTube and in YouTube-related video tutorials. My analysis will draw on the so-called "production of culture approach" as it has been developed in cultural sociology to research professional practices of production. According to this approach, the "explanation of cultural practices depends on the identification of the discursive fields providing the 'constitutional infrastructure' that enables actors to construct the knowledge frameworks upon which action is based."[8] Similar to other defining discourses, such as the economic, legal and technological powers materialized in the interface and the protocols of use,[9] I take here the "quality of discourse" as one of the cultural forces that construct YouTube as a new space of cultural participation.

Who Cares about Quality?

According to a traditional dichotomy, the "quality discourse" would be identified as a top-down force that maintains the cultural elite's control of an emerging field of creative practice—whereas new groups of users, probably identified as "the people," challenge and question established hierarchies based on traditional notions of aesthetic norms and standards. But there is also evidence that not only academics, educators, and full, semi- or pre-professionals contribute to a discourse in teaching "dabblers," "novices" and "amateurs" how to make a professional-looking video clip. Actually, many of the "contributing users" on YouTube themselves engage in the quality discourse on discussion boards, even if this is hardly done in an articulated and sophisticated manner.

In her inspiring study of social networking in small communities of video sharers, Patricia G. Lange documents some reflections on the quality of videos, probably provoked through the formal setting of her ethnographic research. Though Lange argues that "critics fail to understand that video quality is not necessarily the determining factor in terms of how videos affect social networks," her study reveals that some participants are "dismissive of the standard *of other* people's videos. Their objections are often related to technical issues (including poor editing, lighting, sound, or some combination) or content (too many videos about people sparring)."[10] Lange's accurate wording implies that quality certainly *can* be a determining factor and that—even if it is not determining—is actually a matter of reflection even among groups of "contributing users" that are first and foremost interested in building and maintaining small-scale networks. This is not astonishing, given the fact that aesthetic styles are determining factors of community building in many areas of youth and popular culture.

One of Lange's informants seems to reflect explicitly on this mechanism when he explains that what Lange calls "privately public behavior" is to be read as a deliberate strategy. "He cloaked himself in a character in order to develop video skills, garner a fan base, and then reveal himself, once successful, to his old friend RJ,"[11] Lange writes. Skills are in this user's perspective directly associated with the dream of making successful, if not viral, videos that would help him to gain the appreciation of his friend and other peers. Against the background of ethnographic studies like Lange's, I argue that it is unproductive to create an opposition between social aims and aesthetic means. Users who engage in small-scale social networks are also sensible of the quality of clips shared online. Though these users' motivation might be more socially than aesthetically grounded, the means to achieve social recognition among peers and maybe beyond is often articulated in terms of videomaking skills and product quality. Therefore, it is more productive to generally assume that users are conscious of aesthetic quality, even if not in an articulated and reflected way.

In fact, discussions on quality emerge on different levels and on different occasions at YouTube: the interface asks users to rate clips and to add comments, and many users actually express their affinity with feelings, experiences and preferences on the YouTube forum, or mock a video's poor quality.[12] There is the official YouTube award, where the YouTube staff calls out some of the most popular videos and asks users to rate them and indicate which ones deserve extra recognition. Beyond that, there is the genre of instructional videos and "how-to books" teaching the art of YouTube videomaking to those users who aim at larger, diverse audiences. Tutorials, then, can be understood and analyzed as a discourse that articulates and negotiates aesthetic sensibilities and ideas of what defines the quality of a YouTube video.

"Quality" According to YouTube Tutorials

Since 2006, there has been a growing number of printed tutorials on how to make effective use of YouTube. Titles such as *How to Do Everything with YouTube; 15 Minutes of Fame: Becoming a Star in the YouTube Revolution* and *YouTube: An Insiders Guide to Climbing the Charts* all contain separate chapters teaching the ploys for creating attention for a clip and making it circulate widely, if not a viral hit. Next to these types of general introductions, there are tutorials that advise businesses how to exploit the possibilities of advertising and marketing on YouTube: *Plug Your Business! Marketing on MySpace, YouTube, Blogs and Podcasts and Other Web 2.0 Social Networks; YouTube: Making Money By Video Sharing and Advertising Your Business for Free;* and *YouTube for Business: Online Video Marketing for Any Business.* Getting as many hits as possible is, according to these tutorials, the currency of videos on YouTube. However, widespread circulation of a video does not only imply popularity and thus potential economic revenues; traditionally it is also associated with the notion of publicness and thus with a framework that triggers certain collectively acknowledged norms and conventions. This is the rationale behind printed YouTube tutorials like *Wired* magazine's above-quoted short reference in six steps or the book-length *YouTube for Dummies.*[13] *Wired magazine's* tutorial, though very condensed, is a prototypical example of the genre. It reminds the maker of a few things to keep in mind: "Choose your weapon; Record clear audio; Keep it steady; Light your subjects; Film multiple takes; Edit edit edit."[14] Except for the first imperative, the other five read like a professional critics' advice about what mistakes to avoid.

As Martina Roepke has suggested with regard to handbooks on amateur filmmaking, tutorials can be read as professional interventions into amateurs' and dabblers' home-movie practices.[15] For example, Michael Miller's book-length *YouTube 4 You* explains what to pay attention to in a short chapter of only ten pages. Most of it is devoted to technical aspects of convenient video standards, questions of recording television footage and ripping fragments from DVDs, whereas only three pages address original videomaking. However, the question of quality is addressed specifically. Here, too, the structuring question is: "What makes a great YouTube video?" According to Miller, a clip should target a small audience; should address a specific topic from a personal point of view; should be funny and attractive for some other reason; should be original, since "the world of YouTube needs innovators, not imitators"; and should be as short as possible. Reading tutorials as reactions to poor practices, Miller's tips in reverse would give a description of the average home-made video on YouTube: thematically and stylistically unfocused, not providing any personal or original perspective, not entertaining and far too long.[16]

Obviously, the aesthetic norms Miller draws on are based on the concept of authorship, and thus in sharp contrast to what, for example, José van Dijck has described as the characteristic of the "snippet" on YouTube. Van Dijck uses the term snippet to refer to the transient status of a clip within the potentially endless process of reusing, recycling and remaking on YouTube.[17] However, handbook authors like Miller draw not only on authorship as a defining concept, but also on craftsmanship when addressing more technical skills of videomaking. Miller explicitly advises users to professionalize their practice by taking into account basic aspects of camera, lighting and sound when filming. "In general, it pays to be professional. If you're shooting your own videos, use adequate lighting, set up attractive camera [angles], and definitely make sure that your sound quality is up to snuff. Even amateur videos can look good and better-looking videos attract more viewers than do dimly lit poor-sounding ones." Next to the concepts of authorship and professionalism, Miller draws on a third concept traditionally associated with the artistic mastery of a medium or art form when he advises to "Play to the medium's strengths. Know that your video will be seen in a tiny window on a small computer screen and then shoot it accordingly. Use lots of close ups, keep the background plain, avoid long shots, and employ simple images with high contrast. Visual subtlety is not your friend."[18]

As Miller recommends, videos made for YouTube should acknowledge the very characteristics of the medium. The quote makes clear that such remarks are based on the traditional idea that an emerging medium is defined in a process of aesthetic differentiation. Interestingly enough, Miller's recommendations read like some of the early reflections on the nature of the small screen from the 1950s, when film was the established medium television was compared with. The idea of medium specificity is accordingly linked to the discourse on how to achieve aesthetic quality. Thus, a video playing to the characteristics of YouTube in an original way, and at the same time meeting the professional standards of production, proves authorship and, vice versa, would show that YouTube is an artistically specific medium.

The concepts of authorship, professional craftsmanship and medium specificity are defining components of the "quality discourse" in printed tutorials for YouTubers. Online tutorials, available on YouTube itself, do not differ fundamentally from printed versions. YouTube's "own" official tutorial covers the familiar topics, traditional handbooks or Websites of video filmmaking address. Short clips averaging 40 seconds explain the basic features of lighting, camera, sound and special effects. These clips, too, seem to point at—from a professional perspective—the most common shortcomings of the "average" video on YouTube. Not surprisingly, these clips are provided by and linked to the website of *Videomaker*, a magazine for film amateurs that advertises on YouTube's website. The presenters in these online tutorials use a rather informal way of addressing the audience, as if they were talking to a community of peers:

"Hi, I'm Issak from *Videomaker* and I'm going to give everyone a tip out there to make their YouTube videos a lot better looking."[19]

9 "Of course, you need a camera!": One of Youtube's own video tutorials

Probably the most traditional of these how-to videos on YouTube is a classical instructional clip of ten minutes produced by the retired local radio and television columnist Jim Carter, notorious on YouTube as the producer of more than 250 videos for "do-it-yourselfers." As a former professional, he raises in his tutorial "How to make a

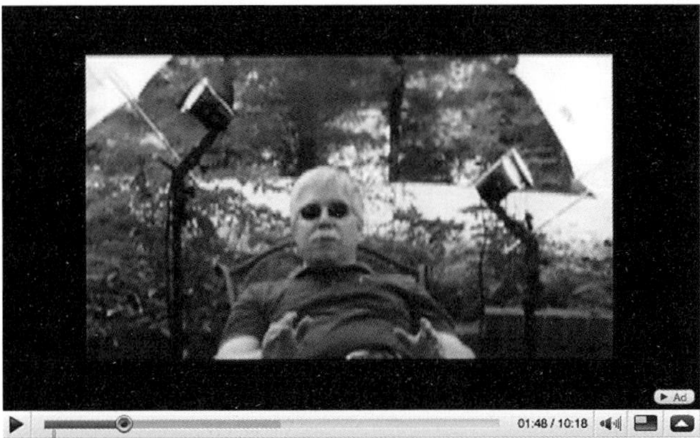

10 "How To Make a Video": James Carter knows

Video" the typical topics: the selection of equipment, the actual filming, decoupage and editing, scriptwriting and acting in front of the camera. Particularly interesting regarding the online tutorials is the dialogic dimension, when users comment on the tutorials and react to the makers' tips and advice. For example, Carter receives some mocking comments for his old-fashioned sense of humor. At the same time, there are users who express their thankfulness in short responses like "great vid, it helped," or in longer comments that seem to underline the need for professional interventions: "Sweet, I saw a lot of my friends' problems in this video's solutions, good job." Carter, obviously enjoying his authority deriving from his professional experience, reacts in a rather untypical way for YouTube. He uses the maximum space of 500 characters to answer questions accurately, adding some extra advice. To a users' disrespectful comment "10 minutes? WAY to long dude," a comment that reaffirms the norm that a video online has to be short and to the point, Carter responds in a demonstratively polite way, again using his old-fashioned sense of humor: "Thanks for your comment. I went to your channel. No wonder you said my video was too long. Your videos are as short as the miniskirts women wore in the 70's. I have a challenge for you. How about covering the same topics I did and see how long your video turns out."[20]

It is obvious that different styles of communication meet here. Some younger producers of tutorials on videomaking for YouTube have created different styles of presenting themselves and addressing their

11 Mark Apsalon on chroma key and his DVD

viewers as peers. Examples are Mark Apsalon's short videos addressing specific questions such as the use of chroma key, or the tutorials of Mr. Safety who, such as in "How to Improve Video Quality The Cheap Way," addresses videomaking novices in particular who are unable to spend a lot of money. Whereas Tim Carter, a retired cameraman, is a post-professional, Mark Apsalon and Mr. Safety can be characterized as semi-professionals or pre-professionals who use YouTube to promote their own work. Apsalon's tutorials, for example, are teasers for his one-hour instructional videos on filmmaking that can be ordered on DVD.

12 "That's the color it should be!": Mr. Safety

Apsalon and Mr. Safety both receive many laudatory comments for their tutorials and are addressed as authorities by a community of users who want to improve their skills in videomaking. Such hierarchies and the discourses maintaining them are characteristic for traditional amateur cultures, and YouTube is all but free from traditional cultural hierarchies—obvious, for example, in the following comment by user EA060: "Some of these things seem hilarious to me, being a professional cameraman and video editor. But those advices are good for the amateurs. An interesting way to make people understand some things. About 'white balance' on VX cameras don't use the auto function because it's not JVC to work properly. You better make the white balance manually, or use the presets (int/ext) because you will have to work more on an editing software. The same thing for DSR 150 and DSR 170 from Sony. Good luck!"[21]

What is interesting here is not so much the specificity of information exchanged, but more the style of user EA060: by introducing himself as a professional cameraman whether this is true or not, he creates a hierarchy between "the amateurs," the pre- or semi-professional whose advice is useful for amateurs, and himself as a true professional who possesses the superior ability to evaluate the tutorials. The common ground of this discourse recreating traditional hierarchies is the culturally shared belief that the better the quality of a public utterance, the bigger the audience and the stronger the impact of the message will be. And quality derives, according to the rather traditional discourse, from authorship, craftsmanship and the professional use of the mediums' specific features. The quality discourse thus perpetuates traditional cultural norms even with regard to the open and easily accessible space of participation that YouTube offers.

Conclusion: Sharing versus Participating

This article's analysis of the quality discourse on YouTube aims at a better understanding of (some of) the cultural powers that define YouTube as a cultural space of participation. Like in other cultural realms where the professional world and the world of the consuming audience is mediated by a rich, differentiated and powerful amateur culture,[22] quality discourses function not only to create taste hierarchies, but also to professionalize dabblers and novices and make the public and professional world more accessible for them. Users with different backgrounds and interests in YouTube contribute to and maintain this quality discourse. Full, semi-, pre- and post-professionals use YouTube to share *and* promote their knowledge, and dabblers, novices and amateurs contribute to the same discourse through their questions and comments. As opposed to the era of mass media—with producers on the one side and consumers on the other—there is a diverse field of positions in the space of participation YouTube creates. From the few tutorials I have discussed in this article, it is obvious that they draw on traditional media aesthetics and cultural conceptions of authorship and publicness, and can thus be characterized as sort of a conservative power working to format YouTube as a space of participation.

One could characterize this discourse as a disciplinary one that works to domesticate "ordinary" users' original creativity and to subordinate the open, participatory space of YouTube to the regime of hierarchical mass media and traditional cultural norms. But this would be a romantic misconception of users' "authentic creativity." All users are without any exception part of already existing cultures and have to work through these cultures' norms and conventions to develop their own creative interests and skills. Tutorials in videomaking are a means to develop such skills, especially for those whose engagement on YouTube aims not just at sharing moments and experiences, but at contributing to and participating in a broader audiovisual culture. Far from blurring the boundaries between the spheres of production and consumption, online video culture redefines and institutionalizes the relationship between these spheres in a more differentiated way. The quality discourse is one powerful force within this process of redefinition and differentiation. Although video-sharing sites allow for more diverse forms of participation than traditional mass media ever did, the quality discourse on YouTube works to structure possible acts of audiovisual participation according to well-established conventions and standards.

Endnotes

1 Jim Feely, "Lights! Camera! Vodcast! How to make your own viral clip," *Wired,* 5 May 2006.

2 See advertisement for the camera at www.focus.de/digital/foto/digitalkameras/tid-6811/allround-digitalkameras_aid_130827.html [last checked 15 February 2009].

3 Patricia G. Lange, in her contribution to this volume, addresses a type of YouTube video that aims at connecting people with shared interests. Since such "videos of affinity" are not meant to be watched by a diverse audience, they don't have to be original and well crafted. These videos, according to Lange, are often "stereotypical, spontaneous, and contain many in-jokes" and can still fulfill their social function, though they seem to "draw undeserved attention" from viewers who do not share the specific interest.

4 On the need for of a better differentiation of types of users and forms of participation, see José van Dijck, "Users like you? Theorizing agency in user-generated content," *Media, Culture & Society* no. 1, 2009, pp. 41–58.

5 Henry Jenkins, *Confronting the Challenges of Participatory Culture: Media Education for the 21st Century* (Chicago: MacArthur Foundation, 2006), p. 3.

6 Henry Jenkins, *Convergence Culture. Where Old and New Media Collide* (New York: New York University Press, 2006).

7 For a detailed discussion of the concept of "spaces of participation" see Eggo Müller, "Formatted spaces of participation: Interactive television and the reshaping of the relationship between production and consumption," in *Digital Material – Tracing New Media in Everyday Life and Technology*, eds. Marianne van den Boomen et. al. (Amsterdam: Amsterdam University Press, 2009).

8 Jarl A. Ahlkvist, "Programming philosophies and the rationalization of music radio," *Media, Culture & Society* no. 3, 2001, pp. 339–359.

9 See for a thorough discussion of regimes shaping participating online Mirko T. Schäfer, *Bastard Culture: User Participation and the Extension of Cultural Industries* (Utrecht: Utrecht University, 2009) and the contribution of Frank Kessler and Mirko T. Schäfer in this volume.

10 Patricia G. Lange, "Publicly private and privately public: Social networking on YouTube," *Journal of Computer-Mediated Communication* no. 1, 2007, pp. 361–380; see her article in this volume also.

11 Ibid.

12 See Patricia G. Lange's contribution in this volume.

13 Chris Botello & Doug Sahlin, *YouTube for Dummies* (Indianapolis: Wiley Publishing, 2007).

14 The tutorial is quoted from Jim Feely's article "Lights! Camera! Vodcast! How to make your own viral clip," *Wired*, 5 May 2006.

15 Martina Roepke, *Privat-Vorstellung. Heimkino in Deutschland vor 1945* (Hildesheim, Germany: Olms, 2006).

16 Michael Miller, *YouTube 4 You* (New York: Que Publishing, 2007), p. 87.

17 José van Dijck, "Homecasting: The end of broadcasting?" *Vodafone Receiver* no. 18, 2007 – http://212.241.182.231/rcb1/?p=36 [last checked 15 February 2009].

18 Miller 2007, p. 87.

19 See www.youtube.com/handbook_popup_produce_light?pcont=lightbasics [last checked 15 February 2009].

20 All quotes are reactions to Tim Carter's instructional video entitled "How to film a video" – www.youtube.com/watch?v=3zFePU1uvtc [last checked 15 February 2009].

21 Quoted from EA060's comment on Mr. Safety, "How to Improve Video Quality The Cheap Way" – www.youtube.com/watch?v=OePFgmyvnWo [last checked 15 February 2009].

22 In contrast to the general perception, professional and semi-professional productions usurp, as Green and Burgess argue in their contribution to this volume, more and more space and attention on YouTube and are starting to define the site's cultural meaning.

Bjørn Sørenssen

Breaking the Age Barrier in the Internet Age: The Story of Geriatric 1927

In documentary film the relationship between technological innovation, democratization and audiovisual aesthetics has always been a major factor. It is easy to concur with B. Ruby Rich when she states that "documentary history sometimes reads like a patent-office log in terms of its generations of machinery [...] with endlessly renewed promises of enhanced access that occasionally really does follow."[1] One might add that one of the promises most frequently connected with the technological equipment available to the documentary filmmaker has been the wish to democratize the medium. This development may be described within the paradigm of what is usually referred to as the "public sphere" in English, a key concept for describing the development of the relationship between society and the individual originally coined by Jürgen Habermas in 1962[2] and later extended to denote alternative forms of public spheres defined by Oskar Negt and Alexander Kluge.[3]

In the years following World War II, there were attempts at using available amateur technology to establish alternative, oppositional filmic public spheres through the American avant-garde movement and within the independent documentary movement. The main problem was, of course, that since these movements existed well outside the public sphere of the film industry, they would start out and remain marginalized phenomena. Attempts at establishing alternative distribution and exhibition channels through the 1960s and 1970s usually ended up as interesting, though isolated movements that resounded better with cineaste groups than a general audience. In the context of film history, however, these marginalized "mini-publicities" were to have an impression vastly larger than on their modest audiences in a form that could be referred to as aesthetic counter-publicities. One such case is the British

Free Cinema documentary movement in the 1950s, which became influential not only in the field of documentary, but also for British feature-film production in the ensuing years, inspiring a new everyday "kitchen-sink realism." The groundbreaking short documentary subjects of Free Cinema, produced as a response to the perceived conservativism of the Griersonian documentary movement, were only shown on six occasions at the National Film Theatre in London, something that hardly may be termed a mass-media context. However, the films became influential in the ongoing public debate about documentary and feature film in postwar Britain.[4]

Today, we can see how amateurs producing digital video within an experimental frame—video blogs, newsgroups, etcetera—on the Internet often have an impact on commercial and institutional audiovisual forms. In the same vein, the expanded possibilities created by new media technology, in this case lightweight recording equipment for 16mm sound film, revolutionized the field of anthropological film and brought about the concept of cinéma vérité. This direction, with its ambition of getting closer to everyday life than the classic documentary was able, originally addressed a specialist audience in the field of ethnology and anthropology, but it is now recognized as the precursor of the mass-media phenomenon of reality TV.

In terms of history, we have been able to examine how different forms of alternative publicities have emerged in a media context, movements and phenomena suggesting a far wider scope than Habermas' original use of his public-sphere concept. According to Douglas Kellner, there is a considerable widening of the public-sphere concept in contemporary society due to the application of new media technology. This implies that it is necessary to go beyond the defined historical context of Habermas and view the "new" public sphere as "a site of information, discussion, contestation, political struggle, and organization that includes the broadcasting media and new cyberspaces as well as the face-to-face interactions of everyday life."[5]

It is possible to discern this convergence of the great publicity and the many counter-publicities in what Kellner terms the new cyberspace, that is the World Wide Web and its repercussions on contemporary life. The millions of personal computers in the industrialized world have long ago been changed from one-way communication receivers to potential media production tools, supported by a similar number of mobile telephones that can record sound and moving images. The web on the Internet has become a rupture in the wall between the private and the public spheres, challenging the dystopia of Habermas—where the forces of the mass-media industry more or less successfully invaded the private sphere—and presenting a more optimistic view, where the individual can and will contribute to public discourse. However, Habermas still seemed to maintain a pessimistic attitude towards the supposed expansion of public discourse on the Internet. In his acceptance speech when receiving the Bruno Kreisky Prize in 2006, he stated:

> Use of the Internet has both broadened and fragmented the contexts of communication. This is why the Internet can have a subversive effect on intellectual life in authoritarian regimes. But at the same time, the less formal, horizontal cross-linking of communication channels weakens the achievements of traditional media. This focuses the attention of an anonymous and dispersed public on select topics and information, allowing citizens to concentrate on the same critically filtered issues and journalistic pieces at any given time. The price we pay for the growth in egalitarianism offered by the Internet is the decentralized access to unedited stories. In this medium, contributions by intellectuals lose their power to create a focus.[6]

This double-edged character of online society, vacillating between democratic potentiality and superficial vulgarity, is expressed in several of the new forums of production-empowered Net users. YouTube is, of course, a good example of how—and how fast—innovation happens in the new online media, and has for many come to represent the kind of utopian role for moving images that Alexandre Astruc envisioned in his famous 1948 essay *The Birth of a New Avant-Garde: La caméra-stylo*. In this essay, Astruc's point of departure was the recent progress in cinema aesthetics represented by directors like Orson Welles and Jean Renoir, and the two recent advances in media technology: the 16mm film format and television. Astruc envisioned a real breakthrough for film as a medium, no longer only as an entertainment medium, but as a fundamental tool for human communication. "With the development of 16mm and television, the day is not far off when everyone will possess a projector, will go to the local bookstore and hire films written on any subject, of any form, from literary criticism and novels to mathematics, history, and general science," he wrote. From this moment, which at the time didn't seem far off, "it will no longer be possible to speak of the cinema. There will be several cinemas just as today there are several literatures, for the cinema, like literature, is not so much a particular art as a language which can express any sphere of thought."[7]

It is safe to say that Astruc's technological vision in 1948 managed to give an accurate description of the general access to audiovisual material through DVD players and the local bookstore as a source of films "written on any subject"—admittedly supplanted by present-day supermarkets. In addition, there are now personal computers with broadband connections in the majority of homes in Western Europe and North America, making it possible to fill the virtual shopping bag with a plethora of audiovisual offerings. Astruc's vision of literary criticism, novels and general science as the main content of the shopping bag is, however, more dubious. Nevertheless, one may assume that in terms of film aesthetics, the offerings of the local supermarkets and video stores are closer to the kind of superficial entertainment the young Astruc polemicized against in 1948. However, the plain wishful thinking of a French postwar intellectual also played a part. "A Descartes of today would already have shut himself up in his bedroom with a 16mm camera and some film, and would be writing his philosophy on film: for his *Discours de la méthode* would today be of such a kind that only the cinema could express it satisfactorily."[8] When that was written, the medium Alexandre Astruc discussed was a little more than half a century old and had undergone what to Astruc and his contemporaries appeared to be astonishingly fast development. The leap from the images in Edison's Kinetoscope or the Lumiéres' Cinématographe to an entertainment industry that in the postwar year of 1948 was at its apex was indeed impressive. Astruc also had the foresight to mention what in the ensuing years would challenge and surpass the cinema as the primary audiovisual medium: television.

Today, the Internet and the Web have opened up yet another channel for active mass participation and production of audiovisual material. In a media-historical sense, YouTube seems to promise what Astruc hoped for half a century ago. The main reason for the enormous success of YouTube lies in the fact that it operates as an open channel for the teeming millions of prospective content producers who, thanks to the technological and economic development of digital media production equipment, can now exchange meanings, experiences and—perhaps most importantly—ways of expression through moving-image media. Every day, YouTube sees the debut of new pieces of audiovisual expression, from film snippets to entire feature films, some generating millions of hits by digital word of mouth. By registering as a director with the service, there is also the possibility of opening up a new "channel," where visitors can log on and contribute commentaries in text or in the form of new video material. In this way a network of thousands—perhaps the auteurs of the 21st century, to use a parallel in film history—has been established, and these new auteurs have found a mass audience that would have been inconceivable for an earlier amateur without economic and technological access to mass media. The key here is, of course, the concept of interactivity, signaling a significant departure from the concept of the auteur as an isolated individual, which has been inherent to the view of authorship over the last two centuries. Although usually connected with the more literary blog, the people who choose to share their ideas in audiovisual form on YouTube often cooperate in enhancing the contributions of others, emphasizing the collective.

The main problem with YouTube as a distribution channel, however, is the signal-to-noise ratio: every item has to contend for space with an avalanche of homebrew video snippets of laughing babies, stupid dogs and an endless number of popular film and TV show emulations, in addition to the fact that the entertainment industry has now acknowledged the power of YouTube and is swamping the website with promotional material. Thus, the site fully illustrates Habermas' worry about the loss of focus in a sea of individual contributions heavily reliant on the various hegemonic forms of expression. However, there are also numerous examples of innovative formal experiments on YouTube, several of which have been able to benefit from the word-of-mouth viral promotion encouraged, among other factors, by the website's rating system.

Intergenerational Communication

An interesting phenomenon among the YouTube new "auteurs" is the user Geriatric1927 and his video posts. After a short personal introduction entitled "Geriatric Grumbles," users come face to face with an elderly British gentleman using a simple webcam to declare his enthusiasm for the YouTube community, a quite odd appearance on a

13 The geriatric's "first try"

site dominated by a youthful audience. Geriatric1927 declares his intention to share his life experience with his younger audience. Responding to the fact that more than 4,000 YouTubers have sent him positive feedback—as of November 2008, the video has been registered with 2,789,508 views on YouTube—Geriatric1927 started a series entitled "Telling It All" that by August 2008 had reached some 60 episodes.[9] In this autobiographic monologue, the audience is informed about growing up in pre-World War II class-dominated England and about the person behind the pseudonym, whose name, one later learns, is Peter Oakley. At the age of 79 he posted his first video on YouTube. Apparently a widower, he was educated in the field of mechanical engineering and worked in the British health sector prior to being self-employed and later retiring. Oakley leads off every new episode with a short vignette of text and music—mainly classic blues—before addressing his audience with: "Hello YouTubers!" From this point the webcam remains focused on him as he continues his monologue, with an ample number of digressions, about growing up in another age. The response from his audience, which seems to have stabilized at around 20 to 30,000, comes in the form of text and videoblogs addressed to him, parodies—most of them good-natured, with a few exceptions—and responses sent to his new website www.askgeriatric.com. The average viewer seems to be of very young age, a fact perhaps mirroring Generation Y's need for a kind of grandfather figure. With a grandparent generation living in Florida or Arizona (or Spain in the case of North European youths), it is possible that new living patterns in the middle class have produced an unexpected deprivation.

With media exposure comes fame, and Peter Oakley has been awarded considerable attention in the regular media, with coverage, for example, on BBC radio and in the *Washington Post*. However, he has refused to appear on regular television and has managed to maintain relative anonymity. On several occasions he has broken off his autobiography to comment on the kind of pressure that public media exerts. He maintains his loyalty to "his YouTubers" and insists that the qualities of the conversation and personal correspondence are preferable to being exposed in the regular mass media—a point of view that undoubtedly appears sensational to an audience led to believe that exposure via the mass media is more or less the meaning of life. During 2007 and 2008, however, Oakley "branched out," adding informal talks about current affairs to his running autobiography under the title "Geriatric thoughts." He has also, apparently, become somewhat of a senior citizen activist. Oakley, who is an avid blues fan, got involved with the "geriatric rock group" The Zimmers—who took their name from the Zimmer chair—during the spring of 2008. This group was the brainchild of documentary filmmaker Tim Samuels, and it made its first appearance in the third part of his documentary series *Power to the People* on BBC in May 2008. *Power to the People* is, according to the BBC, "a three-part series of mischievous documentaries presented by Tim Samuels, who helps some of the most disenfranchised people in society make their voice heard."[10] The video, featuring the Zimmers' rendition of The Who's "My Generation," became an instantaneous hit on YouTube with more than two million hits and placed 26th on the UK singles chart the same week the program with the video was shown on BBC2. Later the same year, Oakley was the lead singer for a version of Alan Parson's "Old and Wise" on the Zimmers' first album, *Lust for Life*. Oakley, in fact, had his "new media celebrity status" confirmed when he was asked to attend a reception at Google UK headquarters with Queen Elizabeth, something that was, of course, duly commented on in his video blog.

In a recent article Dave Harley and Geraldine Fitzpatrick studied Geriatric1927 in the context of globalized and intergenerational communication.[11] In addition to pointing out that Oakley's activities highlight the discrepancy between the increased life expectancy in present-day

14 "This is the first time I have done this, by the way": The Zimmer's "My Generation"

society and the distribution of Internet use in age groups over 60, the authors draw attention to how the YouTube community may serve as a learning tool for the would-be digital video producer. Oakley's confidence in his own abilities appears to be faltering at this point, both in terms of his ability to express himself through his videos and in terms of producing and uploading content onto the YouTube website. What began as an individual effort by Oakley soon developed into a collaborative endeavor through the comments he receives from his viewers. They give him feedback in a number of ways that help him to develop his video presence within YouTube. The following are examples of viewers' comments that critique the technical aspects of his video production and give him technical advice on how to improve it. "Try putting music into the video through the program you are using, it would sound much better :)" was a comment made by ZS9, 19, US, in response to Oakley's first video post. At a later stage Gt, 21, US, writes, "You can also change the colors on Windows Movie Maker. When you are typing your text down by where it says animation or what ever to change the display of your text it should be right there. Just click that and you can change the font and then color is right under the font."[12] Oakley is quick to take advantage of the advice given, and the changes in production qualities and techniques in subsequent videos provide evidence of the results of his learning. Harley and Fitzpatrick state that, all in all, "it is remarkable to what extent the videoblog of Geriatric1927 appears as a collective enterprise actually enhancing the highly individual character of the project."[13]

Oakley's solid fan base seems to have provided him with continuous feedback on form and content, and that has helped him in establishing and maintaining a website. This dual character of collective support and individual presentation presents an interesting contrast to Astruc's individualized vision of the future Descartes holed up in his room with his camera. Oakley is, thus, writing his life with a camera pen—but he is not doing it alone. In *The Subject of Documentary* Michael Renov points out that over the past few decades we have seen a shift in individual self-expression from written media (diaries and other written material) to a culture of audiovisual self-presentation both inside and outside the institution of the documentary. One might ask oneself whether this tendency toward audiovisual self-presentation is a "turn inwards," a retreat from the traditional societal role of documentary, and thus a turn from Paul Rotha's "documentary as pulpit," to the documentary as a confessional testimony. Renov, however, does not see it that way:

> Video confessions produced and exchanged in nonhegemonic contexts can be powerful tools for self-understanding, as well as for two-way communication. [They] afford a glimpse of a more utopian trajectory in which cultural production and consumption mingle and interact, and in which the media facilitate understanding across the gaps of human difference rather than simply capitalizing on these differences in a rush to spectacle.[14]

Conclusion

Through Oakley's series *Telling It All* we can glimpse the contours of an innovation in the relationship with the "classic" documentary, an innovation that may be ascribed to the change in forms of distribution represented by digital audiovisual narrative. A recurring problem within documentary theory and practice is the question of representation—or the burden of representation. The Griersonian project of the 1920s and 1930s was, to a large extent, a pedagogical project. Grierson wanted to use the medium of film in order to illustrate the extent to which modern society was a result of a complicated pattern of interaction among its citizens. The problem, as critics of Grierson have pointed out, was that British documentary tended to reduce the subjects of the films to deindividualized, representative figures subjected to a master narrative they had no control over.

This problematic has led to several experiments in letting the subjects in the documentary express themselves more directly, as in the Canadian social-documentary project *Challenge for Change* in the 1960s, in which enthusiastic filmmakers passed out cameras and sound equipment and experimented with inclusive editing and distribution formats. The reason this and other similar projects failed was that the distribution link was marginalized and that however democratic the intensions were, the initiative and control of the film project came from outside and from above. In *Telling It All* we have a case where the subject controls his own narrative from the very first moment. In this way Peter and his video autobiography represent a dramatic challenge to a film genre that at times may seem at odds with its own proclaimed democratic potentiality. Paula Rabinowitz sums up this problematic in the title of her book dealing with how social conditions have been described in theater and television documentaries throughout the 20th century: *They Must Be Represented.*[15] The title denotes a "they" and a "we," where all good intentions of acting on behalf of others often leads to a cementing of existing social constellations—the subject of the documentary invariably becomes trapped in the role of a victim.

This brings us back to Alexandre Astruc and his vision of the future author or auteur—one who writes with a camera instead of a pen. A major point for Astruc was that the perceived new media situation would open up for alternative ways and means of audiovisual expression, hence his insistence of connecting the new technology with the aesthetics of the avant-garde. For him, the new technological possibilities meant more than just a democratization of the media; in fact, he regarded it as a necessary rejuvenation of film form, liberating it from the old. Maybe parts of this vision are being realized today, in the unlikely figure of an 80-year-old auteur in the worldwide digital network who transfers the experiences and narratives of his generation to a younger one.

Endnotes

1 B. Ruby Rich, "Documentary Disciplines: An Introduction," *Cinema Journal* no. 1, 2006, pp. 108–115.

2 A recent Google search for "Habermas+blogosphere" yielded over 40,000 hits. Jürgen Habermas, *Strukturwandel der Öffentlichkeit* (Frankfurt am Main: Suhrkamp, 1962). The title of the English translation is *The Structural Transformation of the Public Sphere: An Inquiry Into A Category of Bourgeois Society* (Cambridge, MA: MIT Press, 1991). In this context it should be noted that the English translation of the German *Öffentlichkeit* carries some translation problems that public sphere does not quite cover. In her introduction to Oskar Negt and Alexander Kluge's *Public Sphere and Experience*, Miriam Hansen expresses it in this way: "The German term *Öffentlichkeit* encompasses a variety of meanings that elude its English rendering as 'public sphere.' Like the latter, it implies to a spatial concept, the social sites or arenas where meanings are articulated, distributed, and negotiated, as well as the collective body constituted by and in this process, 'the public.' But *Öffentlichkeit* also denotes an ideational substance or criterion glasnost—or openness (which has the same root in German, 'offen')—that is produced both within these sites and in larger, deterritorialized contexts; the English word 'publicity' grasps this sense only in its historically alienated form. In the dialectical tension between these two senses, Negt and Kluge develop their concept of *Öffentlichkeit* as the 'general horizon of social experience.' " Miriam Hansen, foreword to Oskar Negt & Alexander Kluge, *Public Sphere and Experience. Toward an Analysis of the Bourgeois and Proletarian Public Sphere* (Minneapolis: University of Minnesota Press, 1994), pp. 8–9.

3 In *Öffentlichkeit und Erfahrung* (1972), a book strongly influenced by the 1970s discourse on ideology, the authors emphasize the necessity to take into consideration how the European working class related to various public spaces according to experiences of its members. Habermas referred solely in passing to this "plebeian Öffentlichkeit." Negt and Kluge, however, give several examples of how alternative forms of public spheres were organized in the years between the world wars in organized labor movements in Germany and Austria, characterized as a "Gegenöffentlichkeit"—public spheres set in response and opposition to the dominating public space, or counter-publicity as it has been referred to in English. Yet, as Negt and Kluge point out, these attempts soon led to

situations where they would merely establish parallel institutions emulating the bourgeois public sphere, thus ending up as isolated social organizations, what the authors refer to as "Lageröffentlichkeit"—literally encampment public spheres.

4 Sarah Street, *British National Cinema* (London: Routledge, 1997), pp. 78–80.

5 Douglas Kellner, "Habermas, the Public Sphere and Democracy: A Critical Intervention," in *Perspectives on Habermas*, ed. Lewis Edwin Hahn (Peru, IL: Open Court Publishing, 2000), pp. 259–289.

6 Jürgen Habermas, *Preisrede anlässlich der Verleihung des Bruno-Kreisky-Preises für das politische Buch 2005* (Vienna: Renner-Institut, 2006), p. 4 – www.renner-institut.at/download/texte/habermas2006-03-09.pdf [last checked 15 February 2009].

7 Astruc is quoted from Peter Graham, ed., *The New Wave. Critical Landmarks* (London: Secker & Warburg, 1968), p. 19.

8 Ibid.

9 The number of video postings by Geriatric1927 reached over 100 as of January 2008, with less emphasis on *Telling It All* and more on contemporary issues, especially conditions for the elderly in Great Britain.

10 See http://news.bbc.co.uk/2/hi/programmes/power_to_the_people/about_the_series/default.stm [last checked 15 February 2009].

11 Dave Harley & Geraldine Fitzpatrick, "YouTube and Intergenerational Communication: The Case of Geriatric1927," special issue, *Universal Access in the Information Society* (forthcoming).

12 For comments about Geriatric1927, see for instance www.youtube.com/watch?v=p_YmigZmUuk [last checked 15 February 2009].

13 Harley & Fitzpatrick 2009.

14 Michael Renov, *The Subject of Documentary* (Minneapolis: University of Minnesota Press, 2004), p. 215.

15 For a discussion, see Paula Rabinowitz, *They Must Be Represented. The Politics of Documentary* (London: Verso, 1994).

Form

Joost Broeren

Digital Attractions: Reloading Early Cinema in Online Video Collections

Considering its complete absorption into contemporary culture, it is sometimes hard to believe that YouTube is really only a few years old. Despite the plethora of copycats, YouTube's brand name has become synonymous with online video. This quick rise may lead one to believe that YouTube has no history, and indeed both academic and popular investigations of YouTube and its ilk have mostly focused on their future development. However, the emphasis on YouTube's future blinds us to meaningful historical connections. This article is an attempt to sketch out one such connection: the one between YouTube's online video collections and early cinema, or to be more precise: the earliest forms of cinema which Tom Gunning has termed the "cinema of attractions."

When Gunning published his article in 1986, he could hardly have imagined the success and influence his approach to early cinema would have. Today, the concept is still central to early cinema research, a fact most succinctly illustrated by the recent publication of *The Cinema of Attractions Reloaded.*[1] Most of the essays in this anthology remain focused on early cinema, but a few use the concept of "the attraction" to examine cinematic objects outside this sphere proper. Proceeding from Gunning's assertion that "in some sense recent spectacle cinema has reaffirmed its roots in stimulus and carnival rides, in what might be called the Spielberg-Lucas-Coppola cinema of effects,"[2] some articles attempt to bring the concept of cinema of attractions to the present day, tracing the attractional mode of presentation to various genres, from the 1930s musical to present-day action films.

Yet, somewhat oddly—considering the connotations of the "reloading" metaphor—most articles never move outside the cinematic paradigm. To a certain degree this makes sense, considering the centrality of the term cinema in Gunning's concept. Yet it seems to me that the attractional mode constitutes a *dispositif* (to borrow Frank Kessler's usage of the notion) that can be applied to other media as well. Prior to 1905, for example, cinema was not always considered a medium of its own. Slides and moving pictures were just different forms of projection techniques displaying more or less attractional content. Indeed, if one continues through media history it is precisely outside the cinema that the attractional mode has remained in the most frequent use, with genres such as the television commercial or the music video clearly falling into this category. However, I would argue that the attraction resurfaces in its fullest form in streaming-video websites such as YouTube. As I will show, in this media environment it is not only the attractional mode of address that resurfaces, but also the original objects themselves (early film fragments) as well as the context in which these were shown, albeit in modified form. Before elaborating on this further, however, it is necessary to examine the constitutive elements of what for the purposes of this article may be called the *attractional dispositif*.

Defining Early Cinema (as) Attractions

In his contribution to *The Cinema of Attractions Reloaded*, Warren Buckland tries to reconstruct "the conceptual structure of, and assumptions underlying" Gunning's original essay.[3] According to Buckland, Gunning deals with three basic problematics. The first is the re-examination of the relation between early cinema and (contemporary) avant-garde cinema. This problematic is approached by dealing with two secondary problematics: the "strangely heterogeneous relation" between film before and after 1906, and the "hegemony of narrative films."[4] According to Buckland, "Gunning uses the primary problematic (the link between early cinema and the avant-garde) to address and solve problematics 2 and 3 (periodization and heterogeneity/hegemony). The as-yet unstated concept of the attraction is the gel that binds together and solves these problematics."[5]

So what exactly is this attraction? The term was first used by Sergei Eisenstein, who applied it in the context of the theater. However, Gunning also emphasizes that "then, as now, the 'attraction' was a term from the fairground."[6] Principally, it is a cinema that shows rather than tells. "Contrasted to the voyeuristic aspect of narrative cinema analyzed by Christian Metz, this is an exhibitionist cinema."[7] This exhibitionism exerts itself in the same way the cinema of attractions constructs its relationship to the viewer. Gunning deliberately removes his definition from the "Méliès vs. Lumière" dichotomy, which casts Méliès' effects films in a narrative light and dismisses the Lumières´ actualities as non-narrative. For Gunning, they are two sides of the same coin: "One can unite them in a conception that sees cinema less as a way of telling stories than as a way of presenting a series of views to an audience."[8]

Heide Schlüpmann has extended the analogy between fiction and non-fiction by looking at the content of these films. She questions the applicability of the modern-day distinction between fiction and non-fiction to early cinema, seeing both as essentially *documentative* in this period, as "the early fiction films were fuelled by the same interest as the documentary films, and [...] they also represent a kind of documentation, albeit by other means."[9] This leads her to the claim that (narrative) *fiction* film in this period was partly a pretext for being able to show scenes of intimate home life, which were taboo in non-fiction film.[10] According to Gunning, the centrality of *showing* is also reflected in the modes of exhibition in early cinema. Taking his lead from Charles Musser, Gunning characterizes early cinema exhibition as a showman's cinema, harking back to fairground conventions: "The early showmen exhibitors exerted a great deal of control over the shows they presented, actually re-editing the films they had purchased and supplying a series of off-screen supplements, such as sound effects and spoken commentary."[11]

In a reaction to Gunning's article, Musser provides an alternative to the way Gunning employs his theories. One of the points he makes is that the showman and/or lecturer in fact often had a narrativizing function. For Musser, the distinction between early cinema and that which follows it lies not in the distinction between narrative and non-narrative, but in the locus of narrative control. "In this period [the 1890s] creative responsibilities were divided between motion picture producers and exhibitors. What we now call postproduction was almost completely in the hands of the exhibitors."[12] Musser's objection is part of a larger criticism of Gunning's theory, which can be seen as generally typical for criticisms of the cinema of attractions. It largely boils down to two points, both visible in Musser's article. The first issue is the extent to which there *is* narrative in early cinema; Musser's point about the lecturer is part of this issue. The second issue is periodization. While largely agreeing with Gunning's definition of cinema of attractions as typical of cinema before 1903 to 1904, Musser (and many others like him) objects to the fact that Gunning extends this definition to all early cinema, up until 1915.

The question of periodization has led to the previously homogeneous era of "early cinema" to be broken into two distinct periods, the first an era of attractions, the second a transitional era in which this attractional mode slowly gave way to the classical Hollywood system. This periodization often implies a difference in length, implicitly making a distinction between "attractional" short films on the one hand and "narrative" long films on the other. Most discussion has centered on exactly when these changes occurred: Charlie Keil dates the transitional period as taking place between 1908 and 1917 in the American context.[13] Ben Brewster, using a slightly different terminology and looking at the European context, sees the changes starting in 1906 and 1907 and running through to World War I.[14]

In re-examining the cinema of attractions as a concept, Frank Kessler claims that both the question of whether or not early cinema had narrative and that of periodization are, to a certain degree, beside the point. Since any periodization is by definition a historiographical construction, it is "much more their usefulness and productivity that is at stake than their 'correctness.'"[15] As for the question of narrative, Kessler reminds us that the cinema of attractions is defined by its mode of address—by the way it enters into a relationship with its audience. The differentiation that Gunning (with André Gaudreault) makes between the "cinema of attractions" and the "cinema of narrative integration" should therefore not be seen on a narratological level, but in the way they address the audience. In light of these two points, Kessler proposes that it "might be preferable to rather conceive this conceptual couple in terms of a 'cinema of narrative integration' versus a 'cinema of *attractional display*.' "[16] My analysis will follow this reformulation of Gunning's original concept. This new attractional mode of display has consequences for both the content of the films as the context in which they are presented, and the way they address their audience.

Online Video: Attractional Mode of Address

Kessler notes three characteristics of the cinema of attractions (and thus the cinema of attractional display) which "appear to be directly linked to this general orientation towards the spectator," namely "the gaze and gestures of actors directed towards the camera, the temporality, the frontality."[17] These characteristics are truly visible in online video as well. However, before specifying the similarities, let us focus on another, at first glance more superficial, comparison: that of the films' length. Both films of early cinema and online video clips are *short films*, mostly staying well under ten minutes in length. While this might seem to be a similarity that is so superficial as to be inconsequential, it might indeed be worth taking note of, not least in the light of Corinna Müller's remark that the terms "cinema of attractions" and "narrative film" in fact "imply the short film on the one hand and the long film on the other."[18] The basic understanding of early film as short film, and film after 1915 as (predominantly) long film, is indeed visible in the literature dealing with early cinema. The analogy may be extended further regarding the fact that for early cinema as well as for online video, the short length of the material is in part regulated by technological specifications. The early cinematographs were prone to jam or break down when using spliced film strips, thus dictating the maximum length which could be used. In online video collections, it is the bandwidth of both the website and the user—as well as the buffer size of the user's PC—which limit the possible length of films.

However, in both media these technological limitations are apparently not the only thing dictating the length of the films, since even when these limitations are removed lengths don't automatically change. The transition from "cinema of attractions" to "narrative cinema" was not done in an instant. Brewster, like Gunning, also makes the important distinction that this transitional period does not consist of films becoming more and more narrative gradually, over a certain period of time, and therefore longer and longer. Instead, "the institutions for each type of cinema being essentially different from one another, they could and did exist side by side for quite long periods."[19] The same can be said about online video. Although bandwidth and hard-disk space have both increased rapidly over the last few years, most online clips still run a few minutes at the most. This is true even when longer lengths are possible and indeed encouraged. While YouTube allows for video clips with a running time of up to ten minutes, it is rare that this length is used. An unverified but fair approximation indicates that the average film length on YouTube lies around three to four minutes. Apparently, the short length of films is not simply due to technical limitations, but rather a conscious choice by the creators. In making this choice, they align themselves less with some tradition of narrative integration, and much more with the tradition of the music video, the movie trailer, the television advertisement—in short, with a mode of attractional display. Another similarity with early cinema is that these clips often work specifically to *show*. This concerns the showing of the self—the exhibitionist aspect of the cinema of attractions getting a literal dimension. Using webcams, mobile-phone cameras or home-video equipment, users film themselves doing all sorts of things.

A number of these forms of display have a peculiar connection to the vaudeville background of early cinema. The musical display, for example, consisting of people recording themselves performing songs, harks back directly to a vaudeville context. Naturally, the setting differs: instead of a theatrical stage, most of these video clips are recorded in people's own homes. The genre can roughly be subdivided into three categories: people lip-synching original recordings of popular songs, people recording their own cover versions of songs by their favorite artists, and people recording their own songs. One could also include (illegal) video recordings of performances by professional artists in this category. However, since these films differ from the others in that the performance itself is not specifically staged for display through these websites, even though the video clip itself was, let us first focus on the other three categories. All three are made with slightly different motivations; for instance, miming is mostly done in duets, thereby giving it a social function outside the display to unknown others. But while the aural aspect obviously would seem to take dominance in these types of films, it is in fact the visual that is most important, since the aspect of literally showing oneself is central to all three. Audience address is also strong in all three categories, with the performers usually looking directly at the camera and often introducing their song to the audience.[20]

The element of showing oneself is even more strongly present in the second category: the physical display. Of course, every display is physical. But the term "physical display" is meant here in a more narrow sense, as a display of physicality. This category mostly consists of people performing stunts or tricks—bike stunts, magic tricks, etcetera. In the stunt videos especially, the aural aspect is of almost no consequence, usually being limited to the use of music or someone behind the camera either cheering (when a stunt goes right) or laughing (when one goes wrong). In fact, most of these videos use music played over the visuals, making them more directly comparable to silent cinema (which was often accompanied by what we would now call "source music"). In this type of video clip, spectator address can be direct, but is not necessarily so. In the case of magic tricks the performer usually looks directly at the camera, and thus at the audience; with bike stunts the performer (for obvious reasons) usually does not address the viewer. Yet even in the last case, shots are framed to provide the audience with the most satisfactory *view* of the action, and the films sometimes even include action replays.

15 Early Attractions: "Rough Sea at Dover"

Another type that can be included in the category of physical display is the presentation of natural physicality: a display of the power of nature. Examples of this are films of waves breaking onto a rocky beach in a storm, heavy thunderstorms, and water thrown and turning to snow instantly at very low temperatures. These might be compared to early films of similar phenomena. The image of waves breaking onto a beach especially is one that recurs over and over in the earliest years of cinema; "Rough Sea at Dover" (1896) is just one example of many in the so-called "rocks-and-waves" genre. The majority of videos presenting natural physicality are more or less documentary; what little fiction is available is mostly limited to parodies of, or tributes to, existing television programs or films by their fans. Since these videos usually do not (re)tell a story per se, instead focusing on well-known aspects of their source material, either to jokingly parody them or to lovingly recreate them, these might be called attractional as well. The relative lack of fiction might be partially explained by referring back to Heide Schlüpmann's thesis that early cinema fiction was in fact a way of showing the taboo subject of home life (with non-fiction showing the audience other aspects of modern life).[21] The same taboo does not exist in the modern day; in fact, as mentioned earlier, a large percentage of the video material available online is recorded in a home setting. Fiction thus does not serve any purpose in this medium of attractional display.

The non-original content available through online video collections is also mainly in the attractional mode. This consists mostly of the most attractional genres in cinema and television: music videos, movie trailers and advertisements. Partly, this involves copyrights issues. While other, more "narrative integrational" films are their own product and therefore cannot be given away freely online, these three types of video are primarily created to sell something else—the more people see them, the better. Yet there is another dimension to this as well, since the attractional aspects of these forms integrate fully with the context offered by the websites and their original content.

Online Video: Resurfacing Early Cinema

If these videos mostly seem to work in an attractional mode, online video websites such as YouTube also enable a resurfacing of early films themselves. Browsing the YouTube collection, one can find many examples of this. Most, if not all, of the films available are from the established canon (i.e. by Porter, Méliès, Griffith). Most likely this is due to the fact that these films are readily available to YouTube's users for uploading, for instance through their availability on videotapes or DVDs, or through television broadcasts (mostly within the context of documentary series on early cinema). The online video collections, then, (again) reinforce the established canon and (further) neglect films that have not been preserved in other media either. The relatively prominent presence of early cinema's films in online video collections must, as in the case of advertising or music videos, partly be attributed to the issue of copyright. Early cinema is old enough to be in the public domain, and can therefore be uploaded to various collections without problems. But again, as with advertising and music videos, equally important is the fact that the films seem to feel at home here. This is perhaps most clearly articulated through the linkage between films. Early films do not constitute a category of their own; when viewing Méliès' *Le voyage dans la lune* (1902), the menu of related films not only consists of other films by Méliès, but also includes a video of two Spanish boys firing a rocket and modern-day shots of the full moon. When viewing the Lumières' *L'Arrivée d'un train à La Ciotat* (1895), the list includes other films of arriving trains from various periods—as well as links to videos of the band Lumière. The website's collection system thus establishes a dialogue between examples of early cinema and modern-day films.

16 Out of a sudden: The famous train arrives at La Ciotat

This film-historical dialogue—or sort of a narrative—is more or less constitutive of an afternoon spent browsing the collection. For, just as Musser has drawn attention to the fact that early films were not shown independently but as programs, structured and therefore "made narrative" by a lecturer or programmer, the same goes for online video. It is rare that users watch one film specifically; one film tends to lead to another in a potentially endless string of more or less associated clips.

Hence, it is not only the attractional mode of address that resurfaces in these online video collections. To a certain degree, the attractional mode of display can also be traced to the new medium—brought into the "digital age" to comply with elements of what might be called the *digital dispositif.* Even if various video websites present films to audiences in different ways, YouTube has established the default mode of presentation. While layouts and surface functionality may differ from other, similar websites (such as former rival, present owner Google Video), the underlying functionality and assumptions are, to a large extent, the same for all. Typically, these pages offer two entrances to the collection. The first is an entrance selected by the system, showing lists of videos organized by status ("most popular") or chronology ("most recent"). The second entrance is the search box, with which the user starts a keyword search of the collection, thus, an entrance selected by the user. A third possible entry point is of course a direct link to a specific video. In all three cases it should be noted that these are indeed *starting points.* As we have seen, the fact that one film leads to numerous others is inscribed into the system of these collections. The films' display pages typically link to other films, either thematically related or added by the same user. Additionally, the space in which the video itself is shown changes, once the film has run its course, to a link space showing thematically related films as well. The viewing system thus encourages the user to keep viewing, an encouragement that leads to a much-reported "addictiveness" of these types of websites: once you start watching, there's no end in sight.

Conclusion

Video journeys through online film collections echo the attractional mode of display. This is primarily the case since the grand narrative is not dictated by the *producer* of the films. The users adding video clips to the collections have no say in the larger narrative of the site, although he or she can attempt to offer some guidance in the description of the film (in a way similar to the descriptions movie producers gave in film catalogues). But it is the "system" itself that ultimately selects the context in which it puts these videos, sorting them predominantly through thematic comparisons based on the titles, tags and descriptions that the "producer" adds to his uploaded film. Proceeding from Musser, the narrative control is thus a negotiation between the "producer" (the user adding the film) and the "exhibitor" (the website showing the film). It is as if the owner of the cinema (YouTube) is jostling for control with the projectionist (the user). Yet in a digital context, there is one more participant in this negotiation—the audience. The website ("exhibitor") structures the pathways a user may take by offering a certain selection from the database and by offering this selection in a certain order. The producer can influence this structuring somewhat by means of the title, tags and descriptions. But the decisions of where to start the journey, what film to watch next and when to stop watching are made by the audience. Here, the attractional *dispositif* meshes with one of the central elements of the *digital dispositif*—interactivity.[22]

Endnotes

1 Tom Gunning, "The Cinema of Attraction[s]: Early Film, Its Spectator and the Avant-Garde," in *The Cinema of Attractions Reloaded*, ed.Wanda Strauven (Amsterdam: Amsterdam University Press, 2006), pp. 381–388.

2 Ibid., p. 387.

3 Warren Buckland, "A Rational Reconstruction of 'The Cinema of Attractions,' " in *The Cinema of Attractions Reloaded* 2006, pp. 41–56.

4 Gunning 2006, p. 381.

5 Buckland 2006, p. 45.

6 Gunning 2006, p. 384.

7 Ibid., p. 382.

8 Ibid.

9 Heide Schlüpmann, "The Documentary Interest in Fiction," in *Uncharted Territory: Essays on Early Nonfiction Film*, eds. Daan Hertogs & Nico de Klerk (Amsterdam: Stichting Nederlands Filmmuseum, 1997), pp. 33–36, 33.

10 Ibid., p. 35.

11 Gunning 2006, p. 383.

12 Charles Musser, "Rethinking Early Cinema: Cinema of Attractions and Narrativity," *The Cinema of Attractions Reloaded*, pp. 389–416.

13 Charlie Keil & Shelley Stamp, "Introduction," in *American Cinema's Transitional Era: Audiences, Institutions, Practices*, eds. Charlie Keil & Shelley Stamp (Berkeley: University of California Press, 2004), p. 1.

14 Ben Brewster, "Periodization of Early Cinema," in *American Cinema's Transitional Era: Audiences, Institutions, Practices*, pp. 66–75, 73.

15 Frank Kessler, "The Cinema of Attractions as *Dispositif*," *The Cinema of Attractions Reloaded*, pp. 57–69, 58.

16 Ibid., p. 59.

17 Ibid.

18 Corinna Müller cited in Brewster 2004, p. 66.

19 Brewster 2004, p. 73.

20 Jean Burgess connects this performativity to the participatory nature of YouTube in her work, e.g. " 'All Your Chocolate Rain Are Belong to Us?': Viral Video, YouTube and the Dynamics of Participatory Culture," in *The Video Vortex Reader: Responses to YouTube*, eds. Geert Lovink & Sabine Niederer (Amsterdam: Institute of Network Cultures, 2008), pp. 101–109.

21 Schlüpmann 1997, pp. 33–34.

22 While I will not venture a definitive prediction to the development of YouTube, its launch of the Screening Room is interesting in relation to this article. The new dedicated area within YouTube makes room for long-form videos (up to ninety minutes) in high quality, made by professional independent filmmakers. While online video thus seems to be slowly following its older brother cinema into the territory of longer and narrative film, for now the era of the online attraction seems far from over. This viewer, at least, will be watching avidly how the exhibitionist *dispositif* of the attraction is further developed in an interactive environment.

Thomas Elsaesser

Tales of Epiphany and Entropy: Around the Worlds in Eighty Clicks

This article is concerned with the changing function of narrative, that is, with the question of what happens when one of the central cultural forms we have for shaping human sensory data as well as information about the "real world" finds itself in a condition of overstretch. Or more precisely: what kinds of asymmetries occur when much of this perceptual, sensory and cognitive data is being produced, i.e. recorded and stored, by machines, in cooperation with humans, which has been the case since the beginning of the 20th century, but which is being fully acknowledged only since the beginning of the 21st century. Photography, cinema, television and the Internet are all hybrids in this respect: they gather and store sense data that is useless without the human interface, but exceeds in quantity what humans can make sense of, and also what narrative can contain, i.e. articulate, "linearize" or "authorize." Second, the same potential overstretch affects the modes of spectatorship, of participation, of witnessing that are entailed by the display of and access to this data, especially in an environment which is common, public and collective (like cinema), but also "dynamic," discrete and "interactive" (like the Internet), which—in other words—allows for feedback loops, for change in real time, and thus potentially is both endless and shapeless. Narratives are ways of organizing not only space and time, most commonly in a linear, consecutive fashion: they also, through the linguistic and stylistic resources known as "narration," provide for a coherent point of reception or mode of address: what used to be referred to as a "subject position," or "reader address." Narratives, in other words, are about time, space and subject, or the "here," the "now" and the "me."

One must therefore start from the notion that linear sequencing, though quasi-universal, is not the only way to make connections of continuity and contiguity or to plot a trajectory and provide closure. It follows that if time's arrow is only one of the axes on which to string data and access it, then stories with a beginning, middle and end are only one such cultural form. In the era of simultaneity, ubiquity and placeless places, other cultural forms are conceivable and do indeed exist. Computer games are often cited as the competitors for the hegemony of narratives, and so-called scripted stories or spatial narratives increasingly gain attention even outside gamer communities. Henry Jenkins, for instance, thinks of both narratives and games as "spatial stories." He argues that "spatial stories can evoke pre-existing narrative associations; they may embed narrative information within their mise-en-scène, or provide resources for emergent narratives," yet they do not have to take the form of classical narratives.[1]

17 "Honda Accord Cog"

What scripted stories or spatial narratives, then, does YouTube offer, once a user engages with the site's dynamic architecture, sets up a few ground rules (both narratives and games need rules), and then lets him/herself be taken to different sites, spaces and places: not by the logic of an individual character's aims, obstacles, helpers and opponents, but by the workings of contiguity, combinatory and chance? In other words, what happens when neither the causal chain of action and reaction, nor the temporal succession of locales determines the direction or trajectory of the journey, but when one is guided by keywords or tags, tag clouds or semantic clusters, embedded links, user's comments and of course, one's own "free" associations?

Constructive Instability

As a site for exploring scripted spaces, YouTube still stands among some of the major traditions of narrative (the novel, cinema). Close to cinema in its use of visual segments extracted from different (narrative, performative) media, YouTube also gives the illusion—like the realist novel, but also like YouTube's owners, Google—of a kind of totality, a full universe. With the difference that a novel suggests *one* world (among many), while Google suggests *the* world: if you cannot find it on Google or YouTube, many people now seem to believe that it either doesn't exist, or is not worth knowing or having.

Most of us are well aware of the dangers of relying on such a monopoly of information, but we also know, from our frequent, if shamefaced use of say, Wikipedia, how seductive it is to take as reliable fact what has been written, rewritten, amended, deleted and once more rewritten by many hands in a single Wiki entry. We accept the convenience such ready-to-use knowledge affords, and we align ourselves with the implied consequences of a potentially momentous development: the so-called post-human condition, which "configures human beings so that they can be seamlessly articulated with intelligent machines."[2] In the post-human, there are no essential differences or absolute demarcations between bodily existence and computer simulation, between cybernetic mechanisms and biological organisms, between robots running on programs and humans pursuing goals or quests. In the words of N. Katherine Hayles, a prominent representative of the post-human view: "What [is] happening, is the development of distributed cognitive environments in which humans and computers interact in hundreds of ways daily, often unobtrusively."[3]

Even if one rejects the full implications of such a post-human position,[4] one is well-advised to reflect on the definitions of "culture" and "nature," both of which stand under the sign of *techné*—but of a *techné* which must itself to be refigured around the notion of "art" and "artifice": practices that are best situated between "design," "engineering" and "programming." This raises an interesting prospect and may even hold out a promise: as "life" becomes more "artificial" by being both engineered and programmable, the possibility arises that "art" has to become more life-like (by emulating processes of reproduction, replication, random generation, mutation, chance and contingency), in order to remain "art," that is, "human," in the sense of "un-adapted" and sensitive to "failure" (which in this context would be another word for finitude, that is the certainty of death, or closure).

Similarly in the sphere of knowledge production and dissemination: if the principles of "art" and "life" collapse, coalesce or converge around replication and repetition, if they are organized by self-regulation and feedback, and shaped by aggregation and clustering, what kind of knowledge arises from the "convergence culture" that is the Internet?[5] In order to test this question I conducted an experiment: accepting, for the sake of the argument, the post-human "human-machine symbiosis" as fact, I aligned myself with the logic of the auto-generated Web links, and their embedded information. At the same time, I imagined myself a Web 2.0 flaneur, while falling back on an old-fashioned avant-garde technique popular among the Surrealists: automatic writing.

To give some indication of the results of the experiment, I shall introduce the concept of *constructive instability*. What interests me about the term, derived from engineering, is the idea that "instability" and even "failure" must have a place in the narratives of adaptive, dynamic or emergent situations. For one obvious point to make about self-regulatory systems is that they involve risk and imponderability. As, among others, the "Internet guru" Jaron Lanier, in his attack on Wikipedia as "digital Maoism," has pointed out, there is real concern about the kind of agency and the measure of control individuals and collectives are handing over when "intelligent systems" run so much of everyday life, in the area of medicine, the government or on the financial markets, and in the conduct of modern warfare. Information systems such as we have them are considerably more fallible than is usually realized, as can be seen from electricity power-station failures, the knock-on effects that come from a local disturbance in the international air-traffic systems. Of course, one could argue that these are not self-regulatory phenomena, but hierarchized and top-down, while the Internet was conceived and built precisely in order to minimize the domino effects typical of linear forms of communication. It is indeed due to the general success of this package distribution system that we feel so over-confident in the workings of all complex systems and circuits. A spectacular example is the financial markets, where the more advanced trading instruments, such as futures and derivatives, are inherently unstable: how dangerously so has been proven by the "crashes," "meltdowns" and "credit crunches" in recent times. One working assumption of my experiment, in other words, was that the principle of instability and volatility, and indeed, fallibility must be regarded as "systemic" in the human-machine symbiosis: not as a design fault, to be eliminated, but specially engineered as a calculated risk, and maybe even as a design advantage.

Performed Failure — Narratives of Collapse

Let me now report where the idea of constructive instability took me in a more circumscribed field of application, namely film and media studies, and the "future" of narrative. I understand the term "constructive instability" primarily in its most literal form, namely as the property of an artifact constructed and built for the purpose of drawing maximal use from the processes engendered when it collapses or self-destructs. My focus of attention for this new field of force centered on constructive instability as a systemically precarious equilibrium on the Internet was YouTube: as mentioned, exemplary for the social networking and user-generated-content websites, where the monopoly of information (as controlled by Google) is constantly modified and amplified by the users' own sense of what is important, useful, amusing or of what simply exists: modified in other words, by a thoroughly pragmatic understanding of what is "true" and what is "real."

Utilizing what I understand to be the underlying algorithmic structure and feedback dynamics of these "open socials" or "social graphs," i.e. the combination of search terms—the tag clouds—with the cluster mechanisms and sort algorithms of the YouTube site, I began to follow the semantic trail of the terms *collapse, instability, chain reaction*, etc. to see where it would take me, and eventually decided to make my starting point a two-minute British advertisement. In 2003, it had "made history" not only because its fame and success proved the power of the Internet as a "window of attention" for advertisers, but also because its production values—it cost around six million dollars to produce—put it squarely in the league of Hollywood blockbusters. It also demonstrated the ambivalence of the idea of *collapse*, when understood as a bipolar principle of destruction and creation, with moments in-between: of transition, of balance, of interlinked concatenations, or—to use a favorite term of urbanists and sociologists, but also of ecologists and climatologists—of *tipping points*.[6]

"The Honda Cog"

The advertisement is for the Honda Accord car, and is generally known as the "Honda Cog." It generated an enormous amount of Internet traffic, and also serious coverage in the press. In short, it had a substantial crossover effect into the traditional media as well, and became, in fact, an "urban legend." Looking at the original advertisement more closely, it is clear that the setting connotes a gallery space: white walls, wooden parquet floor, no windows, controlled light sources. It also alludes in a playful, but unmistakable fashion to the work of several canonical artists of the 20th century. Fitting, too, is the fact that a Japanese car maker should have commissioned this ad, for it was Japan that first showed Europe and the US how to make cars with robots, how to reduce costs by just-in-time delivery: in short, it was Japanese auto firms that pioneered several of the principles we now lump together under the term "post-Fordism," but which could just as well be called "Toyota-ism" or "Honda-ism." What we see, then, is the ironic mise-en-scène of a meta-mechanic assembly line which says "Look: no hands! Pure magic" or—as the Honda slogan has it—"the power of dreams." The director, Antoine Bardou-Jacquet, is a well-known creative artist of high-concept ads and music videos.

The links on YouTube relating to the "Honda Cog" quickly lead to an extract from a "making-of" video, which gives some glimpses of the immense effort that went into the production of such an effortless and yet inevitable concatenation of collapsing moments and obedient parts. The making-of video—which, by a nice coincidence, has as its motto Soichiro Honda's famous "Success is 99% failure"—ends up celebrating in the language of cinema our fascination with the engineering marvels that are contemporary automobiles, but it also mimics the generic features of a nature documentary, concerning the patience it takes to train animals (here: car parts), in order for them to perform for humans. Back to the "Honda Cog": besides the allusions to Japan and post-Fordism, there is the voice at the end, intoning the tag line: "Isn't it nice when things just work?" I associated it immediately with Sean Connery and James Bond, and so did the users of YouTube. Very soon I discovered tags that led from the Honda Accord to the Aston Martin DB5, Bond's famous car; the link immediately connected the "life" of the Honda Accord's parts to the Aston Martin's gadgets, and especially those fabulous demonstrations given at the modifications workshop in the belly of the MI-5 headquarters, by the immortal engineer-inventor Q. Another link brought me to a French mashup of this scene, which gives it a quite different subtext and cultural atmosphere: references are now to Christopher Lambert, Bob Marley, the Rastafarians, Californian beach culture and air-lift suspension, Rizla cigarette paper, rolled joints, all played out against intense homophobic/homoerotic banter between Q and Bond.[7]

One immediately associates the gruff boffin engineer from MI-5 who "never jokes about his work," but visibly delights in his playful as well as lethal modifications, with another obvious father of the "Honda Cog," namely Rube Goldberg. The name stands for a kind of machine that does simple or humble tasks (like sneezing into a handkerchief) in an especially complicated, ingenious or roundabout way, utilizing common principles of traction and transmission, but in a manner that makes them meta-mechanic (reminiscent of both Marcel Duchamp and Charles Chaplin).

Apart from the voice, it is the words that hold another key to the ad's cultural layers: for besides Bond and automotive gadgets, "Isn't it nice when things just work?" cannot but evoke—for a British listener, at least—one of the most famous political campaigns ever. "Labour isn't working" was the 1979 slogan that brought Margaret Thatcher to power and made advertising chic and hip, thanks to Charles Saatchi (head of the company that devised the poster, and for whom the director Antoine Bardou-Jacquet has also worked), who in turn "made" "Young British Artists" chic and hip, and to this day is one of the most influential collectors of modern and contemporary art: precisely the sort of art the "Honda Cog" gently mocks as well as generously celebrates.

"Der Lauf der Dinge"

However, the words of the "Honda Cog" nod-and-wink not only at the knowing cognoscenti but also anticipate possible legal problems (which did indeed arise) by acknowledging (not so obliquely) where the makers had "appropriated" the idea for the ad: not from a London gallery, nor a billboard, but the Kassel documenta of 1987. There, one of the most popular art pieces was a half-hour video, entitled "Der Lauf der Dinge," generally translated as "The Way Things Go," but better rendered as the "The Life of Things." Its makers are two Swiss artists, Peter Fischli & David Weiss, who have been working together since the early 1970s. This videotape was their international breakthrough.

18 "The Life of Things"

The rough, para-industrial setup, the processes put in motion as well as the materials used inevitably recall many of the key elements of modern sculpture, conceptual art and other avant-garde practices, notably (but not only) from the post-WW II period: the concern for balance and suspension (Suprematism and Constructivism); assemblage art (from the late 1940s); kinetic art (from the 1950s and '60s); trash objects, garbage and recycled materials (from New Realism and Pop); ready-mades and small wasted energies made useful (Marcel Duchamp); and finally, the energies inherent in apparently inert matter from the work of Carl Andre, not to forget the macho-engineering skills of

Richard Serra and the action paintings—here duly automated and pre-programmed—of Jackson Pollock.

The connections between the "Honda Cog" and "Der Lauf der Dinge" (just as the ironic allusions to their respective predecessors in art, cinema and popular culture) are of, course, the very stuff of cultural history in both its modernist and post-modernist variants. The echoes and allusions can be accommodated within the traditional parameters just this side of plagiarism: of "homage," "remediation," "pastiche" and "appropriation." The saturation with puns and arcane references to inter-media phenomena is furthermore the trademark of the smart ad, as pioneered and made global by, among others, Saatchi & Saatchi in Britain since the 1970s and '80s. Smart ads are seen by many as part of the problem of the cultural collapse of distinctions, rather than as part of the (democratizing) solution or rescue of high culture, even though such cheekily in-the-know ad campaigns have been widely adopted not only for cars and other commodities, but are a staple promotional tool for museums and other traditional temples of high culture also.

Yet the point to make in the present context is that the majority of these cultural references, genealogies and associations were suggested to me not by critical essays, but by the YouTube tags and user comments themselves: in other words, by a different, much "flatter" mode of linkage and hierarchy, in which the pop-cultural, topical, taste-driven or art-historical knowledge base of the users and up-loaders is cross-hatched with a good deal of contingency and chance, while nonetheless seeming to form part of a discernable design, a "narrative": a totality-in-the-making, however amorphous or blob-like it may appear in its early stages of formation. If I were to draw some preliminary conclusions, I would highlight the following points: first, the "Honda Cog," while serendipitous in its media effects (no one anticipated quite what an Internet phenomenon it would be), is very traditional in the ideology of its creation: in the making-of video one recognizes all the clichés of commercial filmmaking (money and labor invested equals aesthetic value and authenticity) as well as of auteurism (the artist's vision is paramount, he is a driven and relentless perfectionist: success—the perfect take—finally rewards his perseverance).[8]

Second, and as a counterargument, one can also observe a new frame of reference at work: that of the test, or test run,[9] as a new paradigm, situated between Gilles Deleuze's "control society" and the concern with the post-human. In the "Honda Cog" it manifests itself in the take, the re-take, here amplified and exaggerated to become its own parody: it took 605 takes to "get it right," eloquently illustrating the "99% failure" rule. Likewise, the lab conditions, the stress tests of man and machine are frequently mentioned, humbly put in the service of perfection, excellence and self-improvement. As if to respond to this challenge, there is now a making-of video for "Der Lauf der Dinge," specially compiled by Fischli & Weiss for their major Tate Modern retrospective that opened in October 2006. It too concentrates on the endless trials, the recalcitrance and resistance of the materials, emphasizing performativity now in the mode "performance of failure" as a goal in itself, rather than any emphatically asserted "artist's vision" (as with the "Honda Cog").

19 "Took 606 takes to get right": Honda spoof

A third point, worth highlighting because it brings the "Honda Cog" and "Der Lauf der Dinge" in line not only with each other, but aligns them with major issues in film studies and film theory, is that both are the work of bona fide filmmakers. I already highlighted this in my comments on the "Honda Cog" and its proximity to the Hollywood blockbuster, but it is worth pointing out that "Der Lauf der Dinge" only exists as a film/videotape: it is not the filmic record of a performance of machinic self-destruction, but an event staged specifically for the camera. The mise-en-scène in each case is that of an auteur director, who decides exactly where to place the camera, when to move it, how to frame and reframe each action and its (con-)sequence. A half century of film theory comes alive in these mini-films with maxi-budgets, around the "long take" and "montage," and the implication of opting for "staging in depth" or "cutting in the camera." While some "invisible edits" are discernable, long-take classic continuity editing is the preferred choice in both pieces.

Finally, in both works, one notes a studied anachronism, a retrospective temporal deferral at work. This has two aspects: one concerns their respective artistic technique, the other their (meta-)physics. Regarding technique, the "Honda Cog" team are proud to certify in the making-of video that they engineered this extraordinary concatenation "for real" and not with the aid of digital effects, which in the aesthetic they are committed to would have amounted to "cheating." And yet, by 2003 digital effects had already become the norm in advertising, so that their decision is a deliberate self-restriction such as one knows it from minimalism or concept art at the highpoint of Modernism. Likewise, Fischli & Weiss produced their tape around the time when artists were seriously considering their response to the new media technologies of video compositing and digital editing. Their work is clearly a manifesto in favor of materiality and indexicality, an ironic middle finger stuck in the face of the digital to come, and taking their stand in the heated debate about the loss of indexicality in the post-photographic age.

The other studied anachronism concerns the physics used in both works, and the way they figure causality. Causality in these films operates at the familiar middle level and within human proportions. Rooted in Newtonian physics, the makers celebrate a visible, tangible world, fast disappearing into invisibility at both ends of the scale (at the macro-astronomic as well as at the micro-nano level), but also insisting on a linear causality vanishing in the media in which one now encounters their work: the Internet and YouTube are, precisely, non-linear and rhizomatic. The "old physics" on display are in the case of the "Honda Cog" highly stylized and deliberately tweaked for humorous effect, while in "Der Lauf der Dinge" the concatenation of buildups and disasters has also a more somber, cosmic dimension, as if one were invited to be present at the moment of the Big Bang, i.e. the birth of our own physical universe
.

Around the World in Eighty Clicks

Fischli & Weiss have as their motto "Am schönsten ist das Gleichgewicht, kurz bevor's zusammenbricht" [balance is most precious just before it collapses]. While clearly applying to their work as a whole,[10] this aesthetic of the tipping point also encapsulates the main challenge that my experiment with tagging and user-generated links on YouTube poses. For at this juncture in my test, the following question arose: where would this semantic knot or node around "constructive instability" and the performativity of failure take me once I had chosen the "Honda Cog" and "Der Lauf der Dinge" as my epicenters, once "collapse," "concatenation" and "chain reactions" became my search criteria, and once YouTube's tag clouds defined my self-imposed constraints? One answer was: nowhere at all; a second one: all around the world; and a third answer would be: back into the problems of narratology.

Nowhere at all: following the YouTube tags puts one on a cusp over an abyss: of hundreds, if not thousands of similar or even the same videos, commented on and cross-referenced to yet more of the same and the similar. In Foucault's epistemic terms, the Internet is "pre-modern" in its regime of representation: resemblance rules. The more you move, the more you come to a standstill. *All over the world:* searching the "Honda Cog" and "Der Lauf der Dinge" on the Internet and YouTube started off several other chain reactions, which opened up wholly unexpected avenues in a wonderful efflorescence of rhizomatic profusion, beckoning in all directions and sending me on a most wonderful journey of discovery. Not all of these journeys or forking paths can be retraced here, so for convenience's sake I have sorted and bundled some of them into clusters and allowed the clusters to become small "cluster bombs," ignited and radiating outwards from the "Honda Cog" and "Der Lauf der Dinge."[11]

Clusters and Forking Paths

That the tags from Fischli & Weiss should quickly bring one to Rube Goldberg was to be expected.[12] But little did I suspect that "out there," the idea of building such elaborate mechanical contraptions serving a very simple purpose has an enormous following. With the camcorder always at the ready, geniuses of little more than eight or ten years of age try filling a cup of Coke from a bottle catapulted by a mousetrap snapping tight, or show us how to use the vibrations of their mobile phone's ringer to set off a chain reaction that switches on the radio. A different kind of task preoccupies a New York artist by the name of Tim Fort, who spends his time devising Rube Goldberg hybrids which turn out to be little allegories of cinema itself. His homage to the beginnings of cinema once more evokes the celluloid strip, and its transport by and through machine devices, unseen by the spectator, are made visible here in their mechanic simplicity. Fort himself calls his works "kinetic art movement devices, using an extended repertoire of impulse transmission techniques and the magic of montage," and this originary idea of cinema as pure mechanical movement hovers, like a phantasmagoric ghost, over many of the Internet's Rube Goldberg meta-mechanical contraptions: so much so that their clustered presence on YouTube makes of the site something like the cinema's reverential funeral parlor.

From the Rube Goldberg connection it was but "one degree of separation" that led—"laterally" but also by the simple addition of an adjective in one of the user comments—in an apparently quite different direction. The unlikely combination "Japanese Rube Goldberg" landed me among a cluster of videos from a Tokyo-based educational television program, collectively known as *pitagora suicchi*. This is the Japanese pronunciation of Pythagoras Switch, and is aimed at children. It shows simple but ingenious combinations of everyday objects aligned in such a way as to allow one or several small balls (or colored marbles) to travel in a circuitous but steady downward motion. Subjecting the ball to the laws of gravity (Newtonian, for sure), the objects create intricate obstacles, which interrupt but cannot finally stop the ball's trajectory. The journeys always end with a tiny flourish, a point of recursiveness and self-referentiality. Signaled by the moment when the ball falls into a receptacle or hits a mini-gong, the flip confirms the identity of the show and plays a maddeningly addictive jingle. A Pythagoras Switch is a minimalist exercise in creating closure from indeterminacy, miraculously conjoining the pleasures of free play and the strict rules of physics.

Why is it called Pythagoras Switch? The makers merely hint at "the Eureka experience" that children are supposed to have, thanks to a sort of category switch: " 'Pythagoras Switch' wants to help kids have that moment of A-HA!" Granted that these short performances do indeed flip a switch, I nevertheless tend to think of the name Pythagoras as a misnomer and even a para-praxis, a failed performance: namely, not only is "Eureka" usually attributed to Archimedes (and not Pythagoras), but it should be called the Archimedean Switch for another reason also. After all, the principle of *pitagora suicchi* resembles the famous fulcrum associated with Archimedes' name: the single point of equipoise that he said could lift the universe from its hinges. But the fact that it is called Pythagoras leads one in yet other no less intriguing directions: to geometry and to Euclidean solids, as well as to the so-called Pseudo-Pythagoreans, the first important Gnostics of the ancient world, who survived right into the Middle Ages and beyond, and whose main analysis of the universe was in terms of the magic of numbers and the mysteries of mathematics. Pythagoras would have been a fitting grandfather of the power of algorithms, and thus the appropriate patron saint not so much for the Pythagoras Switch as for the sort and cluster algorithms of YouTube that made me discover pitagora suicchi in the first place, right next to Rube Goldberg.

If the Pythagoras Switch is minimalist and haiku-like in its elegant economy and delicate epiphanies, a close cousin, by contrast, is all on the side of excess, the incremental and of the nearly "getting out of hand": I am referring to that other major Japanese pastime, having to do with knock-on effects, namely domino toppling. Here, too, Japanese television is in the forefront, since it appears to stage regular domino telethons. One of these televised Japanese shows on YouTube features a high-tech contraption where the steel ball's trajectory is only one phase that releases other mechanical agents and sets off further reactions, including small explosions in the manner of Fischli & Weiss, but also gravity-defying underwater action in goldfish bowls. Once again, it is worth noting the aesthetic that oscillates between the cinematic and the televisual: while the Pythagoras Switch program prefers long takes, with a camera that pans and reframes rather than cuts, the Japanese Rube Goldberg contest and the domino telethon, by contrast, favor the typical action replays of televised sports events, but with their spoken commentary they are also reminiscent of the *benshi* tradition of silent cinema.

Conclusion: Between Epiphany and Entropy

The domino toppling contests also brought home another lesson of globalization: "Don't follow the flag, follow the tag." Just as commodities, trade and labor no longer "respect" the boundaries of the nation state, the tags´ "chain reaction"—or "domino telethon"—easily cross borders and even continents. So it is fitting to interrupt this "Tour of the YouTube World" with an image, and one of totalitarian domination: the domino toppling championships, where millions of dominos fall in order to form themselves into simple images, reminiscent of thousands of sportsmen and -women flipping colored boards to reveal a portrait of Mao to the God's eye television camera. While multitudes (whether of dominoes or of young athletes) forming a recognizable likeness highlight the coercive, normative power of such software as operates the Internet at the level of the algorithms, of the codes and protocols (mostly hidden from view and in any case incomprehensible to the ordinary user), the idea of an "image" also reminds us of the fact that in the man-machine symbiosis, two very different kinds of system are expected to communicate with each other. For this "image" is nothing but the filter, membrane or user-friendly face—the "interface," in short—between stupid but infinitely patient (and performative) machines, running on programs relayed to gates and switches (electric-electronic dominoes, one might say), and intelligent but increasingly impatient (as well as accident-prone) humans, requiring visual representations that give a sense of recognition and self-presence, relayed through words, sound and, above all, through images.

The concept of the interface at this juncture raises more issues than can be tackled here, but it allows me to return to the question I started with, namely the place of *narrative* as interface between data and user. As the logic of the time-space continuum, i.e. the diegesis, is transformed into clusters of multiply interrelated and virally proliferating semantic links (the *syuzet* or "story"), narrational authority, i.e. the (uneven) distribution of information, and the order or sequence in which it is accessed (the *fabula* or "plot") seems to pass from "narrator" to "narratee," from storyteller to user. Yet since the user depends on the "machine" to generate the access points, by way of sort algorithms and tag clouds (whose internal logic generally escapes him/her), a new "authority" interposes itself, both "stupid" like chance and "all-knowing" like God.[13] How can one describe the consequences of this unlikely contact space?

Fischli & Weiss see the encounter in both ethical and aesthetic categories. That they are aware of the problem of who or what is in control and who or what has agency and responsibility is shown by their remarks on "Der Lauf der Dinge." By fully implicating "the things" themselves, they comment meta-critically on the dilemma that agency poses for the human-machine symbiosis.[14] In the context of narrative, Fischli & Weiss suggest that the "worlds" which open up as a consequence of following the semantic trail of "The Honda Cog" and "Der Lauf der Dinge" both have a creator-narrator (multiple and anonymous, but nonetheless singular-in-plurality) and do not (to the extent that they are self-generated). By bringing together various individuals and their activities, skills and obsessions at very different locations, they can be called "scripted spaces" (since their coming to my attention is at least in part "scripted" or "programmed"), but they are neither directly comparable to the classic novel, nor do they resemble a video game or a virtual world like Second Life. Yet what one encounters is nonetheless a story world of sorts, rich in human interest, detail and characters, full of humor and wisdom: in the genre of what one could call *the digital picaresque*.

YouTube is a user-generated-content site with a high degree of automation, where nonetheless a certain structured contingency obtains, as suggested by the semantically quite coherent clusters that I was able to extracts via the tags attached to my videos. My "Travels with YouTube" led a series of forking-path narratives, where the multiplicity of strands made up for some weak plotting and meandering storylines, which together nonetheless make out of exquisite corpses a lively clutch of shaggy dog stories, reminiscent of Borges' *Garden of Forking Paths* and Buñuel's *The Milky Way*.[15] This leads to the paradox alluded to above: the structured contingency is, on the one hand, strongly informed and shaped by mathematics, via the site's programming architecture and design, based on its search and sort algorithms. On the other hand, the chaos of human creativity, eccentricity and self-importance prevails. My clusters around "collapse" were only small islands of sense carved out of a sea of boiling magma, made up of human self-presentation and self-performance, the trials and errors of the collective "me," which is YouTube. But who is to say that this performative persistence "to be, to be present and to be perceived" does not mimic certain forms of narrative self-reference, while creating a cast of believable characters, and even generating a particular mode of narrative address?

20 Sato Masahiko's "Bubble Sort"

Narrative self-reference: the rhizomatic branching or viral contagion propagating in all directions, while non-hierarchical and "flat" or "lateral" in its linkage, nonetheless seems to produce a surprisingly high degree of self-reflexivity and auto-referentiality, no doubt due to the effects of "positive feedback." The demonstrations of chain reaction, mechanical concatenation, Pythagoras switches and falling dominoes are performative also in the sense that they either enact their own conditions of possibility or remediate a previous stage of their own mediality, as nostalgic or ironic pastiche and repetition. For instance, via the Pythagoras switch another meta-dimension emerged, which brought one of the core mechanisms of YouTube into view. One of the creators of the Pythagoras switch series is the video artist Sato Masahiko, one of whose installations, called "Bubble Sort," I was linked to. The piece, which shows a line of people waiting, rearranging themselves according to size in fast-forward motion, completely baffled me, until its tags led to several other videos, also having to do with sorting. Masahiko's video, it transpires, visualizes a popular sorting algorithm, called indeed "bubble-sort," explained on YouTube by tens of videos, all manually "remediating" or graphically "interfacing" the different sorting algorithms (insertion sort, selection sort, shell sorts, etc.), apparently a favorite pastime for first-year computer science students.

The cast of characters, as we saw, included some well-known names, such as "Rube Goldberg," "Pythagoras," "James Bond"; others become known because they "sign" their work: Antoine Bardou-Jacquet, Fischli & Weiss, Tim Fort, Sato Masahiko; many more merely present themselves to the camera in low-resolution homemade videos. Thanks to all of them, however, the YouTube ways of showing and telling are ludic and reflexive, educational and participatory, empowering and humbling; in short: they mark an unusually soft dividing line between creative design and hard-core engineering, storytelling and role playing, singularity and repetition. To put this in the terms of another discourse, more germane to the post-human: it is to find oneself in the presence of strange organisms, pulsing, moving and mutating, depending on the tags one enters or encounters, as YouTube sorts, filters and aggregates the choices I am not even aware of making. That they cluster themselves semantically is partly a concession to the "human interface," but partly also because of a special heuristic value: it is where the cultural noise of verbal language encounters the information of the mathematical program, providing the constructive instability of performed failure, and throwing the grit of human creativity and dirt of human unpredictability into the machinery of perfect human-machine adaptation.

The traditional asymmetry of the single point of origin (the author, the narrator) addressing a potentially infinite number of readers or viewer was already deconstructed by Roland Barthes' "writerly text" and many other narratologists since. Hence, the multiple authorship of the YouTube tales, when joining up with the selectivity and serendipity of the user, make YouTube a very "writerly" experience. But the mode of address that I am trying to focus on is also different from the "writerly" in that it creates an empty space of enunciation, to be filled by the anonymous, but also plural "me." On the one hand, a site like YouTube is inherently addictive, as one video drags one along to another and another and another. Yet after an hour or so, one realizes how precariously balanced and delicately poised one is, between the joy of discovering the unexpected, the marvelous and occasionally even the miraculous, and the rapid descent into an equally palpable anxiety, staring into the void of an unimaginable number of videos, with their proliferation of images, their banality or obscenity in sounds and commentary. Right next to the euphoria and the epiphany, then, is the heat-death of meaning, the ennui of repetition and of endless distraction: in short, the relentless progress of entropy begins to suck out and drain away all life. "Epiphany" and "entropy," one might say, is what defines the enunciative position or "subject effect" of YouTube, encapsulated in the recursiveness of its own tagline "broadcast yourself," which, being circular, accurately describes its specific "mode of address" as an infinite loop. YouTube's scripted spaces or picaresque narratives are held together not by a coherent diegesis nor a coherent subject-position, but by a perpetual oscillation between the "fullness" of reference and recognition and the "emptiness" of repetition and redundancy, the singularity of an encounter and the plurality of the uncountable in which the singular occurs.

Whether there is a better name for this oscillation I do not know, but it puts me on notice that my experiment would be incomplete and even misleading if I did not emphasize *both* epiphany *and* entropy, and instead were to give the impression that it was either possible or responsible to gather my clusters like floral bouquets, or cherry-pick the gems like "Honda Cog" or "Der Lauf der Dinge" while ignoring or even disavowing the rest. Like the high-wire acrobat sensing at all times the trembling tightrope beneath her feet, the pleasure of YouTube as narrative lies in its referential expanse, but its downside is the crash and the void. Epiphany and entropy remind us that the post-human always comes up against our mortality and finitude. Held against the open horizon of our "stupid God," the Web 2.0 feedback loops, with their unimaginable, yet palpable magnitudes, suspend us between infinity and indefiniteness, a state made only bearable and livable, in short human, thanks to constructive instability and the performativity of failure, which is art; for as Fischli & Weiss so wisely remind us: *am schönsten ist das Gleichgewicht ...*

Endnotes

1 Henry Jenkins, "Game Design as Narrative Architecture," in *First Person*, eds. Noah Wardrip-Fruin & Pat Harrigan (Cambridge, MA: MIT Press, 2004), p. 121.

2 Katherine N. Hales, *How We Became Posthuman: Virtual Bodies in Cybernetics, Literature, and Informatics* (Chicago: Chicago University Press, 1999), p. 3.

3 "Computers aren't just in boxes anymore; they are moved out into the world to become distributed throughout the environment. 'Eversion,' my colleague Marcus Novak has called this phenomenon, in contrast to the 'immersion' of the much more limited and localized virtual reality environments." N. Katherine Hayles, in a conversation with Albert Borgman on humans and machines, see www.press.uchicago.edu/Misc/Chicago/borghayl.html [last checked 15 February 2009].

4 According to many recent studies of evolutionary biology the smooth transition model of the human/machine interface is too large an assumption to make.

5 See Henry Jenkins, *Convergence Culture: Where Old and New Media Collide* (New York: New York University Press, 2006).

6 Malcolm Gladwell, *The Tipping Point: How Little Things Can Make a Big Difference* (New York: Little Brown, 2000). See also Ian Bremmer, *The J Curve: A New Way to Understand Why Nations Rise and Fall* (New York: Simon & Schuster, 2005), about "how to turn authoritarian regimes into stable, open democracies." Ian Bremmer, whose Eurasia Group advises on political risk, sums up the challenge in a simple graphic that is this year's tipping point.

7 Thanks to Fabrice Ziolkowski for providing the translation and cultural commentary on the clip.

8 "In 2003, he directed the internationally acclaimed and multi award winning Honda 'Cog' commercial for London's Weiden & Kennedy. This is a two-minute commercial showing Honda parts bumping into each other in a chain reaction. It took months of meticulous planning and trial and error, with a four-day shoot at the end. It was shot in two takes and was all done for real. It was a victory for patience and passion! It first caused a stir running throughout the entire commercial break during the Grand Prix and went on to win a Gold Lion at Cannes, Best commercial and Gold at BTAA and a Gold Pencil at D&AD to name but a few." – www.partizan.

com/partizan/awards/?type=Commercials&year=2004 [last checked 15 February 2009].

9 For more on the new regime of the test as a paradigm of the control society, see Avital Ronell, *The Test Drive* (Bloomington: University of Illinois Press, 2005).

10 As demonstrated, for instance, by their series *Equilibres - Quiet Afternoon* (1984), part of the Fischli & Weiss "Flowers & Questions" retrospective at the Tate Modern in London October 2006 to January 2007.

11 A "Warp" function in the "TestTube" section of the YouTube platform now allows one to "explode" such clusters around the selected video and see the tag clouds scatter. Thanks to Pepita Hesselberth for drawing my attention to this feature.

12 There is an excerpt from "Der Lauf der Dinge" appearing as an "Amazing Rube Goldberg Fire Machine" on YouTube – www.youtube.com/watch?v=pX8fpPf7Y0g).

13 "What's the difference between God and Google? God—as revealed through Jesus Christ—is the finite infinite, and Google—as experienced by its users—is the infinite finite." Father James Schall, S.J., in a personal conversation, New York, February 2007.

14 "GOOD and EVIL are often very close, for example when the candle on the swing sets fire to the detonating fuse. Because they are nice and childish, the candle and the swing tend towards the good, whereas the detonating fuse is evil because you don't need it for harmless things. On the other hand, every object in our installation is good if it functions, because it then liberates its successor, gives it the chance of development." Fischli & Weiss "Flowers & Questions" retrospective at the Tate Modern in London October 2006 to January 2007.

15 The link between interactive storytelling and Buñuel has been made before, most systematically by Marsha Kinder, "Hotspots, Avatars and Narrative Fields Forever: Buñuel's Legacy for New Digital Media and Interactive Database Narrative," *Film Quarterly* no. 4, 2002, pp. 23–45.

Kathrin Peters and Andrea Seier

Home Dance: Mediacy and Aesthetics of the Self on YouTube

"After all, isn't the body of the dancer precisely a body dilated along an entire space that is both exterior and interior to it?"
(Michel Foucault)[1]

Whatever we know about ourselves we know through and from the media.[2] Every self is bound to an exterior, which it addresses and in which it is reflected. The Internet platform YouTube naturally offers potential for media-based self-referentiality. At the moment, YouTube is probably the most prominent example of a media practice that allows the individual to record the minutest details of his or her life and to distribute them. By introducing a gap between self and world,[3] media enable a distance required for any relation to the self. Various technical apparatuses—from the quill to the webcam—place the self at a distance and at the same time bridge that distance to the extent that they make it accessible and accessible for alteration. Seen in this light, historically different media have always played a decisive role in historically different self-relations. Processes of mediation are, thus, not only intimately linked to processes of subjectification; they are also their prerequisite.

Just as media apparatuses on the one hand and practices of self-treatment on the other hand are not simply givens, the relation between the two is subject to constant shifts that cannot be attributed to the transformation of the apparatuses themselves. Instead, it seems sensible to posit complex networks in which apparatuses and individuals interact without mutually determining one another. The partial and highly selective self-referentiality that YouTube allows raises questions that we will explore in the following article by looking at a specific genre: dance performances of individuals of both genders on YouTube, where performers play back pop songs in private and dance to them. Remakes, interpretations of pop songs, and in part the presentation of music composed by the performer him or herself represent a large portion of the videos on YouTube. As a subgroup of these musical appropriations, the "home dances" form an interesting example that combines questions of relations of the self, body practices and media technologies. In short, can YouTube dance videos be seen as technologies of the self? How can this form of mediated self-practice be discussed? Do YouTube videos introduce new aspects of self-constitution, and if so, which ones?

The discussion concerning Web 2.0 often focuses on an increasing practice of self-staging and self-stylization, which in turn is considered a trademark of digital mass culture. Facebook, MySpace, Flickr and Twitter, blogs and personal homepages can indeed be considered plausible evidence for the multiplication of possibilities for public self-thematization. Findings from the realm of governmentality studies on the practice of self-management also seem to support this conclusion. In this context, practices of self-staging are not primarily evaluated as media processes, but above all as political and social processes of transformation. Furthermore, the context is posited as a growing "economization of the social" that turns the self into an infinite project involving strategies of optimization and revision, thus motivating comparisons of achievement and constant self-observation.[4]

21 "Private dancer" by aurorabean

22 "Video killed the radio star" by ziamb05

Arguments from media history and the social sciences seem here to coincide almost too perfectly. To sketch out the problematic: on the one hand, the positing of an increasing compulsion to self-represent and -stage often entails an under-defined concept of superficial masquerade, simulation or deceit, raising the question of the authentic subjectivity that provides the foil for comparison.[5] On the other hand, the discussion about the increasing mediation of everyday and professional life involves a presumption of a new and fundamental saturation of these realms by the media. This assumption in turn implies that work and private life were previously media-free spaces that are now subject to mediation. Early works of cultural studies, however, problematized this assumption. Studies in the realm of television research, for example, referred to the mutual effects of everyday life and television programming through the structuring of times of day, weekdays and weekends.[6]

Thus, one needs to take a closer look at the relationship between practices of the self and media apparatuses. In so doing, it becomes clear that processes of subjectification in new media necessarily repeat and vary older and other forms of mediated processes of subjectification. The points of comparison are thus not unmediated subjects, but relations of the self that are mediated in a different way. To account for the current variety of media self-models, Jörg Dünne and Christian Moser have developed the concept of "auto-mediacy." They propose a concept of self-referentiality that both historicizes and accounts for media differences. "The increasing technologization of the media has not caused an impoverishment in subjective interiority; on the contrary, it has generated a greater variety of self-referentialities."[7] In this article we will hence investigate YouTube videos as a form of automediacy, exploring the specific intersection of processes of subjectification and mediation. Central to our exploration of home-dance videos are above all their media-specific, aesthetic, governmental and utopian potentials.

"Video Killed the Radio Star": Remediation and Reenactment

There are several combinations of music and image, sound and vision. They stretch from classic formats like musicals or music films to the latest developments of VJing in clubs. In VJing, there is an overlapping of music, image and dance in which all three media mutually enrich and amplify one another, thus creating a synesthetic experience. With the invention of the Walkman in 1979, a portable device was able to turn a listener's surroundings into a kind of moving image, an image track that seemed to accompany the soundtrack on the headphones. The listener's movement insured the emergence of constantly new images, like the individual's very own "film." This is probably why portable listening in transportational situations is so popular. The car radio could once be considered an early form of audiovisual reception, in which the speed of travel caused an animated sequence of images on the windshield. The Walkman—which has since been replaced by MP3 players and iPods—now belongs to the prehistory of a fusion of sound and vision, which began with the music video in the early 1980s.

When it began broadcasting in 1981, MTV presented as its first video clip "Video Killed the Radio Star" by the Buggles. The clip shows men in satin jackets playing keyboards, while a woman in a 1920s outfit dances in a plastic tube. A song of departure is sung to an allegory of radio. "We can't rewind we've gone too far/Pictures came and broke your heart, look I'll play my VCR." Today, no VCR is necessary to see the video—it is of course available on YouTube with other appearances by the Buggles. In a critical vein directed at both the self and the media, some commentaries on the site state that "YouTube killed the video star." Of course, this is not really true, because we are still dealing with video formats, albeit digital ones. YouTube does not seem to be killing off the video star, but rather preserving and multiplying this phenomenon. An overwhelming number of performances of this song can in fact be found on the site. In one video, two very young men mockingly imitate a Buggles performance, with a green wall as their backdrop. In another, two sisters do a remake—which is pretty advanced in terms of choreography and post-production—in what is probably their parents' house. Decisive in this remake are the dance performances before living-room walls as well as the sunglasses—both references to the '80s, yet a bit off-target.

23 Boffopy's "Video killed the radio star"

These remakes are attempts at reenacting what is now a historical music video, which itself declares another medium historical. That is a "classic new wave music video," as one user writes. To be able to decide who really was there, the users ask one another, "How old are you?" But of course, in the process of remediation taking place here, that is, in the process of gaining something "new" from imitating, quoting and varying the "old," [8] it hardly makes a difference whether the video was actually seen on TV in 1981 or on YouTube in 2009. For "Video Killed the Radio Star" awaits with a series of allusions, reminiscences and condensations that describe and initiate a break in the history of media. In many ways the key transformation introduced by YouTube has to do with the possibility of creating remakes or reenactments as home videos and distributing them easily. Movement and dance are not just elements of the video clip that is being consumed, but can be added in home videos as an activity of the "prosumer." [9] What was previously done with pop songs at home using mobile audio devices, be they on record, cassette or videotape, can now be recorded and presented to a major audience as an audiovisual file.

But what does the audience get to see? The props, costumes and setting are usually quite minimal in these home videos, and this often includes a funny T-shirt, a wig or a pair of sunglasses. Backdrops for playbacks are often simply the rooms as they are. The "filmic" space depends on the possible camera positions, and cameras built into laptops are often used.[10] This naturally results in limited possibilities when it comes to set design, hence the genre displays an endless series of private spaces, especially teenager's bedrooms: full shelves in the background; the edge of a desk at the bottom of the image; posters, sofas and houseplants. Artemisbell, a famous YouTube cover dancer, performs in her stocking feet, in front of a floor-length curtain or a white wall. On the right we see a detail of a painting. Others dance while sitting in front of their computers, set to record their performance. The dance floor is simply constituted by the performers' own four walls: here, no disco lighting submerses the surrounding space in obscurity—which is necessary in club culture for liberating people from everyday life and allowing them to "make an appearance" on the dance floor. The pragmatism in design could be attributed to a lack of aesthetic ability, or even ignorance when it comes to questions of composition. And of course, the interiors usually attest to a certain average taste—and how could it be otherwise? Furthermore, in adapting the image to the conditions created by the available space and technical equipment, a certain

24 Minimal setting in "Video killed the radio star"

aesthetic randomness is apparently accepted easily: this randomness contrasts profoundly with the thoroughly designed video clips to which the performances refer. But it is precisely this lack of self-consciousness that leads to considerations that not so much emphasize the amateur status of the YouTube video,[11] but makes their very mediacy the center of attention.

For instance, a logic of recording is clearly active here, one to which the digital or digitalized video is still subject. Naturally, a video camera registers whatever is visible from a certain angle, even if it is contrary to the maker's intent. While the focus is solely on the performance of the actors, the framing of the images reveals much more: the room décor thus supplements the video. This supplementary aspect of the image in turn forms the aesthetic surplus of the YouTube video. Moreover, these videos find their way into VJ sets[12] as artifacts of an "authenticity" that can scarcely be achieved professionally; they are also broadcast on MTV or reused in advertising.[13] These remediations make it clear that the break between analog and digital media is based less on the materiality of the recording process than the increased and instantaneous possibilities of distributing what is recorded.

However, it also becomes clear that home dances are not just about amateur self-alteration along professional aesthetic standards. The difference between professional and amateur does not seem particularly applicable here, for it is questionable whether the so-called amateurs judge themselves according to professional standards, or according to the commentaries and answers of other users listed on the YouTube website. In fact, the obvious imperfection of the videos creates a kind of archive of poses and images, its range of elements played repeatedly and varied. This archive is accessible by means of a computer only, through YouTube to be specific. The computer is thus the center of events. As a consequence, there are hardly any home videos that negate or conceal the digital device to which they are addressed. Either the action takes place directly in front of the computer, or computers are more or less explicitly part of the image. The computer is thus always a node in this arrangement—as a medium of reference to existing texts, poses and videos already in circulation—and at the same time as a medium of distribution of the performer's own performance in the future. It could also be said that the actors are engaged with symbolic structures and mediation while a new media structure is in the process of inauguration at the same time. This disperses any clear references to superstars or competition winners, rather establishing referential chains or a spreading network among video clips and commentaries, where the goal is to attract attention. Without striving for direct communication with a concrete partner, the dancing takes place quite concretely before the computer itself, in the light of the ceiling lamp.

"Dancing with Myself": Ranking and Competition

While techniques of competition and ranking serve as the dramaturgical foundation of entire television shows like *Pop Stars* and *Pop Idols*, the logic of competition also plays a central role in YouTube home dances, for YouTube does not consist of videos alone. As on other sharing sites, symbols, signs and lists that lead to other sites and other content are arranged around these videos. Beside the clip itself, there are (to the right) lists with similar videos, and beneath it responses and comments; that is, a writing-image relation with a web of paratexts established by the functionality of YouTube. The hit numbers reflect the video's popularity, and the stars that can be given, up to a maximum of five, represent an average evaluation. Even though YouTube lets the user community as a whole function as the televisual jury, common ranking techniques develop their normalizing effectiveness precisely in the exclusion of expert opinions. In effect, evaluation by mouse click, points and written comments serves as a motor. An informal struggle for recognition is thus taking place as expressed by a user: "One of the best on Youtube. The wrong people get recognition. Try again gents. Too funny." From the community of users, so-called YouTube stars emerge, and in 2008, they were given a live stage and a live stream on a YouTube gala. Despite the quirkiness that is typical of YouTube stars, the popularity ranking culminates in a star system which has washed away countless videos under a wave of attention.

However, perhaps even more interesting are the commentaries on users' performances. This is also the place where aesthetic critique is expressed. Two aspects are regularly up for debate: on the one hand, the value of the original song and its singer, and on the other hand, the quality of the YouTuber's performance. While in the case of the first, the memories of the commentators themselves always play a role, the comments about the latter often revolve around "talent": "This is my favorite vid, you're so talented," or "Talent. Pure, raw talent." Like talent competitions in other media, here talent is established as a basic quality that one either has—or does not. It is a kind of ultimate explanation that encourages the fantasy that the greatest talent need only be found among an endless flood of candidates in order to produce stars. Work on the self, practice, failure and the significance of networks in achieving recognition no longer seem to be of any importance.

25 Julia Nunes' version of "It's raining men, the weather girls"

While YouTube comments follow this contextual logic also, the frequent use of the word "talent" can be understood in an entirely different way. Expressed in this writing style are not least the difficulties of formulating aesthetic criticism, since what is needed here is not just talent, but also knowledge, practice and work that go beyond spontaneous expressions of approval or disapproval. Seen in this way, it is much less an omnipresent excellence and talent scouting perpetuated amongst the users; rather, talent is used as a basically empty signifier whenever the writer is at a loss for words, whenever an aesthetic critique cannot be formulated. Series of exclamation points or the repetition of a single letter often also point to the void of not having anything substantial to say: "Rock it cutie!!!!!!!!!", "Hmmmmmmmmmmm ..."

Comments thus stand in the context of a subjectification that takes place through the expression of thrill, agreement or rejection. Roland Barthes once made a list of things that he loved, and a list of things that he did not love. These lists have no normative character, they are subjective in the best sense: "I like, I don't like: this is of no importance to anyone; this, apparently, has no meaning. And yet all this means: my body is not the same as yours."[14] Similarly, YouTube commentaries lead to the formation of preferences and communities that at times diverge from the concept of clearly defined subcultures based on music or dance styles. Far more diffuse, fleeting and unpredictable units, like specific movements, gestures, poses, views and facial expressions, come into focus instead. In responses to the videos, they are met with declarations of approval or displeasure from other users, and this usually means, in the realm of dance, answered, imitated or varied with their bodies. Self-constitution and self-transgression go hand in hand: with the help of YouTube home dancing, the individual body is both rendered open to experience and deterritorialized, and also inscribed in a general archive of gestures, poses and images through imitation and procedures of repetition.

26 JemessandEm's "Abba-dancing queen"

For the specific form of circular reference and activities within the user community, the structure of the YouTube page is important. It pools the activities of the prosumer and makes rapid links between videos possible. Without the portal function of YouTube, the circular activity of receiving, producing and commenting would be theoretically possible, but much more complicated, and thus not very enticing. Regarding the situation of reception, YouTube realizes in contrast to television a form of media use that appears both self-driven and controlled. "Flow" here does not consist in the avoidance of interruption, as is standard for television, but results from a bundling of dispersed elements. The next click to the next video is not prescribed, and in that sense can be considered self-chosen. But it also does not require an independent search among the endless data available on the Internet. The linking of individual pages is even controlled by the prosuming activity of the users to the extent that previous pages viewed prestructure the website's setup. It is thus the classic principle of liberal governmental technology that seems to be at work when surfing through the offerings on YouTube. The impression of an autonomous and individual state of reception is solely due to the control exercised by the link structure. Bundling and dispersal, autonomy and control remain dependent on one another. But the Web portal does more than enable and evoke the networking of users. The aforementioned composition of the page, which has links from one video to numerous others that are "similar," needs to be considered a constant discursive summoning and restating of a concept of networking.

"Everyone's a Winner": Transgressions

On YouTube there is both a "female" and a "male" dance version of the 1978 Hot Chocolate song "Everyone's a Winner"—both by LilyKerrigan. In the female version, pink shirts hang in the background, the dancer is wearing a low-cut, black dress and a pageboy haircut. In the male version, the corner of the room is bathed in blue light, the protagonist has her hair tied back and is wearing a blue T-shirt. In the first video, arms and hair fly about, in the other legwork dominates. The repertoire of movements that LilyKerrigan uses cannot be pinned down precisely. Instead of quoting concrete individuals, an imaginary is cited within which gender poses are constantly repeated and perpetuated. In so doing, these gender poses are always linked to cultural spaces and media modes of representation: in the home dances, the setting of pop music, which has formed over decades—from the disco ball to the dancing crowds to the DJ—is brought up to date. Subjective experiences are inseparably fused with media reception as a result. Pop's horizon of knowledge and experience includes both sweating in the disco and watching MTV. Technologies of the self and media technologies are mutually determinant. For not only are disco nights or raves themselves complex media arrangements consisting of sound systems, records, orders of space and fashion, lighting and actors, they also form new media imagos that are then processed in video clips. Gender-specific dance moves and dress codes are embedded in this structure, and realized, exceeded and even shifted within it.

Even if LilyKerrigan's female version of "Everyone's a Winner" is watched ten times more often than the male version (as one would

27 Female and male: LilyKerrigan´s "Every 1's a winner"

expect), the differences between the two can only really be seen in a direct comparison (which is made easier by a split-screen version that the user also uploaded). That the gender coding of dance movements, despite all their sexual equivocalness, can also result in ambiguities is made clear by an additional example. In a corner of his room, a teenager performs Prince's "Kiss" from 1986, wearing a three-quarter T-shirt and a leather jacket and precisely imitating the singer's hip movements. Then a friend comes into the image from the side, playing air guitar, his stature still relatively untouched by puberty. As the word "kiss" is sung, the older boy kisses the younger one, who giggles and retreats from his advances, and the sexual tension immediately explodes into fragments of a childish game, unspoken homoeroticism and intense embarrassment. What moves into the image here is the teenager's room as the "narcissistic cell of star/fan subjectification," as Tom Holert writes, but who is a fan of whom remains unclear.[15] Even beyond the realm of traditional dance forms, dance movements have always been learned through practice, and this was done in the privacy of the teenager's bedroom.[16] And this has always contained a specific ambivalence of self-control and self-forgetting, discipline and pleasure. For social discipline and aesthetic subjectification are equally dependent on practice, on repetition, the setting of different levels and the production of difference.[17] The corrective within this setting of practice might be a mirror or a friend, now it can also be a YouTube video.

28 The teen remediation of "Kiss"

If we wanted to define teenager's bedrooms as heterotopias as described by Foucault, they might be understood as equally private *and* public, actually existing *and* utopian, performative *and* transgressive spaces. At issue in this utopia is not an imaginary that appears in strict separation from the given as its "beyond," but the transgression and transformation potentials of the given. In a radio version of the heterotopia essay, Foucault explores in quite emphatic terms heterotopias as counterspaces:

> These counter-spaces, these localized utopias, the children know them perfectly. Of course, there is the garden, there is the attic, or rather the Indian tent in the attic. And, on Thursday afternoon, there is the parents' bed. [...] These counter-spaces were not truly invented by the children alone, quite simply because it seems that children never invent anything. On the contrary, it is the adults who have invented the children

> and whispered to them their wonderful secrets, and then the parents, the adults are surprised when the children blurt them out.[18]

Accordingly, would not playing air guitar in a teenager's room represent one of the most wondrous heterotopias? But what happens when playing air guitar on YouTube is inscribed in an evaluative ranking of air-guitar playing? Does it lose its utopian potential if it appears on a Web portal that combines the professional and the private? Does the empowerment to engage in self-performances, which initially suspends the usual prejudice of affirmation and critique, automatically lead to a loss of distinction, to a leveling of difference? Or does this not amplify the utopian potential of transgression through the possibility of all-embracing dispersal and multiplication? The answer does not lie in reading the performances of the home dancers as either a form of media-generated empowerment *or* an example of self-governance, where the sole issue is using the self as a creative and economic resource. Neither the genre of the home-dance video as a whole nor the individual contributions can be clarified in this sense.

Conclusion: "Dance Me to the End of Love"

The questions posed at the beginning of this article were as follows: how could a concept of automediacy be productive if practices of self-constitution in digital media cultures are not automatically suspected of superficial masquerade or neo-liberal self-marketing? How can the portion of these self-practices involving media, aesthetic and cultural technique be analyzed without claiming the priority of the media or the self? The home-dance videos offered an opportunity to discuss the intersection of subjectification and mediation on YouTube. Without being able to provide definitive answers, or even wanting to, we would like to sum up our considerations in three arguments.

Firstly, YouTube's "home-dance videos" represent a specific form of self-practice based on the playful practice and expansion of the physical technique of dance. At issue in these dance videos are an aesthetic and existential self-reference[19] as well as pleasurable performance and transgression. The ambivalence of dance between constitution and transgression of the self seems to amplify itself once more through the practice of recording and distribution, because it results in a clear form of mediated self-alienation. Home-dance video production can thus be understood as self-performances in which not just internal and external rule overlap, but where the self is equally situated and transgressed on the basis of the repetition of references from popular culture. In this way, body and media techniques and those of the self all fuse in home-dance videos. They form in this fusion an agency in which the dancers, the video images, website functionality, the images of existing performance interact, whereby it is impossible to predict the goal or aim of these acts.[20]

Secondly, in forming an intersection of physical practices, self-relations and media techniques, the home-dance videos can be understood as an "automediated" practice that not only represents a model of the self, but generates and multiplies self-referentialities. Prior forms of subjectification, or those taking place in other media, are again picked up on YouTube, whereas at the same time they shift in their repetition. This remediation takes place above all in quoted pictures, gestures and poses. The homemade remakes in front of living-room shelves and in teenagers' bedrooms produce—whether intentionally or not—new aesthetic forms that for their part flow into a pop and media-culture archive. Which bands and music and dance styles deserve to be archived in such a way is the subject of constant debate in the commentaries. The question of the canon's legitimacy becomes a point of constant negotiation.

Thirdly, the YouTube home-dance videos represent a governmental practice of self-regulation and self-management that is closely linked to the logic of competition and ranking. At the same time, we should note that the almost excessive evaluations, rankings and commentary, anchored in the software, in contrast to the widespread television contest practices, do not target the best "adaptation" to a given model (such as a professional music video), but often unforeseen criteria which also vary greatly depending on the priorities of individual communities. The attraction of placing videos of performances on YouTube seems to inhere in a certain self-expression, and thus self-distantiation beyond the exhaustive, hierarchical procedures of traditional media institutions. This makes it interesting to question which direction the potential of an aesthetic of the self will develop if the creation of YouTube stars becomes established.

Endnotes

1 Michel Foucault, "Utopian Body," in Caroline A. Jones, ed. *Sensorium. Embodied Experience, Technology, and Contemporary Art* (Cambridge, MA/London: MIT Press, 2006), pp. 229–234, 232.
2 This can be read as a rephrasing of one of Niklas Luhmann's best-known formulations: "Whatever we know about society or the world in which we live, we know it from the mass media." Niklas Luhmann, *The Reality of the Mass Media* (Stanford: Stanford University Press, 2000), p. 1.
3 Christoph Tholen, *Die Zäsur der Medien. Kulturphilosophische Konturen* (Frankfurt am Main: Suhrkamp, 2002).
4 See Ulrich Bröckling, Susanne Krasmann & Thomas Lemke, *Gouvernementalität der Gegenwart. Studien zur Ökonomisierung des Sozialen* (Frankfurt am Main: Suhrkamp, 2000).
5 For example, discussions in dating forums often revolve around the subject of participants not presenting themselves as they really are—but as they want to be.
6 See John Fiske, *Television Culture* (London: Routledge, 1987).
7 Jörg Dünne & Christian Moser, eds. *Automedialität. Subjektkonstitution in Schrift, Bild und neuen Medien* (Munich: Fink, 2008), p. 14.
8 Jay David Bolter & Richard Grusin, *Remediation: Understanding New Media* (Cambridge, MA: MIT Press, 2000).
9 This term refers to a type of cooperation that subverts the distinction between passive consumption and active production. Alvin Toffler developed it in the 1980s with an eye on the coming technoculture of the 21st century. For a discussion, see Alvin Toffler, *The Third Wave. The Classic Study of Tomorrow* (New York: Random House, 1989).
10 However, at issue here are not closed-circuit installations; in other words, the actors cannot follow their performances on screen.
11 See Ramón Reichert, *Amateure im Netz. Selbstmanagement und Wissenstechnik im Web 2.0* (Bielefeld, Germany: Transcript, 2008).
12 See for example the YouTube parties of the artist Bjørn Melhus.
13 See for example the advertising campaign of Stiegl, an Austrian beer, that uses YouTube performances of "ski jumps" on escalators for an advertising clip. Many thanks to Jana Herwig for this reference.
14 Roland Barthes, *Roland Barthes by Roland Barthes* (New York: Hill and Wang, 1977).
15 Tom Holert, "Digitale Ich-Maschine," *Jungle World,* 22 January 2009.

16 On YouTube there are many videos that teach specific dance moves, for example hip hop.

17 See Christoph Menke, "Two Kinds of Practice: On the Relation between Social Discipline and the Aesthetics of Existence," *Constellations* no. 2, 2003, pp. 199–210.

18 Michel Foucault, "Les Hétérotopies. Radio France 7. Décembre 1966." Quotation taken from Michel Foucault, *Die Heterotopien. Les Hétérotopies. Der utopische Körper. Le corps utopiques* (Frankfurt am Main: Suhrkamp, 2005), pp. 40–41.

19 Michel Foucault, *Aesthetics, Method, and Epistemology*, ed. James D. Faubion (New York: New Press, 1999).

20 See Ilka Becker et al., eds., *Unmengen – Wie verteilt sich Handlungsmacht?* (Munich: Fink, 2008).

Christian Christensen

"Hey Man, Nice Shot": Setting the Iraq War to Music on YouTube

In all my dreams, before my helpless sight,
He plunges at me, guttering, choking, drowning.
If in some smothering dreams you too could pace
Behind the wagon that we flung him in,
And watch the white eyes writhing in his face,
His hanging face, like a devil's sick of sin;
If you could hear, at every jolt, the blood
Come gargling from the froth-corrupted lungs,
Obscene as cancer, bitter as the cud
Of vile, incurable sores on innocent tongues,
My friend, you would not tell with such high zest
To children ardent for some desperate glory,
The old Lie: Dulce et decorum est
Pro patria mori.[1]

Some ninety years before the introduction of YouTube, the British poet and soldier Wilfred Owen produced a series of works depicting the horrors of World War I. His poems stood in stark contrast to the propaganda produced by pro-war poets and the British government in which the battlefield was portrayed as a place of honor, loyalty, courage and patriotism. Owen used poetry to provide readers with a soldier's view of the trenches, with *Dulce et Decorum Est* as perhaps his most powerful indictment of the futility and brutality of military conflict (the last line of the poem—the "Lie"—translates as "It is an honor to die for one's country"). This memorialization and documentation of warfare through verse is but one example of how soldiers throughout history have used a variety of media (from print to photography to music) to record their experiences, and soldiers in Iraq and Afghanistan setting videos of military activity to music and uploading them to YouTube is an extension of Owen's method of documenting warfare.

Literary scholars might be aghast at the very notion of equating the works of Wilfred Owen with a two-minute YouTube clip, uploaded by a soldier, which shows an attack on Fallujah and is set to the industrial rock band Filter's "Hey Man, Nice Shot." It is very easy, of course, to fall into the trap of waxing dramatic over the development and rapid uptake of new forms of communication hardware and/or software, especially when that uptake has been nothing short of explosive.[2] This article, however, is not about comparing (qualitatively) one form of personal or artistic expression with another, nor is it to suggest that one tool for communication (for example, YouTube) is more "effective" or "influential" than another (such as books of poetry). Rather, my intent here is to consider these ad hoc, highly intertextual "soldier productions" in relation to a number of core issues: YouTube as a site for the documentation and memorialization of soldiers' activities; YouTube and "ephemeral communicative space";[3] and, finally, views of war on YouTube as entertainment.[4]

Rooted in earlier research in which I have examined the presentation of "dissonant" representations of warfare in Afghanistan and Iraq via videos uploaded to YouTube,[5] my intent here is to move away from a discussion of clips containing little or no narration or audiovisual additions and showing strictly "military" activities (bombings, street fighting, tanks). The US occupations of Iraq and Afghanistan have spurred a particular genre of YouTube material depicting, in various forms and in various styles, war and military conflict. Many clips show troops engaged in violent battle, with deaths and casualties either implicitly suggested or explicitly shown. Some of the most popular videos and clips—attracting millions of views and generating thousands of comments—within this genre, however, are those set to music, depicting US soldiers in Iraq in action, at play or communicating with friends and loved ones back home. It would be easy to dismiss these clips as nothing more than an interesting byproduct of a horrific war, yet in July of 2006 no less a pop-culture giant than MTV aired a documentary on troops' uploaded music videos from Iraq, entitled *Iraq Uploaded*. Reminding viewers of the title of the classic *MTV Unplugged*, *Iraq Uploaded* played off the exotic, edgy and "raw" nature of music videos from a combat zone, undoubtedly thinking of the inherent appeal to younger males in key demographic groups.

Intertextuality, Music and War

While it would always be much simpler to take a technologically deterministic position regarding YouTube, the root of any discussion of it, war and music should really begin and end with a discussion of intertextuality and street-smart digital literacy. What becomes clear when watching music video after music video by soldiers serving in Iraq and Afghanistan (as well as those created by friends, family, and pro- and anti-war civilians) is the degree to which the producers are familiar with, and can easily adapt, well-established aesthetic and narrative codes and practices, and seem to have little problem creating what are in some cases high-quality audiovisual products made under astonishingly difficult conditions. In his popular book *Generation Kill*, Evan Wright noted the degree to which the soldiers in the platoon in which he was embedded lived and breathed mediated popular culture:

> They are kids raised on hip-hop, Marilyn Manson and Jerry Springer. For them, "motherfucker" is a term of endearment. [...] These young men represent what is more or less America's first generation of disposable children. More than half the guys from the platoon come from broken homes and were raised by absentee, single, working parents. Many are on more intimate terms with video games, reality TV shows and Internet porn than they are with their own parents.[6]

In addition to their absorption of popular culture, and in line with an environment where material for YouTube clips is to be found in abundance, Susan Carruthers has noted that the current US occupation of Iraq is unique in that soldiers themselves are using digital technology to capture everything from the historic to the barbaric. "Yet while civilians [in the United States] snooze, their uniformed counterparts in Iraq are busily shooting everything in sight—digital cameras having become an essential piece of 21st-century kit," she states. In the US no one may be looking, but "over there it seems that everyone is snapping and filming. From the ancient ruins of Mesopotamia to the quotidian tribulations of counterinsurgency soldiering, nothing is off-limits."[7]

Of course, such clips can make up the stock video footage for ad hoc YouTube troop videos. But what of the music? When making the film *Soundtrack to War* (2004), George Gittoes spent 18 months on the frontlines examining the role music played for the troops during the occupations of Iraq and Afghanistan. Gittoes' film illustrated how music—primarily rap and heavy metal—was used by troops as a tool for preparing themselves psychologically for the violence of conflict, and the possibility of killing. Listening to hardcore music allowed the soldiers to place themselves into a mental state devoid of empathy or fear. In yet another study on music in the Iraq War, Jonathan Pieslak also reached similar conclusions. "From metal and rap music used by American troops to inspire them for combat missions, to anti-war protest songs on popular radio, music functions in a variety of ways in relation to the Iraq war," Pieslak notes. Some functions are familiar from earlier conflicts, "others are dramatically different in consequence of new recording and listening technologies. While carrying out patrols and missions, for example, American soldiers can listen to music in tanks and Humvees through self-made sound systems, portable CD players, and mp3 players." According to Pieslak, music is even used during interrogation "to break the will of detainees if they refuse to answer questions."[8]

As troops increasingly use music to express their feelings during a time of war, YouTube has entered the picture as a vehicle for relaying those sentiments back home, often with the use of intertextual material. Kari Anden-Papadopoulos has noted that soldiers producing these clips "fall back on contemporary popular culture and its broad repertoire of war as entertainment,"[9] and that the clips are part and parcel of a trend toward a "confessional" culture in which digital media are used for exhibition of the self. Or as MTV put it in promotional material for the program *Iraq Uploaded* back in 2005: "To a generation of soldiers raised on first-person-shooter video games, armed with pocket-sized digital still and video cameras, the Iraq war is coming home in an unprecedented, and sometimes disturbingly graphic, way. A previous generation's soldiers from Vietnam returned mostly with still shots and memories [...] but the military's lax rules on the posting of video on the Internet have allowed Iraq war soldiers to post their uncensored video diaries online for all the world to see. Hundreds of hours of video footage are now on sites like iFilm, YouTube and Ogrish.com, providing a visual document of life during wartime as it's never been seen before."[10]

Setting the Iraq War to Music

There are a wide variety of music videos from Iraq from which to choose. This will not be an exhaustive examination of the scores of music videos uploaded to YouTube by soldiers serving in Iraq and Afghanistan, as the number of clips, the problem of sourcing the clips and the sheer repetition and redundancy of many of the videos would make such an undertaking relatively fruitless. Rather, I would like to discuss two particular genres of military music videos— what I will call "Get Some" and "Reflective"—and give a few examples from each for the purposes of further discussion and consideration. This is not to say, of course, that all of the music clips from Iraq fit into these two categories, or that a video from one category could not be included in the other, but rather that there are clear structural resemblances among clips in the same category. It would be fair to say that these two groupings represent the lion's share of military YouTube material from Iraq and Afghanistan set to music, and as such, make for ideal points of departure.

29 "Slightly graphic": A classic "Get Some" video

The first category, the so-called "Get Some" clips, is named after a phrase commonly used by members of the US military: " 'Get some!' is the unofficial Marine Corps cheer. It's shouted when a brother Marine is struggling to beat his personal best in a fitness run. It punctuates stories told at night about getting laid in whorehouses in Thailand and Australia.

It's the cry of exhilaration after firing a burst from a .50-caliber machine gun. 'Get some!' expresses in two simple words the excitement, fear, feelings of power and the erotic-tinged thrill that come from confronting the extreme physical and emotional challenges posed by death."[11] Consequently, the typical "Get Some" video shows intense, sometimes violent military action, usually involving powerful military hardware, and is almost always set to heavy metal (such as Slayer, Drowning Pool or Slipknot) or rap music (with Tupac Shakur being a particular favorite). The "Get Some" clips are more often than not a rapid-fire series of images or short moving clips set to aggressive, hardcore music.[12] Despite the musical accompaniment, many of these videos include live, original audio and dialogue, often with troops indicating pleasure and exhilaration during the heat of battle.

A classic example of the "Get Some" video would be "A Bullet With a Name on It," uploaded by WilcoUSMC.[13] The video was set to the heavy-metal song of the same name by the band NonPoint. The video opens (in silence) with a quote from the Bible's 23rd Psalm: "I will fear no evil, for you are with me," followed by the start of the music and a fade-in to a US soldier pointing a rifle out a window. The video is a typical compilation of still images and video footage, including a large number of clips showing gunfire and large explosions. The clip ends with a fade to black and the words "Semper Fidelis" ("always faithful"). "USMC/Iraq Video (Graphic)"[14] by gyleake also opens with a section (albeit a paraphrase) of the 23rd Psalm ("We shall fear no evil") set to the song "This Is the New Shit" by Marilyn Manson. The video is a skillfully edited piece of work, with the tempo of the still images edited to coincide with the tempo of the music. As the music reaches the climax (sexual connotation intended), the video shifts from still images to live action showing the troops. Unlike "A Bullet With a Name on It," "USMC/Iraq Video" contains extremely graphic images, footage of dead Iraqi soldiers and thermal-imaging footage of individuals being killed on the ground. The clip concludes with images from the September 11, 2001, terrorist attacks on New York (an association made in a number of such videos)[15] and a final picture of a piece of heavy artillery with the words " 'livin' the dream' '07. "

There is one "Get Some" video that is worthy of particular attention, as it has been posted and re-posted on a number of occasions. Footage of the November 2004 siege of Fallujah, shot by Corporal Jan M. Bender, a "Combat Correspondent" with the United States Marine Corps, is set to the song "Out of My Way" by the South African "post-grunge" band Seether. The video appears under a number of different titles, but is usually presented in the original format. To use the example posted by marine87devil,[16] the clip opens with the following information:

> "Operation Al Fajr"
> Aka Phantom Fury
> Footage Shot and Edited
> By Cpl Jan M. Bender Combat Correspondent/USMC
> On the Mean Streets Of Fallujah
> Nov 7-Nov 25, '04

The clip then shows a red light flashing to the rhythm of a heartbeat, and you hear (what you assume to be) two soldiers speaking about the US assault on Fallujah: "Soldier 1: This is what people joined the Marine Corps to do. You might be in the Marine Corps for twenty years and not get this chance again: To take out a full-fledged city full of insurgents. Soldier 2: Pretty much we said, 'Hey, we are going to be here at this time, you know. If you want some you can get some. Fuck 'em up.' " The clip is then roughly four minutes of relatively uncommon footage from the siege on Fallujah, showing US soldiers firing upon and blowing up a variety of buildings. At no point in the video are casualties (US or Iraqi) shown. The end of the clip, as the song fades out, has the following message: "To those who lived the good life, fought the good fight and made the ultimate sacrifice. May we never forget." While Bender is often credited as the video's maker, it is not as widely known (based on the YouTube postings) that he also set the footage to music for the men in his platoon and distributed it, because, as he described it, "I felt a responsibility. This was their own history."[17]

Unlike the knee-jerk aggression and war porn[18] of the "Get Some" clips, "Reflective" music videos offer exactly what the title suggests: a view of time spent in Iraq and Afghanistan from a more thoughtful, personal and/or reflective perspective. The videos within this category tend to be set not to speed metal, older heavy metal or rap, but music that creates an environment for a more contemplative state of mind. The "Reflective" videos address a wide variety of topics, from messages to family back home to the nature of military service and support for fellow troops. These clips are occasionally critical of the war or the conditions under which troops are expected to serve but, more often than not, the uploaders indicate that they are attempting to show a side of warfare that is often hidden from civilians back in the United States: tiredness, work, loneliness, sadness, camaraderie, boredom, love of country, love of family and loyalty.

In "Welcome to Iraq (A-Btry 2/114th FA)," for example, a soldier with the login name cnine posted a clip with the following description: "This is the highlight music video I made of our time in Iraq. We were reverted to infantry. The footage takes place in 2005. All images are from cameras of the soldiers of alpha battery 2-114th." Then follows a dedication list: "To Tommy Little, Greg Tull and all the friends, family and comrades lost over there. Enjoy. Leave comments. Send the link to your friends. Let everybody see what its all about through our perspective, not CNN's."[19] The video comprises still and moving images set to the song "So Cold" by the band Breaking Benjamin and "Until the End of Time" by Tupac Shakur. The opening shot, timed to coincide with the mood-inducing opening of the song, is a poignant still image showing the following message/graffiti on a wall located in an undisclosed military building (with an arrow under the message pointing downward): "Welcome to the US Army deposit center. Please place your family, hopes, dreams and life into the amnesty box below."

While this somber opening could be taken as a critique of the war (and military life in general), the video attempts to show a multifaceted view of warfare. In the clip, cnine has interspersed video footage of battle, heavy artillery and explosions with softer images of soldiers playing with children, Iraqi children in school, civilians getting medical checks, and fellow soldiers smiling. While the song "So Cold" is one that could best be described as hard rock bordering on alternative metal, it is not the type of song typically heard in the "Get Some" videos, nor is "Until the End of Time" by Tupac Shakur (which has samples and remixes of the very soft tune "Broken Wings" by Mr. Mister). This video is striking because of the ways in which cnine has mixed traditional images of warfare with more humanitarian fare, thus creating a personal music video in which the emotional complexity of war (from the perspective of the individual soldier) is presented. The clip ends with a list of "credits" set to the song "So Far Away" by Staind.

30 Shot on location: "Stuck"

The goal of "telling the story" of Iraq (from the perspective of the troops) to civilians back home is pervasive in the "Reflective" videos, and the soldiers are often overt in their intentions. Written statements in the opening seconds of the music videos are a common vehicle for making these goals clear. In "This is our story—US Marines in Iraq,"[20] set to the songs "Fix You" by Coldplay and "The Space Between" by the Dave Matthews Band, louieizme starts his clip with the following tribute: "For those who served, those who perished, those who continue to serve and those who will. This is our Story. SAEPE EXPERTUS, SEMPER FIDELIS, FRATRES AETERNI." The Latin phrase at the end is a US Marine slogan (often tattooed onto the arms of soldiers) translates as: "Often tested, always faithful, brothers forever." This video presents an interesting and moving chronological arc of war, from opening images of troops leaving home (with tearful family members watching), to their arrival in Iraq or Afghanistan, to battle scenes, to the end of the tour and reunion with friends and family. Rather than ending on this note of joy, however, the video concludes with powerful images (taken, it appears, with a personal digital camera and not stock footage) of flag-draped coffins being loaded onto a plane, relatives overcome with grief and hugging the coffins upon their arrival, and as the music fades away, a final image of several US flags planted in a military graveyard. After the music has ended and the credits have rolled, there is a shot from the air of US troops in a formation spelling out: "9–11 We Remember."

A final, very original example of the "Reflective" video is "Iraq War Music Video 'Stuck,' " uploaded by zerechakfilms. The film, shot and directed by filmmaker Jeremy Zerechak, is an MTV-style music video featuring solder/musician Jonathan Geras playing his own song, "Stuck." The film was unique in that it was shot and produced on location in a US Army camp in Baghdad. In his description of the video and the song, Zerechak[21] wrote:

> Stuck, a real wartime music video recorded and produced entirely in Baghdad, brings to life the despairing loneliness and isolation of the true human behind the soldiers serving in the front lines and headlines. Its message musically and visually advocates the voices of thousands of soldiers separated from their homes and loved ones. Stuck harmoniously combines documentary-style imagery of environment and performance with a lyrical acoustic sound to create a moving and original piece.

In the video, Geras is shown singing while on his bunk, atop military vehicles, perched on a rooftop and sitting in front of a bullet-riddled mural of Saddam Hussein. Unlike other "Reflective" videos in which a mixture of original and copied images and footage is combined with music by well-known artists, "Stuck" combines original music and original film, making it a rather unique wartime pop-culture product.[22]

Conclusion: YouTube & Owen

Moving beyond the mere description and categorization of the music videos from Iraq and Afghanistan, one might ask how these videos fit and might be regarded within specific theoretical and conceptual contexts. One notable aspect is that the clips function as a form of historical marker, or memorial of the *living* (rather than the dead). In his research on the use of the Internet for the creation of the online Iraq war memorial,[23] Nicholas Grider has stated that "what is most interesting about the online exhibition, and most importantly the website that serves as an online version of it, is how and to what end it redefines what a memorial is and does, as well as how 'the memorial' has moved, in the current media landscape, from physical site to dematerialized and endlessly reconfigurable remembrance." According to Grider the online memorial "is no longer simply a proxy—an eternal marker meant to commit to public memory a past event—but an ongoing process that depends less upon the implied eternity of a built physical environment than on the entirely different eternity of circulating information."[24] Grider's point regarding the fluid nature of the war memorial when converted into online form, as well as the notion that memorial is becoming a process, is important when thinking about YouTube as a site for the documentation of war. This fact has not been lost on the soldiers who served in Iraq and Afghanistan, and used digital video cameras and YouTube to mark their place in history. A soldier interviewed for the MTV documentary *Iraq Uploaded* noted that the music videos proved to be both a form of historical documentation for the broader population, and a personal confirmation that experiences in battle were, in fact, real: "You look at World War II and Vietnam and the Holocaust. It's hard to [imagine] that those events actually look place because it's just unbelievable. Even now, when I look back on some of the things we experienced, I'm like, 'Man, did that really happen?' And when I look back at those videos, occasionally I'm like, 'That really happened,' and it's still hard to believe."[25]

In a recent article, Miyase Christensen and I proposed the concept of "ephemeral communicative spaces" for explaining and examining the discursive slots that emerge following particular local, national or international events: slots that are open for a finite time (hence their ephemeral nature), but within which topics of sociocultural or political importance are addressed and debated.[26] The US occupation of Iraq is clearly a geopolitical event that has gone beyond the ephemeral, yet there were instances during the conflict—the initial invasion, the fall of Baghdad, the execution of Saddam Hussein, the siege of Fallujah, Abu Ghraib—where such ephemeral communicative spaces did open and topics such as US imperialism, torture and the legality of war were addressed. The occupation of Iraq will one day end (we assume), and so the YouTube music videos created by soldiers as a form of personal expression can also be seen as a product created within a specific communicative space that, while far from ephemeral, is certainly temporally finite. When the occupation ends, and members of the military go home, the music videos will remain in suspended online animation as cyber-relics: their novelty value gone, but their personal, subjective testimonies to history intact.

George Gittoes brings this article full circle when he writes that the war in Iraq was "The first war that has been driven by poetry [...] this urban poetry of rap and rock 'n' roll."[27] This brings us back to Wilfred Owen and his war poetry. His work raises a number of interesting questions regarding not only the relationship between art and war, but also the sensitive issue of the relationship between art, war and entertainment, which is also salient when discussing the music videos uploaded to YouTube by soldiers. While Owen is firmly embedded within the Western literary canon and has achieved an unofficial position as the commentator on the horrors of World War I, there remains the thorny question of voyeurism. Owen, just as the young men and women who upload their clips to YouTube in Iraq and Afghanistan, observe war from a position both unique and unimaginable to those who have never seen a single man or woman killed, let alone in battle and in their tens, hundreds or thousands. This position, while horrific, also taps into the very mythologies of war that Owen was attempting to discredit: bravery, loyalty, courage and violence. While Owen wrote poetry to crush notions of "glorious" war, some troops in Iraq produced videos extolling the virtues of patriotism and valor in battle. In the end, however, one could argue that both extract curiosity precisely because of the horrific nature of their subject.

One need only read the viewer comments under many of the clips discussed in this article to understand the degree to which their use is often linked to something other than honoring those who fight or a desire to "witness history." Often, there is the simple desire to see explosions, weaponry and US troops "kicking ass," and many of the comments posted by viewers are racist and xenophobic. The addition of aggressive music and patriotic symbolism to the videos (US flags, images of the Twin Towers collapsing, military graves) only serves to fuel those fires. Paul Rieckhoff of the group Iraq and Afghanistan Veterans of America said that most of the people looking at these videos are most likely civilians who are "into military stuff or guys who play video games," and that they are people who want to "live vicariously through soldiers—guys who want to be able to experience it without losing a leg."[28] If YouTube is a site for the documentation and memorialization of war, the musical clips uploaded from the battlefields of Iraq and Afghanistan are disturbing, violent, sad and sometimes entertaining additions to that virtual repository.

Endnotes

1 Excerpt from Wilfred Owen, *Dulce et Decorum Est,* in *The Collected Poems of Wilfred Owen* (New York: New Directions, 1965), p. 55.

2 Christian Christensen, "YouTube: The Evolution of Media?" *Screen Education* no. 45, 2007, pp. 36–40.

3 Christian Christensen & Miyase Christensen, "The Afterlife of Eurovision 2003: Turkish and European Social Imaginaries and Ephemeral Communicative Space," *Popular Communication* no. 3, 2008, pp. 155–172.

4 See for example, Robin Andersen, *Century of Media, A Century of War* (New York: Peter Lang, 2006).

5 Christian Christensen, "Uploading Dissonance: YouTube and the US Occupation of Iraq, " *Media, War & Conflict* no. 2, 2008, pp. 155–175.

6 Evan Wright, *Generation Kill: Devil Dogs, Iceman, Captain America and the New Face of American War* (New York: G. P. Putnam, 2004), p. 5.

7 Susan Carruthers, "No One's Looking: The Disappearing Audience for War," *Media, War & Conflict* no. 1, 2008, pp. 70–76.

8 Jonathan Pieslak, "Sound Targets: Music and the War in Iraq," *Journal of Musicological Research* no. 26, 2007, pp. 123–149.

9 Kari Anden-Papadopoulos, "US Soldiers Imaging the Iraq War on YouTube," *Popular Communication* no. 1, 2009, pp. 17–27.

10 See www.mtv.com/news/articles/1536780/20060720/index.jhtml [last checked 15 February 2009].

11 See www.rollingstone.com/news/story/5938873/the_killer_elite/ [last checked 15 February 2009].

12 Anden-Papadopoulos 2009.

13 See http://se.youtube.com/watch?v=ZnmsGYk1adw [last checked 15 February 2009].

14 See http://se.youtube.com/watch?v=bJwlR6HMcKw&feature=channel_page [last checked 15 February 2009].

15 The failure to prove any link between the attacks of September 11, 2001, and Saddam Hussein's regime seems to have had no impact on the practice of making 9/11 a point of reference in a large number of clips.

16 See www.youtube.com/watch?v=0N8PDBwve6g [last checked 15 February 2009].

17 See www.courierpress.com/news/2008/jul/13/on-airwithtri-statemarine [last checked 15 February 2009].

18 For a discussion on the notion of "war porn" see Jean Baudrillard, "War Porn," *International Journal of Baudrillard Studies* no. 1, 2005 – www.ubishops.ca/BaudrillardStudies/vol2_1/taylor.htm [last checked 15 February 2009].

19 See http://se.youtube.com/watch?v=UtE0HPrTylU [last checked 15 February 2009].

20 See http://se.youtube.com/watch?v=uoQdNDYU4Fw [last checked 15 February 2009].

21 Jeremy Zerechak was a documentary film student at Pennsylvania State University at the time of his deployment. In addition to the video in question, Zerechak also shot 56 hours of raw documentary footage during his tour of duty, material that would become the basis for an award-winning feature-length production, *Land of Confusion*. For a discussion see http://zerechakfilms.com [last checked 15 February 2009].

22 There are naturally other examples of musicians producing their own music and videos in Iraq, for example the rap group 4th 25 (Fourth Quarter).

23 See www.facesofthefallen.org [last checked 15 February 2009].

24 Nicholas Grider, "Faces of the Fallen and the Dematerialization of US War Memorials," *Visual Communication* no. 3, 2007, pp. 265–279.

25 See www.mtv.com/news/articles/1536780/20060720/index.jhtml [last checked 15 February 2009].

26 Christensen & Christensen 2008.

27 See www.youtube.com/watch?v=3y_5vxM8PYM&feature=related [last checked 15 February 2009].

28 See www.mtv.com/news/articles/1536780/20060720/index.jhtml [last checked 15 February 2009].

Malin Wahlberg

YouTube Commemoration: Private Grief and Communal Consolation

YouTube offers an alternative culture of commemoration where private loss finds articulation in video tributes made in memory of loved ones. Social and ritual aspects of commemoration are often expressed in memorials as public sites of trauma. On YouTube, however, the commemoration is virtual and the posted message not necessarily engraved forever. Another difference lies in dedication; traditional memorials are regularly created as official monuments of celebration, but Web memorials often represent cultural expressions effected by personal trauma (terminal disease, suicide, incest, child abuse, etcetera). These events that permanently change private life stories also evoke experiences with a high degree of intersubjectivity. This article will address, exemplify and contextualize "the memorial video tribute" as a contemporary phenomenon of "vernacular memory," as well as a ritual of grief that embraces a wide spectrum—from the obituary as kitsch to the social promises of communal action.[1] In my account of the virtual memorial and, more specifically, video tributes on YouTube, I suggest a reassessment of *commemoration* and *memorial* from the perspective of personal loss, Web-based communication and the intersubjective realm of grief culture.

The Memorial Video Tribute

Despite a growing number of memory videos and related expressions made in other countries, the memory video is primarily an American invention. In a commercial context, this genre is first of all associated with the amateur documentation of weddings and other greater moments in life. However, it also includes the memorial video tribute which, sadly enough, and according to the site of Memorial Lane Productions, seem to represent a flowering business in the shadow of war. The site, for example, makes a special offer for memorializing war victims, "50 percent discount on all memorial tributes for Members of the Armed Forces!"[2] Together with the "funeral video," which is a memorial video tribute produced by the funeral home to be shown at the service, the memorial video tribute represents a scarcely acknowledged phenomenon within the American culture of grief. On YouTube it stands out as a representation and practice extended into the global realm of the Internet. Video tributes are suggested and encouraged by funeral instruction books at Amazon.com, and as a product offered by many funeral homes, the memorial video tribute also exemplifies "the funeral as mega-industry."[3] The overlap of the personal tribute and the funeral video may explain the predictable quality of many YouTube examples, which, with some important exceptions of elaborate amateur achievement, may seem to be a grotesque corpus of sentimental kitsch. Regarding the funeral business, photo companies and others who offer the video tribute as a product, the phenomenon exemplifies the abiding influence of commercial interests on amateur culture.[4] When looking at the video tributes on YouTube, it is sometimes hard to tell if they are amateur videos or funeral videos made on demand. As Luc Pauwels concludes regarding the related phenomenon of the family website: "non-media professionals" are being encouraged "to extend their family album into the Internet and, hence, using 'free' websites implies exposure to a sophisticated 'Web' of commercial offerings."[5]

Despite the function of a private shrine for public use, the memorial video tribute is not necessarily a representation excluded from world history and current affairs. The point of intersection between a historical event and a private tragedy is evident in the large number of video tributes made in the aftermath of, for example, the 9/11 catastrophe in 2001, Hurricane Katrina in the fall of 2005, or the increasing amount of tributes dedicated to the US armed forces in Iraq and the memory of soldiers lost in action.[6] As Christian Christensen's article in this book testifies, there is a growing corpus of soldier videos on YouTube, including videos that express patriotic feelings and even tributes made by the US Army to comfort and honor the families of killed soldiers. In other videos a strong antiwar message is added to the honoring of the dead, which indicates the subversive potential of the amateur video as a tool for media activism. The soldier tributes deviate from the majority of memorial videos because in terms of amateur culture, they are part of an extensive and varied context of videos made by American soldiers based in Afghanistan and Iraq.[7]

For reasons of demarcation, the remainder of this article will focus primarily on video tributes made in memory of individuals unexpectedly dead after accidents, illness or suicide. In this context, expressions of grief and loss meet with idealized portraits of the dead, and in many cases a will to bring communal attention to the private and shared grief caused by, most notably, cancer and suicide. The cause of death makes the subject of the video tribute a victim, and as a victim she or he is represented as a symbol of problems of a more general, communal concern. Unimaginable is the number of names that would be on display if national memorials were constructed for cancer victims, or all the people who struggle to overcome and survive the suicide of a close relative.

31 "Rest in Peace," in memory of Tracy Pagani

Video tributes are commonly entitled "In Memory of X," "For X," or "X's Funeral Video," i.e. the loss and commemoration is immediately suggested by the title. In combination with the music, which in most cases seems to have been chosen to emphasize the sad fact of death or the pride with which the memory of the deceased is celebrated, family images transmit the temporal dramaturgy that Roland Barthes ascribed to the affective impact of the photograph. "He is dead and he is going to die" – yet images show somebody uncannily unaware of the approaching ending.[8]

A series of photographs presenting a person from early childhood to a recent moment preceding her or his death has an existential impact, reinforced by the chosen score, to stress the unique narrative of each individual life story, and to deplore the loss and missed opportunities of a life that was ended too soon. The presence of absence enacted by photographs, and the contrast between the happiness suggested by family footage and the irrevocable fact of death, represent *the* universal content of the memorial tribute video. Reinforced by the rhythmic and affective frame provided by the music, this representation brings attention to the uses and functions of traditional family footage, within and beyond the context of digital media.

A closer look at a single example will illuminate some of these general characteristics in relation to the particular Web context of reception and immediate communication. The video is entitled "The Letter." To the sound of Robert Plant and Alison Krauss' song "Please read the letter that I wrote" the title is presented in a red caption. A blurred shot reveals the back of a man approaching a tombstone, followed by a closeup view of the inscription "Melinda Ann Smith Beachy." As the song plays, the video presents a series of photographs showing Melinda in her wedding gown, vacation snapshots, as well as fragments of everyday life: Melinda playing with the dogs, reading on a sofa, looking up from her computer, or driving a car. The moving sequence from the beginning of the video reappears once, and there are a few photographs of the grieving husband before the screen darkens as the song fades away.

Aside from the video, there are about 40 commentaries posted in reaction to it on YouTube—the spontaneous feedback by some of the video's 26,263 viewers.[9] Vern Beachy made this tribute in memory of his wife, and in answer to his audience he reveals that Melinda committed suicide. One commentary testifies to the coincidental discovery that usually characterizes the reception of YouTube material, and the existential impact and possibly cathartic relief or morbid voyeurism involved in glimpsing the pain of others:

> I have to thank you for the reply. I didn't expect it. I was having a somewhat "bad" day at work, took a lunch break to look at a video, and was looking for the video that goes with that song and yours came up. After

> looking at it, crying, I started to think that my day wasn't all that "bad" after all. I can imagine you miss your love very much. That must be very hard. Take care, Pattie.[10]

The formal consistency of the memorial video tribute is striking, although there are differences and subgenres related to the cause of death, the point of view expressed by the filmmaker, the use of commentaries, and the level of communal interest and call to social action. Some examples include moving images and even sequences recorded at the funeral service, but most videos consist of a slideshow of photographs accompanied by music and captions. Music is fundamental for providing an apt emotional ambience for the series of stills, where grief blends with the proud sentiment of remembering and celebrating the dead. As indicated by the example above, music is key in terms of identification and chance-like access, because a particular song often provides the link connecting the unaware YouTube user to the memorial video. The modes of accessing these tributes do not differ in any significant way from the YouTube culture at large, where videos reach viewers by means of personal recommendations, the cutting and pasting of links, and by the thematic clustering of material provided by the YouTube interface itself.

Commemoration as Ritual Act and Media Event

In the extensive field of academic work dedicated to social and cultural practices of commemoration, *the memorial* is a place where ritual acts meet with the politics of preservation and historical representation. Its symbolic value materializes in the architecture of grief, which stresses the difference between a memorial and a monument. "Monuments are not generally built to commemorate defeats," Marita Sturken notes, rather "the defeated dead are remembered in memorials. Whereas a monument most often signifies victory, a memorial refers to the life or lives sacrificed for a particular set of values."[11] The distinction is commonly made in reference to the Vietnam Veteran's Memorial in Washington that was designed by Maya Lin in 1982 and provoked a massive debate regarding war monuments in general, and the historical representation of the Vietnam War in particular. In American studies of public memory this example brought attention to the memorial as enactment of social disdain and conflict; a problem that was further illustrated by the NAMES Chicago Project AIDS Memorial Quilt, "the largest piece of folk art ever created," which was initiated in 1985 by the gay-rights activist Cleve Jones in San Francisco.[12] Different from predominant memorials, the Quilt consists of more than 37,400 three-by-six-foot panels made by individuals and groups from around the world. Together, the assembled panels constitute a collective manifestation of grief and anger—an immense field that visualizes the innumerable victims of AIDS while inspiring social action.

Contemporary research on public memory in film and media studies center mainly on three major fields of interest.[13] The first involves the construction of memory in practices, representations and material artifacts. Secondly, commemoration in relation to trauma has often been subject to studies that almost exclusively deal with the Holocaust and other genocides.[14] Finally, a third approach to commemoration focuses on the role of media in the reproduction of public memory. With reference to media events, such as the death of Princess Diana in 1997, commemoration has also become a discourse on image and affect where public practice and official memorials increasingly seem to fuse with a variety of unofficial and spontaneous shrines at the site of mourning. The memorial itself turns into media event, and, as Erica Doss emphasizes, since the invention of television we have become accustomed to an excessively material and visual mourning culture.[15] Sturken makes a similar reflection regarding the spontaneous memorial, in contrast to the official memorial. With reference to examples such as the Oklahoma City National Memorial and Ground Zero in New York, she describes a culture of grief where the memorial is at once a tourist attraction and a site of spontaneous, unofficial commemoration.[16] The Oklahoma City National Memorial was set up five years after the bombing. It deviates from other national memorials in the sense of being a tribute to the lives of ordinary citizens, and in that the memorial was preceded by the unofficial counterpart referred to as The Memory Fence. In the immediate aftermath of the bombings a fence was raised to demarcate the area devastated by the bomb, and it soon transformed into an unofficial memorial. In a few days the entire fence was covered by flowers, flags, messages and teddy bears.[17]

The large number of objects left on the fence in Oklahoma (50,000 in 1999) exemplifies the material and visual aspect of national trauma and shared grief. A similar manifestation of loss was notable in the aftermath of 9/11, where memory fences appeared at Ground Zero and outside each affected police and fire department in New York City. A particular brand of tourism in the shadow of national trauma is of course not unique to the American context, but Sturken convincingly shows that the scope of national and international pilgrimage to, for example, the Oklahoma Memorial and Ground Zero should be understood in relation to a "comfort culture, with its attendant politics of affect" which is crucial to grief culture in the US.[18] Similar to related examples of vernacular Web memorials, the video tributes on YouTube point at the discursive struggle of the memorial as a site where, according to Erica Doss, "versions of history and public memory are in dispute."[19] Generally, commemorative sites "produce action within their viewers, be they visitors at the site or mourners for lost loved ones," although private commemoration on the Web extends this action into communication and interactivity.[20] The context of communication and media culture demands a deepened consideration regarding the public reception of the video tribute and the interactive element of its realization. The memorial video tribute provides an alternative conception of public memory that is somewhat aligned with, for example, the "signature squares" of the NAMES Project AIDS Memorial Quilt, where visitors are encouraged to write commentaries.[21] Also, the memorial as visual attraction and a site of cathartic pleasure seems to represent an aspect of contemporary grief culture, whether the memorial is physical or virtual.

Traces of Death and Loss in Cyberspace

The memorial video tribute stands out as a continuation and renewal of previous expressions and practices of *the virtual memorial*, which is the overall label for this Web culture of commemoration.[22] Web pages honoring the dead represent the classical example, which is commonly referred to as virtual memorials or Web memorials. According to Pamela Roberts, these cyberspace obituaries started to appear shortly after the creation of computer-based communication. Web cemeteries initiated in the 1990s still function as sites of commemoration and a practice of expressing loss and honoring the dead. For example, the popular British site Virtual Memorial Garden is dedicated to the memory of "people and pets," and the garden's philosophy is posted on the opening page:

> The Virtual Memorial Garden is not a place of death, but somewhere [sic] people can celebrate their family, friends and pets; to tell the rest of us about them and why they were special. People's attitude to death in Europe and North America has undergone a radical change in the last one hundred years. Death is no longer the commonplace event that it was when we were less healthy and medical care was not as effective. Certainly we have lost touch with the idea of remembering, though perhaps the fact that many people feel the urge to trace their family tree is a remnant of the powerful respect for ancestors that can still be found in countries like China, Japan and Korea. We need to celebrate the Day of the Dead just as they do in Mexico![23]

Today, personal tributes to the dead appear in various cyberspace community venues, and as the memorial video exemplifies, the creation and functions of shrines on the Internet now go beyond websites (and interconnected sites) to include amateur videos. Virtual memorials seem to provide "a sense of place and, to many, a sense of community."[24] These are acts of remembrance that may also reflect the sentiments and opinions of local communities. In the corpus of videos reviewed for this article, the importance of religious communities reverberates in viewers' commentaries, and various foundations and organizations are present in related links and sometimes even part of the film.[25]

The memorial video tribute is most commonly based on family photography, which also makes it a form of domestic representation in line with, or a combination of, the family website and the family film. The family website exemplifies the long-standing practice of family photography converted into "the semi-public space of the Internet."[26] Domestic image culture, such as the family album, the home movie or the family website, is characterized by the ritual of idealized self-representation and the universal content of its endlessly recycled motifs: smiling family members posing for the photographer at Christmas parties, marriages and birthdays. For obvious reasons, children and childhood have always been at the heart of the family album. The crucial function of family photography, scholars often claim, is to construct a unified image of the past.[27] Another important dimension, described beautifully by

Susan Sontag, is our desire to freeze an irrevocable moment, to make "a neat slice of time."[28] The existential aspect of the photograph as a trace of the past is further intensified in these video tributes, which also exemplifies the persistent function of (analog and digital) photography as a mnemonic and therapeutic tool for dealing with trauma.

32 "In Tribute to Jeff Soriano," a patchwork of photographs

Aside from the important aspect of domestic representation, the memorial video's filmic quality of animated photographs accompanied by sound suggests a reference to the history of amateur film. Similar to the family film, the video tribute often reproduces the blurred images of the home movie. In terms of social representation it provides a fragmentary, anonymous and incomplete record, while nevertheless indicating obvious markers of class, race and gender. Yet, there are decisive differences between the memorial video tribute and the home movie that go beyond the different media technologies per se. The maker of a memorial video does not typically consider videomaking a hobby, nor does she or he make a record of the happy "now" of family life to be reviewed later on. However, there are examples that bring attention to the interrelated practices of the home movie, the video tribute and amateur filmmaking.

"In Tribute to Jeff Soriano" was made by one of his cousins who, in 2007, shortly after a lethal car accident, added this video on YouTube under the name of RegiSor94.[29] It begins with an image from the accident site, where somebody put a piece of wood with the name and dates of the deceased. A text insert clarifies: "On April 20, 2007 Jeff Nielson Santodomingo Soriano died tragically in a car accident." Soriano's tombstone is shown in the following image, and then a caption informs the viewer that "June 22, 2008 would have been his 20th birthday [...] but we, all of his friends and family will always remember the good times with him." The ensuing montage of snapshots show Jeff as a baby, Jeff and his cousins growing up, Jeff as a student, and party images of Jeff and his friends. Different from the regular funeral video, this is an elaborate collage of a large amount of photographs that rhythmically appears to the music in singular frames, or by two or several in the same image. In the final sequence, the camera pulls back to reveal an immense patchwork of photographs, which finally morphs into one big portrait of Jeff. A final caption ends the video: "We will never forget you, Jeff." So far, the video has been seen by 351 viewers, although the small number of text commentaries are mostly posted by other friends and relatives, all positive and encouraging. RegiSor94 reads and answers the questions written in response to his work, and he recently made a new tribute to Soriano. In the introduction that appears below the title of the video, he writes:

> This is a video that is long overdue. I edited the original version for a commemorative DVD for my cousin, but I always wanted to upload it for all of his friends and family. I wanted to make people aware of this truly tragic event, which was only triggered by that other incredibly tragic event at Virginia Tech. But I truly re-edited this to insure that we all never forget Jeff, a truly wonderful person. To Jeff, this one's for you, cousin. We all miss you very much. You were one of the good ones. And special thanks to his brother Eugene for keeping Jeff in our hearts and minds. And to Jana, for rekindling his memory in me so that I could create this video for everyone. The music is Switchfoot's "This is Your Life."[30]

Apparently, the contributor is not only a grieving relative, but an amateur interested in montage technique and cinematic effects. In contrast to the majority of video tributes on YouTube, the latter tribute to Soriano consists of home movies depicting the cousins at various family events at different points in the young Soriano's life. It is an example where the videomaker has chosen to explore the dramatic impact of intertitles while editing the home-movie fragments into a narrative that brings forth the historical coincidence of public tragedy in relation to the private grief of a family tragedy: "Jeff Soriano was lucky to survive the school massacre at Virginia Tech on April 16, in 2007, only to be killed in a car accident later the same week on April 20." RegiSor94 combines brief contextual remarks with clips from the TV news to interrelate the two events. This tribute brings attention to the home movie as social representation and alternative archive. In contrast to the previous photo collage, the visual markers of class, ethnicity and gender are intensified because the recorded scenes and gestures unfold in "approximate realtime."[31]

The second, more elaborate version of RegiSor94's tribute has attracted 1,660 viewers. Again, there are only some ten text commentaries, most of which seem to have been written by friends or by people from the same neighborhood. For example, Cups4Us added the following commentary in the typical lingo of YouTube condolence: "dang... yo... imma miss my dude ... Ive been knowin Jeff since like 3rd grade... Me and him were the flag boys in our class room ... Jeff always seemed to be happy... in doing that everyone around him stayed happy... Imma miss u man..."[32] Regarding the common grounds of the video tribute and amateur culture on the Web, RegiSor94 offers an illuminating example. There is a link from his latest video to another site on YouTube where RegiSor94's work and ambitions are spelled out in more detail. There is a disclaimer regarding the illegal use of music in his work and a section where RegiSor94 expresses his wishes to become a professional filmmaker: "I've always wanted to get into the film industry... for as long as I can remember. I love telling fascinating stories. I love dazzling people with visual effects. I love all types of animation."[33]

From Grief Culture to Rhetorical Construction

"The suicide memorial" is the label of a specific category of video tributes on YouTube. Similar to websites organized by, and in support of, relatives struck by the loss, grief and desperation caused by the suicides of loved ones, the suicide memorial most clearly offers a private shrine for public use which is at the same time a site that may provide comfort, or communal consolation, to a virtual community based on shared loss. Similar to videos made in memory of dead children (death by accident or criminal acts), the suicide memorial on YouTube is often interlinked with other videos or a series of funeral videos edited by organizations and foundations. In this context, the rhetorical construction of Web memorials calls for attention. The aims and goals of interest groups or private foundations make the individual memorial subordinate to specific themes and an explicit call for action. To quote Aaron Hess, the Web memorial should be acknowledged both in terms of performance and social text.[34] A rhetoric of communal interest is added to the video tribute, although it may only be manifest in details such as the logo of a foundation or a rubric that implies murder rather than suicide, such as "Bullied to death."[35] Links to individual websites make the suicide memorial an extension of the Web ring. In this sense, the video tribute may potentially provide a therapeutic tool for grief and a possible channel of shared experience and communal action.

33 "Teen Suicide" - A memorial video

According to the information provided by organizations and fundraisers in connection with suicide memorials on YouTube, harassment and school bullying represent an important social problem that also explains the high rate of teenagers and young adults who commit suicide in the US every year. "Bullying leads to bullycide" is a typical message conveyed by the organized suicide memorial. In the fragmentary account of an interlinked series of photographs, the actual life story of the deceased can only be imagined, and a description of the complex reality of mental illness and suicide is nowhere to be found. Lack of information and critical reflection, or even statements regarding social ills, add to the rhetorical construction of the suicide memorial. Funeral videos may easily be used to bring attention to, for example, the social problem of school bullying, whether or not this actually caused the suicide in question. The video "They committed suicide because of bullying" was edited to commemorate eight teenagers who committed suicide in 2003-2005.[36] Portraits of eight separate youths are accompanied by The Readings' "Wanda's Song," the lyrics of which refer to bullying. In 2007 the song was used frequently in related Web memorials, which the same year resulted in The Wanda Project, dedicated to the problem of "bullycide."[37] A similar example is the video entitled "Teen Suicide Web Tribute," which so far has been seen by 78,018 viewers.[38] Photographs of 12 young boys and girls are presented in a series together with a close relative's commentary for each obituary. "In the United States alone, over 10,000 teens will die by suicide each year. These rates continue to RISE. [...] It's time to change how we think about suicide and what it does to those left behind."

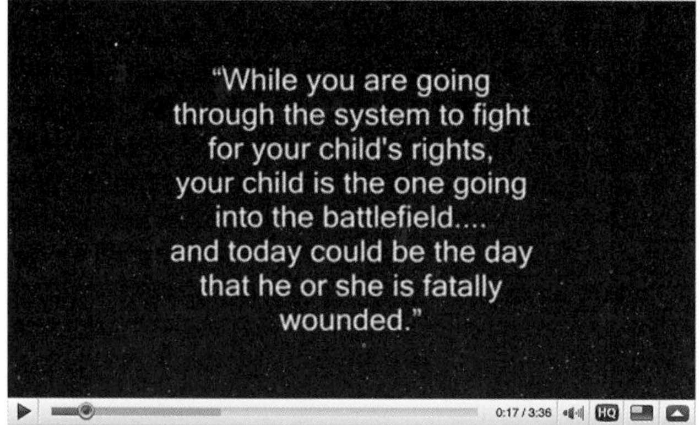

34 "In Loving Memory": Brandon Chris Swartwood (1982–2000)

Research findings have indicated the social and psychological importance of the Web as a communal site where private grief can be expressed and responded to by others with similar experiences. Sites such as www.1000deaths.com provide an entire community of grief dedicated to the victims of suicide, interlinking a number of individual websites.[39] However, YouTube commemoration is a phenomenon that is highly different from the enclosed Web community of a support group's correspondence and text-based testimonies to loss, grief and frustration. The suicide memorial on YouTube seems rather to add to an underground culture of cathartic pleasure, where many commentaries are posted by accidental viewers and by people alien to the grief and anguish experienced by the relatives of suicide victims. Commentaries may express compassion, but they may just as well express contempt, and there are many rude and aggressive remarks as well. In response to a suicide memorial, one of the viewers reacts to the disrespect and scorn expressed in many commentaries:

> I am disturbed and upset by all the mean careless, rude, ignorant, self righteous, and know it all comments on here. I am someone who suffers from several very debilitating psychological conditions and who has attempted suicide more than once in the past, this is a struggle of mine. I have read allot of the comments on here and am amazed at how quick people are to grudge. I am struggling with it right now and found this video looking for something to watch that could help me think straight, It's not easy.[40]

The possibility of immediate response on the Web may help the makers of video tributes in the sense that the subject of their loss is acknowledged by an audience. Also, there are comments written in sympathy and support of the videomaker and messages that convey that deeper sense of understanding only extended by someone who has endured a similar hardship. Meanwhile, by putting family images and private grief on display in the form of a video tribute, individuals also expose themselves to mere voyeurism and the fact that, on YouTube, total strangers will look at their private tragedy, and whether or not they cry when looking, there is also the thrill of the real, the inexplicable attraction of spectacular deaths, and a sense of relief. On YouTube, the perverse voyeurism implied in the suicide memorial is emphasized by the archival logic of sorting videos into a cluster according to a specific theme. As a result, tributes to victims of suicide appear side by side with videos promising spectacular suicides in realtime.[41]

Conclusion: YouTube Commemoration

Similar to the Memory Fence in Oklahoma, Web memorials represent a site where individuals are encouraged to express emotions, to share common experiences, and also to imagine the grief and terror of others. Commentaries to video tributes posted on YouTube reveal a related ritualistic behavior to that of placing flowers, teddy bears, photographs and messages on a memory fence or at the site of accidents and murders. Although national trauma is replaced by the trauma of personal grief, and although the material objects of commemoration are replaced by a virtual counterpart, the Web memorial is also a site of attraction that invokes both catharsis and redemption in the visitor. Erika Doss refers to Georges Bataille to speculate about the possibility that the American public, in its fears of death and dying, may have "equated the visual and material culture of grief with the transformative milieu of the sacred [...] 'a privileged moment of communal unity.' " People go to these places, she further writes, "to see and touch real-life tragedy, to weep and mourn and *feel* in socially acceptable situations. As shrines to trauma, these sites memorialize the horrible events that occurred there, and also the grief of relatives, survivors and complete strangers who feel kinship with those who died. Ghoulish fascination with inexplicable death, with the death of innocents and unfortunates, is accompanied by feelings of guilt and gratitude."[42]

The official memorial is constructed to commemorate the collective loss of national trauma, although the spontaneous rituals conducted at the site of mourning suggest a cathartic act through which the historical event and the "mass body" of victims are replaced by objects and messages that speak of "the dead as individuals."[43] Memorial video tributes on YouTube represent a virtual counterpart in the sense of providing a shrine and an expression of loss that is widely accessible: to the accidental viewer, fellow grievers and users who are attracted by the experience of relief and consolation in crying at the misfortune of others, or in identifying with the grieving parent or partner. The memorial video tribute thus offers a private celebration of the dead to be shared by anybody in cyberspace, a virtual memorial by means of photographs and the affective, nostalgic power of a favorite song, which most of all mirrors a vain attempt to fill the void of loss and grief. Based on family photographs, the video tribute often presents an idealized, retrospective image of family life. In contemporary Web culture, the memorial video tribute stands out as a practice of private commemoration in public, not seldom with a clear therapeutic function for the maker and a cathartic, consoling or even mobilizing function for the viewer. In line with the various websites as shrines to trauma, the video tribute represents an unofficial memorial where the private and existential sphere of grief fuses with the semi-public sphere of amateur culture on YouTube.

Endnotes

1 I borrow the term "vernacular memory" from Aaron Hess, who has studied the difference and overlap between "official and vernacular voices" in the example of 9/11 web memorials. Aaron Hess, "In digital remembrance: vernacular memory and the rhetorical construction of web memorials," *Media Culture & Society* no. 5, 2007, pp. 812–830.

2 See www.mlvp.com/Armedforces.html [last checked 15 February 2009].

3 See, for example, Melissa Abraham, *When We Remember: Inspiration & Integrity for a Meaningful Funeral* (London: Three Things, 2007). The funeral video as a service offered by the funeral business is also exemplified by some examples on YouTube, where the funeral home is indicated at the end of the film.

4 Thomas Lynch, "Funerals-R-Us: From Funeral Home to Mega Industry," *Generation* no. 2, 2004, pp. 11–14.

5 Luc Pauwels, "A private visual practice going public? Social functions and sociological research opportunities of Web-based family photography," *Visual Studies* no. 1, 2008, pp. 34–49.

6 See for example the videos www.youtube.com/watch?v=lHstQv8C2zQ and www.youtube.com/watch?v=-acQZ9ldvQQ&feature=related [last checked 15 February 2009].

7 Kari Andén-Papadopoulos, "US soldiers imaging the Iraq war on YouTube," *Popular Communication. The International Journal of Media and Culture* (forthcoming in 2009).

8 Roland Barthes, *La chambre claire* (Paris: Éditions de l'Étoile, 1980), pp. 148–49.

9 See www.youtube.com/watch?v=SJkmeLULQ2o&feature=related [last checked 15 February 2009]. The video is no longer available due to a copyright claim by WMG].

10 Commentary by bucks932 at www.youtube.com/watch?v=SJkmeLULQ2o&feature=related [last checked 15 February 2009]. This video is no longer available either.

11 Marita Sturken, *Tangled Memories. The Vietnam War, The AIDS Epidemics, and the Politics of Remembering* (Berkeley: University of California Press, 1997), p. 47.

12 For example, see Jacqueline Lewis & Michael R. Fraser, "Patches of Grief and Rage: Visitor Responses to the NAMES Project AIDS Memorial Quilt," *Qualitative Sociology* no. 4, 1996, pp. 433–451.

13 For a critical reassessment of memory as a key word in postmodern theory and what may be described as the "new cultural history," see Kerwin Lee Klein, "On the Emergence of Memory in Historical Discourse," *Representations* no. 69, 2000, pp. 127–150.

14 See for example Dominick LaCapra, *Representing the Holocaust: History, Theory, Trauma* (Ithaca: Cornell University Press, 1994).

15 Erika Doss, "Death, art and memory in the public sphere: the visual and material culture of grief in contemporary America," *Mortality* no. 1, 2002, pp. 68–82. See also Marita Sturken, *Tourists of History. Memory, Kitch, and Consumerism from Oklahoma City to Ground Zero* (Durham and London: Duke University Press, 2007).

16 Sturken 2007, p. 10.

17 Ibid, p. 107.

18 Ibid, p. 5.

19 Hess 2007.

20 Ibid.

21 Lewis & Fraser 1996.

22 Pamela Roberts, "Memorial, Virtual," *Macmillan Encyclopedia of Death and Dying*, ed. R. Kastenbaum (New York: Macmillan, 2003).

23 The Virtual Memorial Garden is located at http://catless.ncl.ac.uk/vmg/.

24 Reiko Schwab, "Acts of Remembrance, Cherished Possessions, and Living Memorials," *Generations* no. 2, 2004, pp. 26–30.

25 See, for example, "The Jessica Marie Lunsford Foundation. Helping Children in Crisis" at www.youtube.com/watch?v=Z2Y7b8EBGBg&feature=related. See also the video "Bullied to Death (Music: Lithium)," which is dedicated to "victims of bullies" [last checked 15 February 2009].

26 Pauwels 2008.

27 Marianne Hirsch, *Family Frames: Photography, Narrative, and Postmemory* (Cambridge, MA: Harvard University Press, 1997).

28 Susan Sontag, *On Photography* (New York: Penguin Books, 1977), p. 17.

29 The video "Tribute to Jeff Soriano" is located at www.youtube.com/watch?v=Jko5P06L2hl&NR=1 [last checked 15 February 2009].

30 See Chicago www.youtube.com/watch?v=Jko5P06L2hl&feature=related [last checked 15 February 2009].

31 For a more extensive account of approximate realtime and documentary representation, see Malin Wahlberg, *Documentary Time. Film and Phenomenology* (Minneapolis and London: University of Minnesota Press, 2008).

32 See www.youtube.com/watch?v=Jko5P06L2hl&feature=related [last checked 15 February 2009].

33 See www.youtube.com/user/regisor94 [last checked 15 February 2009].

34 Hess 2007.

35 See www.youtube.com/watch?v=gE5ylNOn4N4 [last checked 15 February 2009].

36 Ibid.

37 The Wanda Project was initiated in 2007 by Brenda High, whose son is thought to have committed suicide because of bullying.

38 See www.youtube.com/watch?v=FXqocdThk8s [last checked 15 February 2009].

39 See, for example, Erica Michaels Hollander, "Cyber Community in the Valley of the Shadow of Death," *Journal of Loss and Trauma* no. 6, 2001, pp. 135–146.

40 Commentary by Abu Born92587 at www.youtube.com/watch?v=dnyOEm7GIHE&feature=related [last checked 15 February 2009].

41 Looking at the "related videos" listed with the suicide memorials examples above, several clips perform or mimic suicide acts, explicitly playing with actual death as screen attraction on YouTube. See, for example, "My Last Video," www.youtube.com/watch?v=w3z-8QLUEG4&feature=related [last checked 15 February 2009].

42 Doss 2002.

43 Sturken 1997, p. 173.

Markus Stauff

Sports on YouTube

While sports is an important topic on YouTube, it seems to be one among many others. The procedures of uploading and accessing videos lead to a heterogeneous agglomeration of topics and styles. Clicking and commenting relate and rank videos in ways that don't adhere to strict classifications of genres. "Sports" is one of fifteen default "categories" of YouTube, and although there are even some channels specializing in sports, they are not remotely as prominent as sports channels are on television (this applies to "most subscribed" as well as to "most viewed"). Videos that depict sports in one way or the other show all the typical forms and variations of other topics on YouTube and are linked to clips that don't deal with sports but show related emotions, gimmicks, ideologies or visual pleasures. Of course, there are innumerable clips that focus on the "sexy" (mostly female) bodies of athletes.[1] If such a clip is selected, the "Related Videos" overview lists videos of sports competitions (without focusing on "sexiness") and videos of "sexy bodies" (unrelated to sports). There are thousands of clips that show funny and bizarre examples of sporting life, from programs featuring bowling with a frozen turkey to "Funny Sports Bloopers" that show mishaps during actual sport competitions—be it amateur tennis or professional ice skating.[3] And there are also numbers of appropriations that change the meaning of professional sports footage through re-editing, image processing or comments.

The often mentioned features of YouTube, for example the de- and recontextualization of short clips, the individual appropriation, the coexistence of professional and amateur footage, and the attention seeking through "fun" and "sex" affect the depiction of sports as that of any other topic. This raises two interrelated and quite simple questions. If we look at other media—press, film, radio, television—sports has always been (in economic and aesthetic terms) an especially important topic for the development of these media, while the respective specifications of the different media shaped sports at the same time. In this article I want to discuss if and how sports—despite the described indifference of YouTube—uses or accentuates features or aspects of YouTube that other topics don't. Complimentarily, I want to ask how the procedures of YouTube contribute to the public image of and communications about sports. The underlying assumption is that because of the historically well-established sports-media complex, the research of sport representations in a particular medium (and especially a "new" one like YouTube) can contribute to our understanding of the specificities of this medium as they relate to the specific representational features of sports in general.

35 "Turkey Bowling": Practicing sports in inapproriate surroundings

Sports is not understood here as a topic, but rather as a field of knowledge and communication that follows specific rules. My main argument is that the established modes and procedures in "media sports" are still retraceable on YouTube (and contribute some of their dynamics to it), but that the dynamics of YouTube somehow subvert the main procedures of media sports. Thus, sports on YouTube is in some aspects tied to other media but in others detached. Insofar as it is detached from other media content and defined dominantly by YouTube's own procedures and practices, sports becomes, interestingly enough, less and less sports—at least in a more narrow sense that will be elaborated upon below.

Media Sports: Comparison and Knowledge Production

In traditional mass media, sports has become one of the most common topics; sports is integrated into news (more systematically than other arrays of popular culture) and quiz and talk shows, and is a recurrent theme in fictional productions as well. References to sports come in any format and thus in any aesthetic mode the media has at its disposal. Nevertheless, there seems to be not only a specific and outstanding array for sports in many media, but also a very specific function of sports in the historical development of mass media. Newspapers and magazines have had sports pages since the end of the 19th century; radio and television have regular sports programs in addition to special live events. These special arrays of media sports have a significant look—be it the photographs of bodies in motion, the accumulation of statistics or the mix of slow-motion replay with graphic inserts—thus highlighting specific aspects of the media.[3]

It would be an exaggeration to say that sports has always been a decisive factor when establishing a new medium. Yet, it was regularly an early topic—for film, radio as well as television.[4] Sports, no doubt, contributed to formal and technical innovations and also to a kind of (self-)reflection of media. The reason for that is not only the sheer quantitative importance of sports in popular culture (and thus its relevance as a tool of attention economy), but also the specific structures of perception and modes of knowledge that are established by sports. Here, it becomes important to have a clear definition of what sports is. In common language, fitness culture, hiking with friends, and climbing a mountain on your own may all be called sports—and there are of course YouTube clips on all these activities listed under the heading or keyword "sports." Still, these heterogeneous activities don't provoke special treatment by the media or special formats and technological solutions. Only a more narrowly defined notion of sports, i.e. as organized, rule-guided, repeated competition, produces a significant form of media display, thus becoming an incentive for defining, reflecting and developing media further. This is not to say that hiking, aerobics or going swimming with some friends shouldn't count as sports; still, when researching the significance of media sports, making distinctions remains important. The way the word "sports" is used in contemporary society (especially since it has also become a major metaphor for talking about politics, business and so on), somehow distracts from the fact that the kind of sports that was constituted by modern mass media as a particular (if also heterogeneous) field is not just another form of entertainment, but implies a specific use of media.

Such a distinction and insight into the specific conjunction of media and sports can be further clarified by looking at sports' origination and development in the 19th century. Tobias Werron argues that modern competitive sports is constituted by the public comparison of performances and thus is, from its beginning, a media sport.[5] The decisive difference between modern sports and older forms of games, of ritualistic competitions, of occasional or spontaneous contests lies in the very existence of a broad media audience beyond the audience in the stadium. It is this public communication about sports that leads to the integration of the single contest into a continuous comparison of performances, a significant trait of contemporary media sports. This originated in the second half of the 19th century, when the combination of telegraphy and mass-circulation newspapers not only provided reports on individual competitions and their results, but also related—on one page, in one table, in one article—competitions from different times and places to each other. The continuous flow of similar contests organized by the newly established leagues and the constant coverage of events are obviously dependent on one another. It is well known that the second half of the 19th century saw a standardization of rules and playing grounds that is closely connected to the serialized and hierarchical organization of competitions. Both aspects—standardization as well as serialization—only make sense because "the telegraph-press-alliance opened up the horizon for the invention and testing of such institutions [as leagues, records, world championships] and, by doing so, first initiated the trend towards standardized rules and new modes of competition which has remained at the heart of the sport system."[6]

While the contingent course of the individual event is still an important source of sports' attraction, this attraction is itself defined by the relation to non-present performances and achievements. This doesn't refer solely to the results (where a win can be worth more or less depending on the result of distant games involving competitors), but also to the way the result is achieved. Because the competitions are separated, it becomes imperative to compare not only the bare results, but also the circumstances of the achievements and parts and aspects of performances to which results can be ascribed. If you want to compare two teams that have not yet played each other, it is not sufficient to know their previous results; rather, it is important to know where the results came from (a coach training his or her team, or a fan discussing the future chances of his or her team). If, then, modern sports is constituted partly by the communication about and especially the comparison of performances, the visibility of the performance and the possibility of attributing the results to isolated components are of special importance. Here again, it is media that produce sports by providing "criteria of observation and evaluation such as statistics, records, historical narratives, legends, etc., thereby widening and refining the scope of comparison."[7] As is always the case with knowledge production, the media technologies that are used define the objects of knowledge. This means that the narrative and statistical sophistication decides "how complex, universal and global a competitive culture can possibly become by reflecting performances and evaluating them."[8] Media are thus constitutive for modern sports because they define what can be recognized as a relevant aspect of a performance and an achievement.

Without going into further detail, it can be argued that media sports became a distinctive format, genre or mode of representation not only because of its economic success, but also because of different aesthetic characteristics. As modern sports is constituted by media that relate the distinct performances and make them comparable in detailed ways, media sports became outstanding in its use of the most heterogenic procedures—from statistics and slow motion to biographical information and ethnic ascriptions—to make the athletic achievements transparent and comparable. Media sports is, hence, specific in the way knowledge has to be produced again and again: some event—a competition—is not merely shown but dissected into its particular elements. In contrast to history or science programs on television, the goal of knowledge production in sports is to enable audiences to form their own opinions. Contrary to the common idea that media sports has over time become sort of a spectacle—if not a complete simulation—sports is in fact marked by a highly referential aspect: it not only shows external happenings but uses all the available tools to find out something about them. Media sports can be characterized by its intense procedures of knowledge production that combine specialized information (like medical, technical and tactical data) with popular and commonly accessible modes of knowledge (such as speculations on psychological or personal reasons for a given performance).[9]

Accessing the Events: YouTube as Secondary Medium

The question is, then, how YouTube inserts itself into this dynamic. How does YouTube, for instance, contribute to and transform the comparison of performances? How does this desire of media sports to compare performances make use of (and thus transform) YouTube? Two significant features of YouTube are of special interest here: first, its highly intermedial and remediating character, and second, its principles of relating and comparing different items. While sports is always constituted by a whole constellation of different (and quite heterogenic) media, YouTube (still) exists as a reworking and reconnecting of prior products of different media. Sports is constituted by mediated (but in a way systemized and standardized) modes of comparison, but YouTube functions more as a machine that relates items (and makes them comparable) in multiple and often unexpected ways.

Being part of the constellation of media sports, YouTube works above all as a secondary resource, making accessible what is defined as relevant by other media. More than any other topic, sports structures a regular and direct production of and access to YouTube clips, while YouTube provides sports with the possibility of revising its most important moments. On any given Monday, for example, the goals of most European football leagues are available up on YouTube.[10] They are easily accessible by their dates, the names of the teams and the players, and they are hierarchized and preselected by, for example, newspapers or Internet sports portals that hint at the most sensational scores. As a kind of archive, YouTube mixes different materials and modes of production: while some sports organizations, like the NBA, have their own channel on YouTube where they post highlight clips, others are not present at all. In such cases, users may upload television footage or their own recordings (from cellphone cameras for instance). While sports facilitates a direct access to material, it also makes evident the restrictions of YouTube, especially the removal of clips due to copyright infringements. During the Beijing Olympics in 2008, all postings of regular television material were removed in the course of one or two days. However, users anticipated this procedure by posting clips referring to other Web pages where clips not allowed on YouTube could be found.[11] Even if YouTube does not work as a comprehensive archive for media sports, it is nevertheless structured according to a quasi-archival mode of access.

As a consequence, YouTube is secondary in the sense that other media determine the relevance of the happenings that are looked up on the site. It is live television broadcast that define the moment of importance. A significant portion of the material posted on YouTube is taken from television, often only slightly modified. Even for sports competitions that are not shown on television, other media mainly structure the access to YouTube clips. If a sports event is reported on in newspapers or in online forums, clips (of a competition which was not broadcasted) often get higher click ratings than otherwise. A recent European basketball game between Alba Berlin and KK Bosna Sarajevo serves as a case in point. There was no television broadcast of this game; however, it turned out to be not only the longest game ever played in European professional basketball—five overtimes—but also the one with the highest final score, 141 to 127. The game was, hence, reported in media that normally don't write anything about basketball, and as a consequence, the YouTube clip recorded by a fan received much more attention than the usual clips on European games.

As other features of sports on YouTube that will be dealt with below, the structure of the quasi-archival access is deeply dependent on the kind of sport, with occasionally completely different structuring of time, space and events as well as, of course, a completely different structure of copyright and availability—an aspect that cannot be elaborated on appropriately here.

Referentiality, Condensation and Reinterpretation

Sports periodically generates well-defined events that are objectively (in quantifiable terms) outstanding and present in all media. While different media depictions of sports are closely related, together they claim to refer to an external event. The highly referential mode of media sports becomes especially noticeable in the fact that there are different broadcasts of one and the same event—often from different countries with commentary in different languages. As a result of the complicated and highly restrictive copyrights of sports broadcasts, users can at times only find scenes from some international competition in languages they don't understand. However, on YouTube the main focus is often the depicted performance. This means that grainy images can be important also, such as if they depict an outstanding performance worth watching even if only outlines of the athletes are recognizable.

The externally defined need or desire to see something very often contributes to an ongoing reflection on the way the media work. The quality of the images and the ways the television sportscasters make their comments is discussed very often. Of course, this problematic revolves around various copyright issues that also become especially apparent in the field of sports and are explicitly discussed by fans. Hence, user-generated clips that show a competition as a sequence of still photographs or as an animation using Playmobil or Lego figures are not only a funny or artistic appropriation of professional material,[12] they are also reminders of the fact that the "real" event is not accessible and are very explicitly only approximations of this "real" event. Thus, sports contributes in a direct and specific way to what Thomas Elsaesser has described as the "necessary performance of failure" that accompanies the "constructive instability" of emerging media.[13]

While YouTube's depiction of sports is closely related to television (and other media), it nevertheless changes the way sports is shown and accessed. The most obvious issue here is the highly selective aspect of YouTube, which reduces sports to remarkable moments (or to series of such moments) and finally recontextualizes these moments in different ways. In a sense, YouTube pursues only the different levels of condensed repetition that are already established in television (and my argument would be that sports on YouTube is, here again, more directly structured by traditional mass media than a similar reworking of other media material). During live broadcasts, some scenes are made more valuable by an instant replay. The same goes for post-game interviews and highlights programs, where the performance often gets reduced to single moments. In all these cases the definition of some moments as highlights changes the meanings of these moments that, on the one hand, have to represent the whole game; on the other hand, fragmenting the continuity of the performance opens it up for more production of heterogeneous meaning.[14] It is no wonder that YouTube not only continues this process but also does so by using similar criteria as television. The communication of sports always deals with the question of what the most decisive moments of the competition actually were. While there is an incentive to discover hidden aspects, the search for decisive happenings is nevertheless common to different kinds of sports. The preponderance of goals, fouls, tricks, etcetera on YouTube is not only due to the endeavor to pick the most spectacular, but also adheres to the fact that these are the most evident moments of relevance. This becomes even clearer when YouTube clips deal with disputable happenings, above all with referees' decisions.[15] The clips, then, are meant as pure evidence for a specific type of action. If it is indeed completely indisputable, as when a ball hit Brazil's Rivaldo on his leg during the World Cup in 2002 and he pretended it struck him in the face,[16] such clips rapidly become a joke related to other "funny" videos. But if a situation isn't as unambiguous as the author of the description proclaims, a furious discussion might arise in which images are interpreted in contrary ways. If television reduces the partisanship characteristic for sports—mainly because of the demand for objectivity[17]—YouTube seems to reintroduce this partisanship into media sports. Most clips that are posted don't aim at a non-biased view of a competition, but at the praise (or denunciation) of a team or athlete. The discussion about a clip often becomes rude, not seldom outspokenly nationalist or racist. YouTube doesn't offer many other possibilities to react than by anonymous comment or a related video; it doesn't integrate tools for appropriating and reworking the given video, or for chatting. Ways of using clips to discuss "actual" happenings are, thus, clearly restricted.[18]

Modes of Comparing

In all the examples mentioned above, sports seems to underline the database logic of YouTube.[19] Particular items are addressed because there is an external reason to view the clip and because it is possible to access items directly by name, date or category of event. This becomes especially obvious when the database is used not for a repetition and reviewing of—or compensation for—an important event whose live broadcast on television is now either gone or didn't exist at all, but as a tool for assessing future possibilities. Fans who discuss the chances of their team against the next competitor or the qualities of a player who will join their team for the next season use YouTube clips to gather information or support their argument. The short and condensed form of YouTube clips, especially "best-of compilations" that have already compiled the most remarkable scenes with a certain team or player, fit the requirements of such usages. Again, there are external incentives for this kind of use and the discussions mainly take place in more specialized online forums. Furthermore these discussions, referring to a reality beyond the clip, assess not only the depicted performance but also the reliability of the clip itself, i.e. if it is a "representative" selection of situations and so on.

36 Stylization of real sports using computer games

As a consequence, the referential and intermedial dynamics of media sports highlight YouTube's function as a database. At the same time, the site modifies access to sports, especially, as Cornel Sandvoss argues, its spatial determinations. "The coverage of sporting events on the Internet contributes to the dual tendencies of cultural 'homogenization and fragmentation' in that it has aided the formation of transnational sports fandom while simultaneously eroding the coherence of national sporting cultures that formed in the post-war era of nation state-centered broadcasting."[20] Still, YouTube places sports performances in a different context than other media, and its specific mechanisms of comparison and interrelation change the depiction as well as the communication related to sports in a more profound way. While such online formats as live tickers, sports portals or fan chats feature modes of knowledge production quite similar to those of television sports—in fact, they are based on the knowledge and also the imaginations generated by television[21]—YouTube features dynamics that just don't fit media sports. The heterogeneous relations built up inside YouTube detach the sports clips from the modes of communication established by other media.

37 Zidane vs. Materazzi

Most clips on YouTube that can be related to the topic of sports do not contribute to the communication on sports in this narrower sense. One of the typical modes of appropriation in YouTube takes cultural products, be it a film or a sports competition, and transforms its meaning by re-staging or re-editing it. These kinds of clips are interesting because they are somehow between the database logic defined by the sports discourse and YouTube's dynamic of recontextualization that goes way beyond sports' comparison of performances. The decisive scenes of the 2008 Super Bowl, for example, famous for its surprising outcome and also for the most remarkable performances, can be watched as "real" video as well as an animation done with an early, now nearly "classic" football computer game.[22] Still, it is significant for sports that these appropriations are used to understand and discuss the "real" happenings and to criticize the television commentary. The more weird appropriations of sports events don't aim at the most accurate re-staging of the happenings, but they can still be related to sports' incentive to discover how it happened. Take the innumerable video comments on the infamous headbutt by Zinedine Zidane during the World Cup final of 2006. Using visual effects, videos commenting on the "event" replace, for example, one of the two players involved with a lamppost, an armed "terrorist," and so on. Thus, they still contribute, at least on a metaphorical level, to the ongoing speculation concerning what really happened on the field and what the reasons were for this behavior.

While these examples, then, are still connected to the communication on sports, using various remediations to gain insight into "real" happenings, they obviously go beyond mere comparison of performances. Naturally, YouTube is a huge machine for relating and comparing; even a single clip often presents sequences or rankings of comparable items, from the best touchdowns and the most embarrassing knockouts to the sexiest athletes. YouTube's various mechanisms of linking different clips guarantee that there are no clear criteria and no borders for comparisons. This means, for example, that the worst fouls or the sexiest athletes are compared, that changes from different leagues and different levels are comparable, and of course, it also means that the appropriation of a sporting event by means of a computer game is related to similar appropriations of a film or anything else. There is, quite simply, no specific means of comparison that fits the very systematic requirements of sports. Where YouTube contributes to the comparison of sports performances, it does so on the basis of and in close connection with other media. The embedding of videos in online forums, blogs, etcetera involves them in a communication on sports that is not identifiable as a distinct field on the pages of YouTube.

Conclusion

While YouTube is, as a database, well integrated into the media sports complex, the site's way of relating and comparing are at the moment of no particular use for modern competitive sports. This doesn't mean that YouTube's modes of comparison are chaotic, unreliable or of no use at all. Rather, it remains significant that practices that are somehow connected to sports but can't be considered sports according to the more narrow definition benefit from the dynamics of YouTube—and might even be dependent on them. Significant examples are some dance cultures or the subculture urban performance of Parkour.[23] Both are developing into global phenomenona because of YouTube's possibilities for comparing the movements of other practitioners (whether as historical examples or innovative advancements). The mode of comparison, however, aims not at the same amount in a (quantifiable) comparison of performances, and it surely doesn't aim at the (referential) decision of whether this or that movement was right or wrong, decisive (for a final result) or not. Furthermore, it is precisely the fact that these forms are not already pre-structured by other media, television in particular (through its aesthetic and economic forces), that enables their presence on YouTube to give them a specific organization.[24]

While sports, as has been shown in this article, accentuates specific aspects of YouTube and contributes to its structure (at least the structure of its access), there are at present no procedures in YouTube that contribute to the comparison of sports performance in a more specific way. YouTube has adopted several of the dynamics of media sports, but the site itself is not a medium participating in the definition and production of sports. Rather, it (more often than not) subverts the modes of communication that constitute modern sports. This can be explained by the "deficits" of YouTube—the absence of possibilities for a more structured discussion and more systematic and meaningful relation between clips. Yet, it can also be explained as a result of the unobstructed operation of YouTube's most significant features: the accumulation of relations that are defined by a wide range of practices, semantics and technologies. Looking at YouTube, it becomes clear that sports is based on a specialized, defined and also hierarchized form of communication. Looking at sports on YouTube, it also becomes clear how undifferentiating YouTube's modes of listing, comparing and ordering actually are.

Endnotes

1 See e.g. "The 10 Hottest Female Athletes" – www.youtube.com/watch?v=u_KvIzo3cFc&feature=channel_page [last checked 15 February 2009].

2 See http://www.youtube.com/watch?v=mfAsibkCmZw; and www.youtube.com/watch?v=1796OXXdVzs; and finally www.youtube.com/watch?v=0iks s1fGCZE&feature=related [last checked 15 February 2009].

3 For an historical overview, see Janet Lever & Stanton Wheeler, "Mass Media and the Experience of Sport," *Communication Research* no. 1, 1993, pp. 125–143.

4 See Dan Streible, *Fight Pictures. A History of Boxing and Early Cinema* (Berkeley: University of California Press, 2008) and Douglas Gomery, *A History of Broadcasting in the United States* (Oxford: Blackwell, 2008).

5 Tobias Werron, " 'World Series'. Zur Entstehung eines Weltereignisses," in *Weltereignisse. Theoretische und empirische Perspektiven*, eds. Stefan Nacke et al. (Wiesbaden, Germany: Verlag für Socialwissenschaften, 2008), pp. 101–140.

6 Tobias Werron, "World sport and its public. On historical relations of modern sport and the media," in *Observing Sport. System-Theoretical Approaches to Sport as a Social Phenomenon*, eds. Ulrik Wagner & Rasmus Storm (forthcoming).

7 Ibid.

8 Ibid.

9 Markus Stauff, "Zur Sichtbarmachung von Strategie und Taktik. Die mediale Organisation des Kollektivs in Sportwissenschaft und Fernsehen," in *Strategie Spielen. Medialität, Geschichte und Politik des Strategiespiels*, eds. Rolf F. Nohr & Serjoscha Wiemer (Hamburg: LIT Verlag, 2008), pp. 162–188.

10 As I am interested in the main intersections of YouTube and sports, I focus on the most prominent examples, i.e. the kinds of sport that are televised on a regular basis. It would, of course, be necessary to research not only why some sports are generally less prominent (often a question of national success and also of historical coincidences), but also what kinds of sport better fit the procedures of YouTube.

11 See e.g. www.youtube.com/watch?v=LznMSKpEWz8 [last checked 15 February 2009]; this one uses some stills from a football game following the preliminary caption: "YouTube's Terms of Service doesn't allow me

to post this video here! CLICK on the link in description to watch FULL video!!!" For a more general survey on copyright infringements, see the contribution by Paul McDonald in this book.

12 See www.youtube.com/watch?v=xh8WQUJNcKE [last checked 15 February 2009].

13 Thomas Elsaesser, " 'Constructive Instability', or: The Life of Things as the Cinema's Afterlife?" in *The Video Vortex Reader. Responses to YouTube*, eds. Geert Lovink & Sabine Niederer (Amsterdam: Institute of Network Cultures, 2008), p. 19.

14 Travis Thad Vogan, "Football-Highlights. Zur Politik der zusammenfassenden Sportberichterstattung," in *Mediensport. Strategien der Grenzziehung*, eds. Felix Axster et al. (Munich, 2009).

15 Typical examples are traveling and double dribbles in basketball (www.youtube.com/watch?v=Uo9TyFCEz1k&NR=1 and www.youtube.com/watch?v=ty6DA8SGGYg&NR=1) and fouls or dives in football (www.youtube.com/watch?v=Eu90rhU4Pi0 [last checked 15 February 2009]).

16 www.youtube.com/watch?v=UgfRCa71Kmw [last checked 15 February 2009].

17 Geoffry Nowell-Smith, "Television – Football – The World," *Screen* no. 4, 1978/79, pp. 45–59.

18 A more in-depth analysis of these limitations of YouTube can be found in Jean E. Burgess & Joshua Green, "Agency and Controversy in the YouTube Community," in *Proceedings IR 9.0: Rethinking Communities, Rethinking Place –Association of Internet Researchers (AoIR) conference* (Copenhagen: IT University of Copenhagen, 2008) – http://eprints.qut.edu.au/15383/1/15383.pdf [last checked 15 February 2009].

19 Lev Manovich, "Database as Symbolic Form," *Convergence* no. 2, 1999, pp. 80–99.

20 Cornel Sandvoss, "Technological Evolution or Revolution? Sport Online Live Internet Commentary as Postmodern Cultural Form," *Convergence* no. 3, 2004, pp. 39–54.

21 Ibid.

22 Examples of animations done with the computer game Tecmo SuperBowl can be found at www.youtube.com/watch?v=m1VPaEjks2U and www.youtube.com/watch?v=KQU8p40qcuQ&feature=related [last checked 15 February 2009].

23 Samantha Carroll, "The Practical Politics of Step-Stealing and Textual Poaching: YouTube, Audio-Visual Media and Contemporary Swing Dancers Online," *Convergence* no. 14, 2008, pp. 107–120; Rebekka Ladewig, "The rabbit hole is deeper than you think! Zur medialen Inszenierung von Parkour," in *Mediensport. Strategien der Grenzziehung*, eds. Felix Axster et al. (Munich, 2009).

24 This might in part also be the case for some kinds of sports that are indeed defined by the mediated "comparison of performances," but that are also not on television (at least not very prominent). In this context it would, for example, be worth scrutinizing more carefully the case of poker (this was pointed out by Tobias Werron) or the practice of "stacking," where people reorder plastic cups in a specific succession as quickly as possible – www.youtube.com/watch?v=U951R_r-3fM [last checked 15 February 2009].

Vinzenz Hediger

YouTube and the Aesthetics of Political Accountability

In late March 2009, Senator Jim Webb, a first-term Democrat from Virginia, Vietnam veteran, former journalist, bestselling author of novels and history books and a former Secretary of the Navy in the Reagan administration, took the floor of the Senate to propose a sweeping reform of the US prison system. Webb pointed out that the United States is home to five percent of the world's population—and 25 percent of its prison population. He went on to link the high incarceration rate to a failed drug policy that criminalizes consumption and leads to the imprisonment of legions of otherwise harmless and innocent people as drug offenders. Webb's move was generally hailed as utterly courageous, and as a move from a politician who obviously cared for the common good more than for his own political future.[1]

Webb comes from a conservative Southern state and won his seat in the 2006 mid-term election by a narrow margin of just a few thousand votes. His victory was all the more remarkable because the incumbent was a relative heavyweight: George Allen, a former two-term governor of Virginia and, at the time of his re-election campaign, one of the front-runners for the Republican party's presidential nomination in 2008. Allen had led Webb by double-digit margins for most of the campaign but lost narrowly after a harrowing finale. There is a consensus that one single element, more than any other, contributed to Allen's loss.[2] On August 11, 2006, at one of his campaign rallies in a rural area of Virginia, Allen spoke to a crowd of supporters. At one point he addressed an Indian-American in the audience, S.R. Sidarth, who worked for the Webb campaign and was following him with a video camera, as a "macaca." Media commentators later argued that "macaca" was a Northern African slur for dark-skinned people which Allen may or may not have picked up from his mother, a native Algerian (who was, as it turned out shortly after Allen had gotten into trouble for his supposedly repeated use of racial slurs, of Sephardic Jewish descent[3]), but which was not a common racial slur in rural Virginia.

Nonetheless, the intent to offend the dark-skinned young man and to expose him to the ire of the crowd was transparent in Allen's comments as they were recorded on tape. Allen not only introduced Sidarth, a Virginia native, to the crowd as "macaca," but went on to welcome him to America, marking out a difference between the "real America," represented by Allen and his followers, and some other America to which, he implied, Sidarth belonged. To Allen's lasting chagrin, his remarks were not only recorded—but instantly made available to a large audience on YouTube.[4]

38 "Welcome to America": George Allen's "macaca moment"

Sidarth's tape furnished incontrovertible proof of Allen's racist slip-up and was picked up by national television networks, creating a major political controversy that dominated news coverage for several days. Allen, in fact, had to go on *Meet the Press*, the flagship of the Sunday morning political talk shows, and try to explain his way out of what he had said at his campaign rally. But to no avail. The meme of Allen's subliminal racism was set, and in short order investigative journalists dug up stories of other examples of racists outbursts from friends and former colleagues. They even found out that Allen had something of a fetish for the Confederate flag, which he had used to decorate his home and office ever since his arrival in Virginia in 1967. To a large extent, then, it would seem that Jim Webb owes his Senate seat, and George Allen the end of his political career, to S.R. Sidarth and his videocamera. It should not come as a surprise that "macaca moment" has now become a standing expression in the American political lexicon.[5]

YouTube and Political Statistics

One way of summing up the story of George Allen's political demise is to say that he succumbed to YouTube. A number of factors explain how Allen went from a double-digit lead early in the race to defeat and from being the Great White Republican Hope to political oblivion. Due to the Bush administration's indisputable incompetence and the Iraq war, Republicans had become unpopular even in some of their erstwhile strongholds by the fall of 2006. In addition Virginia, one such former stronghold, had gone through a demographic shift, with the state's North effectively becoming a large suburb of Washington, DC, as large groups of relatively wealthy, politically liberal new residents moved in. In a situation already unfavorable to the incumbent senator, the "macaca moment" probably just delivered the death blow. Exposure of Allen's racist invective on YouTube prompted the mainstream media, and in particular cable news channels and political talk shows, to pick up the story and air the tape, giving it much broader play and a larger audience than it had already gained on the Internet. A critical number of Virginia voters may then have decided to turn out and vote for Jim Webb, thus defeating a politician who clearly represented the Grand Old Party in all its fading glory.

From the evidence of George Allen's travails it would seem that YouTube has changed the political process. The question is how. One way to account for the impact of YouTube on the political process would be to try and measure it.[6] One of the attractive features of YouTube is that it generates its own statistics and lists the number of viewings below every video posted. For instance, Barack Obama's April 2008 speech on race in Philadelphia was viewed a combined 7.5 million times—there are two versions on Barack Obama's YouTube channel alone. While 7.5 million is still a far cry from the 30 or 35 million viewers Obama was able to reach with his 30-minute infomercial broadcast over four networks a few days before the November 2008 election, this is a significant figure. As of this writing, in spring 2009, will.i.am.'s famous "Yes We Can" video, which was based on an excerpt from Obama's New Hampshire primary concession speech, had been viewed a combined 24.1 million times.[7] This is still only slightly more than half of the 43 million viewings for the video of Paul Pott's original performance of "Nessun dorma" on *Britain's Got Talent*, and it is less than the 25 million viewings kitchen-help-turned-singing-sensation Susan Boyle generated with one video of her first appearance on *Britain's Got Talent*'s series 3 in April 2009 in less than a week.[8] Still, it is a big number. But what do these numbers mean?

Commentators generally agree that Obama's speech on race marked a pivotal moment in his campaign. With it, the candidate managed to defuse the issue of race for the remainder of the campaign.[9] But how much of the speech's impact can we attribute to YouTube? Obama's speech on race is a 40-minute piece of oratory, and viewing it represents a considerable investment in terms of time and attention. The fact that 7.5 million viewers were willing to make that investment is certainly indicative of something. But of what? Similarly, the will.–i.am video was considered one of the key motivational tools for young Obama supporters, a YouTube rallying cry of sorts. But once again, one would be hard pressed to come up with a specific assessment of the video's impact. Roughly one third of the 24.1 million viewings actually came after November 4, which seems to indicate that viewing this video has a ritual and celebratory aspect that does not directly translate into any measurable action.

Sidarth's video recording of George Allen's "macaca moment," by the way, registered almost 390,000 viewings. Given the size of Virginia's population of approximately 7.65 million, and the fact that Webb won by less than one half of one percent of the total vote—less than 15,000 votes—this is still statistically significant. But it is also safe to assume that the video owed its impact not only to YouTube, but to a feedback effect as well. The video became an online sensation only after it had been picked up by television news programs. It would seem, then, that YouTube statistics are of little value for an inquiry that seeks to establish a causal relationship between YouTube and certain outcomes of the political process. If such an explanation is indeed what one has in mind. Probably the most exact statement that can be made about Obama's YouTube viewing statistics is that they do not contradict other statistics that have emerged in relation to the Obama phenomenon. Both polling during the campaign and the ballot returns indicated that Obama was the overwhelming favorite among young voters. This demographic also goes online more than other segments of the population and prefers social-networking and interactive sites such as YouTube. At best, this is a case of statistics that reinforce each other by not contradicting one another.

But perhaps the key to the meaning of YouTube playlist figures is observing the observer—that is, reading the readings they generate. When the McCain campaign released its now infamous "Biggest celebrity" attack ad that equated Barack Obama with Britney Spears and Paris Hilton in August 2008, the viewing statistics shot up very quickly and reached a level above any of those for the other videos released on the McCain YouTube channel.[10] A McCain spokeswoman read this as an indicator that the political tide was turning and that McCain was now reaching the youth vote, a key demographic that had hitherto eluded the aging Vietnam veteran. It took the acumen of left-wing bloggers to point out that many of these viewings likely came from Obama supporters who watched the video out of general interest, if not in order to motivate themselves to work even harder for their candidate.

Thus, all the YouTube viewing statistics mean is that the video in question has meaning to a certain group of people. As sociologist Jeffrey C. Alexander argues with regards to the will.i.am "Yes We Can" video, YouTube becomes a site for a symbolic fusion of actor and audience, a symbolic site in the civil public sphere where the audience affirms the political actor's success at addressing the key political issues of his moment.[11]

With access to YouTube's internal traffic data, one could of course come up with very specific indications as to the geographic location of those viewers, as well as other kinds of information.[12] But for good reasons this information is not available to outsiders.[13] And if it were, it would still not teach us much about why these people watched the clip. You can of course turn to the comments section and read the posts. There are usually a lot fewer comments than there are viewings. But the comments often contain explicit statements as to why and how the viewers viewed a particular video. Bloggers such as Andrew Sullivan have developed a way of reading comments with a statistical eye. If they want to gauge the impact of a particular statement by themselves or another blogger, they routinely turn to the comments section and perform what you might call a spontaneous content analysis, weighing the numbers of positive and negative responses. But while such exercises may aspire to the scientific, the results they yield fail to be more than indicators of something that remains essentially undetectable.

YouTube statistics, then, pretend to be exact but remain opaque. They are primarily symbolic indicators of cultural relevance. They mark out nodes of cultural discourse saturated with meaning. As such, they establish and enact a difference between surface and depth to the Internet. They indicate that something is happening, and we need to figure out what. Or, to phrase it more academically, they present a symbolic surface that calls for political and cultural hermeneutics, an analysis that reveals their hidden meaning and suggests a theoretical model such as the one proposed by Jeffrey Alexander that explains their social and cultural dynamics.

Performances on Camera

But then again, the political meaning of YouTube also resides in what is plainly visible, the videos themselves. After he had secured the Republican nomination for president, John McCain gave a televised speech that became instantly famous for two aspects of its delivery. McCain finished every sentence with a forced smile that looked like an awkward grimace, and he delivered the speech in front of a green background. Not only did the green background make McCain look sick, it also provided an opportunity for digital remix artists to seamlessly insert backdrops from other films and television programs. After all, "green screen" is the technical term for neutral backgrounds that allow an actor's performance to be combined with any footage you choose. Political satirist Stephen Colbert seized the opportunity and launched a "green screen challenge," inviting his viewers to remix the McCain speech with any material they pleased.[14] While Colbert broadcast the best entries on Comedy Central's *Colbert Report*, most of the selected and many of the rejected videos also showed up on YouTube, finding an audience in the hundreds of thousands among a constituency that was probably not interested in the videos primarily because it cared for John McCain so much.[15]

39 The McCain "greenscreen challenge": Star Trek version

No such videos exist for Barack Obama. In fact, except for a few videos that mock Obama's sometimes hesitant delivery and catch him losing his train of thought in a campaign speech, there seems to be very little footage that allows remix artists to portray him in a defamatory way by rearranging words, sentences or facial expressions. It would be naive to assume that this is a coincidence. In his second book, *The Audacity of Hope*, Obama tells the story of how his Republican opponent, a politician who went on to self-destruct about halfway through the campaign, not unlike many of Obama's other opponents so far in his career, hired a young videographer to follow him around for days on end. The idea was to tape every occurrence that might portray Obama in an unfavorable light and hurt his electoral prospects, precisely the setup that Jim Webb used to entrap George Allen two years later.[16]

Obama tells the story to illustrate the kind of tactics that political campaigns use, without condemning or condoning the tactic as such (after all, he went on to campaign for Jim Webb in Virginia in 2006; these appearances are amply documented on YouTube too). But for Obama, the story is also a metaphor for the constant scrutiny he was and still is under. For him to lose his cool in front of a camera would have meant morphing into the stereotype of the angry black man, thereby endangering any aspiration he could have to appeal to white mainstream voters. In fact, as one can tell from the relevant passages in his first book, he developed early on in his life a sense of how to behave amongst white people to make them feel safe and secure.[17] It is probably not too far-fetched to speculate that this particular sense of self-awareness not only helped Obama develop a successful media personality as he entered the political stage. It also helped him gain, or rather retain, almost complete control of himself as a YouTube personality. His performances on camera are always pitch-perfect as he alternates between a trademark look of bemused detachment and a pose of engaged earnestness, occasionally throwing in his now world-famous smile for good measure.

Accordingly one could argue that YouTube introduces a new discipline of politics as performance. YouTube creates a public sphere, or sub-sphere, that is relentlessly unforgiving to those who slip up. It forces a new degree of restraint and self-control on politicians who want to appeal and succeed beyond their core constituencies. But then again, as in the case of Barack Obama, one could argue that the world that YouTube made favors those who already possess such restraint and self-control. It would seem that George Allen, much like the regrettably addled John McCain, represents the contrary case: a politician who did not understand the new discipline of politics as performance, who lost his self-control on camera and was punished for it. However, if you look at the "macaca moment" video clip closely, it becomes evident that George Allen clearly knew what he was doing. He did not just insult a dark-skinned bystander and get caught in the act. He knew who Sidarth was, that he worked for the Webb campaign, and that he followed him around to tape precisely the kind of occurrence that Allen: one is tempted to say: almost generously—produced for him. Of course, one could still try to read the "macaca moment" as a case of lack of restraint, and even an understandable one at that: the pressure became too much for Allen, he lost his cool and threw a tantrum.

But that is not what happened. The insult is couched in a relatively elaborate argument about the difference between Jim Webb's Virginia and the "real" Virginia, the conservative parts where Allen's constituents live. Allen is making fun of Webb for sending his videographer rather than coming to visit these parts of the state himself. By doing so, Allen is merely rehearsing a standard argument from the Republican campaign arsenal, carving out a difference between "real," i.e. conservative, white Southern Americans, and everyone else, particularly brown and black people. Marking out this difference is the rhetorical essence of Nixon's famous "Southern strategy," whereby the Republican party moved to provide a new political tent to disenfranchised Southern Democrats in the wake of Lyndon B. Johnson's civil rights legislation of the mid-1960s.[18] One could argue that the Southern strategy marks the precise moment when the party of Lincoln, the party of 19th century Abolitionists, ceased to be just that.

While it would be reductive to brand the Republican party and the conservative movement as inherently racist, the "Southern strategy" helps to understand a number of key tenets of Republican policy, particularly the party's opposition to taxes. As Kevin M. Kruse has demonstrated in *White Flight. Atlanta and the Making of Modern Conservatism*, a study of residential politics in postwar Atlanta, conservative anti-tax policies emerged in part from local and regional resistance to desegregation in the South.[19] The "macaca" invective and the argument he couched it in cannot have struck Allen as out of line, then, quite simply because it was very much *in* line with the overall political strategy that made the Republican party so successful over the last thirty years: mark out the difference between "us" and "them" and extol the "values" that make "us" American. Allen probably thought that he could do this because he knew from experience that it worked. As of 2006, this was, and from his perspective in all likelihood would continue to be, the way Republicans won elections and decided political conflicts in their favor.

Only this time he lost. What Allen found out, albeit too late, was that he was not, or no longer, in the position that he so self-assuredly assumed in the video: a position to determine who belonged and who did not, who was a "real" American and who was not. What we see play out in Sidarth's video is a political moment of conflict, of politics par excellence as described by Jacques Rancière. In his book *Disagreement. Politics and Philosophy*, Rancière defines politics as conflict, and more specifically as conflict about the question of equality, as opposed to policy, which covers the entire realm of governance.[20] Carl Schmitt famously defined politics as a conflict between friend and enemy.[21] For Rancière, the conflict is not between friend and enemy, but between equals in principle who are not—or not yet—equals in actual fact. Rancière finds the "ur-scene" of the political in Aristotle's *Politics*, in the conflict amongst Athenians about whether the poor should be granted equal rights with the wealthy and those in good social and economic standing. This conflict reemerges in modern democratic societies. Most, if not all, modern societies subscribe to the principle of equality in one way or another, a principle that is of necessity in conflict with the myriad social and economic differences and stratifications that these same societies produce. For Rancière, politics is the "game" of dramatizing such differences in the public sphere, at least those that are in obvious contradiction with the principle of equality. But where an orthodox Marxist would seek the resolution of this conflict in the elimination, if necessary by force, of all differences, and particularly the economic differences, that contradict the principle of equality, Rancière subscribes to what you might also call the Ghandian approach to politics. As the Mahatma said, in order to overcome injustice you must make it visible.[22]

Conclusion

For Rancière, then, the political and the aesthetic are inextricably linked. But so are politics and media. One of Rancière's interests is in flyers and leaflets and the role they played in 19th century social and political movements. Had YouTube been around when he first wrote his book, he could have turned to the Web for his material. In a sense, the "macaca moment" is the purest political moment YouTube could produce. For George Allen, it was not a gaffe—and for Sidarth it was more than an insult. For both, it was an intensely political moment, a moment of conflict which was all about the principle of equality, and a conflict that, thanks to video and YouTube, was plainly visible for all to see. What Sidarth's video did was make the underlying injustice in Allen's partition of America in "real" and "non-real" portions visible. However difficult to measure that contribution was, it signaled a step towards overcoming this injustice.

In light of Rancière's point about the alliance of aesthetics and politics, and in light of Gandhi's statement about making injustice visible, it seems ironic that Allen picked not just any bystander, but a videographer, and an Indian-American at that. But he could not have made a better choice had he wanted to demonstrate what the conflict was about, and how it was going to be played out, than to get into a fight with a non-white individual with a video camera and access to YouTube. Sidarth, his video camera and YouTube together produce what you might call a new political aesthetic of accountability. Holding people accountable to the principle of equality by making their injustices visible on a public stage is not new per se—it is a profoundly democratic and also a specifically modern game. But with YouTube, this game has just entered a new stage, one with a much larger audience.

Maybe, one day, former prison inmates who were incarcerated for negligible offenses such as possession of marijuana and freed in the wake of Jim Webb's proposed prison reform will commemorate the day George Allen picked on S.R. Sidarth and helped propel Webb to the US Senate. And just maybe they will go online and watch the video, adding to the film's viewing statistics and underlining the fact that YouTube is both a medium of politics and an archive for, and in some cases even a monument to, genuine political moments.

Endnotes

1 See *The Economist*, "A Nation of Jailbirds," 2 April 2009.

2 See for instance Brooke Fisher Liu, "From aspiring presidential candidate to accidental racist? An analysis of Senator George Allen's image repair during his 2006 reelection campaign," *Public Relations Review* no. 4, 2008, pp. 331–336. A general assessment of YouTube's impact on the 2006 elections is given in Vassia Gueorguieva, "Voters, MySpace, and YouTube. The Impact of Alternative Communication Channels on the 2006 Election Cycle and Beyond," *Social Science Computer Review* no. 3, 2008, pp. 288–300.

3 For the story about the Jewish background of Allen's mother's see www.cbsnews.com/stories/2006/09/26/politics/main2039589.shtml. The story came out in September 2006, roughly a month after Allen's run-in with S.R. Sidarth. It's safe to assume that the Allen campaign circulated this information in an attempt to control the damage wreaked on Allen's public image by the disclosure of what was allegedly a history of using racial slurs. A case of reverse anti-Semitism, if you will. The underlying argument would run something like this: being a Jew according to Jewish genealogy, Allen is really a victim and not a perpetrator. Therefore he cannot possibly be a racist.

4 See the clip *George Allen introduces Macaca* – www.youtube.com/watch?v=r90z0PmnKwI [last checked 15 February 2009].

5 See for example the entry for "macaca" on Wikipedia – http://en.wikipedia.org/wiki/Macaca_(slur) [last checked 15 February 2009].

6 For one see Christine B. Williams, "Congressional Candidates' Use of YouTube in 2008: Its Frequency and Rationale" – http://blogsandwikis.bentley.edu/politechmedia/wp-content/uploads/2009/01/youtubejan21_final-2.pdf.
7 See for example www.youtube.com/watch?v=jjXyqcx-mYY [last checked 15 February 2009]. In addition, the video has sparked more than 100,000 comments.
8 For a study of clustering effects as they relate to the relative shortness of YouTube videos and networks of related videos, see Xu Cheng, Cameron Dale and Jiangchuan Liu, "Understanding the Characteristics of Internet Short Video Sharing: YouTube as a Case Study" – http://arxiv.org/pdf/0707.3670.
9 See for example Elisabeth Corville, " 'Our Union Grows Stronger': The Poetic Persuasion of Barack Obama," *Anthropology* News 49, no. 8, 2008, pp. 4–5.
10 See www.youtube.com/watch?v=oHXYsw_ZDXg&feature=channel_page [last checked 15 February 2009]. On McCain's YouTube site the "celeb" video is still by far the most viewed as of this writing in April 2009.
11 Jeffrey C. Alexander, "The democratic struggle for power: the 2008 Presidential campaign in the USA," *Journal of Power* no. 1, April 2009, pp. 65–88.
12 For a study of YouTube traffic on a specific university campus network where the researchers had access to the university's internal network data, see Michael Zink, Kyoungwon Suh, Yu Gu and Jim Kurose, "Watch Global, Cache Local: YouTubeNetwork Traffic at a Campus Network – Measurements and Implications" – www.cs.umass.edu/~yugu/papers/zink-08mmcn.pdf [last checked 15 February 2009].
13 YouTube's parent company Google went so far as to refuse to cooperate with the US government on an effort to track down users of child pornography on the Internet. The Department of Justice demanded information on Internet searches relating to child pornography, a request that Google fought in court. In all likelihood, Google's rationale was demonstrating to users that their data would not be made available to government agencies under any circumstances. See "Google defies US over search data" – http://news.bbc.co.uk/2/hi/technology/4630694.stm
14 For a collection of videos made for "the Colbert Report make McCain interesting green screen challenge," see www.youtube.com/view_play_list?p=DA7FA635FCA74754 [last checked 15 February 2009].

15 One current empirical study of the 2008 presidential campaign assesses the impact of editorial cartoons on political preferences. A study of network TV satire in the Jon Stewart/Stephen Colbert mold has yet to be undertaken. See Jod C. Baumgartner, "Polls and Elections: Editorial Cartoons 2.0: The Effects of Digital Political Satire on Presidential Candidate Evaluations," *Presidential Studies Quarterly* no. 4, pp. 735–758. Baumgartner's key finding is that editorial cartoons do not change political preferences. This result brings to mind Howland, Lumsdaine and Sheffield's classic study on World War II propaganda and instructional films. While testing the impact of the *Why We Fight* film series on the political attitudes of enlisted members of the US armed forces, the researchers found that the films improved viewer's understanding of the conflict they were engaged in but did not affect their overall attitudes, particularly not their political attitudes. It is safe to assume, then, that YouTube videos do not change attitudes either. Rather, they function as a tool of mobilization. The "macaca moment" video probably reached voters who would not have voted for Allen anyway but were motivated to register and go to the polls by the video. See C. Howland, A. Lumsdaine and F. Sheffield, *Experiments in Mass Communication* (Princeton: Princeton University Press, 1949).

16 Barack Obama, *The Audacity of Hope. Thoughts on Reclaiming the American Dream* (New York: Three River Press, 2006).

17 Barack Obama, *Dreams from My Father. A Story of Race and Inheritance* (New York: Three Rivers Press, 1995).

18 For an in-depth study of white Southern residential politics, desegregation and the "Southern strategy," see Matthew D. Lassiter, *The Silent Majority: Suburban Politics in the Sunbelt South* (Princeton: Princeton University Press, 2005).

19 Kevin M. Kruse, *White Flight. Atlanta and the Making of Modern Conservatism* (Princeton: Princeton University Press, 2005).

20 Jacques Rancière, *Disagreement. Politics and Philosophy* (Minneapolis: University of Minnesota Press, 1998).

21 Carl Schmitt, *Der Begriff des Politischen* (Berlin: Duncker und Humblodt, 1932).

22 As is well known, other contemporary political theorists in the post-Marxist vein such as Ernesto Laclau and Chantal Mouffe prefer to draw on Carl Schmitt to account for political conflicts relating to the question of who belongs and who does not in modern democratic society. See Ernesto Laclau and Chantal Mouffe, *Hegemony and Socialist Strategy. Towards a*

Radical Democratic Politics (London: Verso, 2001). See also Mouffe's later work on Carl Schmitt, in particular her *The Challenge of Carl Schmitt* (London: Verso, 1999). It is also important that the pathos of making injustice invisible permeates *Das Kapital* as much as it does the political thinking of Gandhi. One could argue, then, that Rancière has not moved all that far from his neo-Marxist origins. But he has certainly dropped any pretense of revolutionary action. On the problem of visibility and injustice in *Das Kapital* see my "Thermodynamic Kitsch. Computing in German Industrial Films 1928/1963," in Vinzenz Hediger and Patrick Vonderau, eds., *Films that Work. Industrial Films and the Productivity of Media* (Amsterdam: Amsterdam University Press, 2009).

Storage

Rick Prelinger

The Appearance of Archives

Maybe we can begin by stating that YouTube is not itself an archive. Preservation is neither its mission nor its practice. But what good does it do us to insist on this point? When hardly anyone remembers the distinction between film and video; when a soon-to-be-majority of younger people has grown up in an environment where video is born digital; and when degraded, low-resolution and immersive, high-quality media coexist without conflict, the fine points of archival definition disintegrate in the noise. This article argues that YouTube might as well be an archive; that in the public mind it is not simply an archive but an ideal form of archive; and that it problematizes and threatens the canonical missions of established moving-image archives throughout the world.

Online video became a mainstream possibility almost a generation ago in 1992 with the widespread introduction of QuickTime software. A growing number of tools and applications enabling the convergence of video and computing sparked almost continuous discussion in the moving-image archives field, but words led to little action until the first few years of the new century. The archival world lost its sense of mission while reiterating what seem to be eternal cultural divides between access and openness, between control of records and proliferation, and between casting archivists or archival users as central figures in archival practice. Worries about copyright holders (whether known, unknown or suspected), about "losing control" of collections, and about the qualification of members of the public to see and use archival materials kept most archives from offering materials online. If they took steps to make collections accessible digitally, they were usually baby steps.

In all fairness, there were a few bright exceptions to this trend. The Library of Congress made a significant number of pre-1915 historical films available for unrestricted downloading through its American Memory Project.[1] The Internet Archive, a San Francisco nonprofit digital library, made its first large moving-image collection, the Prelinger Archives collection, accessible for free use at the end of 2000. The collection has grown to over 2,000 items and spawned an estimated 30 million downloads.[2] On local levels in the US, and elsewhere in the world, a few other online collections came together. Many, however, were restricted to users at specific institutions or within the educational sector.

Towards a Default Clip Culture

While most archives and archivists dithered, commercial services rushed to transport video to personal computers. Copyright maximalism and a long chain of restrictive business models influenced the development of online video architecture. Most online video services followed some kind of streaming paradigm, presenting video in an evanescent manner, leaving no trace of the video file residing on the viewers' disks. Though streaming files could be captured and saved by expert users, to most people streaming video was the most ephemeral of all media, incapable of being downloaded, edited, annotated, referenced, indexed or remixed. One danger of building access restrictions into software and hardware is that minimum standards of access tend to devolve into maximum standards, and in fact commercially motivated limitations crossed the nonprofit/for-profit border, infecting the consciousness of public and nonprofit moving-image archives. To this day there are relatively few online audiovisual collections that allow users to freely download materials.

Hundreds of commercial online video sites sprang up in the early 2000s. Most perished due to competition and unsustainable business models, but YouTube, a latecomer, got traction relatively quickly after its founding in February 2005. By summer 2008, YouTube had over 140 million videos online and morphed into a mainstream cultural phenomenon.[3] I would argue that in the eyes of the public, YouTube had become the default online moving-image archive. Much of archives' labored steps toward providing public access counted for naught when placed next to YouTube's simple, low-functionality service. Without even knowing that a competition was on, archives had lost the contest to determine the attributes of the future online moving-image archives.

But what made YouTube so attractive to the public, and what did it do that archives had not seriously tried to achieve? First, it was a complete collection—or at least appeared to be. During its first two to three years, a search for almost any topic, television show or person on YouTube would return at least one clip or clips. Enabled by a corporate disregard for the niceties of copyright, YouTube quickly came to be a site that offered the illusion of comprehensiveness and even turned up unsuspected surprises. A high percentage of videos offered by YouTube were not available for sale, loan or simple viewing through any other channel or service.

Second, YouTube was open to user contributions. Without special permission or credentialing, anyone's video could find a place in the same repository where favorite programs and actors resided. I believe that this mix of personal and corporate expression made YouTube tremendously attractive to neophyte and emerging mediamakers, who felt privileged to be able to host their work in the same repository used for the work of famous makers and famous shows. The mystique of archives as rarefied and impenetrable containers of cinematic masterworks suddenly disappeared. Mashups and remixes of commercial film and television often appeared in search results adjacent to the works they'd appropriated, which constituted a kind of recognition of the remixer by the remixed.

While many users chose to upload copies of commercially produced material rather than works they themselves had produced, it's important to say that in most cases users curated selections based on what they liked or thought was important. In fact, YouTube's collection of commercially produced video segments constitutes a vast popular encyclopedic effort comparable in some aspects to the Wikipedia project, in other words a massive, crowdsourced project to index, categorize and contextualize the corpus of world television. By choosing and uploading specific segments from videos in their collections or programs grabbed off the air, users were in fact acting to segment and add coherency and value to a vast, undifferentiated continuous stream of commercial video. Though this may not be legally protected authorship due to the copyright status of this material, it is authorship nonetheless, a broad-based popular effort to add coherency to and contextualize material left without context by its copyright owners. Akin to the cataloging and documentation work performed by canonical archives, this user-based effort rushed in where with few exceptions archives had not been able to go.

Third, YouTube offered instantaneous access with very few limitations other than reduced quality. In contrast, the world of established physical-media archives takes pride in offering the highest-quality material, but is characterized by latency and significant limitations on access. Because of the fragile nature of many archival documents and severe limitations on resources, most members of the public are not welcome in most moving-image archives unless they are pursuing a project that will have a public, scholarly or production impact. If a user wishes to reuse a document held at a moving-image archives, he or she is likely to encounter significant permission, copyright and clearance barriers. As a result most potential public users have never had contact with an established archive. In contrast, hundreds of millions of people have used YouTube and its access paradigm has been naturalized as the logical modality of archival access. This cannot help archives that bear the burden of maintaining (and explaining) a suite of access limitations.

Archives are beset with problems stemming from a historical proliferation of media formats. Many archival holdings are difficult and expensive to copy and almost impossible to view because they are fixed in outdated formats. By reducing all video to a lowest-common-denominator Flash format, YouTube presents the illusion that these problems do not exist while making it very easy to watch videos. No client software is required of the user, and no skills are necessary. And while no one could call YouTube's video presentation high-quality, I would argue that the low-res appearance of most YouTube videos map help foster a sense of immunity among users, a sense that YouTube viewing doesn't really violate any owners' rights because it's just watching a picture of a video. YouTube places the viewer in permanent preview mode. In fact, many commercial rights holders have turned their cheek and winked, knowing that YouTube often functions as a publicity machine for their programming.[4]

Fourth, YouTube offered basic (if not overly sophisticated) social-networking features. It's possible to link individuals to their uploads and favorite videos, to send favorite videos to other people, and to maintain friends. Such features are de rigueur for content-oriented websites today. But YouTube's facilitation of these basic networking functions may imply more, perhaps an understanding that archival access is inherently social, that it has passed beyond the classic paradigm of the lone researcher pursuing private studies. In a time when legacy archives are fighting for public mindshare and fiscal survival, they would do well to encourage any possible manifestation of fan culture by influencing their users to identify as a group with shared interests.

Finally, though it takes some skill to download a video from YouTube, the videos were very easily embeddable. You can easily paste a YouTube screen into your own website or blog and bracket the video as part of your own page. Though this does not constitute actual possession of the video file, it implies the freedom to cite and quote video segments, a function that was not previously provided by any other Web service. Television clips on YouTube are now used to make broadcasters more accountable for their coverage and by political bloggers seeking to support or damage particular politicians. In this sense YouTube functions as a valuable assistant in the maintenance of civil society.

Rethinking Archives

For reasons mentioned above, I argue that YouTube quickly fashioned itself into what most members of the public regard as the world's default media archive. This puts established media archives into a paradoxical situation: as they insist on the importance of classical archival missions, they will appear to be less useful, less accommodating, less relevant, and ultimately less important than YouTube, the pretender. Everything that anyone does to bring media archives online is now going to be measured against YouTube's ambiguous legacy. And though YouTube (the service) may not remain the same forever or even continue to exist, all online video efforts will be assessed in context with its pioneering innovations, which have altered public expectations of what television is and can be.

So what is next for archives? Most have refused to collaborate with YouTube. Others have jumped on the bandwagon, making low-quality digital surrogates of selected materials available through customized channels. The overall reaction seems to be one of retrenchment. I am reminded of the advent of home video in the early 1980s. While many archives protested at the threat video posed to the continued maintenance of the cinematic exhibition experience, ultimately most archives made materials available on videotape, videodisc and ultimately DVD. Today, DVD is the primary means of public access to materials held by archival institutions. It's unfortunate that archives have to rely on a flawed and inefficient commercial distribution system to get works out to audiences, but they have chosen not to create their own alternatives. It may well be that YouTube or its successors become the primary means of public access to archival holdings.

But what if archives choose not to play in this sandbox? It's possible that the YouTube paradigm will prove so objectionable to archives and content gatekeepers that there will be a reaction against online video distribution in all its forms. This would likely be self-defeating. The problem is that audiences are much more sophisticated now than they once were, and there is widespread expectation that archival material should be accessible. Retrenchment will equal obscurity and irrelevance. Alternatively, there are more publicly minded entities like the Internet Archive, which might perhaps morph into the PBS of online video sites. There are also walled gardens, like the British online cinema studies sites. In the US, a current proposal for an AVAN (Audiovisual Archives Network), which is architecturally and intellectually influenced by the ARTstor project, is now in process. Alternatively, archives might leverage mass digital distribution systems already in existence and use them to their own ends. Of course, we already have the Internet, and moving-image archives have yet to "use it" as they please.

YouTube will not exist forever without change. It is already remaking itself to accommodate the marketplace and as a consequence of its continuing negotiations with business adversaries. Many user-created or user-segmented videos that incorporate supposedly copyrighted material have disappeared, and YouTube has deployed technology to prevent such videos from appearing on their public site. Many HD-quality video and downloadable videos are being offered. But none of these changes lessen YouTube's disruptive effects upon moving-image archives, whose share of public attention vis-à-vis commercial online video services continues to diminish.

Like libraries, publishers and record labels, moving-image archives suffer from clinging to outdated paradigms of access and distribution. Change is urgent. But the developments that have weakened archives' status in the public sphere and threaten to subvert the consensus that keeps them alive aren't primarily consequences of their own actions or inactions. Rather, their loss of status is a result of powerful externalities over which they have no power. Though YouTube is not an archive killer, and though archival material forms a mere fraction of the hundred million-plus YouTube videos, the site embodies a paradox: at the same time that it offers the greatest potential for the public dissemination of historical and cultural images and sounds, it threatens to make redundant the institutions that actively preserve these materials.

YouTube implicitly recognized that archives were not the end of the media lifecycle, but rather a new beginning. Corralling the labor of millions of users to curate, select and upload videos from every kind of source, YouTube gave new life to the moving-image heritage and exposed archival material to a vast audience. It is now up to archives to decide how best to fulfill their canonical missions in a changed world.

Endnotes

1 See http://memory.loc.gov/ammem/index.html [last checked 15 February 2009].

2 See www.archive.org/details/prelinger [last checked 15 February 2009]. Other moving-image collections available from the Internet Archive total approximately 160,000 items.

3 See http://beerpla.net/2008/08/14/how-to-find-out-the-number-of-videos-on-youtube/ [last checked 15 February 2009]. The site estimates the total number of videos on YouTube between 141 and 144 million as of August 2008.

4 As of early 2009, YouTube has offered HD-quality (720p) playback in 16:9 format, provided that compatible videos have been uploaded.

Frank Kessler and Mirko Tobias Schäfer*

Navigating YouTube: Constituting a Hybrid Information Management System

"We no longer watch film or TV; we watch databases." Geert Lovink uses this statement to address the shift emblematized by, among others, YouTube in the introduction to *The Video Vortex Reader*.[1] The so-called "database turn" that Lovink presents seems to him a fundamental shift in the way in which moving images are being experienced today. Talking about YouTube in terms of a database is without doubt an adequate description of the technological basis allowing users to upload, search, find and retrieve moving-image files on the site. This, however, is not the only conception users (or scholars) have of YouTube, and probably not the one that intuitively comes to mind, as the digital objects that one deals with are in fact perceived not as data sets, but rather as films, video clips, TV shows, etcetera—in other words: moving images. So before we continue our discussion of this platform's function as a database, we will have a brief look at some other conceptualizations that try to consider YouTube in analogy to other cultural institutions that collect and make accessible sounds and images.

YouTube as Archive or Library

In another article from the *Video Vortex Reader* Thomas Thiel discusses an installation by Wilhelm Sasnal consisting of a 16mm loop projection showing various video clips filmed from the screen of a laptop presenting "the historic and diverse contents of the media archive

YouTube."[2] Referring to a video-sharing website as an archive of highlights, on the one hand, the fact that among the millions of clips that can be found there, a non-negligible number present, and thus make accessible, historic material. Such a point of view is perfectly illustrated by a post on the *McGill Tribune* website by someone called Bryant, who states: "Now YouTube is an archive; just the other day I watched an educational film that was made in the 1950's, that, without youtube I would've never seen."[3] On the other hand, the archive analogy stresses the possibility that users can find material there and reuse it for their own purposes, as is the case with Sasnal's installation mentioned above. Similarly, Henry Jenkins declares that "YouTube functions as a media archive where amateur curators scan the media environment, searching for meaningful content, and bringing them to a larger public (through legal and illegal means)."[4] The term "archive" is used in both cases in a rather straightforward way, pointing towards a collection of audiovisual material that is stored and can be retrieved through appropriate search operations, rather than, for instance, in the more epistemological sense in which Foucault uses it.[5] Here, the term "archive" is furthermore associated with the general possibility of storing data collections and does not refer to the traditional understanding of archiving as an institutionalized practice. Online data collections labeled archives could in fact be better characterized as perpetual transmission rather than permanent storage. Some moving-image archivists, therefore, clearly reject the analogy because of at least one fundamental difference emphasized by Leo Enticknap:

> I don't see any evidence that YouTube is attempting to undertake long-term preservation of any of the material it hosts, which is surely a core function of an archive; one which distinguishes an archive from other types of document or media collection. Indeed, it'll be interesting to see what happens to the less frequently viewed content once YouTube's server capacity is filled. As far as I can see, YouTube is essentially an infrastructure for the distribution of video content for end user viewing.[6]

Enticknap marks a decisive difference here, indeed: questions of preservation do not play any kind of role on such a video-sharing website, and neither does the question of precisely identifying the status of a document, or the issue of different versions of a film, its registration and cataloguing according to certain standards, etcetera. This leads Rick Prelinger to conceive of YouTube rather as a library: "Actually, I think your description of what YouTube does shows that it's more of a library than an archive. I understand the difference to be that an archive ('archos'—'first') is charged with the permanent preservation of original documents, whereas a library simply exists to make copies available for access."[7] But this proposition, too, is rejected by a different AMIA (Association of Moving Image Archives) member, Andrea Leigh, because of yet another important aspect that is lacking on YouTube, namely rules and regulations, that is ethics, with regard to the material aspects of a document that govern the work of archivists and librarians alike. "Libraries are oriented around a code of ethics [...] and a core set of values," she writes. These provide "communities with comprehensive access to both information and entertainment resources, not entertainment resources only that lack selection criteria, principled organizational methods based on over 100 years of practice and tradition, and a high service orientation. So not only is YouTube not an archive, it is not a library, either."[8]

While such debates might be seen as traditional archives setting up defense lines against new practices and especially new organizational forms appearing on the Internet, there are also obvious differences between both as regards goals, procedures and ethical commitments. And there are obvious differences between Web-based projects as well, for instance between archive.org and YouTube. But clearly, archives and libraries are institutions that function according to relatively strictly codified lines of conduct, that have to observe standards defined by professional associations, often on an international level. More importantly for our analysis here, however, what this discussion shows is that whatever analogy is drawn to existing institutions or functions (this might even be valid for the more neutral term "repository" that is also used regularly to describe YouTube) will fall short on one level or another, only partly covering the rather specific way in which such a video-sharing facility functions.[9] It may thus, indeed, be more productive to let go of such comparisons and start with the technological foundations of the platform, that is, as suggested by Geert Lovink, its being a database.

YouTube as Database

Lev Manovich has identified the database as a crucial aspect of digital media as such. Going beyond the computer sciences' definition of the database as a structured collection of data, Manovich considers it a cultural form that follows its own logic and exceeds operations such as the storage and retrieval of data. "They appear as a collection of items on which the user can perform various operations—view, navigate, search."[10] In addition to this, YouTube, as well as other services generally referred to as Web 2.0, offers the possibility of adding items to databases, improving the information management through user-generated meta-information as well as synchronizing them through so-called Application Programming Interfaces (API).[11] In this respect, YouTube as a database is in fact more accurately described as an infrastructure, as its scope goes well beyond the YouTube Internet site proper. The website "The programmable web" lists more than 330 so-called mashup sites employing video feeds and other data from YouTube. These facilities make accessible specific selections from the YouTube database that YouTube itself does not offer its users, sometimes combining them with other Web applications such as, for instance, Google Maps, Flickr, and also other video-sharing sites or music distribution services such as LastFM.

40 "Kutiman mixes YouTube": funky mashup site

Another option YouTube offers are the so-called "embedded links" that facilitate integration of YouTube videos into all types of other environments, from personal websites and amateur or professional blogs to the online services of traditional media such as newspapers, magazines and television channels. YouTube even explicitly encourages such embeddings, as is evidenced by the proposed links to several other Web 2.0 platforms.[12] The YouTube database, in other words, is accessible not only through the one interface that Google manages itself. While surfing the Internet, a user can encounter moving images branded with the company's logo almost anywhere. When a video has been watched through an embedded link, the viewer is offered the possibility of looking at so-called related material, too. The user can thus navigate the database from an external site also, albeit with fewer options.

The YouTube database, however, does not only consist of video files, but also contains titles, brief descriptions called "info," tags, hyperlinks to the uploader's site or to related material, as well as user comments of variable, and sometimes quite extensive, proportions. In addition, it stores data concerning the number of views, popularity ratings, flagging rates, recursive links and other kinds of statistical information. In fact, video retrieval and management depend fundamentally upon such user-generated input provided as text. Since moving-image files are not machine-readable—meaning that the program cannot identify the semantic content of this kind of file—information management relies on metadata that names, describes or categorizes whatever there is to be seen. This is an essentially hybrid constellation, since users provide semantic input, which the machine then processes algorithmically, producing different types of clustering with a corresponding organization of video files and metadata.[13] Ultimately, this technological infrastructure can be seen as a specific affordance enabling new forms of media practice. In a way, thus, understanding YouTube means describing it in terms of a "hybrid interaction" where humans and machines—users and information management systems—are inextricably linked.

One could also refer to the approach formulated by the so-called Actor-Network theory, according to which human and non-human actors have to be considered equally important in the constitution of social interaction.[14] As the way in which YouTube and other Web 2.0 applications such as Flickr, Facebook and other function depends fundamentally on the way in which they succeed in channeling user activities into software design, one could describe them in terms of what Tim O'Reilly addressed as "architecture of participation," which is also in a way akin to Bruno Latour's analyses of translations of social protocols into technological design.[15] Consequently, Web 2.0 applications thrive on stimulating user participation on various levels, which subsequently is translated into input feeding the information management system.

YouTubing: View, Navigate & Search

Doing YouTube can mean a number of things: one can simply watch one (specific) or a whole series of clips; one can rate, flag or comment on videos; or one can upload, categorize, annotate and tag one's own moving images (either self-produced or found and appropriated). These operations imply different levels of activity on the part of the user, but even a simple viewing (either on the YouTube site or embedded somewhere else) leads to an invitation, or proposition, to watch more. Right from the start, the YouTube interface offers various choices. In addition to the search facility it shows which videos are being played at that very moment, it presents a number of "promoted videos" (proposed by the YouTube company) as well as "featured videos" that are highlighted for their qualities (having been selected for this category is one of the "honors" subsequently flaunted among the "Statistics & Data" information for the clip).

Viewing, in other words, is but a default aspect of navigation. The act of watching YouTube is in such a perspective only the practice of navigating through the database's content, exactly as claimed by Lovink. This, however, differs fundamentally from the activity of zapping from channel to channel on a traditional TV set, since the various television programs are not linked to each other by any semantic relations, and are simply related by the fact of their being broadcast simultaneously. The YouTube suggestions do not really compare to the program structures of early cinema, either. Thematically organized programs would also present some kind of overarching narrative, whereas the dominant format would present some sort of structured variety.[16] By contrast, viewing YouTube actually consists of navigating from one video to another, semantically related ones. This practice is not confined to the Youtube.com domain, but has been implemented into many other Web services and websites by means of open APIs that allow users to stream contents from the YouTube database into different applications, and where every viewing leads to a list of related clips.

In order to search the database for video clips, the YouTube interface, to begin with, includes a common search bar. However, the API also offers the possibility to automate search processes and retrieve videos according to a certain search string in order to implement them into a different application.[17] As mentioned, YouTube's information management relies on machine-readable information describing the video clips that permits their retrieval according to key terms. A video clip of Madonna, in other words, can only be recognized as such when there is an explicit textual marker. This so-called meta-information is initially generated by the users uploading the videos and consists of the title users give a clip, the information added to an info box in order to provide background information or a summary of the clip, and the tags, that is a number of keywords one can select freely according to what one assumes to be appropriate labels for these images. Users viewing videos also provide meta-information implicitly, since the viewing rate is a criterion for the order of videos that match a given keyword.[18] The activities of users, either those supplying information about videos they upload in the form of a title, additional information and tags, or those viewing, rating, commenting on or flagging videos, do affect the responses of YouTube to search requests. Navigating the YouTube database is therefore also intrinsically related to the activities of the numerous other users providing the necessary meta-information for efficient information management. Furthermore, a specific media practice emerges here, where users create meta-information in order to receive more views of the material they have uploaded, and by the same token they improve information retrieval processes within the database. Meta-information, in other words, is crucial for the information management on Web platforms that host non-machine-readable content such as videos or images. In order to function, YouTube, and also Flickr and other services of that type, in fact "crowdsource" the labor that is necessary to supply the meta-information, benefiting from the various ways in which users willingly or unwillingly, explicitly or implicitly provide them with input.

The success of searching moving-image files thus relies upon the different types of metadata provided by the person who uploads a clip as well as by other users. Search results consist of a selection of videos that match the request in a presumed order of relevance, but may in fact not include the item one has looked for. Users can then either renew the search or click on one of the suggested clips in the hope that the "related videos" listings will get them closer to their goal. These kinds of operations would be utterly inefficient for a traditional moving-image archive where search criteria are defined as precisely as possible, where categories and keywords are fixed in thesauri, often as a result of cross-institutional or even international agreements, and where catalogues contain similar information for each item.[19] In other words, the kind of metadata produced and used by archival institutions aim for maximum clarity and efficiency, whereas the search-as-navigation procedures characteristic of YouTube and similar platforms derive from a form of media practice that follows a different rationale.

Creating YouTube: Upload, Tag, Comment and Flag

YouTubing in many ways goes beyond the activity of merely watching videos. The interface at the youtube.com site already offers many possibilities for users to partake of its functioning. The ensuing activities can be divided into operations resulting in either explicit or implicit participation. Users participate explicitly by, for instance, starting a channel and uploading videos to the database. This activity includes the creation of meta-information and addition of title, tags, and other information to the uploaded video clip. Users watching those clips can either react to them by posting a video response or commenting on them in writing. Both forms of comments will be intrinsically related to the initial video, but may also offer additional possibilities for navigating to other user sites and videos. When uploading a video, users are requested by the YouTube interface to select a category that fits the video clip.[20] Since these rather broad categories do not sufficiently describe the video clips to allow efficient search operations, users can additionally add tags to formulate more specific categorization of their content.[21]

The choice of tags is supposed to be related to what the images present, but the meta-information can also be employed strategically for other reasons. Obviously, YouTube can be used in many different ways. As indicated above, it can serve as some sort of repository, enabling users for instance to copy and upload material from TV and add them to an existing, rather incoherent collection of memorable televisual moments, featuring incidents from TV shows such as *The Jerry Springer Show, Idols, The Colbert Report, Late Show with David Letterman,* etcetera. Here, YouTube constitutes something like a dense compilation of television highlights. Tags refer to the title of the TV program as well as to the noteworthy aspect of the fragment in question (e.g. such as Jerry Springer, bizarre, cheater). Another function YouTube fulfills is serving as a channel to explain the way in which one must proceed in order to achieve a given result. This takes the form of videos illustrating various do-it-yourself practices. Such files are then associated with the How-to category, but additionally tags refer to the practice in question and even to related issues (e.g. Little Brother book, How to make a shirt print). Yet another way of using YouTube has been labeled self-presentation.[22] Often such videos provoke or explicitly ask for video responses, which constitute an additional set of video comments on the original video. This area of self-presentation could also be understood as some kind of commentary users make on popular culture or political trends.

41 Tagging as misinformation

For political reasons especially, tags are often chosen with the strategic goal of luring others to view a given video file. In such cases the practice of tagging is in a way appropriated and turned into a form of deliberate misinformation. The clip entitled "XXX PORN XXX" by user AbolishTheSenateOrg, for instance, is tagged with a variety of keywords that can refer to pornography, while the video itself is a plea to abolish the US Senate. User scottstone567 tries to attract views by adding pornography-related tags, title and info to videos that display instances of rather unskilled painting and related activities. It appears that the use of tags, title and description is actually quite frequently appropriated in order to increase the number of views for such videos, which show content that does not at all correspond to what the metadata suggest. Referring to complaints about this practice, user Redsoul76 comments in the info box of his video "Paris Hilton new Sex Video": "RoflMonkeys-Copter stop complaining and searching for porn on youtube and next blame for not finding it lol..."[23]

Users take ample advantage of the option to comment on uploaded material. In some cases, and not always in direct proportion to the number of views, clips may provoke tens of thousands of reactions. Sometimes mere statements of approval or disapproval (in many cases just a simple "lol" or "wtf"), there also are strings of discussions among users, which by the way do not always involve the content of the clip in question. In some cases, it is an aspect of a comment that leads to a reaction and discussions of an entirely unrelated issue. In practice, probably but relatively few viewers will read through all these comments, especially if there are thousands of them. However, the commentary section is an integral part of the database and generates metadata that are relevant to the overall functioning of YouTube, even though the content of individual comments may be of interest to the commentator only. As for the generation of metadata, the number of comments feeds into indications of popularity and relevance. When searching for a video, the search engine seems to favor those that have obtained high numbers of views and also received many comments.[24]

YouTube also offers the possibility for a very specific type of user comment, namely the so-called flag button for "report[ing the] video as inappropriate." While making such an option available to users may originally have been inspired by the idea that this might help the efficient and rapid removal of pornographic, racist or otherwise extremist content from the site, it can also lead to various forms of censorship when people declare that they feel "offended" by a clip, for whatever reason. As the YouTube staff has the final authority in this question without having to argue about or justify such decisions, there are some concerns about hidden forms of censorship resulting from abusive flagging.[25]

All these operations that YouTube offers its users—or rather which must be used for YouTube to generate the metadata necessary for its functioning—are at first sight ancillary options and additional services. Quite on the contrary, however, they actually provide the indispensable basis for the database's information management. In part, this requires acts of deliberate participation—uploading, tagging, commenting, flagging—where users choose to actively contribute to the YouTube website. But in addition to such actions, which one could label "explicit participation," any such operation is also a contribution to the database, even though the latter aspect may be for users just a side effect of what they consider their main purpose, namely to interact directly or indirectly with others. In fact, every single click on one of the links to a clip, however random or accidental this choice may be, does feed into the database as well. Every interaction with the YouTube site leads to a trace in the system and becomes a record relevant to the statistics that can be read at the surface as an indicator for "popularity." Such acts of "implicit participation," of which most users are probably unaware, are actually the backbone of the entire operation. The participation, in other words, is implemented into the software design.[26]

YouTube as Resource: Mashups and Spin-off Services

Given the enormous amount of uploaded video clips as well as the specific software design, YouTube functions in many respects as an infrastructure and cultural resource. This is the case for the artists or other users for whom, according to Henry Jenkins and Thomas Thiel, YouTube functions as an archive, that is as a reservoir of material they can appropriate and reuse according to their own needs. But in addition, as Tim O'Reilly points out, it is crucial for Web-based services to provide synchronizable databases in order to have their service implemented in as many third-party applications as possible. The activities that we have labeled "Creating YouTube" in fact also include the implementation of the contents of its database into other Web applications. The YouTube API is frequently used for building so-called mashup websites. This term designates sites that "mash" various data streams from different Web applications together to create a new format.[27]

Mashups such as Tagbulb use APIs of various Web services such as YouTube, Yahoo Video, Flickr, Google, del.icio.us and others in order to present related content from those different sources, or in this case resources, corresponding to a given key term.[28] Mashups, in other words, make available combinations of material from various services organized according to specific zones of interest in ways that the original platforms do not provide. Reversing, in a certain sense, commercial enterprises' practice of opening their own channels on YouTube as an additional distribution outlet, mashup websites comb through all sorts of collections of material and make selections targeted towards relatively well-defined groups of users.

The continuous circulation of YouTube material, together with the aforementioned fact that identification of particular clips depends on the meta-information added by uploaders and other uses, results in the fact that the database can be described as a repository for audiovisual material that is simultaneously stable and unstable. Instability results, to begin with, from the rather incoherent and unorganized way in which videos are indexed, labeled and filed. But at the same time, and in fact by the same token, stability is generated through the organization of content in the form of a dense layer of meta-information consisting of titles, tags and descriptions. Another factor characterizing YouTube as an unstable repository is the uncertainty as to whether or not uploaded videos remain on YouTube. Any video may disappear from the site for a variety of reasons: material can be removed by the person who posted it originally, or it can be deleted by YouTube staff members for violating the terms of use. But popular videos that have been removed often reappear, either on YouTube or other video-sharing platforms. Here an unorganized, rather anarchic and accidental practice of users copying and re-uploading videos results in redundant storage.[29] This practice creates at least some kind of stability countering the unstable nature of digital repositories. The inherent instability, in other words, seems to stimulate practices for compensation. One example here is the MIT project YouTomb, which monitors videos uploaded to YouTube and identifies those that have been removed for violating terms of use.[30] YouTube is therefore more than a mere Web platform where videos can be uploaded and viewed. Rather, it seems to be an infrastructure and a cultural resource that can be used in numerous ways. It constitutes the raw material for a new media practice of perpetual uploading, viewing and deleting of material, as well as streaming it to a variety of other Web services and sites.

Conclusion: YouTube as a New Media Practice

While Geert Lovink clearly identifies a central and crucial point of the phenomenon YouTube when he claims that "we no longer watch film or TV; we watch databases," this statement in a way short circuits the basic infrastructure of YouTube and the variety of ways in which it functions for its users, both at its surface and even beyond, as is the case with mashup sites and the embedding of clips within other sites. As we have tried to show in this article, YouTube constitutes an intrinsically hybrid system of information management, where users provide all sorts of input, among which the uploading of audiovisual material most certainly is the site's raison d'être. However, making video clips available to others is not sufficient for YouTube to operate. The material has to be described, indexed and categorized in various ways in order to be storable, identifiable, retrievable and thus viewable or, in a literal sense, to become *visible*. Once made visible in this emphatic sense, thanks to the software design a clip becomes related to other videos, ranked in terms of its relative popularity according to the number of views, and it may even become a "featured video" because of whatever qualities have been ascribed to it; others comment on it; it may trigger approval, disapproval or debates; it may also get flagged and consequently removed for being judged inappropriate.

While description, indexing and categorization are standard operating procedure for traditional archives—albeit in a different and more systematic and normative way—the different acts of explicit and implicit participation, the generation of metadata by various kinds of user activities constitute a new media practice that represents a challenge to our established conceptions of media use. In order to analyze a phenomenon such as YouTube, one needs to take into account its fundamental heterogeneity and hybridity, its technological infrastructure as well as what is happening on its surface or its interface. The multifunctional interfaces of YouTube, providing numerous possibilities of use and reuse, form a perpetual stream of data that goes well beyond the YouTube Web platform and appears in a multitude of other websites and services. Using YouTube is a practice of navigating through the database of stored contents, either by direct search requests on the YouTube website, or by clicking through lists of videos provided on YouTube or any other website that streams videos from its database. The hybrid information management is crucial, as it determines the retrieval and the relational presentation of videos. Apparently, users quickly learned how to affect search results through keywords (tags) and additional text-based information. The versatility visible in the technical design meets the miscellaneous practices to make YouTube a platform and a channel for "shameless" self-representation, but also educational videos, political propaganda, informative documentaries and commercial programs, as well as grassroots journalism, alternative news services and political debate. Hence, YouTube obviously provides a platform for viewing all sorts of audiovisual clips, but also a forum for various kinds of interaction between humans, and perhaps even more importantly, an infrastructure for generating data that can be treated as metadata. To understand YouTube, one needs to go deep into YouTube.

Endnotes

* The authors would like to thank the members of the Utrecht Media and Performance Seminar for their valuable comments on an earlier version of this text.

1 Geert Lovink, "The Art of Watching Databases. Introduction to the Video Vortex Reader," in *The Video Vortex Reader. Responses to YouTube*, eds. Geert Lovink & Sabine Niederer (Amsterdam: Institute of Network Cultures, 2008), p. 9.

2 Thomas Thiel, "Curator as Filter/User as Creator," in *The Video Vortex Reader*, p. 184.

3 Post by Bryant dated 1 July 2008 – www.mcgilltribune.com/home/index.cfm?event=displayArticleComments&ustory [last checked 15 February 2009].

4 Henry Jenkins, *Convergence Culture. Where Old and New Media Collide* (New York: New York University Press, 2008), p. 275.

5 See Michel Foucault, *L'archéologie du savoir* (Paris: Gallimard, 1969), pp. 169–173. See also Wolfgang Ernst, *Das Rumoren der Archive* (Berlin: Merve, 2002).

6 Post by Leo Enticknap on the Association of Moving Image Archivists (AMIA) discussion list, "The YouTube issue" thread – http://palimpsest.stanford.edu/byform/mailing-lists/amia-l/2006/10/msg00274.html [last checked 15 February 2009].

7 Post by Rick Prelinger, ibid.

8 Post by Andrea Leigh, ibid. This position, however is nuanced by another librarian: "A library is simply a collection of materials made for use by a particular population—that's the dictionary definition. [...] Does YouTube hold a collection of materials? Yes. Do they provide comprehensive access? Yes (to those who have computers). Is there any organization? Probably very little, but I haven't spent enough time on there to figure that out. Do they have selection criteria? No I don't think so, but in this case it makes it all the more interesting ... which is the objective I believe. The point is ... I think there is definitely strong argument that it is not an archive ... but not a library? Hmmmm." Post by Brena Smith, ibid.

9 For YouTube itself, however, such analogies are rather profitable in terms of its cultural legitimation. Hence the comment of one AMIA member: "I'm sure Google would be thrilled to know that professionals are spending their days discussing whether or not YouTube is an archive, library, or neither. $1.65 billion well spent. Ha ha!" Post by Brena Smith, ibid.

10 Lev Manovich, *The Language of New Media* (Cambridge, MA: MIT Press, 2001), p. 219.

11 See Tim O'Reilly, "What is Web 2.0" (2005) – www.oreillynet.com/pub/a/oreilly/tim/news/2005/09/30/what-is-web-20.html [last checked 15 February 2009].

12 YouTube and other video websites stream their videos in the Adobe flash video format. Various additional applications, so called add-ons, for the frequently used Mozilla Firefox Browser enable downloading video clips and saving them as flv files—on a Mac you simply press Command-Option-A and then save the flv file. Videos downloaded from YouTube thus constitute an "unknown" data collection that is extending the YouTube database into the hard drives of a multitude of users, where videos might be stored even long after their removal from the YouTube database itself.

13 Among others, these metadata offers the possibility of placing advertisements that correspond to the content of a clip and thus generate additional income for YouTube's mother company Google.

14 See Bruno Latour, *Reassembling the Social. An Introduction to Actor-Network-Theory* (Oxford: Oxford University Press, 2005).

15 See Bruno Latour, "Technology is Society Made Durable," in *A Sociology of Monsters. Essays on Power, Technology and Domination*, ed. John Law (London: Routledge, 1991).

16 See contributions to *KINtop. Jahrbuch zur Erforschung des frühen Films 11. Kinematographen-Programme*, eds. Frank Kessler, Sabine Lenk & Martin Loiperdinger (Frankfurt am Main: Stroemfeld Verlag, 2003).

17 This also goes for the already mentioned so-called mashup websites "mixing" content from YouTube with other databases or streaming selected videos into an interface different from the YouTube interface.

18 The ranking of videos provided as results for any given search request are also affected by the popularity of the video, ranking more popular videos higher. As Ann-Sophie Lehman has pointed out in her review of the category of How-to videos on YouTube, the search phrase "How to iron a shirt" retrieves a list of videos showing how to iron a shirt, but also ranked within the top five results the video "Hillary Heckled Iron My Shirt" of an incident during the Hillary Clinton campaign. The video has had a high number of viewers, the title contains the keywords "iron" and "shirt," which in combination with the high viewing rate (99,313 views as of January 2009) and a high number of comments (988 as of January 2009) probably identified it as a video relevant to the search request "How to iron a shirt." See also Ann-Sophie Lehmann, "How to YouTube. Aneignung und Repräsentation kreativer Prozesse als Performanz von tacit knowledge" (unpublished paper presented at Jahrestagung der Gesellschaft für Medienwissenschaft 2008, Bochum).

19 See for instance Harriet W. Harrison, ed., *The FIAF Cataloguing Rules for Film Archives* (Munich: Saur, 1991).

20 YouTube makes users choose between the following fifteen categories: Cars & Vehicles, Comedy, Education, Entertainment, Film & Animation, Gaming, How-to & Style, Music, News & Politics, Non-profits & Activism, People & Blogs, Pets & Animals, Science & Technology, Sport, Travel & Events. While there most certainly is some kind of logic behind this, the categories definitely read as a rather random attempt to create classifications.

21 Frequently used tags are keywords such as video, sexy, sex, music, rock, rap, funny, news, pop, dance, film, short, and TV. The majority of the uploaded videos are categorized as Music, Entertainment, People / Blogs, and Comedy. See a survey on the most recent uploaded videos of March 12, 2007, conducted by Michael Wesch at Kansas State University – http://ksudigg.wetpaint.com/page/YouTube+Statistics [last checked 15 February 2009].

22 See for instance Birgit Richard, "Media Masters and Grassroot Art 2.0 on YouTube," *The Video Vortex Reader*, pp. 145–146.

23 The video does not display any pornographic content but non-nude pictures of Paris Hilton and footage of monkeys. It is tagged "Hot, XXX, Adult, Action!, Extended, version, real, though including, paris, hilton, and, pamela, anderson, sex, tape, clips, uncensored" – http://nl.youtube.com/watch?v=u8rkZxfoZNA [last checked 15 February 2009].

24 For a quantitative study on the construction of popularity on YouTube videos and the way this is carried out by the information management system see Meeyoung Cha et al., "I Tube, You Tube, Everybody Tubes: Analyzing the World's Largest User Generated Content Video System," in *Proceedings of IMC 2007* (San Diego: ACM Internet Measurement Conference, 2007), pp. 1–14.

25 With regard to censorship concerns regarding material relating to homosexuality, see Minke Kampman, "Flagging or Fagging. (Self-)Censorship of Gay Content on YouTube," *The Video Vortex Reader*, pp. 153–160.

26 For a discussion of this and similar phenomena as aspects of an "extended cultural industry," see Mirko Tobias Schäfer, *Bastard Culture! User Participation and the Extension of Cultural Industries* (PhD diss., Utrecht University, 2008).

27 At the time this article was written in December 2008, the website The Programmable Web lists 334 mashups for the YouTube API – www.programmableweb.com/api/youtube [last checked 15 February 2009].

28 See Tagbulb – www.tagbulb.com/ [last checked 15 February 2009].

29 This, however, has side effects with regard to the automatic ranking by the information management system. As several identical clips can be uploaded and they are considered separate, the popularity status of the same video may vary considerably. See Meeyung Cha et al. 2007, p. 13.

30 See YouTomb – http://youtomb.mit.edu/ [last checked 15 February 2009].

Pelle Snickars

The Archival Cloud

Late in the fall of 2006, *Wired* published an article on the new information factories of the future. These binary plants were supposedly beginning to establish an online infrastructure with the potential to store all data ever produced, and according to the author George Gilder, the dawning of the petabyte age would inevitably lead to the death of the desktop. In the years to come, local computing power would not stand a chance. If mainframe computers were once superseded by minicomputers and PCs, the latter two would now, in their turn, be rapidly replaced by an Internet cloud of shared networks with immense computational power and made up of millions of machines and servers.

Gilder's article was interesting in many ways, particularly because the notion of "cloud computing" was frequently being explained and elaborated upon. Local-area networks apparently belonged to the past, and were being replaced by an "architecture [where] data is mostly resident on servers 'somewhere on the Internet,' " as Google's CEO Eric Schmidt put it in a quoted e-mail exchange. Schmidt was also confident that the contemporary architectural IT shift would lead to "the return of massive data centers."[1] The Googleplex's estimated 200 petabytes of storage at the time seems to have been a first step toward creating the cloud. However, as Gilder stated, past performance was no present-day guarantee, because even "bigger shocks" of data were predicted to be on their way. "An avalanche of digital video measured in exabytes," as Gilder metaphorically put it, seemed currently to be "hurtling down from the mountainsides of panicked Big Media and bubbling up from the YouTubian depths."[2]

It is not likely to surprise anyone that, in fall 2006, YouTube was more or less synonymous with the video avalanche that characterized the Web at the time. During the summer of that year, YouTube had grown at an inconceivable rate of 75 percent a week. The website already had 13 million unique visitors every day who watched more than a hundred million video clips.[3] Naturally, this colossal success was also the reason why Google, at the juncture between October and

November 2006, purchased YouTube for 1.65 billion dollars in Google stock, a deal announced shortly after Gilder's article appeared in print. "Video is powerful. And it's amazing," as Eric Schmidt would later put it in a TV speech.

In many ways, Google is a company that, right from the start in 1997, was designed on the premise that users would want to move from the local desktop to the virtual cumulus in the not-so-distant future. In the eyes of Schmidt and Google founders Sergey Brin and Larry Page, YouTube was therefore perceived as a form of cloud-computing site *avant les mots*, where access to content was as simple as performing a Google query. In fact, YouTube seemed to have taken into account the most precious of Googlian resources—user time and patience. The uncomplicated infrastructure of the site held users' attention, and fast searches, hyperlinks and an interactive tag structure made video content appear to be just a click away. Prior to YouTube, there were few websites that allowed the user to both easily upload moving images and use the Web as a platform for storage and distribution. To be sure, Flickr had already combined uploading of photographs to the Web, where users could tag, comment on and share their pictures, in 2004. But the idea of moving images being directly accessible in a gigantic Web archive was even more attractive—not least commercially. It is true that YouTube (like Flickr) would remain restrictive in its use of advertisements,[4] yet in the eyes of the Google people, the website's public and commercial potential was enormous.

As is generally known, what YouTube offered users—an elegant and flexible way of sharing moving images—became the very starting point of the wave of "video sharing" that would follow. At present, video sharing has established itself as a central part of Net culture, and today YouTube is the world's largest archive of moving images. YouTube has been and remains the default website for a "clip culture" that is increasingly defining both Web entertainment and online information. At the outset, it was completely user-driven, but TV companies and other institutions joined in almost immediately, quickly upgrading the website to a global media repository with which few traditional archival institutions could compete.[5] If the international ALM sector (archives, libraries and museums) is currently struggling with the parameters of user-generated Web 2.0—the main problem being the inability to take advantage of the distributional potential of the Web due to intellectual property rights—the most striking aspect of YouTube, Flickr and other similar "media-archive sites" is that they actually offer the media storage and distribution model of the future. Access is the guiding principle, and these websites have in fact already changed how media material is used and reused. As is well known, one of YouTube's basic recipes for success is the new remix culture in which older forms of media are molded into new interfaces.

By analyzing YouTube as a sort of archival practice, this article will focus on the current transformation of the storage sector and the various discourses surrounding that alteration. Within publicly funded archival institutions digital storage is sometimes seen as a "black hole," basically since the long-term costs of keeping digital files are substantial. "If funding starts to fade, the information may still be retrieved but after a while it will no longer be accessible due to corrupted files, or obsolete file formats or technology,"[6] as the argument goes. While this is certainly the case, binary files are always also accessible files. In traditional media archives, perhaps ten percent of what has been collected is actually used, but the ease of watching and using videos on, for example, YouTube has meant that almost all uploaded material has been viewed by at least one or two users. Thus, according to the logic of the long tail, new Web-based user patterns run counter to traditional forms of analogue usage. The role of traditional archives is of course to preserve content, but the worst way to protect it is to ignore access. Such denial generates no value, and leaves archives unable to afford preservation projects. Protecting and keeping digital content requires public interest—which only comes from various forms of access. This is why YouTube, with its binary cloud of content, is an important archival media phenomenon. The site, in short, offers completely new ways of thinking about both storage and distribution of information.

Cloud Computing

In the summer of 2008, Apple introduced a collection of services called MobileMe, which was a considerable update of the previous application "dot mac." Unfortunately, it proved to be anything but reliable, and Apple soon experienced problems with its credibility. In an internal e-mail, even Steve Jobs admitted that MobileMe had been released too early and that it "[was] not up to Apple's standards."[7]

Based on "push technique," MobileMe was intended to allow users to directly access synchronized personal information via the Web no matter where they were. E-mail, calendars and files would follow the user like a virtual floating cloud filled with information that could be accessed regardless of operating system. The considerable amount of personal storage space provided ensured that users could access files, given a functioning Internet connection.

MobileMe is an example of what the IT branch has termed "cloud computing." In 2008, cloud computing has become something of a buzzword for a new kind of infrastructure for personified information, which no longer exists locally on one's own computer, but online in the Internet's network. YouTube and Flickr, MySpace and Facebook are well-known examples of a kind of cloud computing, because the content and programs for these websites exist online. Naturally, the same also applies to the widely branched blog culture; in fact, Web 2.0 is in many ways molded in the image of cloud computing.

42 Apple's cloud service Mobile Me: "No matter where you are, your devices are always up to date"

But this new digital cloud can also be seen as something more far-reaching, something that is substantially changing how we view the computer as a machine. The above-mentioned article in *Wired* tried to describe the current computational transformation, but two years ago its contours were still blurry and diffuse. Today, however, it is clear that our computers can be understood less and less as isolated and separate units. Concurrently with the development of the Web, it has become impossible to differentiate one's own computer from the network it has become an unmistakable part of. The fact that increasing numbers of small, simple computers are selling is one sign of this trend; figures show, for instance, that more than five million small devices, such as the Asus Eee, were sold in 2008.[8] One's own computer, music player or cell phone no longer needs to be particularly sophisticated, because these devices can retrieve their power, programs, storage space and the information the user requires directly from the Web and the Internet.

This shift, in which our computers are no longer separate units, applies not only to traditional personal computers. The next generation of cell phones, cameras, music players and consoles will all have "online" as their default setting. This means that there will be no reason to save a photograph locally in one's digital camera, because the picture will instantly and automatically be stored "in the cloud." Yet in several respects, the future is already here. For instance, using the small application Dropbox, one can easily (by placing a file in a folder) use the Web as both a storage place and a file server between different computers. Another example is the popular Swedish site Spotify. This is not a purely Web-based service, but a client installed locally to which music is streamed from the company's servers. Still, the principle is the same: if all music—Spotify is said to contain more than two million songs and instrumental pieces—is accessible as soon as one turns on one's computer, then there is no longer any incentive to own these files or to store them locally.

In an attempt to understand structural changes in the economy, society and culture that appear to be the consequence of an increasingly extensive digital cloud, Nicholas Carr, in his book *The Big Switch*, compares current developments with the business strategies underlying the introduction of electricity. For example, production of electrical current took place on a local basis for a long time. In 1901, 50,000 American companies had their own plants for production of electrical current. Carr's analogy is striking. Modern companies have long had essentially identical IT departments that could be centralized. And this is exactly what happened a hundred years ago when central power plants took over various local electricity markets. Although there are certainly considerable differences between information technology and electricity, both are technologies with a general purpose, that is, both are platforms on which a number of applications can be designed. The point of Carr's historical parallel is to show that decentralization and diversification were, and still are, a bad thing in terms of large-scale investments.[9]

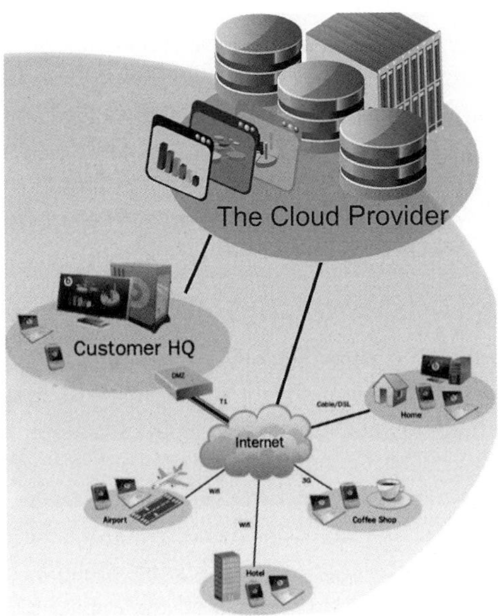

43 The infrastructure of cloud computing

The Internet is, of course, an optimal medium because of its decentralized network structure; in short, it is a cloud made up of different smaller clouds. However, in terms of IT infrastructure and databases that lie below the cloud, it does not seem rational anymore to build separate storage systems at individual archives, to use the ALM sector as an example. The current international trend among cultural-heritage institutions is certainly merging and centralization.

Cloud computing, hence, constitutes a step toward centralizing the information-technology infrastructure, and naturally, the strategic attraction of the cloud is the promise it brings of more cost-efficient IT. While companies and institutions have built and maintained separate PC systems and local networks, so-called client-server systems, for a quarter of a century at huge cost, these systems and networks are now gradually being replaced by centralized IT services delivered directly over the Internet. Google being on the leading edge of this development depends primarily on the fact that Brin and Page realized early on that the Web's network of networks of computers and servers could actually be seen as one gigantic information-processing machine which through sophisticated and superfast communication protocols simply shares bits of data and strings of code. They were not alone in realizing this. In 1993, their present colleague Schmidt (who then worked for Sun Microsystems) pointed out that "when the networks become as fast as the processor, the computer hollows out and spreads across the network."[10]

However, Sun Microsystems's slogan at the time, "The Network Is the Computer," was seen by many as an insult. The network could hardly be one's computer when, with a 28.8 kbit/s modem, one had to look at a blank screen for several minutes while waiting for a website to load. It is rather hard to remember, but Web browsers prior to Netscape Navigator were not able to show anything at all before all information had been read. Thus, connection speed is completely central to the Net's cloud of data. If, on the one hand, Moore's law stipulates that computer processor power doubles every two years, Grove's law indicates, on the other hand, that the bandwidth of telecommunications doubles every decade. Processor speed has developed at a much faster rate—thereby dominating the market—than communication speed in the networks. Insufficient bandwidth has thus regulated the impact of the Net on a kind of infrastructural level.

If speed remains crucial to cloud computing, another decisive factor is reliability. Working in close connection with the Internet requires considerable trust in both the hardware and Internet service providers (ISPs). Saving one's information online may seem unsafe, but with the overlapping data and system redundancy offered by cloud computing, the risks are few. Thanks to modern data encryption, ensuring the integrity of one's information is also no longer a major problem. The crux of the matter is naturally people's general confidence in the Internet. But in reality, the Internet is one of the more protected places for gathering material: the Arpanet/Internet was once created to be the optimal medium, with its digital network of networks designed to survive even a nuclear war. At the same time, backbiters have often stressed that binary code is certainly not to be trusted, and many doubt that digital formats will prove to be as permanent as other storage media. But as Matthew G. Kirschenbaum asserted in his book *Mechanisms*, such criticism is often based on a considerable lack of knowledge of the binary system. The Internet is not only a resistant storage medium by virtue of its decentralized character, hard disks are also considerably more archival in nature than one might think. For instance, what happens after the Ctrl+S command is typed is much more complicated than most suppose, and another equally complex procedure takes place when one empties the "trash." It is not the case that all files in the interface's trash bin disappear once and for all when this is done. In a Windows operating system, this command only means that the computer's FAT (file allocation table) is updated; the files are still on the hard disk. Kirschenbaum points out that when files are used in a computer's operating system, they leave traces of themselves in all sorts of places, like balls in a pinball machine. The same applies to an e-mail message, which leaves dozens of copies of itself during its lightning-fast journey through the Internet's networks. If digital media are sometimes presented as ethereal, this is not the whole truth. Even virtual reality has a material foundation in the form of nanotechnological inscriptions on the computer's hard disk. Strange as it may seem, it is more or less impossible to erase a hard disk; every digital inscription leaves a trace—if only at the nano level.[11]

The new trust in the Web—not the least apparent at the numerous and popular sites offering free online storage—is probably the major reason for the growth of the digital cloud. Today, even Microsoft has realized that a significant change has occurred. "Everything in computer science [has to do with writing] less code," Bill Gates stated in a recent interview. "[Subroutines] is the technique for writing less code. [...] We are [now] in a world ... [where a] subroutine can exist on another computer across the Internet."[12]

In an interview in *Wired*, Microsoft's Chief Software Architect Ray Ozzie stressed the fact that new versions of Office will hardly generate significant revenues in the future.[13] Instead, like everyone else, Microsoft must move out onto the Web, and at the moment, they

44 Try to erase a hard drive—it is almost impossible

are working intensively on an online-based operating system called Windows Azure. Others have been quicker to switch over. Adobe recently launched Photoshop.com, where anyone can now arrange his/her pictures online—something Flickr has offered its users since 2007. Naturally, Amazon as well belongs to the cloud's avant-garde.

Already in August 2006, the company launched the "Amazon Elastic Compute Cloud (EC2) ... a web service that provides resizable compute capacity in the cloud."[14] The service was designed to make Web-scale computing easier for developers, and since the launch, hundreds of thousands of developers and programmers, websites and applications have been paying to use the company's servers. Because Amazon's total computational capacity is used only a few times a year, it is more lucrative to rent out servers that are not used regularly. For instance, about a year ago, the Animoto company, which customizes media presentations of users' photographs and music, was able to serve 25,000 customers an hour using Amazon's cloud of computing capacity. Instead of increasing its own server capacity a hundredfold, which would hardly have been possible technically, Animoto paid ten cents an hour per Amazon server. In fact, cloud computing has been so vital to Animoto's operations that Amazon CEO Jeff Bezos has used the company as an example of how well "EC2 helps web apps scale when their traffic hockey sticks," according to TechCrunch.[15]

Naturally, for actors the cloud's attraction lies in new markets and business opportunities, but with regard to information theory, the shift from desktop to webtop also implies a fundamental change in how we understand binary categories such as "computer" and "Web," "archive," "database" and "sharing." YouTube's model of using the Web as the platform for media content and distribution was hardly the first, but it was a preliminary—and popular—move toward this digital cloud. Of course, this meant initial hassles and nuisances. For instance, in April 2006, Forbes pointed out that the 40 million videos and 200 terabytes of data that were already being streamed from the company's too few servers and undersized machinery certainly constituted a significant element of risk.[16] Three months later, *USA Today* reported that 65,000 videos were uploaded to YouTube daily, and that every day, users clicked on about 100 million video clips. These enormous volumes meant that time spent watching YouTube clips already amounted to almost two thirds of general video watching on the Internet.[17] At the same time, the company's costs for bandwidth were approaching a million dollars a month. Consequently, much of the venture capital YouTube brought in was likely used to finance and optimize the website's technical infrastructure. The deal YouTube made with the ISP Limelight Networks was certainly as advantageous as it was secret, but Forbes nevertheless expressed some skepticism regarding a business model in which so much money was invested in something that hardly generated any revenues at all.[18]

In his book *Planet Google*, Randall Stross claimed that YouTube's phenomenal popularity was technologically grounded in the close timing of three central IT factors. What first enabled YouTube's success was the rapid expansion of broadband. During the dotcom boom around the turn of the millennium, optical fibers that could circle the Earth 11,000 times were being laid down,[19] and YouTube and others were able to reap the benefits of this digital infrastructure. During the period when Web connections were made using 56.6 kbit/s modems, a similar video website would have had no possibility of breaking through. Moving images, even in streamed form, required considerable connection speed, which only broadband could give. Second, as Stross pointed out, the dotcom companies' costs for purchasing bandwidth had decreased substantially by the time YouTube was launched. And *Forbes* speculated that the agreement with Limelight Networks probably meant that YouTube paid as little as between 0.5 and 0.1 cents a minute.[20] From a user perspective, however, the third factor was most important, because it affected the software YouTube relied on. During the ten-year history of the Web, sites with moving images had often experienced problems with playback software. Cross-platform media players such as RealPlayer, Windows Media Player and QuickTime were the established playback technologies for years, but generally they required users to download, upgrade or install various browser plug-ins. YouTube instead decided to use Adobe's new Flash Player, an application created by Macromedia but developed by Adobe after they purchased Macromedia in late 2005. Because Flash plug-ins where preinstalled in almost every personal computer on the market, YouTube reckoned they would experience few problems with Flash. The decision proved to be right, and in fact users have rarely had any problems with incompatible video-encoding formats.

Nevertheless, YouTube's capacity problem was a daily one over a long period of time, at least until Google purchased the company. The mantra "We're running out of storage capacity" seems to have been repeated in the company's hallways.[21] The principal reason was the lack of prescreened uploads, which meant there was actually no control over the website's growth. Naturally, this was never a question of complete laissez faire. It is well known that video material has always been scrutinized and in some cases removed from YouTube. But there has never been any kind of a priori control of content. Besides the limited amount of advertising—which (unfortunately) has become more and more apparent during the last year—this is probably the main reason why YouTube has been the fastest growing site in the history of the Web. At the same time, this lack of control and infrastructural overview meant constant problems with capacity. It was simply impossible to adequately predict the growth in traffic. The fact that YouTube did not examine material in advance has sometimes been presented as pioneering and radical, but the basic idea was not new—and it would later constitute the very basis of Web 2.0 and of social media in general. One of the co-founders of YouTube, Jawed Karim, has pointed out in various contexts that

Flickr, but primarily the dating website hotornot.com, "where anyone could upload content that everyone else could view"[22]—and where this content was ranked (by how attractive various dates were on a scale from one to ten)—was the major inspiration behind the technological infrastructure of YouTube.

At present, ten hours of video material are uploaded to YouTube every minute. Despite this volume, today's technical problems are fewer. Ever since Google entered the scene, YouTube's storage and capacity potential have increased dramatically. The reason, according to Stross, is simply that Google works under the motto of "unlimited capacity."[23] At the same time, fears have been expressed that the Web is heading toward a traffic bottleneck caused by the video trend YouTube established. At the end of 2007, the *International Herald Tribune* reported that the 100 million video clips that were then being streamed daily from YouTube's servers required as much bandwidth as the entire Internet had seven years earlier. Thus, the company stood out as a binary traffic crook, "[since] video is rapidly becoming the most popular thing we do online. But video takes up a lot of space, a lot more than text, and the increased use of video means that the Internet is fast filling up. The result is that if we don't invest soon [...] it could take forever for your photos or video to download or for your e-mail to arrive."[24] Today, however, these fears seem to have been unfounded, thanks especially to the new trend of cloud computing. But fear of traffic jams remains, which is clear in Barack Obama's proposal on net neutrality in terms of Internet speed.[25] YouTube has been criticized for taking up too much of the Web's bandwidth, even though most people agree that the real villains are the global P2P networks whose huge traffic volumes completely dominate the Internet.

Archival Mobility

For the past few years, the "archive" has appeared as a kind of guiding metaphor for the contemporary digital media landscape. According to Wolfgang Ernst it is one of the most essential metaphors "for all kinds of memory and storage capacities."[26] Media archive websites such as YouTube and Flickr are symptomatic of the way in which the Web is recasting today's media forms in an archival direction. Naturally, the digital archive is by nature a database, that is, a structured collection of data stored in a computer system. Database structures are organized according to various models: relational, hierarchical, network and so forth. Regarding YouTube, Geert Lovink has consequently proposed that "we no longer watch films or TV; we watch databases."[27] One consequence regarding this database structure, as well as the digital production and distribution of media, is that the differences between various media forms are disappearing. This is also true of newspapers, photographs and music. The concept of medium specificity is starting to become archaic. On the Web, all media are gray—or more correctly, on the Web there are on closer observation no media at all, just files in databases containing mathematically coded information. Just as 20th century media forms are converging, they are also being replaced by the surface effects of algorithms, that is, by various kinds of programmed content consisting of text, sounds and (moving) images. Filled as it is with binary files, the Internet would seem to be the only channel of communication that still remains.

At the same time, a rather strict division between different media forms still prevails on the Web. For instance, when public service radio or television has been upgraded to digital platforms, the programs are still packaged using the respective media's special signatures, logotype, etcetera. Web-based television is still seen as an *extension* of conventional TV—even though the focus may be changing gradually. The specificity of the medium is, thus, rooted in the analogue past and not in the digital future. But of course there are exceptions; podcasting for example has become a distinct media-specific feature of online radio. Nevertheless, the major difference between analogue and traditional public service and its subsequent online version is indeed the latter's distinct archival character. The motto of Swedish Television's online application SVT Play, for instance states: "More than 2,000 hours of free television—whenever you want!" And the slogan for the BBC iPlayer reads in a rather similar archival fashion: "Making the unmissable unmissable." As of December 2008, more than 180 million programs have been viewed on the BBC iPlayer since its release, hence making a "massive library available to the public."[28]

The new database model or archival mode of online media is also apparent in new media settings disconnected from the Web. Data storage, for example, has become something of a fashionable accessory:

people in the West adorn themselves with white and black iPods or USB memory sticks in shiny design. The mobile iPod culture could also be said to be archival in nature. The foremost variant of an iPod Classic currently has as much as 160 gigabytes of storage space, that is, room for either 40,000 MP3 music files or 200 hours of video. However, selling storage space as an attraction has not always been possible; one never sees a computer's hard disk except as a graphical representation on a computer screen. In fact, data storage has traditionally been completely overshadowed by various glossy interfaces. The Graphical User Interface, the GUI, has essentially got all the attention in descriptions of IT developments. But times change, and Apple is said to have sold about 160 million iPods. The attraction of this little apparatus is not only its impressive design, but also its function as a mobile media archive that lets the user carry around an entire library. Naturally, the library metaphor is even more apt with regard to Amazon's Kindle. The fact that the first version of this portable reading device could store only 200 books was actually completely irrelevant. Kindle 2 can store many more, yet the whole point of this device is its built-in mobile-phone modem that can download, in no time, any book selected from Amazon's cloud of binary books. Consequently, Jeff Bezos has pointed out that his scarcely modest vision for Kindle "is to have every book that has ever been in print available in less than 60 seconds."[29]

Naturally, the founders of YouTube have also shown an interest in the mobile Web. Concurrently with developments entailing that Web surfing is no longer only based only on traditional computers, but has also moved into various MIDs (mobile internet devices), YouTube has invested in making its own website more or less platform and operating-system independent. In May 2006, YouTube launched its "YouTube To Go" service, mainly owing to the growing number of handheld devices capable of recording video.[30] The service enabled users to upload clips directly from their mobile phones to the Web, and half a year later, Chad Hurley announced that yet another mobile service would allow basically everyone to share videos with one another in the YouTube community directly via their cell phones.[31] Furthermore, in February 2007, Nokia and YouTube announced that they were now "global partners," and that the new Nokia Nseries phones would be able to access the sub-site YouTube Mobile from a built-in web browser.[32] More deals followed. In June of the same year, YouTube signed a deal with Apple so that users could

45 YouTube as "killer app" for the iPhone

soon enjoy original content on Apple TV, but more importantly, YouTube became sort of a "killer app" for the new and hyped iPhone.

According to a press release from Apple, YouTube had in fact begun to encode videos in the advanced H.264 format "to achieve higher video quality and longer battery life on mobile devices." Initially, some 10,000 videos would be available, but YouTube promised to continue adding content each week until the "full catalogue of videos was available in the H.264 format."[33]

Apparently, YouTube made great efforts to hook up with the mobile community. Offering video services on mobile devices seems to have been a key opportunity for the company, and YouTube's partner Nokia serves as a case in point. Rumor has it that a Nokia cell phone—due to the company's 40 percent share of the world market—is currently *the* technological device producing the majority of media on a global scale. Consequently, there are innumerable blog posts, sites and online comments on mobile-media usage. For instance, a year ago, thenokiaguide.com stated that YouTube "has made a huge impact on our Web 2.0 lives. Its popularity can best be seen from the amount of [Nokia] apps specifically made for YouTube alone. In a time frame of just a few months we have not one but four apps: Mobitubia, Emtube, YTPlayer and the YouTube Java app." In addition to these, the blog mentioned the mobile YouTube site, as well as the option on some Nokia devices to watch clips directly from the browser with Flash Lite support. "Since when did we have so many apps and services available for just one video service?"[34]

File Sharing

Letting users share videos regardless of place and time was YouTube's main impetus for going mobile. Needless to say, Web 2.0 has been about sharing user-generated content. Consequently, the Web-based participatory culture is rudimentary to understanding YouTube as a cultural phenomenon, as a number of articles in this book reveal. Indeed, "sharing" as a process of dividing and distributing is also an apt metaphor—like the notion of the "archive"—with regard to the new binary landscape. "Sharing is a key feature in the developing field of free software and open source software," Wikipedia informs us, and the dichotomy between "commercial" and "sharing" economies is also central in both Yochai Benkler's and Lawrence Lessig's latest books. According to the former, "sharing" can be seen as "a new mode of production emerging in the middle of the most advanced economies in the world." These new "nonmarket collaborations" are driven by computer networks in which different social relations act as a replacement for pricing mechanisms.[35] As a consequence, according to Lessig, "people participating in creating something of value share that value independent of money."[36]

The primary example of this new "sharing," however, is file sharing. Some see file sharing as the plague of our time, but it is without doubt also a central phenomenon in understanding how the information landscape has changed during the past decade. Already in 1999, the launch of Napster—the first file-sharing program to be spread and used by a wide audience—indicated that media could potentially be shared, stored and distributed in an entirely new way. The power of Napster lay in the network itself, and by the turn of the millennium, almost 30 million people had used the website. The similarities with YouTube are striking, not least regarding the doubtful copyright status of the material, which subsequently led to Napster's fall. Since then the P2P technique has developed, and today's superfast file-sharing protocols stand out (perhaps even more than YouTube does) as a kind of media archive and information distributor of the future. What is technologically remarkable about P2P networks is that while distribution of media material via a website becomes sluggish because when there are too many users, the opposite is the case for P2P. In P2P networks, the more users there are, the faster the distribution. As soon as you download something, you also become *by definition*, and at the same moment, an uploader of those parts of the file you have downloaded. Today, P2P networks represent almost half of the traffic on the Internet. For instance, in November 2008, the company MultiMedia Intelligence reported that "P2P data currently represents 44.0 percent of all consumer traffic over the Internet and 33.6 percent in North America. Much of this data is audio and video files (over 70 percent)."[37]

As the term suggests, file sharing means that users *share* digital information over the network. The same principle applies to cloud computing, and today, several minor actors are building their applications *on* and not *for* the Internet. In other words, the Net *per se* is the new operating system. At the same time, according to critical representatives of various "sharing economies," for example the Open-Source Movement, the digital cloud is a marketing hype. Users are being tricked into uploading personal information into private clouds that are owned and run by companies. Naturally, Google has access to the information users store on its servers—even if Google maintains that it would never use that information. Considered from this perspective, the cloud appears to be considerably darker.

Still, a number of IT gurus, for instance Kevin Kelly of *Wired*, claim that developments toward cloud computing and sharing are inevitable. At the Web 2.0 Summit conference in November 2008, Kelly pointed out that because our media are converging, we will soon have only one common media platform, whether we are talking about TV, the press, radio or film. Everything exists online and is run by the same kind of Web-based machine. In his presentation, which he introduced as "an impressionistic view of what we all are heading towards"—which now of course can be seen on YouTube[38]—Kelly stressed that, in the future, three overall moves will probably characterize the Web: a move up into the digital cloud, a move down into gigantic databases, and a move toward a kind of general sharing. According to Kelly, information that is not part of the cloud and not accessible to everyone will not exist.[39] The latter notion constitutes the foundation of Web-based applications such as Google Maps, which combine the cloud's data or services using "mashup" technology. There are actually those who claim that if Gutenberg's movable pieces of type were the modules on which the art of printing rested, then almost analogous divisible program modules will constitute the foundation of the information landscape of the future.

Conclusion

Kevin Kelly's intentional focus on sharing as the future of the Web and as a fundamental principle for cloud computing is an exciting scenario. Lawrence Lessig is on a similar train of thought in what he calls "hybrid economies," but his vision of the future is considerably darker—and interestingly enough, one of the reasons is YouTube. The site is a kind of "community space—a virtual place where people interact, share information or interest. [But the trick is] to translate these spaces into successful commercial ventures."[40] According to Lessig, community spaces are one of the hybrid economy's three sub-sectors; the other two consist of advertisement-driven collaborative sites (like Slashdot or Last.fm) or various types of Net communities (like Second Life, a virtual game that generates real revenues). Basic to the popularity of these places is the kind of "viral" marketing used, where services, products or messages are so fascinating—like the content on YouTube—that users or customers spread knowledge of them among their acquaintances without being directly encouraged to do so.

Yet the future is uncertain. Particularly concerning possibilities of making money from, for instance, moving images in a digital cloud that has long been characterized by the fact that content is free—although following Chris Anderson's thoughts on "freeconomics" this might well be possible. As this article is being concluded (in January 2009), media reports on YouTube are dominated by the topic of how and when the site will begin making money during the coming year.[41] The eyeballs are there—but how to monetize? Monetization seems to be the number one priority for YouTube during 2009. Strategies involve everything from putting more ads into clips to "click-to-buy" services that take advantage of online ordering mechanisms. But one important factor for getting a hybrid like YouTube to work is having insight into how a social network functions, as well as knowledge of the norms and values that regulate users' activities. Naturally, the people at YouTube know that too much advertisement and too great a focus on sales will lead to decreased popularity. It is nevertheless likely that, in the future, various forms of hybrid economies will constitute the predominant architecture for conducting business in the cloud. If we follow Lessig's gloomier scenario, however, this business architecture will not only reshape the Net's commercial prerequisites, but also radically change how the Net's current gift economy and system of sharing function. It is possible that, in the future, we will have to reckon with a stingier Internet.

Endnotes

1 George Gilder, "The Information Factories," *Wired,* 14 October 2006 – www.wired.com/wired/archive/14.10/cloudware.html [last checked 15 February 2009].

2 Schmidt is quoted from Gilder 2006.

3 Pete Cashmore, "YouTube is World's Fastest Growing Website," *Mashable* 22 July 2006 – http://mashable.com/2006/07/22/youtube-is-worlds-fastest-growing-website/ [last checked 15 February 2009].

4 For a discussion of Flickr and YouTube as variants of hybrid economies, see Lawrence Lessig, *Remix – Making Art and Commerce Thrive in the Hybrid Economy* (New York: Penguin Press, 2008).

5 YouTube contains a great deal of video material from public-service TV channels like the BBC and PBS in addition to material from innumerable commercial TV channels. Today, YouTube has agreements with thousands of partners, but what is most interesting is the actors that have brought suits against YouTube for copyright infringement while simultaneously establishing collaborations with the website. Naturally, everyone wants to be where the users are. This is also the case for the French national media archive, Institut national de l'audiovisuel, an institution that has both sued and cooperated with YouTube at the same time. See, e.g., the blog post, "YouTube en conflit avec Warner Music et l'INA," 22 December 2008 – www.degroupnews.com/actualite/n3115-youtube-warner_music-ina-remuneration-justice.html [last checked 15 February 2009]. It is well know that the relationship between amateurism and professionalism is being renegotiated on YouTube, but thus far, this also concerns the amorphous boundaries between legal and illegal media activities.

6 Jonas Palm, "The Digital Black Hole," 2006 – www.tape-online.net/docs/Palm_Black_Hole.pdf [last checked 15 February 2009].

7 For a discussion, see the blog posts on Arstechnica.com, for example http://arstechnica.com/journals/apple.ars/2008/08/04/steve-jobs-mobileme-not-up-to-apples-standards [last checked 15 February 2009].

8 "Let it rise: a special report on corporate IT," *The Economist*, 25 October 2008, p. 7.

9 Nicholas Carr, *The Big Switch: Rewiring the World from Edison to Google* (New York: Norton, 2008).

10 Schmidt is quoted from George Gilder, "The Information Factories," *Wired*, 14 October 2006 – www.wired.com/wired/archive/14.10/cloudware.html [last checked 15 February 2009].

11 Matthew G. Kirschenbaum, *Mechanisms: New Media and the Forensic Imagination* (Cambridge, MA: MIT Press, 2008).

12 Michael J. Miller, "Exclusive: The Bill Gates Exit Interview," *PC Magazine*, 23 June 2008 – www.pcmag.com/article2/0,2817,2321129,00.asp [last checked 15 February 2009].

13 Steven Levy, "Ray's Way," *Wired*, 16 December 2008.

14 Amazon's official blurb for EC2 can be found at http://aws.amazon.com/ec2/ [last checked 15 February 2009].

15 Mark Hendrickson, "Amazon Funds Animoto Music Video Creator," 15 May 2008 – www.techcrunch.com/2008/05/15/amazon-funds-animoto-music-video-creator/ [last checked 15 February 2009].

16 Dan Frommer, "Your Tube, Whose Dime?" *Forbes*, 28 April 2006 – www.forbes.com/intelligentinfrastructure/2006/04/27/video-youtube-myspace_cx_df_0428video.html [last checked 15 February 2009].

17 *USA Today*, "YouTube serves up 100 million videos a day online," 16 July 2006 – www.usatoday.com/tech/news/2006-07-16-youtube-views_x.htm [last checked 15 February 2009].

18 *Forbes* 28 April 2006.

19 Olga Kharif, "The Fiber-Optic 'Glut' – in a New Light," *BusinessWeek*, 31 August 2001 – www.businessweek.com/bwdaily/dnflash/aug2001/nf20010831_396.htm [last checked 15 February 2009].

20 *Forbes* 28 April 2006.

21 John Cloud, "The Gurus of YouTube," *Time* 16 December 2006 – www.time.com/time/magazine/article/0,9171,1570721-1,00.html [last checked 15 February 2009].

22 Ibid.

23 One of the chapters in Stross's book is, in fact, entitled "Unlimited Capacity." See Stross 2008, pp. 47–62.

24 Elaine C. Kamarck, "Avoiding an Internet jam," *International Herald Tribune*, 27 December 2007 – www.iht.com/articles/2007/12/26/opinion/edkamark.php [last checked 15 February 2009].

25 See, e.g., *Financial Times*, "Surfers should pay congestion charges," 5 January 2009 – www.ft.com/cms/s/0/e6601ef2-da93-11dd-8c28-000077b07658.html [last checked 15 February 2009].

26 Wolfgang Ernst, "The Archive as Metaphor. From Archival Space to Archival Time," *Open* no. 7, 2004, pp. 46–54.

27 Geert Lovink, "The Art of Watching Databases – Introduction to the Video Vortex Reader," *The Video Vortex Reader – Responses to YouTube*, eds. Geert Lovink & Sabine Niederer (Amsterdam: Institute of Network Cultures, 2008), pp. 9–12 – http://networkcultures.org/wpmu/portal/files/2008/10/vv_reader_small.pdf [last checked 15 February 2009].

28 Ian Morris, "iPlayer should be an online Freeview," *cnet uk*, 9 December 2008 – http://crave.cnet.co.uk/televisions/0,39029474,49300271,00.htm [last checked 15 February 2009].

29 Bezos's statement is cited on a number of places on the Web. It was originally published in Steven Levy's article "The Future of Reading," *Newsweek*, 26 November 2007. Whether Kindle will become "the iPod of the book world" is still an open question, but probably about 400,000 units were sold in 2008—though the figures vary—which is an indication that even the book, as the last bastion of the analogue world, is in decline.

30 See www.news.com/YouTube-offers-mobile-upload-service/2100-1025_3-6070527.html [last checked 15 February 2009].

31 See http://news.zdnet.com/2100-1035_22-195998.html [last checked 15 February 2009].

32 See www.engadgetmobile.com/2007/02/12/nokia-teams-up-with-an-unfaithful-youtube-for-nseries-vids/ [last checked 15 February 2009].

33 See www.apple.com/pr/library/2007/06/20youtube.html [last checked 15 February 2009]. For a discussion on formats and codecs used by YouTube, see Sean Cubitt, "Codecs and Capability," in Lovink & Niederer 2008, pp. 45–52.

34 See www.thenokiaguide.com/my_weblog/2008/02/whats-the-ultim.html [last checked 15 February 2009].

35 Yochai Benkler, *The Wealth of Networks: How Social Production Transforms Markets and Freedom* (New Haven, CT: Yale University Press, 2006), p. 6.

36 Lessig 2008, 172.

37 Frank Dickson, "P2P: Contents Bad Boy; Tomorrow's Distribution Channel" – http://multimediaintelligence.com/index.php?page=shop.product_details&flypage=flypage.tpl&product_id=21&option=com_virtuemart&Itemid=80 [last checked 15 February 2009].

38 Kevin Kelly's talk "P2P: Contents Bad Boy; Tomorrow's Distribution Channel" – http://multimediaintelligence.com/index.php?page=shop.product_details&flypage=flypage.tpl&product_id=21&option=com_virtuemart&Itemid=80 [last checked 15 February 2009].

39 Kevin Kelly's talk can be found at www.youtube.com/watch?v=1S0-S36pMo4 [last checked 15 February 2009].

40 Lessig 2008, p. 186.

41 See, e.g., Tom Steinert-Threlkeld, "Time for Change at YouTube: Monetization 'No. 1 Priority in 2009,' " *ZDnet,* 8 December 2008 – http://blogs.zdnet.com/BTL/?p=11142 [last checked 15 February 2009].

Trond Lundemo

In the Kingdom of Shadows: Cinematic Movement and Its Digital Ghost

The cultural logic of the Internet is that it potentially contains "everything." YouTube is perhaps the online "archive" and forum where this myth of completeness has become most pervasive. People from all over the world "broadcast themselves," political projects and presidential campaigns are won and lost; in fact, the entire history of the world since the emergence of the moving image seems to be represented here. With its well over 100 million videos, YouTube appears to assume a potential plenitude. YouTube not only makes new, digitally shot productions available, but to a large extent resuscitates the history of the moving image. It is for this reason also an archive of film clips, functioning as an auxiliary for film history.

What are the consequences, of how we think about the digital as well as the analog, regarding the return of films and excerpts in another medium? What changes in the analog images as they are presented and accessed online—and what remains? How do the files with an analog "alias" differ from the films shot digitally for dissemination on YouTube? To discuss these questions I will first take a look at the myth of the completeness of the Internet at large, and YouTube in particular. The argument then proceeds to a consideration of the changes on the code level, which has lead to important differences between technologies of movement of the analog and the digital moving image. Through a case study of the return of the pre-cinema films made by the inventor Louis Le Prince, generally accessible on YouTube for the first time, this discussion ends in an assessment of connections between archives and storage media in the age of online access and a reconfigured notion of the archive.

The rhetoric of completeness draws upon a spatial concept that has always accompanied "the media": the ether. YouTube is today truly the *Tube of Plenty*, as Erik Barnouw named his account of the evolution of American television—and one of his first paragraphs is on voices in the ether.[1] The broadcast drew extensively on this concept in physics, according to which the ether fills gaps between elements in order to secure random points of connection and to "fill in" the universe. Since the ether is invisible, weightless and intangible, it is phantom matter. Consequently, it is also the matter of phantoms.

The question is, then, whether a concept deriving from early physics, and resurrected in early broadcasting history, can be pertinent to the experience of the Internet? As Jeffrey Sconce demonstrates, the concept of the ether became a property of early wireless transmission media after the streams of transmission cables, like those of the telegraph, were substituted by the flow of etheric signals.[2] Ghostly appearances in the ether are random, singular and ephemeral. Later in broadcasting history, the programming schedules of radio and television stations formed patterns of reception that downplayed the etheric and ghostly properties of the signal. Hence, the concept of the modern breakthrough of new technical media cannot simply be re-evoked in the age of the Internet. Today, the digital video signal is streamed rather than flowing in the ether, and the random connections made when "fishing in the etheric ocean" have given away to a repetitive connecting pattern when surfing the Internet.

Still, the promise of plenitude evokes a world that surpasses and ultimately negates the rational calculability of the information on the Internet. Just as the Library of Babel in Borges' story is architecturally and temporally infinite—all information is potentially located there and it stretches beyond our present and into the future—the popular imaginary of the Internet is that of an archive of archives. Just as the Library of Babel contains the story of our individual futures and therefore our death also,[3] the Internet entails a dimension of virtual reality. As such, its lack of boundaries negates the mastery of the user and renders it incalculable. This is the spectral dimension of the Internet that has informed many fictions in cinema and literature. Cyberspace is a ghostly matter with important connections to the all-surrounding ether of modern media transmissions. These aspects of the Internet may also be more present in the age of wireless, mobile broadband that we are currently entering than in the age of modem and cable connections. The wireless Internet brings the ether back to the popular imaginary. Most of all, the ether is as a concept allied with the rhetoric of plenitude of online image archives. If the ether fills in empty spaces to create a complete universe, it becomes the medium of the infinite, and consequently of the spectral and ghostly.

One might argue that the ether has been "ghostly" because it contains "everything." It includes the past and the future, the deaths of others and ourselves, and consequently ghosts. If new media have been conceived as specters of people who have ceased to exist, it is because their storage and transmission make use of an amorphous substance where the dead still move and speak. There are several studies of ghostly appearances in old media, that is, when old media were new, including the telephone, the gramophone, the radio, cinema and television. In fact, the spectral has often informed electricity itself.[4] Thomas Alva Edison marketed the gramophone as a device to record and to preserve the last words of dying great men, and one of his later projects was to find a way to contact the dead, "on the other side."[5] Early responses to the first film screenings also remark on the spectral; after one Lumière projection, one review claimed that now "one could [...] see one's own acts again long after one has lost them," and another that "death will no longer be final."[6] If the dead and gone continue to speak and move through the new media of the late 19th century, the myth of the all-inclusiveness of YouTube necessarily draws on an idea of the ghostly return of the past also.

However, it is a spectrality of a different order. In early cinema and broadcasting, the ghosts were the return of past events and people who passed away. What returns in early film and broadcasts in online archives is rather the ghosts of a hundred years ago—the ghosts of ghosts. Two aspects are crucial in this analysis of haunted files on the Internet: on the one hand a cultural logic of plenitude—an illusion of completeness, as there are lots of film clips and pieces of music that one cannot find online, which entails a powerful conviction that everything and everybody are potentially within reach. The discussion of the cultural logic of the ubiquity of the world online should, on the other hand, be complemented by an analysis of the technology of movement in digital moving-image files, which evoke a different spectrality. Instead of a plenitude of movement, digital video compression results in a qualitative reduction of movement, where only parts and sections of the image are updated at a time. The digital file is in this sense a mere shadow of cinematic movement, even if this aspect is seldom discussed due to the overwhelming impression of plenitude and completeness. These two spectral dimensions are at odds with each other, and demonstrate how the reception of the Internet often refers to a sort of technological unconscious.

The streaming video of online databases almost exclusively renders an image with low resolution, which is seldom suitable for collective viewing. More importantly for this argument, the MPEG techniques for video compression render the movement only partial. Video compression standards divide each frame into small blocks of pixels in order to analyze changes from one frame of video to the next. A group of pictures (frames) is established around one key frame at regular or irregular intervals (the I-picture, or intra-coded picture, meaning it is spatially compressed like the JPEG standard). On the basis of key frames, P (for predictive) pictures are established in-between to predict the location of each block of pixels. Between I-pictures and P-pictures, in turn, B-pictures use motion compensation from both the preceding and following I- and P-pictures. Just like B movies used to make film programs economical, these "bi-directionally predictive" pictures make moving-image files economical in terms of data storage capacity.

Films returning as digital video are the shadows of cinematic movement. Movement only takes place through updates of certain sections of the image, while the rest of the frame is replayed as is. This ghostly motion of digital video demonstrates how the return of films takes place in *another* medium. This is what distinguishes the viewing of representations of chemical-photographic images on YouTube from the video sequences shot digitally for online dissemination. The (mostly) low resolution and the fact that one often sees only excerpts from films inform each viewing with the spectral presence of the analog "version" of the material. The digital file refers to its analog counterpart, stored in an archive with different materiality and access and indexing principles. Films on YouTube, thus, form a superimposed archive of the digital *and* the analog. An important aspect of online archives, due to JPEG resolution of the still image and MPEG compression of movement, is the experience and technical dimensions of intermedial relations.

Periods of powerful technological change are often thought of as either smooth transitions or absolute points of rupture. In the case of the Internet and digital culture, discourses of remediation and convergence have often proclaimed that media, in the shape of writing, music, still and moving images, etcetera, continue to evolve on a different platform. The transition is often portrayed as a liberation from previous constraints, and for this reason it represents a "logical" development of media. This position can be oblivious to technological change at "code level," and focus on transitions in interaction and reception as smooth and fluent. Another trend is to see technological change as the end of one medium—in our case the often proclaimed "end of cinema"—and the beginning of something radically new. But as we know, moving images in digital platforms rely heavily on the material and cultural forms of analog films. As an alternative to the "smooth transition" model and the "end-beginning" theory of new media, it could be argued that one should be attentive to change exactly through a focused coexistence of technologies, in our case the analog and the digital. It is only by looking at the cultural, material and formal interdependency between the two that one can think critically about their differences. For this reason, new "archival forms" in the digital age, and most typically YouTube, could be thought of as an archive based on the superimposition of the digital and the analog. The digitally shot material on YouTube is, in fact, often haunted by the forms of analog cinema, whereas the digital files converted from analog material constitutes the ghost of cinematic movement.

Le Prince: The Ghost in the Tube

The spectral presence of YouTube becomes especially interesting in the case of uploaded shots of pre-cinema films. One can find several of Etienne-Jules Marey's chronophotographic studies on YouTube, and since they were shot with a camera technique that recorded images at regular intervals, they can be easily synthesized for screening. The animation of Eadweard Muybridge's series of instantaneous photographs are also found in the ether of YouTube. This article, however, will specifically address the return of the films of an inventor who himself is the true ghost of film history: Louis Aimé Augustin Le Prince, born in 1841 and probably deceased in 1890. Le Prince was French, but moved to Leeds in 1869. For the next twenty years, Le Prince traveled between France, the UK and the US, where he painted several panoramas portraying the American Civil War. His experimental work on a camera and projector, however, was conducted mainly in Leeds.

46 Ghostly appearances: Le Prince's "Traffic Crossing Leeds Bridge"

The " 'content' of any medium is always another medium," Marshall McLuhan once explained.[7] The return of film on YouTube in a different medium is, in the case of the inventor Le Prince, a resurrection of the pre-eminently ghostly figure of cinema. His name has always haunted film history for two reasons. The film cameras he invented are among the very first in cinematic history, and he shot films on photosensitive paper rolls as early as the fall of 1888. His cameras have survived and display a working mechanism devised at a very early stage. However, there are uncertainties concerning how his projector worked, and in patent applications and disputes with the famous inventors of cinema, such as the Lumière brothers and Edison, the description of the projector was considered insufficient. Our limited knowledge about Le Prince's projector is most of all due to the second reason for his spectral position in film history, his personal biography. Le Prince mysteriously disappeared on a train journey between Paris and Dijon in 1890.

On YouTube, one can see all three of Le Prince's films from which frames have survived. There is a shot of the Leeds bridge in the summer of 1889, an image of an accordion player and a scene from the

47 "Roundhay Garden Scene"

Roundhay garden with the family of Le Prince's wife. The scene from the garden is central to the dating of his films, as the presence of his mother-in-law in the image verifies Le Prince's annotation of "October 1888," since she died later that month. Thus, in the act of dating the invention, one encounters death and people moving after their disappearance. One important aspect of these films is that they are being seen for the first time on YouTube. They were never shown publicly by Le Prince, as there is no evidence that he had a functioning projector, and there is no record of these films being shown in early film programs. Since only about twenty frames from each film have survived, it would have been difficult to program them in cinema retrospectives.[8] In normal film projection, each shot would last about a second—too short for a viewer to recognize the image before it disappears. But when streamed or downloaded, these images may be repeated and looped, which gives the viewer a different kind of access to the image through repetition. These ghostly frames of pre-cinema thus, in a way, come to life in a new digital setting. When they are animated, be it on film or digitally, it is a resuscitation of something that has never moved, and by extension never lived. Le Prince's films are in many ways ghosts of things that never were.

Each of these films have been (as is usual on YouTube) uploaded in several versions. They are to be found as short files of one to two seconds, in variable resolution and with variable speed of movement. But they are also repeated and re-edited with inserted intertitle jokes, such as "the epic" and "coming to a cinema near you in the fall of 1888" in the case of the Roundhay Garden scene. Re-editing a one-second shot as a trailer, with closeups, repetitions and standard contemporary trailer music, seems to be a popular treatment of the images. This second of movement has also been released as a "director's cut," and many files also have opening and end titles. The jokes made at the expense of this footage are almost all about how these films fail to meet the expectations of "ordinary" cinema today, marketed for example by trailers, and with the properties of the film industry stamped upon them. This demonstrates how these images are almost invariably seen from the perspective of analog cinema, with a classical film tradition in mind, and not as isolated digital files without a history or a home in the analog domain. The return of these images on the Internet, and on YouTube in particular, thus cannot be understood solely from a logic of the digital. They must also be seen in an intermedial and intermediary archival situation characteristic of the moving image in digital interfaces.

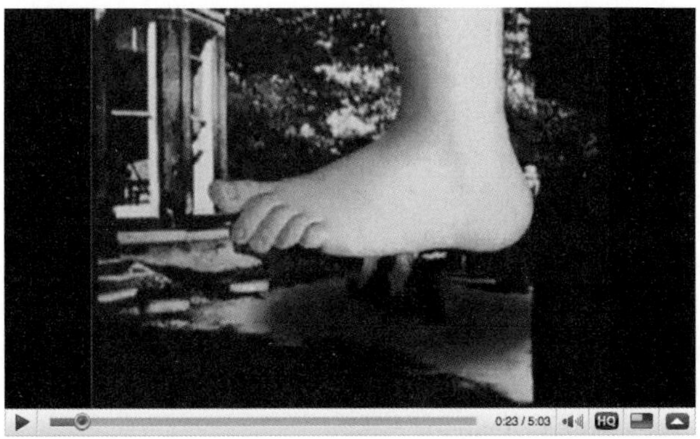

48 "Roundhay Garden Scene" mashup

Not only do the images themselves return in a different medium, the screening mode of the loop becomes accessible in the digital format. If the looping format has to a large degree made the return of these frames possible, this also implies a return of the loop. As demonstrated by the techniques of the Praxinoscope, the Zoetrope and the Vitascope, as well as the Kinetoscope, the loop was a dominant screening practice in the pre-cinema years. Even in the first years of cinema, it was not uncommon to edit shots as loops in order to screen them in multiple repetitions.[9] Even if the linear temporal mode has been dominant throughout cinema history, there is a vein in experimental cinema, in the films of filmmakers as different as Hollis Frampton, Ken Jacobs and Michael Snow, that elaborates on the idea of identical repetitions of a sequence. In the age of the digital image, the loop returns as a common screen technique in computer games, on Web pages and in DVD menus. A major break in the culture of time and space is instigated by the potentially identical repetitions in the phonograph and in cinema, since they affect our memory in new ways.[10] The loop is a virtual property of all sound and moving-image recordings, and the loop of pre-cinema screening modes returns in the digital video files.

Vanishing Tricks

We know that the founding myth of the immersion of moving-image projection is connected to the Lumière film *L' Arrivée d'un train en gare de La Ciotat*. Allegedly, the audience in the left part of the screening room mistook the image of the train for the real thing, and ran out to escape the threatening danger. Of course, the historical veracity of this story is today completely discredited, but the persistence of the myth testifies to the immersive powers of the image. This immersive effect was also underlined by the account of Lumières´ famous screening for a paying audience on December 28, 1895. It started with the projection of a still image, which was then set in motion to underscore the novelty of projected moving photographic images. The projection of the Lumières´ shot of the train—which together with *La Sortie de L' Usine Lumière* is referred to as their earliest films—thus has a history that is ghost-like.

49 How Le Prince disappeared: Fake biopic trailer

The Lumière brothers captured a maximum of movement through the depth of space by filming an arrival and a departure. These figures also distinguish Le Prince's strange fate in pre-cinema.

The train is connected to cinema as an emblem of modernity, and linked to Le Prince's disappearance. In France to arrange financial matters, Le Prince boarded a train in Dijon in September 1890—but he never disembarked in Paris. This famous vanishing act brings together key features of modern time and space in the genres of early cinema. Le Prince's disappearance connects the train films of the first years of cinema with the sudden disappearances in the transformation films made famous by Georges Méliès, Segundo de Chomon, Ferdinand Zecca and others, to make his train journey the quintessential "phantom ride" of cinema. The phantom rides and the Hale's Tours (screenings inside train cars to simulate real journeys) draw on the immersive powers of cinema projection. Le Prince was engulfed in the crowd at the train station, swallowed up by the urban space—never to reappear. Since Le Prince was never seen on the train and his luggage was not found in Paris, and since his body was never discovered on the route between the two cities, there are good reasons to believe that he never boarded the train. This enigmatic transformation cut of Le Prince in the Dijon station—where he was accompanied by his brother—to the station platform in Paris, where he never descended, has invited many theories from film historians. Some claim that he committed suicide, with homosexuality, financial difficulties or lack of success with his inventions as chief motivations. His biographer Christopher Rawlence tests many different theories about Le Prince's disappearance. Le Prince's wife believed he was killed by Edison so he wouldn't pose a threat to the other man's patents. Rawlence finds no evidence to substantiate this theory, however.[11]

Le Prince's cameras still exist, and they inform us that he shifted from a 16-lens camera constructed in Paris in 1887 to a single-lens technique built in Leeds in 1888.[12] This shows that Le Prince was one of the first to record an event on a film strip. He did this at the same time as Etienne-Jules Marey, who also shot chronophotographic images on paper film in October 1888. One could even favor Le Prince's work over Marey's, in a retrospective view, as a precursor to cinema, since Le Prince shot outdoors, in the everyday surroundings that were later so popular in early cinema. Etienne-Jules Marey's movement studies, just like the first films of the Edison company some years later, were shot in the laboratory or the studio. When Le Prince's shots are resuscitated on YouTube, it is partly because the technique of digital synthesis doesn't discriminate between different camera techniques in the same way as projection of a film strip. Since there is no evidence of a functioning projector of Le Prince's invention, he will remain only one of cinema's many inventors. It would nevertheless be convenient to have Le Prince as the sole inventor of motion pictures, since the debates on who invented cinema have been strongly imbued with national fervor. Le Prince, a Frenchman working in Britain, ending his years as both a French and US citizen would have given a bit to everyone.

The artist Matthew Buckingham addresses the works and biography of Le Prince in his installation *False Futures* from 2008. Buckingham projects a scene with the Leeds bridge he shot on 16mm in 2007 from a perspective very close to the one in Le Prince's 1889 film. The historical distance from Le Prince's street scene becomes evident in the abundance of such scenes in contemporary visual culture, above all in the ubiquity of digital surveillance cameras in contemporary urban spaces. Le Prince's shot remains a ghost in the installation, as Buckingham refrains from reproducing its images. The installation thus highlights the disparity between the moving image in a digital age and that of the 19th century's modernity.

Spectral Media

Le Prince's own disappearance is set in the same culture of time and space as the one portrayed in his films. The ghostly return of his films in art installation as well as on YouTube is not a new phenomenon. The first recordings of sound and/or image already drew upon the ghostly return. Maxim Gorky is one of the early commentators who, upon his first visit to the moving pictures in 1896, dwelled on the ghostly appearance of the Cinématographe:

> Yesterday I was in the Kingdom of Shadows. If only you knew how strange it is to be there. There are no sounds, no colours. There, everything—the earth, the trees, the people, the water, the air—is tinted in a grey monotone: in a grey sky there are grey rays of sunlight; in grey

> faces, grey eyes, and the leaves of the trees are grey like ashes. This is not life but the shadow of life and this is not movement but the soundless shadow of movement. [...] Silently the ash-grey foliage of the trees sways in the wind and the grey silhouettes of the people glide silently along the grey ground as if condemned to eternal silence and cruelly punished by being deprived of all life's colours. Their smiles are lifeless, although their movements are full of living energy and are so swift as to be almost imperceptible. Their laughter is silent, although you see the muscles contracting in their grey faces. Before you a life surges, a life devoid of words and shorn of the living spectrum of colours, a grey, silent, bleak and dismal life. It is terrifying to watch but it is the movement of shadows, mere shadows. Curses and ghosts, evil spirits that have cast entire cities into eternal sleep come to mind.[13]

Gorky's account describes an immersive force not unlike that of the wireless' etheric ocean. However, the ghostly return of pre-cinema films on YouTube are of a different kind. It is not the silence and the lack of color of the image that invests the digital kingdom of shadows with a spectral dimension. And it is not human beings that haunt the Internet, but rather early films that return in another medium.

In fact, in the earliest discourses on the documentary powers of cinema, the resurrection of the past through the moving image was already a powerful idea. In his plea for establishment of an archive for the film image in 1898, "A New Source of History," Boleslas Matuszewski wrote of the film image as a material element that at any time could be resuscitated through the light of the projector. "The cinematographic print [...] makes the dead and gone get up to walk. [It] only requires, to reawaken it and relive those hours of the past, a little light passing through a lens in the darkness!"[14] Some years later, Albert Kahn thought of the films in his Archives of the Planet (initiated in 1909) as a resource not for immediate exploitation but for a future that was still unknown. Kahn wanted to make an "inventory of the surface of the globe inhabited and developed by man as it presents itself at the start of the 20th century in order to fix once and for all the practices, the aspects and the modes of human activity, whose fatal disappearance is only a question of time."[15] It is only after these modes of life have disappeared that Kahn's visual inventory found its function. Both Matuszewski and Kahn understood the film archive as a resource for a history of the anonymous and the everyday—or of the crowd as it becomes visible during modernity. The usage of the archive, however, lies in the future, when the movements of the crowd could be resuscitated at a different time.

A century later these images still haunt us in databases and online "archives" like YouTube. In an age when the modes of life in these films are long past and gone, the accessibility of these images fulfill many of the hopes that Kahn and Matuszewski had for their projects. The documentary and evidentiary properties of these images are by no means lost when they are "reawakened" in a different medium. But they return in an age when the platforms, interfaces and material aspects of the moving image have changed, and the notion of the mass and the community has been transformed. Visual usages of these images have changed; online archives of moving images allow for navigation, reappropriation and annotations in unprecedented ways.

It would be a mistake, however, to assume that one medium has simply taken over the existence of another. Digital files do not eradicate films, but are a means of access that in various ways coexist with the analog material. The digital format changes the content of the films, but the altered conditions of the moving image in the age of digital files mean that one must take the relationship between the analog and the digital into consideration. The surviving frames from each of Le Prince's three films also exist as photograms in a museum in Leeds, and Kahn's films in the Archives of the Planet exist as celluloid strips in Paris. The advent of the digital doesn't mean the end of the analog, as is so often presupposed by accounts of the end of cinema, or the end of film, but it entails a different kind of access to and screening modality of these shots.[15] The current archival paradigm is one where the analog and the digital exist in the form of superimposition. These images have received a split identity and a double temporality in digitization; they exist in film archives as analog images, and as digital files for access. The return of these images as "doubles" and as "ghosts of ghosts" has ramifications for their montage and their intermediary connections, as well as for their individual and collective address in the age of the computer.

Conclusion

The detailed accounts of Le Prince's inventions demonstrate how these films return in a different medium on YouTube. The technical properties of the shots are fundamentally altered, as the photosensitive paper strips have been transferred to celluloid, and later converted to digital code. The problem of synthesis was first entirely overcome with the invention of the Cinématographe, and later transformed by the techniques of video compression.

There is an intriguing passage in Martin Heidegger's "The Age of the World Picture" where he argues that the forms of subjectivity belonging to the Modern, based on the "calculability" of the world, result in an incalculability as an "invisible shadow."[16] This shadow is different from the ghostly world of Gorky's cinema. The world within reach as image is connected to the rise of a new dimension of subjectivity. The gigantic aspect of the calculable "world" makes it, precisely for this reason, incalculable. "This becoming incalculable remains the invisible shadow that is cast around all things everywhere when man has been transformed into *subiectum* and the world into picture."[17] This shadow is not an invisible part of the world. It is rather the shadow itself that is invisible, and makes up an aspect in all things visible in the world as picture. As explained by Samuel Weber in his discussion of this concept in Heidegger's text: "But *shadow* here does not name 'simply the lack of light,' or even less its negation. It designates that which escapes and eludes the calculating plans of total representation, of which it at the same time is the condition of possibility."[18] Still, just as the incalculable returns as a shadow in the "Welt-Bild" of the modern world, the rhetoric of the online archives' plenitude returns its users to a gulf of inaccessible information. The feeling that one cannot incorporate the "whole" of YouTube constructs a subject that is incapable of controlling the information.

The subjectivity of the "modern" is not the same in the age of digital machines, and the current ubiquity of screens repositions the constituting processes of the subject. This intermedial position is, perhaps, the invisible shadow in the age of online media. The unlimited calculability and omnipresence of YouTube clips return the user to a shadow that is intermedial and intermediary, like in the superimposition of the analog and the digital. The gap in the modern "world picture" is all the stronger in the face of the infinity of information on the Internet, and makes space for the ghostly and the uncanny. The return of the "lost" films of Le Prince as something different from what they were, in another medium, is part of this uncanny shadow. YouTube contains a finite number of videos, but since this number is rapidly increasing, the archive becomes incalculable. The fact that the information is not permanently accessible (videos are sometimes removed for different reasons) adds to this incalculable dimension. The cultural all-inclusiveness of the Internet, the millions of videos of YouTube together with the participatory imperative in the slogan "Broadcast yourself!" result in this phantom of inaccessible information on YouTube. YouTube is the kingdom of shadows, where the ghostly dwell.

Endnotes

1 Erik Barnouw, *Tube of Plenty. The Evolution of American Television* (New York: Oxford University Press, 1975).

2 Jeffrey Sconce, *Haunted Media. Electronic Presence from Telegraphy to Television* (Durham, NC: Duke University Press, 2000), pp. 63–66.

3 Akira Mizuta Lippit relates Borges' short story to a "Shadow Optics" close to the spectral dimension in my argument. See Akira Mizuta Lippit, *Atomic Light (Shadow Optics)* (Minneapolis: University of Minnesota Press, 2005), pp. 5–9.

4 Carolyn Marvin, *When Old Technologies Were New* (Oxford: Oxford University Press, 1988).

5 Sconce 2000, pp. 81–83.

6 Both quoted in Noël Burch, *La lucarne de l'infini; naissance du langage cinématographique* (Paris: Nathan, 1991), p. 26.

7 Marshall McLuhan, *Understanding Media; The Extensions of Man* (London: Abacus, 1973), pp. 15–16.

8 Christopher Rawlence, *The Missing Reel. The Untold Story of the Lost Inventor of Moving Pictures* (New York: Atheneum, 1990).

9 Mary Ann Doane, *The Emergence of Cinematic Time* (Cambridge, MA: Harvard University Press, 2002), p. 132.

10 Bernard Stiegler, *La technique et le temps 3. Le temps du cinéma et la question du mal-être* (Paris: Galilée, 2001), pp. 40–44.

11 Rawlence 1990, pp. 277–282.

12 Rawlence 1990, plates XVII and XVIII.

13 Maxim Gorky, "The Lumière Cinematograph" (1896), in *The Film Factory. Russian and Soviet Cinema in Documents 1896–1939*, eds. Richard Taylor & Ian Christie (London: Routledge, 1988), pp. 25–26.

14 Boleslas Matuszewski, "A New Source of History" (1898), *Film History* no. 4, 1995, pp. 322–324.

15 Albert Kahn quoted in Paula Amad, "Cinema's 'Sanctuary': From pre-documentary to documentary film in Albert Kahn's *Archives de la Planète* (1908–1931)," *Film History* no. 2, 2001, pp. 138–159.

16 David Rodowick's account of the "end of film" is for this reason, in spite of all the merits of his nuanced discussion, somewhat exaggerated and therefore incomplete. David N. Rodowick, *The Virtual Life of Film* (Cambridge, MA: Harvard University Press, 2007).

17 Martin Heidegger, "The Age of the World Picture" (1938), in *Electronic Culture. Technology and Visual Representation*, ed. Timothy Druckrey (New York: Aperture, 1996).

18 Ibid.

19 Samuel Weber, *Mass Mediauras. Form, Technics, Media* (Stanford: Stanford University Press, 1996), p. 81.

Jens Schröter

On the Logic of the Digital Archive

Nearly ten years before YouTube was launched in mid-February 2005, Hal Foster published the essay "The Archive without Museums."[1] In this 1996 article Foster dealt with the expanding academic discourse on visual culture. Visual culture was seen as an offspring of cultural studies insofar as it eroded the dichotomies between high/low and art/non-art, an issue much debated at that time. Art historians such as Foster and Rosalind Krauss formulated harsh critiques of the new field of visual culture. Krauss for example criticized the loss of specific and differentiated art-historical competences, which allegedly were replaced by a diffuse fog of "vulgar-post-modernist anything-goes."[2] Foster was skeptical also; in his essay he addressed the historical, institutional and technological conditions which led to the emergence of the new field. Let's have a look at Foster's argument first before discussing YouTube and the logic of the digital archive.

Foster's essay begins by contrasting the new conditions of visual culture with those that led to the emergence of art history. According to Foster, the emergence of art history was founded on the foregrounding of the "constructive aspect of the artwork;" the interest in "alien," non-European art fostered by 19th century imperialism; and finally the technologies of photographic reproduction: "Art history relied on techniques of *reproduction* to abstract a wide range of *objects* into a system of *style*."[3] Subsequently, Foster identifies the conditions leading to the field of visual culture; for example, he mentions the "visual virtuality of contemporary media" and the interest in "cultural multiplicity in a post-colonial age." He then, finally, poses the question: "Might visual culture rely on techniques of *information* to transform a wide range of *mediums* into a system of image-text—a database of digital terms, an archive without museums?"[4] Moreover, "what are the electronic preconditions of visual culture, and how long will it take to grasp the epistemological implications?"[5]

Reading Hal Foster's essay a decade later, it becomes obvious that it is a story of loss, with an extremely critical attitude towards the (partial) shift from art history to visual culture. Foster, for example, undertakes an extended discussion of Barbara Stafford's book *Body Criticism*, which he calls a "prominent text in visual culture."[6] Foster not only tries to highlight inconsistencies in Stafford's argument, but also accuses her—quite explicitly—of complicity with hegemonic techno-capitalist powers. "In an academic version of the Stockholm syndrome, some visual culturalists have identified with our technocratic captors; one can imagine the endorsement (the endowment?) from Bill Gates."[7] But what exactly is the point of his critique? Foster's argument becomes clearer when one considers the notion of shifting archival relations. Foster defines "archive" after Foucault as "the system that governs the appearance of statements,"[8] and asks what new archival structures "might enable as well as disable."[9] To him, the "database of digital terms, an archive without museums," is synonymous with a reordering of the form and distribution of information, of cultural memory and therefore of (collective as well as individual) subjectivity. He exemplifies this, quite lucidly, with a cover of *Artforum* from 1995, a magazine Foster calls a "review of visual culture."[10]

50 Cover of *Artforum*, December 1995

On the cover, heterogeneous phenomena are assembled: the *Friends* cast, O.J. Simpson, Courtney Love, *Broadway Boogie Woogie*, a Matthew Barney video frame, a Prada model, a Larry Clark film still, a Gilbert & George montage, a bus advertisement for Calvin Klein, etcetera. The cover's dot structure is reminiscent of the principles of the television image. But Foster insists that television is itself included in the heterogeneous material. Television is itself a part, not an organizing principle, of this disparate archive, whose "implicit order of things is a virtual database. [...] The primacy of the visual in visual culture may be only apparent. Already its order may be governed by a digital logic that melts down other logics of word and image as the computer melted down other machines."[11] One could indeed underline this argument with a reference to Lev Manovich and his notion that the most central cultural form of new media and electronic culture is the database. The logic of the database is the collection of heterogeneous elements, connected not by progress and development, but simply by coexistence and links—just like the different multimedia elements on an average website, or on the cover of the 1995 *Artforum*.[12] Manovich tries to describe this cultural logic in a neutral way—although he links the dominance of "database" to the so-called "end of grand narratives," suggesting a deeper political and ideological force behind the database.[13]

Foster's discussion concerning the "virtual database" and his critique of visual culture ends up in the question of which subject is produced by "visual culture" and its heterogeneous archive. He makes a somewhat surprising claim: "This discourse traces a chiasmus of subject and image. In the first equation of the chiasmus, the subject is defined not only as an image-maker but as *an* image. [...] The second equation of the chiasmus follows from the first: if the subject is defined as an image, the image is defined as a subject, in *its* image."[14] This paragraph is not easy to follow, but I would propose the following reading: the new, shimmering world of the interactive Web, the heterogeneous databases of which we as users are constantly compelled to select (simply by clicking on items and icons), on the one hand behaves like a subject (the websites ask us constantly for reactions and actions), while on the other hand it turns us as users into images—more precisely into consumer profiles stored in cookies, which trace our unconscious desires and connect them to the flows of capital. Using my profile, the recommendations on Amazon address me personally; I am an image on my hard disc, while the website knows me personally, more or less like a friend. Returning to Foster one last time: in the order of the heterogeneous "archive without museums," the "transgression of categories becomes, at the level of 'consumption,' a hip manipulation of signs and, on the level of 'production,' a corporate merger not only of mediums but of entertainment industries: so many clicks on the Web, so many moves on the Market."[15] To sum up: "In the age of electronic information a principal frontier of capitalism is the unconscious."[16]

Interestingly, Manovich also speaks about possible subject effects of the "database." He uses the same metaphor as Foster—"What ideal subject does visual culture model and/or mirror?"[17]—and states: "The modern GUI [Graphical User Interface] functions as a mirror, always representing the image of the user in the form of a cursor moving around the screen. [...] In other words, it functions as a new kind of mirror that reflects not only the human image but human activities."[18] The image on the screen, thus, shows anthropomorphic activities, while my activities, which can be traced and collected, form a "data image" of me. The heterogeneity of the digital archive is therefore a kind of "test scenario" in which the flexible capitalist subject can move freely and display its desires. The subject can find unexpected links—and desires. By freely transforming itself into an image, the subject exhibits its hidden desires and potentially connects them to commercialization. This is the strategy of post-modern capitalism or the precise difference between the "societies of discipline" and the "societies of control," as Deleuze put it.[19]

YouTube is obviously the paradigmatic case of an "archive without museums." It is a vast, highly heterogeneous video archive, a database with snippets from TV shows, movies, music clips, sporting events, etcetera. Departing from Hal Foster's critical stance toward visual culture, this article, then, tries to adapt his critique of the logic of the digital archive—the "aleatory tropes of the web"[20]—to analyze YouTube and the "database subject" the site seems to result in. Given the uncritical hype of Web 2.0, most of which seems to repeat official PR—i.e. new options for liberation, communication and community, be it through YouTube, Flickr or some other social Web gadget—such a critique is perhaps long overdue. Or is a Fosterian critique completely misguided, considering the fact that YouTube does not connect (in contrast to Amazon for example) the subject's floating desires directly to market transactions?

Notes on the History of the Database Subject

One starting point for how databases model their users is the famous article "As we may think" by Vannevar Bush, published 1945 in the journal *Atlantic Monthly*. The article is often quoted as one origin of modern computing. Not in the sense that it is a technical paper, although it proposes a (fictitious) technology, but more in that it describes a problem in the organization of knowledge, which should or could be addressed in a technological way. The article describes, in a way, the concept of a database, as the editor of the *Atlantic Monthly* wrote in his short introduction. "As Director of the Office of Scientific Research and Development, Dr. Vannevar Bush has coordinated the activities of some six thousand leading American scientists in the application of science to warfare. [...] Now, says Dr. Bush, instruments are at hand which, if properly developed, will give man access to and command over the inherited knowledge of the ages."[21]

Bush obviously knew how difficult it was to organize knowledge in an efficient way. "The summation of human experience is being expanded at a prodigious rate, and the means we use for threading through the consequent maze to the momentarily important item is the same as was used in the days of square-rigged ships."[22] He thus suggested a technical solution: MEMEX. While it was and is a fictitious machine, never built, MEMEX exercised a great influence on the subsequent history of hypertext and databases.[23]

In short, MEMEX looks like a kind of desk. On its top are two translucent screens on which documents can be displayed. On the left is a kind of photographic scanner, which can be used to input information. The machine's design is not comparable to today's computing technology, because it was perceived to make use of microfilm.[24] The point is that the user should be able to mark documents that belonged together. By doing this repeatedly the user builds "associative trails" through the vast (and ever-expanding, due to additions) archive. "The real heart of the matter of selection, however," Bush notes, "goes deeper than a lag in the adoption of mechanisms by libraries, or a lack of development of devices for their use." He further states that:

> Our ineptitude in getting at the record is largely caused by the artificiality of systems of indexing. When data of any sort are placed in storage, they are filed alphabetically or numerically, and information is found (when it is) by tracing it down from subclass to subclass. It can be in only one place, unless duplicates are used; one has to have rules as to which path will locate it, and the rules are cumbersome. Having found one item, moreover, one has to emerge from the system and re-enter on a new path. The human mind does not work that way. It operates by association. With one item in its grasp, it snaps instantly to the next that is suggested by the association of thoughts, in accordance with some intricate web of trails carried by the cells of the brain.[25]

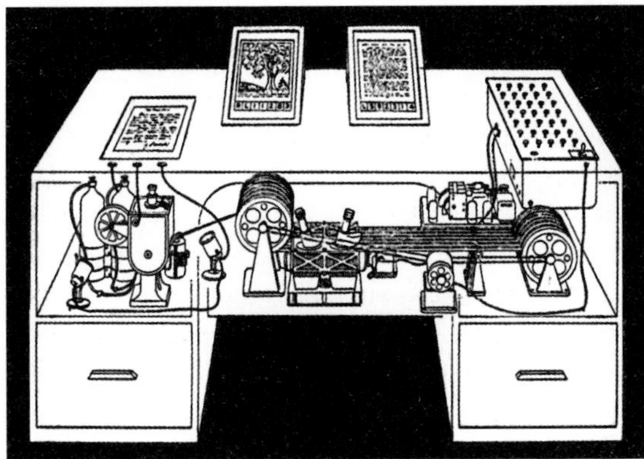

51 The Memex (from: "As We May Think," *Life*, 1945)

In this way a better—as the analogies to the human brain suggest: more "natural"—organization of knowledge should be possible. The problem is of course that trails in the archive produced with microfilm-based technology cannot be erased.[26] A user of the MEMEX would have to be very careful to not build useless or nonsensical trails. Bush describes a scenario of usage: "The owner of the MEMEX, let us say, is interested in the origin and properties of the bow and arrow. Specifically he is studying why the short Turkish bow was apparently superior to the English long bow in the skirmishes of the Crusades." Bush continues to state that such a user has dozens of possible books or articles in his MEMEX:

> First he runs through an encyclopedia, finds an interesting but sketchy article, leaves it projected. Next, in a history, he finds another pertinent item, and ties the two together. Thus he goes, building a trail of many items. Occasionally he inserts a comment of his own, either linking it into the main trail or joining it by a side trail to a particular item. When it becomes evident that the elastic properties of available materials had a great deal to do with the bow, he branches off on a side trail which takes him through textbooks on elasticity and tables of physical constants. He inserts a page of longhand analysis of his own. Thus he builds a trail of his interest through the maze of materials available to him. And his trails do not fade. Several years later, his talk with a friend turns to the queer ways in which a people resist innovations, even of vital interest. He has an example, in the fact that the outraged Europeans still failed to adopt the Turkish bow. In fact he has a trail on it. A touch brings up the code book. Tapping a few keys projects the head of the trail. A lever runs through it at will, stopping at interesting items, going off on side excursions. It is an interesting trail, pertinent to the discussion.[27]

Obviously this user is a kind of scientist who is interested in creating only true and helpful trails, so that there is no problem in that his trails "do not fade." This implies—to cite Deleuze—a certain *image of thought*. "According to this image, thought has an affinity with the true; it formally possesses the true and materially wants the true."[28] This is hardly surprising, since Bush himself was a scientist and his article began with reference to scientists. But Bush also writes: "This has not been a scientist's war; it has been a war in which all have had a part."[29]

However, the MEMEX was not constructed in a way that "all" would or could participate. With everyone participating, a chaotic and finally useless web of trails would probably have been the result. In the 1960s Ted Nelson adopted and revised Bush's ideas and developed the first hypertext systems conceptualized similarly as a kind of associative linking of information.[30] Nelson did develop software for digital computers, so Bush's unerasable trails became *links*, erasable and open to all kinds of change and correction. This would decrease the necessity of "materially wanting the true." Wrong links and wrong (or, for example, offending) documents could be erased and/or changed later. The potential for erasure seemed to open the system for "all" (Bush). Indeed, Nelson's texts actually bespeak a desire for "everything to be in the hypertext." He also coined the term "hypermedia," according to which a hypertextual structure could for example include video and audio material—although this was hardly possible in the 1960s.

However, a new problem eventually emerged. What if documents were erased while some links were still pointing to them? Nelson proposed a central "link table" which administrates the link structure of the archive. When a document was erased, all links on the document disappeared automatically. Nelson thus implied a user subject who could err, that is be driven by uncontrolled and irrational desires. The potential irrationality could, however, be corrected by using a well-ordered software structure; rationality was hence substituted by the software infrastructure of the archive. This instead has a lot to do with today's Web. The World Wide Web was developed in the late 1980s at the European Center for Nuclear Research in Geneva—a truly scientific institution. Tim Berners-Lee was looking for a kind of database which would allow for a better communication of the results produced by different scientists, who numbered in the thousands and were working on highly complex problems. In this respect, the situation was reminiscent of the one on which Vannevar Bush worked. At first Berners-Lee underlined the importance (exactly as Bush or Nelson) of the associative linkage between heterogeneous elements. "One of the things computers have not done for an organization is to be able to store random associations between disparate things."[31] Berners-Lee explicitly stated his goals:

> The dream behind the Web is of a common information space in which we communicate by sharing information. Its universality is essential: the fact that a hypertext link can point to anything, be it personal, local or global, be it draft or highly polished. There was a second part of the dream, too, dependent on the Web being so generally used that it became a realistic mirror (or in fact the primary embodiment) of the ways in which we work and play and socialize. That was that once the state of our interactions was on line, we could then use computers to help us analyse it, make sense of what we are doing, where we individually fit in, and how we can better work together.[32]

In a similar way, Lev Manovich has made the remark that the "rise of the Web, this gigantic and always changing data corpus, gave millions of people a new hobby or profession—data indexing."[33] Berners-Lee, of course, saw this as a positive development, but his appeal to the analysis of "us" and to the optimization of the ways in which "we" work (and "socialize") can also be deciphered as aspects of the "societies of control." One of the conditions for "us" all to be in the Web is obviously that—as in Nelson's work—links are flexible and changeable. But Berners-Lee's design differed in a crucial point from that of Nelson. "Typically, though, hypertext systems were built around a database of links," he stated. This "did guarantee that links would be consistent, and links to documents would be removed when documents were removed. The removal of this feature was the principle compromise made in the W3 [Web] architecture, which then, by allowing references to be made without consultation with the destination, allowed the scalability which the later growth of the web exploited."[34] Berners-Lee hence avoided Nelson's "link table"—the database of links—as the technically substituted consistency of the archive. Other features which Nelson also thought of, e.g. the bivisibility and bifollowability of links, which makes it possible to see which documents link to another given document, were not implemented either.[35] In short, Nelson valued the consistency of the archive, while Berners-Lee preferred the scalability. The gain was of course that the archive could grow—exponentially, exactly as the Web did.[36]

Berners-Lee worked in a scientific environment; scalability and consistency were not contradictions. This became problematic only when the Web was released from the confinements of a closed scientific discourse. And that is what happened some time before 1994 with the advent of the first Web browsers. Soon after that there was no longer a well-ordered archival structure; rather, it became increasingly organized like a supermarket (with a lot of non-profit segments). Because the Web expanded so quickly, an overview (e.g. in the form of an index) was not possible. Instead, sites that attracted users moved towards the center, whereas neglected sites found themselves on the periphery. Attention thus became the key to Web success.[37] The capitalist principle of competition could hence readily inscribe itself into the Web, mainly because of the absence of an alternative structuring principle.[38]

The short history of the database subject as sketched out above implies how the database's structures can involve a certain kind of database subject. These structures can also betray something about the database's compatibility with other structures. The Web, for instance, "fits" competitive-driven capitalism; it is not surprising that after the distribution of the first browsers—only a few years after the "victory" of Western market capitalism over so called "real socialism"—its popularity culminated in ideologies of "frictionless capitalism" (Bill Gates) that were independent of concrete contents.[39] In a sense, Manovich puts forward a similar argument when he connects the structure of the database to the "end of grand narratives." Manovich notes that because no overarching logic structures the Web, this heterogeneity allows any kind of competition. He sees the database logic in general as an end of all hierarchies (except of unproblematic data hierarchies), while in fact most of the real existing databases may simply mirror existing social hierarchies. I would instead argue that specific methods of organizing the digital archive are connected to specific social phenomena— e.g. linking the Web to the still existing and flourishing grand narrative of money.[40]

YouTube as a Digital Archive

In relation to what has been discussed above one might ask oneself what specific type of database (respectively archive) YouTube actually is? Furthermore, what "vacant places" (Foucault) does the site offer us to become "YouTube subjects"? Obviously, these questions might be seen as too general for such a heterogeneous phenomenon as YouTube. But if we dissect the site into handsome analytical pieces—as close readings of specific content or user patterns—we tend lose the big picture. The heterogeneity and complexity of YouTube is in itself an important point, as Hal Foster's discussion of the digital archive as well as the short history of databases has shown. And when we try to locate this heterogeneity and complexity in broader cultural contexts and ask which subjects such a structure prefers, with Foster, we have to ask ourselves: "After photographic reproduction the museum was not so much bound by walls, but it was bordered by style. What is the edge of the archive without museums?"[41]

The very name YouTube is telling, because it seems to be another articulation of the chiasmus of subject and image—you are the tube and the tube is you. And that is the case: in the ocean of heterogeneous audiovisual material the using subject has to make selections to build his or her "tube." Vannevar Bush already stated that "the prime action of use is selection, and here we are halting indeed. There may be millions of fine thoughts, and the account of the experience on which they are based, all encased within stone walls of acceptable architectural form; but if the scholar can get at only one a week by diligent search, his syntheses are not likely to keep up with the current scene."[42] YouTube is sort of a machine for selection from an audiovisual database or archive. Hence, it implies a selecting subject.[43] One function of YouTube might even be to teach users how to select from an ever-growing field of information and sensations. This argument resembles that of Walter Benjamin, who saw in cinema a machine to train the audience in perceptual "chocs." But today the computerized, white-collar workplace has for many (though of course not for all) people supplanted the industrial workplace. You don't have to train perceptual chocs, but you do have to train selection from menus and finding information.

YouTube offers different tools for doing that: you can "personalize" the site to store different forms of preselections so the website becomes a kind of "mirror" of your activities of selection, and you can choose the "most discussed" or the "most viewed" clips. Even the bare fact of watching a clip structures the archive, insofar as the number of viewings contributes to categories such as "most viewed" from which users can select. "You" can also add "commentaries" and react to previous comments, or "you" can flag videos as being inappropriate, which may cause them to disappear. Perhaps most interesting is that "you" can choose a detailed bundle of statistical information about the chosen clip. "You" can get information about how often the clip was viewed and rated, that is: in which rating lists it has achieved high rankings, how many commentaries were made—and even which sites link to a particular video.

Ted Nelson's originally planned bivisibility and bifollowability of links seems to return here—albeit in a transformed way. The bifollowability in Nelson's concept had the goal of securing the archive's consistency. In YouTube it contributes to the *attention* enjoyed by a particular clip. Therefore, when asking what specific type of database YouTube is, one can obviously state that it is not a database as Bush would have imagined it. A given categorical apparatus does not necessarily drive the selection, neither does intellectual interest, as one might expect from Bush's "scholar," although this is of course possible. The selection is normally driven by diffuse desires. A good friend of mine (himself a "scholar") for example often visits YouTube just to see if he can find video clips from the 1980s of which he has diffuse memories. Thus, he uses the archive to actualize his memories. But "desire" may also be a good term for another important aspect of YouTube. You are the tube and the tube is you—permanent additions to the heterogeneous audiovisual material is the second basic operation (it is only secondary because users are not required to add material, but "you" always have to make a selection). The possibility everyone has to upload his or her own idiosyncratic materials doesn't presuppose a "good will" and an "affinity with the true"[44]—no wonder that we can find endless discussions of the "authenticity" of the content on YouTube (a resemblance to the Word Wide Web in general). With the possibility of uploading everyone potentially discovers his or her own "desire" to do so—to show the adventures of one's cat to the world. YouTube therefore implies not only a continually selecting subject, but also a subject which should "freely" express him or herself. Moreover, it presupposes that everyone wants to express his or her personal desires in audiovisual form. According to Deleuze, who extensively criticized the hegemonic "image of thought," we can find here a hegemonic "image of audiovisual desire." In a market economy it is a duty permanently to express one's own desires. Confess "your" wishes and we will fulfill. It is again the chiasmus of subject and image which is moreover doubled in the chiasmus of expression and selection. Unbelievable numbers of videos are uploaded every minute, while an even more impressive number of viewings are reported.

Therefore, the "masses" express themselves audiovisually while structuring the resulting archive through selection at the same time. Before, it was almost impossible for "everyone" to upload their own audiovisual materials and simultaneously rate, comment on and view the materials of others. So one can say that "in the age of electronic information a principal frontier of capitalism is the unconscious"—that YouTube is an effective machine for *mirroring* audiovisual desires. One should of course remember that, for Jacques Lacan, the gaze and the voice themselves correspond to the scopophilic and the invocatory drive.[45] YouTube is a mapping of collective scopophilic and invocatory desire, which can (and will) be exploited by the advertising and entertainment industries.

But if this is the case, why isn't pornography a central content of YouTube? Is it not obvious that pornography should be central when discussing audiovisual desire? Pornography is surely a hegemonic—more or less misogynic—expression of desire. But the sheer existence of pornography as extreme desire makes other forms of audiovisual desire invisible. So the structural exclusion of pornography and nudity on YouTube allows *other* forms of audiovisual desire to appear. YouTube is, hence, a filter for non-pornographic audiovisual desire—the rest is done in the Web. Because the problematic field of pornography is excluded, the (normally) interesting group of younger consumers can be mapped without any exclusions or suspicions. Except for these constraints YouTube is not structured, as a Bushian archive for example, by carefully chosen associative trails, but by a competition for attention—just like any ordinary capitalist market. Even countercultural impulses can easily be absorbed. If they don't attract enough attention (viewings, ratings, commentary) they just disappear in the neutralizing ocean of information and lose every threatening potential (because they simply aren't recognized). If they attract enough attention, they will at first be discredited—for being in no way countercultural, because the sheer fact of getting too much attention is not a convincing sign of "counterculturality"; in general, a "true" subculture would have to resist the logic of attention and competition at all. Yet, when such content attracts attention it will only be a question of time until the "subculture" is exploited by the entertainment or culture industry.

Conclusion

In my view YouTube is as participatory as market research, and as democratic as public opinion polls. The site is a machine for market research and opinion polls driven by various scopophilic and invocatory drives of its users. Hence, it does not transcend the given capitalist logic of competition and attention. In general, this remains the logic of most user-driven digital archives today. But this logic is of course not technologically determined. It only shows that one example of the hyped Web 2.0 platforms do not by the fact of their existence change culture into more "participatory" forms. Which is not surprising. In an important text from 1968, by the computer scientists J.C.R. Licklider and Robert Taylor, who worked directly on the development of the ARPANET, they stated: "The importance of improving decision making processes—not only in government, but throughout business and the professions—is so great as to warrant every effort. [...] A particular form of digital computer organization [...] constitutes the dynamic, moldable medium that can

[...] improve the effectiveness of communication."[46] The participants in the development of modern computing are obviously aware of the fact that computers are by definition programmable "moldable mediums" in which social imperatives—like "government," "business" and "effectiveness"—have to be inscribed.[47] To return to Hal Foster, one has to say that the eroding of the difference between high and low or professional and amateur content in visual culture simply shows that all these different forms today follow the grand narrative of money—the "great leveler," as Marx put it. So it is less the logic of the virtual database in itself that produces the entropic "archive without museums," but the logic of the virtual database already programmed with the logic of selection and expression, competition and attention.

Finally, the answer to the question regarding the "edge of the archive without museums" seems to be that its logic of selection and expression, competition and attention might only be changed by the transformation of society itself. When its deep logic is that of exchange value, then the end of exchange value would be its most general limit—but that presupposes a social change far more radical than most advocates of "participatory culture" ostensibly emerging with Web 2.0 can even imagine. Perhaps *this* edge is even unthinkable—at least for now. But perhaps there is a kind of more mundane edge; there may be a contradiction between the logic of selection and expression, competition and attention and the possibilities of forming communities on You Tube. "Community" is not a positive default value in itself. Rather, by necessity, communities exclude those who are constitutive for being a discernable community—and in Germany especially, the notion of "community" has some troubling connotations due to the sinister role that the *Volksgemeinschaft* once played. But here we may find a first glimpse of the possibility of a democratic archive, structured by common interest and discussion. But it is just a first glimpse, because when you enter the "community" page of YouTube, one of the first words you see is "contests." At least "competition" is still with us. Yet again: the logic of the digital archive today is not caused by technology in itself; strengthening the truly participatory and democratic aspects of YouTube will probably lead to yet another form of digital archive.

Endnotes

1 Hal Foster, "The Archive without Museums," *October* no. 77, 1996, pp. 97–119.

2 Rosalind Krauss, "Welcome to the Cultural Revolution," *October* no. 77, 1996, pp. 83–96.

3 Foster 1996, p. 97.

4 Ibid. See also Jens Schröter, "Archive – post/photographic," Media Art Net, *October* 2008 – www.medienkunstnetz.de [last checked 15 February 2009].

5 Foster 1996, pp. 97/99.

6 Ibid., p. 107. See also Barbara Stafford, *Body Criticism. Imaging the Unseen in Enlightenment Art and Medicine* (Cambridge, MA: MIT Press, 1991).

7 Foster 1996, p. 108.

8 Michel Foucault, *The Archaeology of Knowledge* (London: Routledge, 2006), p. 145.

9 Foster 1996, p. 108.

10 Ibid., pp. 113–114.

11 Ibid. A discussion of the digital transformations of the archive is conspicuously absent from Charles Merewether, ed., *The Archive* (Cambridge, MA: MIT Press, 2006).

12 See Lev Manovich, *The Language of New Media* (Cambridge, MA: MIT Press, 2001), pp. 218–243.

13 Ibid., p. 219.

14 Foster 1996, pp. 116–117.

15 Ibid., p. 114.

16 Ibid., p. 116.

17 Ibid., p. 116. The Lacanian undertones are of course intended.

18 Manovich 2001, p. 235.

19 Gilles Deleuze, "Postscript on the Societies of Control," *October* no. 59, 1992, pp. 3–7.

20 Foster 1996, p. 117.

21 Ibid.

22 Ibid.

23 For the influence of Bush's MEMEX, see Linda Smith, "Memex as an Image of Potentiality Revisited," in *From Memex to Hypertext: Vannevar Bush and the Mind's Machine*, eds. James M. Nyce & Paul Kahn (Cambridge, MA: MIT Press, 1991), pp. 261–286.

24 In 1945, when Bush wrote his article, none of the xerographic technologies we now take for granted were available.

25 Bush 1945, p. 106.

26 Bush realized this himself of course. For a discussion, see the chapter "Memex Revisited" in *Vannevar Bush, Science Is Not Enough* (New York: Morrow, 1969), pp. 75–101.

27 Bush 1945, p. 107.

28 Gilles Deleuze, *Difference and Repetition* (New York: Bantam Books, 1994), p. 131.

29 Bush 1945, p. 101.

30 See Theodor H. Nelson, "A File Structure for the Complex, the Changing and the Indeterminate," in *Proceedings of the 20th National Conference of the Association for Computing Machinery* (New York, 1965), pp. 84–100.

31 Tim Berners-Lee, "The World Wide Web: A Very Short Personal History," in *People of the W3C*, 1998 – www.w3.org/People/Berners-Lee/ShortHistory.html [last checked 15 February 2009].

32 Ibid.

33 Manovich 2001, p. 225.

34 Tim Berners-Lee, "The World Wide Web: Past, Present and Future," in *People of the W3C*, 1996 – www.w3.org/People/Berners-Lee/1996/ppf.html [last checked 15 February 2009].

35 For a Nelsonian critique of the Web see Pam Andrew, "Where World Wide Web Went Wrong," 1995 – www.xanadu.com.au/xanadu/6w-paper.html [last checked 15 February 2009]. Andrew writes the following on the bivisibility and bifollowability of links: "Another significant problem with the current WWW implementation is the design of the hyperlinks. They are embedded within the documents themselves and are unidirectional and univisible. That is, they can only be followed in one direction and can only be seen from the originating end. This makes link maintenance a nightmare, compounded by the lack of unique document identifiers which significantly increases the frequency with which destination documents change their URL."

36 See Tim Berners-Lee et al., "The World Wide Web," *Communications of the ACM* no. 8, 1994, pp. 76–82.

37 For the genealogy of attention, see Jonathan Crary, *Suspensions of Perception. Attention, Spectacle and Modern Culture* (Cambridge, MA: MIT Press, 1999).

38 Although there are of course some structuring instances, for example the very important Domain Name System (DNS) which was introduced in 1983 and updated in 1987. The aim of the DNS is to correlate addressees and IP numbers.

39 See Jens Schröter, *Das Netz und die Virtuelle Realität. Zur Selbstprogrammierung der Gesellschaft durch die universelle Maschine* (Bielefeld: Transcript, 2004), pp. 97–137.

40 On the "grand narrative of money" see Anselm Jappe, *Die Abenteuer der Ware. Für eine neue Wertkritik* (Münster: Unrast, 2005), pp. 80–88

41 Foster 1996, p. 115.

42 Bush 1945, p. 105.

43 The problem of selection in relation to the popular ideological argument that the more options you can (and have to) choose from, the more "free" you are is discussed in Jens Schröter, "8848 verschiedene Jeans. Zu Wahl und Selektion im Internet," in *Paradoxien der Entscheidung. Wahl/Selektion in Kunst, Literatur und Medien*, eds. Friedrich Balke et al. (Bielefeld: Transcript, 2004), pp. 117–138.

44 Deleuze 1994, p. 131.

45 Foster relates the chiasmus of subject and image directly to Lacan. For a lucid summary of Lacan's work on the gaze see Martin Jay, *Downcast Eyes. The Denigration of Vision in Twentieth-Century French Thought* (Berkeley: University of California Press, 1993), pp. 338–370. For his reflections on the voice and sound see Kaja Silverman, *The Acoustic Mirror. The Female Voice in Psychoanalysis and Cinema* (Bloomington: Indiana University Press, 1988); and Mladen Dolar, *A Voice and Nothing More* (Cambridge, MA, 2006).

46 J.C.R. Licklider & Robert Taylor, "The Computer as a Communication Device," *Science and Technology* April 1968, pp. 21–31.

47 For a more detailed version of this argument see Schröter 2004.

Gunnar Iversen

An Ocean of Sound and Image: YouTube in the Context of Supermodernity

In his landmark study, *Non-Places: Introduction to an Anthropology of Supermodernity*, Marc Augé introduced a new category of place: the *non-lieu*, non-place, the negation of anthropological place, whose main characteristic is being transitive and asocial. Augé's main examples were airports, freeways, supermarkets, subways and malls. Although Augé never applied the term non-place to media, his polar terms "places" and "non-places" are useful in discussing such video-sharing websites as YouTube.

In light of Augé's book, Peter Wollen once contemplated whether cinemas were non-places of the kind that Augé discusses. "The lobbies of large multi-screen cinemas are non-places," Wollen writes, "arguably, the cinema auditorium itself is a non-place up to the moment when the film begins."[1] However, the situation when the film itself starts is different, since audiences are transported to another space, a space that is both lived in and at the same time a site of fantasy, a space that combines elements of place as well as non-place. Shifting attention from the old institution of cinema to new media, one might argue that the experience of YouTube has some similarities. When visiting YouTube, you are everywhere and nowhere at the same time, perhaps sitting at home, in an office, or on a train to visit relatives. YouTube is an ocean of images and sound, offering all kinds of experiences. Letting your fingertips do the traveling, you have access to a mobile space that can take you anywhere—and most often takes you nowhere. Speed is important in this transient place; a way station through which one travels to see comedy acts by strangers, check out the latest political comments, or watch music videos of the past and present. Immersed in the videos on YouTube, following numerous links on a journey through the website's attractions, you may visit numerous other places, perhaps occupied by strangers and open to fantasy, but these places combine elements of place as well as non-place.

Writing today, Marc Augé would probably include the Internet and websites such as YouTube in his description and analysis of supermodernity. According to him supermodernity finds its full expression in non-places; non-places are *the space* of supermodernity. YouTube could easily be integrated into an analysis of supermodernity; in fact, many of the aspects of supermodernity described by Augé resemble those of YouTube.

Supermodernity and YouTube

Originally published in 1992, the "supermodern" anthropological thoughts put forward by Augé presented an anthropology of the present and the near. Since then Augé's analysis of modern phenomena—especially his category of the non-place—has been influential and used by many scholars, discussing topics as different as geography, film and archaeology.[2] Augé scrutinizes the institutions, social life and mode of circulation specific to the contemporary Western world with the approach of the anthropologist: observing, gathering empirical data and creating new concepts to describe and characterize "contemporaneity itself, in all the aggressive and disturbing aspects of reality at its most immediate."[3] According to Augé, we are living in the age of supermodernity, a supermodernity that "is the face of a coin whose obverse represents postmodernity: the positive of a negative."[4] If modernity implies the creation of great truths, master narratives and progressive evolution, and postmodernity is intent on the destruction of the master narratives, supermodernity is characterized by excess. Augé employs three figures of excess to characterize the situation of supermodernity: overabundance of events, spatial overabundance and the individualization of references.

The overabundance of events in the world, all demanding to be considered and given meaning, are connected to the shrinking of space as the globe is made smaller by terrestrial travel, and as communication offers "instant" access to any part of the world. The spatial overabundance of the present is "expressed in changes of scale, in the proliferation of imaged and imaginary references, and in the spectacular acceleration of means of transport."[5] The excess of events and spaces has consequences for individuality, and according to Augé, supermodernity implies an overabundance of egos, as individuals free themselves reflexively and subjectively from conventional sociocultural constraints. Supermodernity acts amid the chatter and excess of signification, space and time, and does not concern itself with the creation, identification or destruction of truth values. Although Augé wrote before the explosion of the Internet, and the creation of websites such as YouTube, it is easy to see how the selection of information from the superabundant sources of new media that is useful could support the concept of supermodernity. The construction of websites such as YouTube, interconnected blogs, or Internet search itself, could be seen as examples of the action of the supermodern subject.

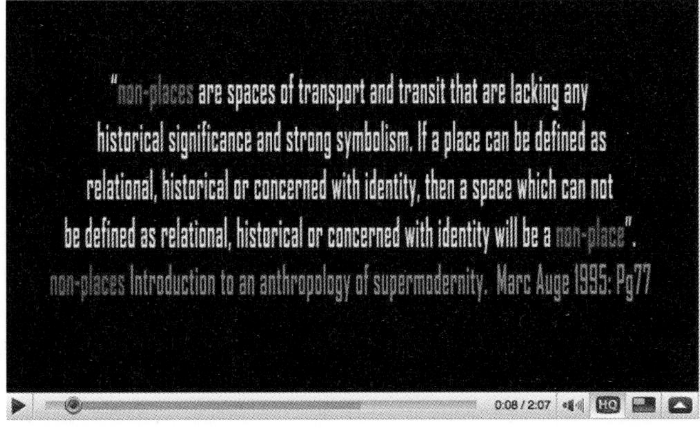

52 Marc Augé on YouTube – stills from "Non-Places | Are Airports Non-Places"

Augé states that the individual, at least in Western societies, "wants to be a world in himself; he intends to interpret the information delivered to him by himself and for himself."[6] He further argues that the supermodernity of our contemporary world points to a need for radical rethinking of the notion of place. He uses the concept of "anthropological place," and contrasts this place of identity, relations and of history to the non-places of supermodernity. "Clearly the word 'non-place' designates two complementary but distinct realities: spaces formed in relation to certain ends (transport, transit, commerce, leisure), and the relations that individuals have with these spaces."[7] Although places and non-places never exist in pure form, the multiplication of non-places is characteristic of supermodernity. Non-places are transient places and meaningless stations through which we travel, and space may thus be the archetype of non-place. Supermodernity produces non-places; spaces where people coexist or cohabit without living together—airport lounges, railway stations, supermarkets, hotels, service stations, clinics, leisure parks, highways, department stores and conference centers. These non-places punctuate space, and change individuals, through the mediations of relations between the self and others.

53 Marc Augé on YouTube – stills from "Non-Places | Are Airports Non-Places"

The opposition between places and non-places derives from Michel de Certeau's distinction between place and space.[8] However, Augé uses non-place in a slightly different way than de Certeau, and his vision of the opportunities individuals have in non-places is more pessimistic. For de Certeau space is a practiced place, and through the tactics of everyday use, the oppositional practices of everyday life, individuals can give different meaning to and change spaces. Augé could be interpreted as stating that non-places generate a new relationship to the world, but this relationship is not always negative, and although the term non-place does have negative connotations, it could also be seen as a new opportunity. Not only for the users, those who pass through the non-places, but also for researchers trying to make sense of new situations or phenomena. Tim Cresswell notes that "Augé's arguments force theorists of culture to reconsider the theory and method of their disciplines. While conventionally figured places demand thoughts which reflect assumed boundaries and traditions, non-places demand new mobile ways of thinking."[9]

Anthropological place is rooted in history, relationships and identity, and the church may be used as an example of an anthropological place. According to Emiko Ohnuki-Tierney the church "embodies the social identity of the people in the same village in their daily social network. It is also a spatial representation of the past, the history of these people and the village."[10] Other similar anthropological places are libraries and archives, places that also embody social identity and history. Non-places, however, are uprooted places marked by mobility and travel; they lack identity, relationships and history. The translation from French to English of the term *non-lieu* has had consequences for interpretation of the possibilities or dangers of dwelling in non-places, and Ohnuki-Tierney has explained that the "term *non-lieu* in a technical juridical sense means 'no ground for prosecution,' that is, the accused is innocent. Those innocent, needless to say, are deprived of their usual identity as social personae and as individuals."[11]

One of the characteristic traits of YouTube is excess. YouTube offers an overabundance of video clips, organized in chaotic ways making precise navigation hard. YouTube is not an anthropological place, defined by identity, relations and history, being closer to a transient non-place, a crossroad where people meet, yet where references are individualized through tags and rating, and where users interpret the information by themselves and for themselves. YouTube is not an asocial place. It is more like a hypersocial place, but the hypersociality of the site is mostly channeled through specific fields or practices, i.e. share a video clip, comment on it, give responses to the uploader, etcetera. As a social process—unless used in a specific way by a local community—YouTube is characterized by the consumption of information. Commercial clips or references are mixed with all sorts of amateur material, and to a certain degree this changes the status of the non-commercial material. This happens in at least two ways. Firstly, it is done by the commercial context itself. Ending up at a commercial site or viewing a commercial clip characterizes many visits to YouTube, and the lack of context makes it hard to determine what kind of clip or site it is. Few or no distinctions are made between commercial and non-commercial clips, and the absence of contexts makes it hard to observe distinctions. Secondly, popularity works as the major attraction and distinction—mainly through rating—and creates an ambiance of competition. Becoming a consumer of information, the YouTube visitor often ends up seeing primarily the most popular video clips, despite the vast archive.

The rating system and the viewer responses is an important aspect of YouTube, not least since the interactive element connects people who share the same interests or the same sense of humor, thus creating social networks. However, the same aspect could also be seen as a negative trait of the site, transforming most clips into spectacles, and highlighting currency and the "latest." "There is no room for history," Augé states, "unless it has been transformed into an element of spectacle. [...] What reigns is actuality, the urgency of the present moment."[12] Augé also proposes that supermodernity makes "the old (history) into a specific spectacle, as it does with all exoticism and all local particularity. History and exoticism play the same role in it as the 'quotations' in a written text."[13] The old and new is hence not interwoven as in modernity; by contrast the old is turned into spectacle—a sort of curiosity where historicity is erased. Many skeptics have been struck by a similar aspect of YouTube, which often has resulted in a condemnation of the website's possibilities. However, lack of context, erasure of provenance, and the essentially performative character of the site make it easy to see that spectacle is an important aspect of YouTube.

54 Early cinema mashup: "Grandpa can dance"

Surfing the Ocean for Early Cinema

Augé's "element of spectacle" in relation to YouTube is for example expressed clearly in relation to the many clips of early cinema found on the site. If one searches for "early cinema" it is possible to choose between more than a thousand clips. Yet, since the tag is broad, a search will include all clips tagged with either "early" or "cinema." On the computer screen, these clips are listed in a seemingly random way, initially organized by "relevance" and not by rating, views or when the clip was added. Of course, all sorts of clips are included in the "early cinema" category. One can find examples of many films by the Lumière brothers and several shorts by Georges Méliès, many film versions of body motions photographed by Marey and Muybridge, and several short documentaries about early cinema in different countries. However, also included are lots of new films, amateur as well as professional, made in the spirit of early cinema, such as promotional clips, experimental films, etcetera.

YouTube is not an ordered and legible space in a traditional archival sense, and although the scholar of early cinema would find plenty of interesting stuff, searching can be time consuming and frustrating. Another problem is provenance and context. The films by Lumière and Méliès, and the excerpts from documentaries, have no information about what sort of films they are, where they were found, if they are complete or where the material is archived. Using "early cinema" when searching for clips will turn up many excerpts from the 1996 television series *Cinema Europe: The Other Hollywood*, but most of the clips are just snippets from the series, and puzzling them together into a whole episode or finding out whether something is missing is nearly impossible without prior knowledge of the material.

Clips from the period of early cinema on YouTube are, hence, regularly presented as spectacles or attractions, without historicity, context or provenance. Nevertheless, the problem is hardly unique to YouTube. In the context of photographic archives, Allan Sekula has noted a similar problematic aspect of archives. In fact, Sekula's words about the relationship between history and photography in regular archives could be used to characterize YouTube. "But awareness of history as an *interpretation* of the past succumbs to a faith in history as *representation*. The viewer is confronted, not by *historical writing*, but by the appearance of *history itself*."[14] However, history is often included in an uncanny and weird way in the peculiar context of performativity prevalent on YouTube. The slogan that YouTube has chosen is, after all, "Broadcast yourself," and the first clip found when entering "early cinema" is for example a video of some old cigarette cards with pictures of old film stars filmed by an amateur that encourages the viewer to bid on a set of cards on eBay, as well as encouraging the viewer to visit a website with an online cigarette-card museum. The clip is thus both a commercial, an extension of an online museum, and an amateur video performance. Often, research queries on YouTube takes one on a dazzling tour through a non-place, to clips whose status is mixed and unclear. These video clips are more performative than memorative; they are not rooted in identity and history, but rather in a fleeting media landscape without fixed borders or temporal traits.

A Celestial Archive

YouTube is interesting as a point of entry into ways of thinking about archives, storage forms and the values that bring these into being. Seen as an archive, YouTube holds promises of a new accessibility of images and sound, as well as fears about a new archival anarchy and problems of information retrieval. Although YouTube is a vast database of clips, it can hardly replace traditional media archives. Only a fraction of analogue media material produced during the 20th century will ever be made available in digitized form. "The Internet is mind-bogglingly huge, and a lot of people seem to think that most of the texts and images and sound-recordings ever created are now available on it—or will be soon," Kristin Thompson has stated. "In relation to music downloading, this idea got termed 'The Celestial Jukebox,' and a lot of people believe in it."[15] Thompson argues against the belief that all (surviving) films eventually will be on the Internet, what she calls a "Celestial Multiplex." Vast though it is, YouTube contains only a small fraction of the films made, so it will never be "The Celestial Archive," and most of the films or videos exist in excerpt form only or without any information about context or provenance. This limits the use value of YouTube and foregrounds its suitability as a site of personalized and ahistorical entertainment. And we may even ask if YouTube, as an example of hyperlinked culture itself, is a non-place, though without the identity and history of other older archives.

Hubert L. Dreyfus has illustrated the opposition of the old and new ways of organizing and retrieving information, and the attraction and positive aspects of each, by contrasting an old library culture with the contemporary hyperlinked Internet culture. For him, hyperlink technology itself seems to be the major problem with digital archives and libraries. Of course, the organizing principle of YouTube is an interconnectedness of clips. No hierarchies other than the rating systems exist; everything is linked to everything else on a single level, and every user can rate videos according to her or his taste. What Dreyfus writes about the Internet itself can be applied to YouTube: "With a hyperlinked database, the user is encouraged to traverse a vast network of information," Dreyfus states, a fact that has led to a situation where everything is "equally accessible and none of which is privileged."[16] According to Dreyfus, an old library culture, which includes traditional libraries and archives, have a meaning-driven, semantic structuring of information. It is stable, hierarchically organized and defined by specific interests. Material is carefully selected, by judging the authenticity, relevance and quality of the texts or films. Texts are part of permanent collections that encourage interested browsing. In contrast to this old library culture, the new hyperlinked culture—of which YouTube is a good example—is flexible, on a single level, and allows for all possible associations. In hyperlinked culture, all editions are included, everything saved and available. This creates dynamic collections, archives or libraries characterized by intertextual evolution, which encourages playful surfing.[17] Dreyfus suggests that the user of a hyperconnected library or archive is no longer a modern subject with a fixed identity, requiring a reliable and complete model of the world. For him, Web surfers instead "embrace proliferating information as a contribution to a new form of life in which surprise and wonder are more important than meaning and usefulness."[18]

Old library culture may be hierarchical and non-flexible, compared with YouTube, but without a way of telling the relevant from the insignificant, everything becomes equally significant. Excess, speed, wonder and personalized references, what Augé probably would call an overabundance of events as well as egos, characterize YouTube. As a new type of archive, YouTube encourages playful surfing, travels through the vast number of video clips, but this enormous "celestial archive" could also be described as a non-place, a place of transition and erasure of historicity. The library culture described by Dreyfus most certainly is an *ideal* archive or library, and not any old library or archive meets these standards, but YouTube is quite different. The flexibility, the dialogue between historical material and modern-day films, and the lack of context and provenance creates in YouTube a different relationship between archive and user, and between historical material and user, compared to old library or archive culture in its best forms.

Conclusion

The default experience of YouTube is one surrounded by too many in the midst of too much, clips of every imaginable style and genre, high and low, old and new, professional and amateur, commercial and non-commercial. YouTube is a place where one can drown, or fight to stay afloat, in a superabundance of meanings. In this article Marc Augé's concept of supermodernity, and his distinctions between places and non-places, have been used in a discussion of YouTube as a social phenomenon and an archive. YouTube is characterized by excess, and obviously, if Augé's terms are applied, YouTube is closer to a non-place than a place.

At his most pessimistic Augé's dark predictions suggest that the non-place "creates neither singular identity nor relations; only solitude, and similitude."[19] Still, on YouTube new digital identities flourish; surprise and wonder are important, and YouTube has many positive aspects, predominantly as a medium for networking. Uploading a video, and encouraging friends or a community to watch and comment, is for example important in various social or political processes. In a critical review of Augé's book, David Harvie points to the possibility of struggle, and how place can be created from non-place through social interaction[20]—which naturally is facilitated by sites such as YouTube. Having access to some examples of early cinema might also be seen as much better than no access at all. New opportunities have indeed been created by YouTube. However, this ocean of sound and images, vast as it is, is a new form of non-place. In 1992, Augé suggested that an ever-increasing proportion of our lives was being spent in non-places, and this might result in a profound alteration of awareness. He argues that we are in transit through non-places for more and more of our time. According to Augé, no organic social life is possible in the non-places of our supermodern world. New social networking sites on the Web might prove him wrong, but YouTube still (at least to me) looks more like a non-place than a place.

Endnotes

1 Peter Wollen, Paris Hollywood: *Writings on Film* (London: Verso, 2002), p. 200.

2 Tim Cresswell, *Place – A Short Introduction* (Oxford: Blackwell, 2004); Wollen 2002; Alfredo Gonzàlez-Ruibal, "Time to Destroy – An Archaeology of Supermodernity," *Current Anthropology* no. 2, 2008, pp. 247–262.

3 Marc Augé, *Non-Places – Introduction to an Anthropology of Supermodernity* (London: Verso, 1995), p. 12.

4 Ibid, p. 30.

5 Ibid, p. 34.

6 Ibid, p. 37.

7 Ibid, p. 94.

8 Michel de Certeau, *The Practice of Everyday Life* (Berkeley: University of California Press, 1984).

9 Cresswell 2004, p. 46.

10 Emiko Ohnuki-Tierney, "The Anthropology of the Other in the Age of Supermodernity," *Current Anthropology* no. 3, 1996, pp. 578–580.

11 Ibid.

12 Augé 1995, pp. 103–104.

13 Ibid., p. 110.

14 Allan Sekula, "Reading an Archive – Photography between labour and capital," in *The Photography Reader*, ed. Liz Wells (London: Routledge, 2003), p. 443.

15 Kristin Thompson, "The Celestial Multiplex," in *Film Curatorship – Archives, Museums, and the Digital Marketplace*, eds. Paolo Cherchi Usai et al. (Vienna: Austrian Film Museum, 2008), p. 216.

16 Hubert L. Dreyfus, *On the Internet* (London: Routledge, 2001), p. 10.

17 Ibid., p. 11.

18 Ibid., p. 12.

19 Augé 1995, p. 103.

20 David Harvie, "Review of Non-places: Introduction to an anthropology of supermodernity," *Capital & Class* no. 60, 1996, pp. 23–25.

Industry

Joëlle Farchy

Economics of Sharing Platforms: What's Wrong with the Cultural Industries?

Over the past few years we have seen the services of the information society expand considerably.[1] Many of these services are based on what has now come to be known as Web 2.0. Though they have some characteristics in common, there is great variety among these services, from community portals and sites for sharing videos or photos to e-commerce platforms and collaborative online encyclopedias. Although there is no single definition of this notion, it might be said that Web 2.0 refers to a set of applications and new uses for the Internet reflecting an evolution that is at once technical, social and economic. From a technical point of view, Web 2.0 is based on technologies aimed at making the Internet truly interactive (RSS, Wiki, Flash). From a sociological standpoint, Web 2.0 involves the distribution or exchange of information and content submitted by Internet users themselves. Once a simple "visitor" or "consumer" of information, the Internet user is more and more becoming a veritable contributor. From an economic standpoint, Web 2.0 is toppling a distributor model and replacing it with one descended from the network economy, based not on control of access via intellectual property rights, but on the abundance of resources available and growth in the number of users.

Even though many sites have not yet attained profitability, various large-scale purchases attest to the trust that economic players have in their valorization potential. A symbol of the dynamic nature of these services, the Google company saw its turnover multiply by a factor of almost 40 between 2002 and 2007. In 2006, Google purchased YouTube and also agreed to pay Fox Interactive 900 million dollars over three years to become the exclusive supplier of sponsored links on the search pages of the social-networking site MySpace. Yahoo! for its part purchased the photo-sharing site Flickr for 35 million dollars. The amount of bandwidth used is another reflection of the dynamic nature of Web 2.0: the amount of traffic generated by YouTube in 2008 equals the amount on the entire Internet in 2000. Using the example of YouTube, the main video-exchange site, this article examines a new model of economics based on the valorization of a Web audience. Web 2.0 promotes a more direct relationship between creators of content and the public, though this does not imply the disappearance of all intermediation. On the contrary, Web 2.0 necessarily entails the advent of new intermediaries whose essential function it is to capture Internet users' attention by guiding them into this economy of abundance. In fact, it is user attention rather than information that becomes the scarce resource in such an economy.[2] After the success of the decentralized peer-to-peer (P2P) networks, Web 2.0 marks the onset of intermediaries providing consumers with rapid means of accessing creative content. What Web 2.0 has in common with P2P networks is making available, without authorization, immaterial products protected by intellectual property rights. This situation poses problems for the content industries, obliging them to come up with new solutions for the future.

An Economic Model of Audience Valorization

Although Internet players' positioning and strategies are always evolving, certain economic models can be clearly identified with them. At the heart of the analysis of the new Internet services is the existence of network externalities.[3] This notion, originally used to describe the characteristics of telecommunications infrastructures, refers first and foremost to positive club effects: the benefit of a good or a service to a user depends on the number of users of this good or service. If the externality depends on the number of users (telephone, fax, Internet), it is said to be direct; if it depends on the variety and the quality of complementary services and goods, themselves a function of the number of users (the utility of a car in relation to the number of garages that repair that type of car), it is said to be indirect. A critical mass of users (the installed base) is formed, and a potent dynamic of demand is set into motion via a viral, snowball effect. Congestion, however, can cause this potent dynamic to run into limitations, such as when the number of users saturates the network's capacity or the quality of services.

The now-classic literature on externalities or intragroups has more recently been supplemented by the analysis of intergroup externalities, a characteristic of two-sided markets which refers to the interaction between two groups of users: the utility for a consumer from group A depends on the number of users in group B. Although this analysis is applied to an outdated reality, the theoretical analysis of two-sided markets appeared in industrial economics at the beginning of the 2000s. A two-sided or multi-sided market is one whose structure supports, and even necessitates, the existence of two very different, but mutually interdependent, customer bases for the products exchanged there.[4] In a two-sided market, a platform such as radio, newspapers, the Web, etcetera offers an intermediary service to two types of customers, to whom it provides a joint product. The intermediary platform is not economically neutral, because it allows players to maximize the gains of their transactions by internalizing the intergroup externalities, as the agents themselves are incapable of internalizing the impact of their use of the platform for the benefit of other users.

The presence of network externalities on a two-sided market has unexpected economic consequences on price formation, level and structure.[5] In order to solve the "chicken and the egg" problem, a platform must have a large installed base, that is, programs to attract viewers. Advertisers, however, will not pay to finance the programs unless they are sure to attract many viewers—the optimal price system implies subsidization of one side of the market to attract users on the other side. In the case of total subsidization, one side of the market becomes accessible free of charge. This is a classic model of advertising-based financing of the media (free television, radio, newspapers). Advertisers value a media company that captures more of the audience. However, the media company, which receives compensation from advertisers, uses these resources to create new programs and provides programs to viewers free of charge on the other side of the market. The media is thus a platform that provides a joint product: media content to viewers—and attention to advertisers.[6]

Financing through Advertising

Characteristic of two-sided market economics, the most widespread model among providers of Web 2.0 consists of providing free services financed by monetization of the audience on the part of the advertisers. This is the model of video-sharing platforms such as YouTube and its French counterpart Dailymotion. Though the two-sided advertising model is a classic model, it makes it possible to obtain additional added value on the Internet. Interactivity provides the ability to track and target Internet users' behavior and interests; the option of segmenting selection by geographic region and new viral marketing techniques both contribute to the effectiveness of the advertising so as to turn a classical mass-media model into advertising that is much more individualized. Another attractive aspect of the Internet for advertisers is the ability to measure with precision the efficacy of a company's advertising investment. On the global level, promotional links, currently on a path of growth, now represent, among the main formats, approximately half of all advertising investments on the Internet. Within the main advertising formats on the Web besides promotional links, traditional banners represent a loss of speed that benefits the "rich media" formats with their visual and audio elements, most notably video.

On sharing platforms as YouTube, advertisements are shown on the site's homepage, which contains elements published or chosen by the platform. They may also appear on a video's viewing page, normally in the form of a banner. The advertiser can also request that the proposed advertisement be targeted with respect to the video's content, in which case higher rates apply. New advertising formats have been developed to have this effect. Thus, the same is particularly true of the insertion of an advertisement at the beginning or end of a video. These sites offer advertisers the option of inserting the advertisement presenting the entire range of one brand's advertisements into the videos of business partners or even dedicated channels. Though certain community platforms, like the media, are derived from a two-sided market model, they are nevertheless not exactly the same: while traditional forms of media are based on a content selection that is limited (if only technically), and focus on one strong audience for each, community platforms are based on the aggregation of millions of audiences—from a few hits to several thousand—of non-handpicked content uploaded by the user.

Many Internet services in fact claim to be part of the "long-tail" model of economics, with regard to both advertisers as well as content publishers.[7] By providing hundreds of thousands of advertisers of all sizes with access to an audience comparable to that of the largest forms of media, the long tail prevails, and regarding content publishers, they of course grant access to an unequalled pool of advertisers. This model relies on the tremendous diversity of content offered as well as on optimization of costs for production and online content publishing, thanks to automation of the process. Though empirically validated by sites as Amazon, Google and eBay, the long-tail model still does not accurately describe sites such as YouTube or Dailymotion. Today, videos from parties with partner rights to the site are the primary sources of revenue. The representatives of these platforms, however, have the economic goal of giving value to very small audiences generated by videos published by more modest players as well.

Yet from an overall perspective, the importance of a global audience in addition to these micro-audiences must be emphasized. In this sense, the platforms are no longer based on the long-tail model, but on a cross-subsidy model in which content providing value through advertising—both content published on the homepage and the partner videos of these sites—serves to finance the hosting of these videos in the absence of advertisements. Thus, the services Google has developed to accompany its search engine—such as Google News, Google Maps and Google Docs—contribute to the growth of a global audience for the company and the associated brand effects, though they do not always bring direct compensation. These services might be considered a building block for the only service Google actually sells: audience access.[8]

Content Industries & Audience Models

To a greater degree than the economic models themselves—the two-sided advertising market for free media has, after all, existed for quite some time—the novelty of content industries lies in the proliferation of services created to make available to the public productions protected by intellectual property rights for the sake of valorizing their audience. The community platforms have been accused by certain rights holders of unauthorized distribution of protected works or excerpts;

these platforms have also been accused of being receptacles for so-called "derivative works" that reproduce text, sound, image or video of an author, artist, producer or distributor without the rights holder's consent. Precise evaluations of this phenomenon have resulted in assessment discrepancies between sites and rights holders.

The proliferation of lawsuits filed against Internet service providers for infringements on intellectual property rights, as well as accused platforms' efforts to curb this phenomenon, lead one to believe that it is far from being negligible. For the rights holders, it is a dual challenge: on the one hand because the protected works distributed by "traditional" media risk falling victim to substitution effects on the global advertising market; on the other hand because the benefits of the new forms of advertising compensation on the Internet are causing conflicts about equal compensation for all parties involved.

Internet Advertising Market

Advertising expenditures around the globe should reach 479 billion dollars in 2008, growth of seven percent compared to 2007. This expansion is the result of the development of markets in China and Russia; the outlook is bleaker for the Western markets. The impact of the global advertising market on GDP is actually diminishing. Internet advertising, though a very recent phenomenon, has become the main growth engine on the advertising market, with progression rates of around 30 percent per year for the past three years. Advertising expenditures on the Internet, which represent almost five percent of total advertising expenditures on a global level, is expected to more than double in 2010. In the US, gross advertising expenditures on the Web reached almost 30 billion dollars in 2007, and are expected to almost double by three years from now.

Of course, the US remains by far the world's most significant market, with American brands historically spending more than their European counterparts for advertising, having made the choice to develop various online strategies earlier. As regards the European market, Jupiter Research predicts that online advertising will nearly double in Europe between 2007 and 2012, from 7.7 billion euros—in net revenues collected by search engines or Internet sites—to 13.9 billion.[9] Thus, the potential of Internet advertising market remains significant. On the one hand, Internet audiences should increase with the penetration of the Net into an increasing number of households, the expansion of broadband and the increase in the average amount of time spent online. On the other hand, the Web's impact within the advertising market remains modest, given time spent online and the advantages of this type of format. The strategies chosen by the sector's major players attest to their confidence in this potential. Defending his company's attempted Yahoo! takeover bid, Steve Ballmer, CEO of Microsoft, predicted that the online advertising market would be worth 80 billion dollars in 2010.[10]

Although the Internet advertising market is on a growth track, for the time being it still remains relatively small. For example, in 2007 the Web represented just 2.3 percent of the French advertising market. Furthermore, the market growth of Internet advertising against the backdrop of the bleak outlook on the global advertising market means that we are seeing an increase in the relative growth of the Internet on the advertising market. Therefore, the Internet has not as of yet helped increase the global market's size; instead, substitution effects have occurred among the various forms of media. Although television remains the primary form of media and maintains a relatively stable impact, Internet media continues to grow, mainly to the detriment of the press, which is experiencing a significant slowdown in the progression of advertising investments. Ultimately, the Internet advertising market remains largely concentrated around the major players, such as Google, Yahoo and MSN, who claim the largest part of the audience. According to some estimates, 30 to 40 percent of global advertising expenditures for "sponsored links" belong to Google's market share.

Thus, one question that arises is whether the content publishers who are experiencing the effects of advertising substitution between the Internet and other forms of media could exploit this new environment to obtain better returns with the help of Internet advertising, or whether, on the contrary, all but the major portals will end up losing in the long run. Furthermore, it is possible that the substitution effects among the forms of media on the advertising market reinforce the negative effect to the cultural industries, in that the traditional forms of media contribute greatly, in terms of audiovisual materials, to financing content creation. These substitution effects could be exacerbated by cache techniques and content-aggregation services; search engines can create exact reproductions of Web pages, storing them on internal servers for easier access. Cache techniques are hence accused of promoting a bypassing of the original site, resulting in the loss of compensation for these sites' publishers and authors. Direct access to content through this parallel distribution network would likely result in fewer visits to the original site, particularly to its homepage, and would thus affect their advertising revenue and, in turn, compensation for the authors of the content. Meanwhile, the search engines benefit from advertising revenue generated by banners on these sites and sponsored links.

Content Industries and Valorizing the Audience

In this economy of audience and traffic, the most important thing is not the information, the content itself, which has become a "commodity," but control of visitor traffic. Unable to control access to the network, the partners of the cultural industry who help capture the Internet user audience do not benefit from any financial transactions that take place as a result, which is a classic externality problem. Moreover, the need to rethink the sharing of added value and the financing of the works serving as a "commodity" to other economic activities is far from new. A famous incident resulted from France's 1847 law intended to protect musical composers' performing rights: the successful composer Ernest Bourget categorically refused to settle his bill in a Parisian concert café where one of his works was playing, defending his position by pointing out that the café was using the music to attract customers without offering him the slightest compensation. Therefore, to his mind, there was no reason for him to pay his bill.

The analysis suggesting that cultural industries remain systematically excluded from the process of valorizing the audience that they help assemble deserves to be explored in even more depth. One the one hand, the idea that cache techniques and content-aggregation services take audience away from the original sites is the source of several criticisms on the part of the Internet intermediaries. Search-engine services exist entirely for the purpose of increasing the number of visits to reference sites whose content is made as easily accessible as YouTube. Furthermore, the cache technique, which has been in existence for over ten years, is entirely optional for the site's publisher (the function can be deactivated on all search engines). The cache generates no profit whatsoever for the search engine, and is not a substitute for referenced media, which remain directly accessible by a link (if the content is removed from the original site, the reference will disappear after a short time); in the end, the cache search continues to generate advertising revenue for the target site.

On the other hand, the audience is a source of revenue and also a source of cost for Internet service providers (ISPs), and although the majority of Internet services share one audience model, their economic interests do not always coincide. Telecommunications companies and Web 2.0 service providers do not necessarily have the same interests. ISPs who charge several dozen euros a month for a subscription hope to become distributors of content themselves in order to ensure long-term profitability thanks to complementary services intending to increase the average revenue per user (ARPU). However, although Web 2.0 sites help stimulate demand for access to rapid broadband so as to benefit telecommunications companies, they also represent a source of direct cost for these same companies through their bandwidth consumption. These factors help explain why telecommunications companies are being driven to consider supplemental charges for data transfer on sites with heavy traffic such as YouTube, and are trying to better their position with regard to advertising revenues. The question regarding future compensation for Internet users posting content on community platforms has also been posed. As of today, Dailymotion, for example, has made the decision not to connect the "motion makers" with advertising resources on the grounds that it is providing them with a free service (bandwidth) and that at this stage, no advertising has been directly inserted into their videos.

Accordingly, it appears that one of the main economic issues lies in the articulation between the solution to the problem of externality—the Internet services benefiting, thanks to an audience monetization model, from the activities of the rights holders who have borne the risks of content creation—and the need to take into account the costs necessary for capturing this audience so as to not penalize the digital economy on its growth track, and to allow for content creation to benefit from real opportunities for distribution.

Conclusion: Solutions for the Future

The tools developed through economic analysis for solving problems of externalities are aimed at requiring the party responsible for the external effect to take this effect into account in its private economic calculations. In other words, the tools allow for an "internalization of the externality." Schematically, these tools can be classified into four major categories. The first involves prohibiting, limiting or making obligatory certain behaviors with regard to the originator of externalities. In our case, this includes all kinds of technical solutions—notably filtering and identification of works—aimed at limiting infringements. The second category consists of establishing rules that address responsibility, here too with the intention of moving the players involved to behave more efficiently. This involves considering a legislative modification to the exceptional arrangement for responsibility. In Europe, the responsibility program currently in effect for Internet services, wherein the intermediaries ensure the transmission and/or storage of information supplied by third parties, in fact stems from the June 2000 guidelines on electronic commerce,[11] which provided for a limited responsibility program for certain types of Internet services. While the use of Web 2.0 services is leading to the proliferation of legal disputes concerning charges of infringement, the difficulties encountered with regard to interpretation and the diversity of solutions in existence begs the question as to whether the current legal framework allows for a correct understanding of an economic, technological and social situation that is different from that which existed at the time of the guidelines' negotiation, in the late 1990s. Engaging the legal responsibility of certain intermediaries involves, for the European nations, either effecting a national reform of the guideline framework, allowing for reduced room for maneuvering, or modifying the guidelines.

The two latter solutions entail coming up with new rules for sharing the benefits of valorization of the audience with those who helped create it. These value transactions could be organized in various ways:

— By taxes levied in proportion to damages incurred, forcing the responsible party to take into account the externality in his decisions. This approach presents the eternal problem of choosing the basis for calculation and for the assigned tax rates, heightened in this case by the instability of the economic model studied and the proliferation of negotiations between the players.

— Through the market agreements which are meant to allow the victims and beneficiaries of external effects to negotiate mutually advantageous agreements, independently of all legal responsibility. The current negotiations between some of the major sharing platforms and various media and content industries lead one to believe that, without abandoning their community dimension, these sites also intend to support the lawful provision of content, and to develop new hybrid models for monetizing the audience. With the help of these kinds of partnerships, the producers and authors' societies could also benefit from new modes of consuming Web material in the future.

It remains to be seen, however, how the opportunities created by each of these solutions will express themselves; in any case, the solutions could not be adapted by all the services in the same way. Thus, for many services, the solution will not involve rules for sharing the benefits of audience valorization with those who help create the audience. For others, the solution will not involve the transfer of value but rather practices that enable fighting the sale of products infringing on copyrights, most notably on online-commerce sites. Yet the solutions are not strictly mutually exclusive. Market agreements can take the form of individual contractual agreements, or they can be "soft laws" (equivalent to industry-wide agreements) which can then be reflected in modifications of the law. Technical measures can serve to prohibit the distribution of works, but they can also make it easier to circulate them and better exploit them. They can also be directly implemented by each partner like "soft-law" agreements such as implementation of video and audio identification techniques, or they can be made mandatory by the government.

Endnotes

1 This article is largely based on a report for the French Ministry of Culture. See Josée Anne Benazéraf, Joëlle Farchy & Pierre Sirinelli, "Les prestataires de l'Internet," *Rapport du CSPLA* (Paris, 2008).

2 See Herbert A. Simon, "Designing Organizations for an Information Rich World," in Martin Greenberger, ed., *Computers, Communication and the Public Interest* (Baltimore: Johns Hopkins University Press, 1971), pp. 71–89 and Richard Lanham, *The Economics of Attention: Style and Substance in the Age of Information* (Chicago: Chicago University Press, 2006).

3 Externality refers to the fact that the activity of one economic agent affects the well-being of another agent, with neither of the two receiving or paying a commercial counterpart for this effect. In the absence of a commercial counterpart, the agent responsible for the externality is not held accountable in these decisions for the influence his actions have on others' well-being.

4 David S. Evans, "The Antitrust Economics of Two Sided Markets," *Yale Journal on Regulation* no. 2, 2003, pp. 645–667.

5 Jean-Charles Rochet, Jean Tirole, "Platform Competition in Two Sided Markets," *Journal of the European Economic Association* no. 1, 2004, pp. 370–390.

6 Olivier Bomsel, *Gratuit! Du déploiement de l'économie numérique* (Paris: Gallimard, 2007).

7 Chris Anderson, *The Long Tail* (New York: Hyperion Books, 2006).

8 Waughty Xavier, "No free lunch sur le web 2.0! Ce que cache la gratuité apparente des réseaux sociaux numériques," *Regards économiques* no. 59, 2008, pp. 589-598 – http://techtrends.eu/files/Nofreelunch.pdf [last checked 15 February 2009].

9 See for example *Business Wire*, "JupiterResearch Finds Recent Consolidation Will Strengthen Online Ad Network Market Despite Negative Reputation Issues," 21 April 2008 – http://findarticles.com/p/articles/mi_m0EIN/is_2008_April_21 [last checked 15 February 2009].

10 See www.microsoft.com/presspass/press/2008/feb08/02-01corpnewspr.mspx [last checked 15 February 2009].

11 Directive 2000/31/CE of the European Parliament and the Council from 8 June 2009 regarding certain legal aspects of e-commerce on the interior market: *JOCE* July 17, no. L 178, p. 1.

Janet Wasko and Mary Erickson

The Political Economy of YouTube

Since YouTube was launched in 2005, many have heralded the video-sharing website as a democratizing media platform that would convert media consumers into producers and reshape the entire landscape of media. Some argue that the site is contributing to a fundamental transformation in political discourse and policy too.[1] From its very early days, corporate organizations have heralded YouTube as a potential goldmine of relatively effortless profit, where millions (and soon to be billions) of eyeballs would translate into huge revenues for YouTube, venture capitalists and advertisers alike.[2] This tension between YouTube's democratizing goals and economic potential is a fundamental question which is often ignored in analyses of the website.[3] YouTube has indeed altered how audiences engage with media, particularly in an online forum, but we cannot ignore the underlying motives of its owners. This article discusses the political economy of the website, presenting the company's history and ownership structure, as well as the efforts made thus far to develop the site's economic potential. Through an evaluation of the power relations that are infused in the structure and operation of YouTube, we can begin to assess whether the site does indeed democratize media production and distribution—or merely serves as yet another media platform intended to generate advertising dollars.

Political Economy of Communication

The discussion in this article draws on a political economic analysis of media. The study of political economy is about how societies are organized and controlled and it is very much about the analysis of power. In the 1970s, Graham Murdock and Peter Golding defined political economy of communication as fundamentally interested in studying communication and media as commodities produced by capitalist industries.[4] More recent theoretical discussions of this approach have been offered by Vincent Mosco, Robert McChesney, Janet Wasko and others.[5] However, in general, the study of political economy of the media is about how the media are organized and controlled within the larger political economy. In other words, it is concerned with who has power to make decisions about the media, and who benefits from these decisions. It is about understanding how power relations actually work within and around the media.

In media studies, critical political economy has grown over the years and is now recognized as a distinct tradition. While critical political economy does not claim to explain everything, political economists have examined a wide range of communication and media issues and practices, including the traditional mass media, and more recently, computers and information technologies. Recent work has focused on issues relating to the growing concentration and privatization of media industries, as well as the implications of commodification and globalization trends for media and culture. Critical political economy is also about challenging the dominant ideology that legitimizes a capitalist system. While we are exposed to a multitude of myths about our society and about the media, political economy is often involved with challenging those myths. In this sense, examining the assertion that YouTube is a democratizing force in new media is an appropriate focus for a political economic analysis.

YouTube's (Short) History

YouTube was officially launched in December 2005 and immediately attracted a huge number of users. At the time the site described itself as "the world's most popular online video community," allowing millions of people to discover, watch and share originally created videos. The founders made a deliberate decision not to include advertising as part of the site, as explained in a 2006 *Time* article. "Early on, Chad and Steve made a crucial good decision: despite pressure from advertisers, they would not force users to sit through ads before videos played. Preroll ads would have helped their bottom line in the struggling months, but the site would never have gained its mythological community-driven status. It would have seemed simply like another Big Media site."[6]

Funds, however, came from other sources. In November 2005, the company received almost ten million dollars in funding from Sequoia Capital, which had previously helped finance Apple, Google and other Silicon Valley companies. Sequoia has invested in a wide range of other companies related to creative industries (Atari, EA and various online sites), although its main focus has been on semiconductor companies, software and other tech services. Sequoia supplies investment funds, which sometimes includes an ownership stake in a company, but it is unclear the amount of control or involvement in the company such investments involve.

55 "The Making of YouTube": last day in the Sequoia office

At the time when YouTube was purchased by Google, the site was delivering "more than 100 million video views every day with 65,000 new videos uploaded daily." The same press release from Google also announced that the acquisition combined "one of the largest and fastest growing online video entertainment communities with Google's expertise in organizing information and creating new models for advertising on the Internet."[7] Thus, from the beginning, Google's intentions seemed clear: to develop YouTube's potential for attracting advertising revenues. Since YouTube is a subsidiary of Google Inc., it remains important to examine the parent corporation more carefully. Founded in 1998 by Stanford PhD students Larry Page and Sergey Brin, Google began as a "Web crawler" or search engine that traverses the Web in search of requested information.[8] The company grew rapidly and is now headquartered in

Silicon Valley with 60 offices in over 20 countries. Google's organization currently includes various divisions such as Google.com—Search and Personalization; Communication, Collaboration and Communities; Downloadable Applications; Google GEO—Maps, Earth and Local; Google Checkout (online shopping); and Google Mobile. The main google.com site has been expanded to include special features, such as Image Search, Book Search, and Google Scholar provides a simple way to do a broad search for relevant scholarly literature, including peer-reviewed papers, theses, books, abstracts and articles. Content in Google Scholar is taken from academic publishers, professional societies, preprint repositories, universities and other scholarly organizations. As is well known, the company has also developed a variety of other tools for users to create, share and communicate.

Google's goal is to organize the world's information and make it universally accessible and useful. To do this, the company relies on advertising to generate revenues. Their advertising strategies include content-targeted ads on google.com, as well as programs such as AdWords and AdSense, which help content owners to monetize their content by adding advertising to content, as well as other advertising strategies. Google is a public corporation—meaning their stock is available to the public—however, they have never paid dividends on common stock. In their latest report to the Securities and Exchange Commission, they stated: "We currently intend to retain any future earnings and do not expect to pay any dividends in the foreseeable future."[9] Control lies firmly in the hand of the founders, executive officers and directors, who hold so-called "Class A common stock." "Class B common stock" and other equity interests represent approximately 70 percent of the voting power of the outstanding capital stock. At the end of 2007, the company's two founders and the CEO owned almost 90 percent of outstanding Class B common stock, representing more than two thirds of the voting power. "Larry, Sergey and Eric [...] have significant influence over management and affairs and over all matters requiring stockholder approval, including the election of directors and significant corporate transactions, such as a merger or other sale of our company or its assets, for the foreseeable future," the most recent 10-K report states. "This concentrated control limits our stockholders' ability to influence corporate matters and, as a result, we may take actions that our stockholders do not view as beneficial."[10] Google's assets for 2007 were around 25 billion dollars with revenues reaching nearly 17 billion.

Google, Inc. Financial Information (in thousands of $)					
	2003	2004	2005	2006	2007
Revenues	1,465,934	3,189,223	6,138,560	10,604,917	16,593,986
Costs & expenses	1,123,470	2,549,031	4,121,282	7,054,921	11,509,586
Net income	105,648	399,119	1,465,397	3,077,446	4,203,720

Information compiled from Google – Form 10-K Annual Report, 31 December 2007.

Advertising revenues have contributed 99 percent of the company's revenues since 2005, with the balance from the licensing of Web search technology and search solutions, plus the sale of other products and services. Interestingly, international revenues accounted for nearly half of Google's revenues in 2007, since more than half of its user traffic is from outside the U.S.

Google and YouTube

Even though Google does not share YouTube's financial information, it is estimated that the latter site generated 200 million dollars during 2008 and perhaps as much as 350 million dollars in 2009. Although this represents only around one percent of Google's sales, it is considerably more than was earned by YouTube in 2007.[11] When it was decided that YouTube was to remain independent from Google, *Forbes* reported that "the Google people are taking over the place, and they've found the buttons on the cash register."[12] YouTube has expanded globally, adding 17 countries between mid-2007 and 2008 and persuasively dominating the online video business. It has been estimated that the site attracted around a billion views per day worldwide in mid-2008, with almost 40 percent of videos streamed on the Web coming from YouTube.

But as of this writing, financial analysts were still claiming that, even though YouTube has a huge audience, it still has an uncertain business model. In fact, one of the fundamental problems that commercial media companies face is how to translate cultural goods into revenue and eventual profit. Nicholas Garnham notes that product scarcity, a foundational element of market supply and demand, is difficult to establish, because cultural commodities are intangible and reusable without much limitation.[13] Furthermore, demand for any given cultural good is difficult to predict, thereby complicating how media companies approach media production and distribution. Companies employ a number of strategies to ensure that commodity value is established through access limitation (most often through distribution and/or the exercise of copyright), constant resupply of media—such as 24-hour news—and the sale of audiences to advertisers. It is this last strategy that most concerns media companies hoping to tap into online audiences.

Social network media, or those websites that provide communities for people to interconnect such as MySpace, Facebook and YouTube, are the latest Internet trend to grab attention from corporations and investors as they explore how to translate potential captive audiences into advertising revenue. Over 16 million people visited MySpace on a monthly basis in mid-2005, prompting News Corporation to acquire the social network site's parent company, Intermix, for 580 million dollars.[14] Facebook, with roughly 15 million monthly visitors in mid-2006, generated interest—and offers—from both Viacom and Yahoo that year; however, Facebook declined both of them.[15] YouTube's 72 million unique monthly visitors viewed 100 million videos every day, was the main reason for Google's purchase, but ever since acquiring YouTube, the company has struggled to see a return on its investment.[16]

The issue of translating these huge audiences into revenue, or monetization—the term that YouTube and Google seem to prefer—has stumped advertisers and media companies alike as more and more people shift their media interaction and consumption from traditional to online venues. Of course, the commercialization of media is not a new story, especially in the US, where there is a long history of profit being prioritized over public interest in the development of media such as radio and television. Yet the Internet represents a challenge to those traditionally held beliefs about commercial media, as it holds the possibility of a truly accessible public-media system. Nevertheless, media industries tend to view any media technology or form as another mode of exploiting captive audiences for profit, with the primary goal of selling these audiences to advertisers.

Google is no different in the pursuit of this goal; however, managing a social hybrid economy as YouTube is very different from running a traditional enterprise. Of course, Google has been a forerunner in trying out new models of monetizing the rapidly growing Internet audience. With the company's investment in YouTube, this goal has become even more urgent, with Google's heavy dependence on advertising revenues. The problem, however, as Google CEO Eric Schmidt admitted in 2008, is that the company doesn't know exactly how to monetize YouTube.[17] While the company is exploring its options, it has also encouraged its advertisers to try different tactics, hoping that someone will finally hit on the magic formula for making money from YouTube's millions of users.

Advertising and Content Control

The industry rhetoric in 2009 is that monetization is essential to the survival of websites like YouTube, despite the fact that most of these social-media websites emerged without the imperative to make a profit. Trade articles with headlines like "We Better Start Monetizing Social Media Before It's Too Late" pointed to an established way of thinking about media and assumed that every media outlet demands advertising, no matter the format or technology; indeed, bloggers and other technology news outlets excitedly speculated about which social media will be the "innovator that leads the way in monetizing social media."[18] Just prior to the Google buyout, YouTube expanded its video offerings by trying to partner with major media corporations to provide content to the website—no doubt an attempt to increase YouTube's value before it settled on a final selling price with Google. Warner Music Group, the world's fourth largest music company, which holds the copyright to over one million songs, arranged to provide its library of music videos, behind-the-scenes footage, interviews and other content. Other media-content providers have been hesitant to sign with YouTube because of the site's perceived lax attitude towards copyright. Warner Music Group addressed this concern by allowing YouTube users to incorporate its music and video footage into their own video compilations, so long as

Warner and YouTube could split revenue drawn from advertising that accompanied any of these user-generated videos. This arrangement fell apart in December 2008, when Warner rescinded its agreement with YouTube, citing the failure to come to licensing terms that "appropriately and fairly compensate recording artists, songwriters, labels and publishers for the value they provide."[19] This suggests that Warner Music Group was dissatisfied with its revenue stream drawing from YouTube.

The video-sharing site has been slow in convincing other major media companies to relinquish control over their content, even after the Google acquisition. As an added deterrent, Viacom filed a one-billion-dollar copyright-infringement lawsuit against Google in March 2007, citing YouTube's unauthorized transmission of 150,000 clips of Viacom media content.[20] A great deal of YouTube's popularity stemmed from users posting their favorite clips from *The Daily Show*, MTV programs and other television shows. But if more people watch these clips online than on cable television, Viacom (and other media conglomerates) risk losing valuable advertising dollars. Signing over content to run on YouTube would, in effect, draw audiences away from content (and corollary advertising) on traditional media outlets. Without any guarantee of significant profit, many major media companies have thus begun to explore their own video-website ventures that could be more controlled in terms of copyright and advertising revenue. Hulu, a joint venture of News Corp. and NBC Universal, is the best example, a site featuring TV and feature films in their entirety. However, by the end of 2008, YouTube had made various deals with MGM, Lionsgate, CBS, The Sundance Channel, HBO and Showtime.[21]

YouTube has been forced to turn to smaller partners, establishing the basic structure of its content business model of providing branded channels or sites within the overall YouTube website that featured a specific company's content. The National Basketball Association, Hollywood Records, Wind-up Records and several independent video producers were among those companies sharing content on YouTube through non-exclusive licenses, although, as in the case of the NBA, some would continue to withhold their most valuable content, featuring it on their own websites instead.[22] Revenue generated through advertising would be split fifty-fifty between YouTube and its partner companies. Advertisers would pay 20 dollars for every 1,000 views of a video, which, for videos that attract tens of millions of views, is more lucrative for content partners.[23] In addition to running banner advertisements adjacent to videos, Google ran advertising before, during and after videos posted on YouTube. Much of this advertising was presented on branded channels, but competitor video-sharing websites like Metacafe and Revver challenged Google in May 2007 to consider bringing the average user into its business model as well. Some of the users with the most-viewed videos on YouTube were invited in early 2007 to join in revenue-sharing deals, whereby YouTube would also split ad revenue fifty-fifty. YouTube executives claimed that users like Lonelygirl15 and HappySlip posted content that "is of equal value to the professional content that is contributed by some of our partners."[24] However, YouTube only invited 20 to 30 users to join its partnership program; meanwhile, it continued to pursue more desirable professional content, signing 150 international media partners by June 2007 and rapidly adding more partners as it spread across the globe. For instance, YouTube signed two dozen new content partners as part of its expansion into India in 2008.[25]

However, advertising that ran before, during or after videos proved to be a less popular option, driving users away from content that hosted this type of advertising. YouTube introduced image-overlay advertising instead, in which a semi-transparent banner would run at the bottom of the video screen for ten seconds; users would be able to click on the ads to receive more information, differentiating it from traditional advertising and providing added value to advertisers. YouTube continued to provide an ad-revenue split with content partners, but still privileged major media companies over individual users (content from 3,000 media partners featured advertising as opposed to roughly 70 independent partners), preferring to run advertising on content that was "safe" for advertisers.[26] Meanwhile, major advertisers began to explore alternative ways to secure revenue from YouTube videos. Some companies like Scripps and HBO began selling advertising space on their YouTube branded channels, thereby enabling them to set their own ad prices. But these companies were still required to split ad revenue with YouTube.[27] Others enlisted individual content providers with hugely popular videos to incorporate their products into newly produced videos. Tay Zonday sang his "Chocolate Rain" and drew 13 million views and the attention of Cadbury Schweppes, which was looking to promote its Cherry Chocolate Diet Dr Pepper soda. Signing a deal for what was, according to Zonday, a "hefty fee," Zonday and Cadbury Schweppes reworked the song into "Cherry Chocolate Rain," and the company's viral marketing approach secured over 2.5 million views in January 2008.[28] In another deal, Warner Home Video's movie *Return to House on Haunted Hill* was featured in the first episode of the popular online serial *Abigail's X-Rated Teen Diary*, an episode that had been watched over 170,000 times.

Product placement carries an added benefit for online advertisers. Viral videos are frequently uploaded to other video-sharing sites and blogs, and while advertisers do not generally obtain revenue from the expanded circulation of these videos, they do allow for the brand name to work for the company beyond paid advertising; this "ensures an ad is married to the video."[29] A video like "Cherry Chocolate Rain" might be posted on any number of websites and blogs and has the potential to secure more exposure for the soda than an image-overlay advertisement might get if run on YouTube alone. In the fall of 2007, YouTube introduced content-identification technology, in part to assuage conglomerates' concerns about copyright infringement. A media company supplies YouTube with what are essentially digital fingerprints of its content and YouTube tracks where that content is being posted (within the YouTube website) and in what form. The media company can then "claim" its content and run advertising with it, splitting ad revenue with YouTube. The user who posted the video receives nothing other than a message from YouTube informing them that "a YouTube partner made a copyright claim on one of your videos" and that "viewers may see advertising on this video."[30] It is estimated that 90 percent of copyright claims made in this manner are converted into advertising opportunities.

Some media companies have jumped aboard the trend of using content-identification technology to push the concept of corporation-sanctioned user-generated content. Users are encouraged to use music or video footage in the creation of videos, without penalty, in order to capitalize on YouTube's viral marketing potential. Various companies use contests to inspire users to create content that falls in line with promotional goals. For instance, Lionsgate Films has promoted numerous films by running contests that ask users to "mash up" video and audio clips to produce new versions of movie trailers. The winning mashup of footage for *Saw V*, for example, would receive a trip to Los Angeles and tickets to "a Lionsgate Horror Film Premiere."[31] These amateur movie trailers become free advertising for Lionsgate and (limited) exposure for the creator of the trailer. So, towards the end of 2008, YouTube was offering a variety of advertising on the site: standard banner ads, homepage video ads, video ads and InVideo ads. An ad on the YouTube homepage cost 175,000 dollars per day, plus a commitment to spend 50,000 dollars more in ads on Google or YouTube.[32] Clearly, the site has become yet another media outlet supported by advertising, despite the enthusiasm and predictions that the Internet would provide a new and uncommercialized "public" space.

Broadcast Yourself (As Long as It's Our Content)

On the surface, YouTube is structured so that anyone's video uploads are not prioritized over others, as indicated by the invitation to "Broadcast Yourself™." However, various techniques adopted by the site—to enhance advertising—privilege some videos over others.

Online audiences tend to be fragmented, thus advertisers have been forced to rethink traditional ways of reaching their target groups. Because media companies and their advertisers want to draw attention to their content, YouTube categorizes its videos, among other designations, into Promoted Videos and Spotlight Videos. Content partners can pay to upload content as a Promoted Video that will then appear on YouTube's homepage with the intent of driving traffic to those videos and accompanying advertisements. YouTube editors choose Spotlight Videos, which follow themes to highlight some of the best videos produced by both YouTube users and corporate content partners. These videos then might secure a status of Most Viewed, Most Popular, Most Discussed, Top Favorites or others, which are categories that function to further drive traffic to these videos. These categories function as promotional devices more than any gauge of what might truly be popular; despite the fact that the Most Viewed videos in fact receive the most views, van Dijck notes, the term "Most Viewed" is relative when video viewings can easily be manipulated by those who can afford to pay for the privilege.[33]

There also is concern that, despite affirmations to the contrary, Google's search engine may privilege Google companies and partners. One advertising executive notes: "Without getting on YouTube, you don't always get picked up by Google search," which thereby might prevent some media content providers from reaching Internet audiences generally, not just those visiting YouTube.[34] But with major media companies still eschewing YouTube as a platform for content distribution, perhaps a space can be opened for smaller, independent companies to reach audiences in ways that traditional media tend to obstruct. Despite the continually increasing popularity of YouTube and the shift of advertising dollars from traditional media outlets to online outlets, content providers are still concerned about copyright issues. YouTube's model of fifty-fifty revenue sharing is backfiring because some of the major media conglomerates are simply starting their own video websites—as is the case with Hulu. The latter site's content providers are paid 70 percent of the revenue generated by advertising on the site, which does not post user-generated content, and they are able to control their content and copyright much more closely.[35]

Clearly, one of the most worrisome aspects of YouTube's monetization strategies is the commodification of labor. This issue arises most acutely when we consider how advertisers and media companies exploit users for profit. While some users might be compensated somewhat more adequately for their work (such as Zonday's "hefty fee" from Cadbury Schweppes), other users are simply guaranteed fifteen (or fewer) minutes of fame. This is, for many, sufficient compensation in an age of easy Internet celebrity. And YouTube is not shy about helping advertisers exploit users to generate revenue. In building brand recognition and value for its advertiser clients, media agency MediaVest works with YouTube to structure collections of user-generated content that align with an advertiser's target audience. "The example I throw out there," notes one MediaVest executive, "is we know kids across the country are submitting their skateboarding videos, so if you have a brand trying to reach a young consumer, we could collect all the best of that footage, have it reside in one area and have the brand wrap around."[36] The overall message is that user-generated content is not as desirable or valuable as professional media content from major companies, unless it can somehow be manipulated to make a profit for media companies and for Google, but certainly not for the individual user.

Conclusion

This article has presented a political economic analysis of YouTube, including its ownership and control issues, and the ongoing efforts to capitalize on the site. Despite the various challenges, it is apparent that Google plans to continue its efforts to monetize YouTube and is willing to try just about anything to ensure that it secures a return on its investment. The company continues to tout YouTube's user-focused reputation, yet has embraced various strategies to privilege corporate partners or established media companies.

YouTube's marketing director has explained that "we're really focused on democratizing the entertainment experience, so whether it's a user-generated content from aspiring filmmakers or from one of the networks, the reality is it's users who are in control. Our users decide what rises up."[37] In promotional material, the site is regularly promoted as oriented to users. "At the end of the day, it's all about the community and we will continue to do what we can to make the user experience a prosperous one."[38] While users may prosper from the YouTube experience, those who are likely to actually prosper in the future—if YouTube's strategies succeed—are the site's owners and their corporate partners.

Endnotes

1 See, for instance, Morley Winograd & Michael D. Hais, *Millennial Makeover: MySpace, YouTube and the Future of American Politics* (New York: Rutgers University Press, 2008).

2 Constance Loizos, "VCs see more than just laughs in goofy Internet videos," *Private Equity Week,* 31 October 2005.

3 See, for example, Don Tapscott and Anthony D. Williams, *Wikinomics: How Mass Collaboration Changes Everything, Expanded Edition* (New York: Portfolio, 2008).

4 Graham Murdock and Peter Golding, "For a political economy of mass communication," in *The Socialist Register 1973*, eds. R. Miliband et al. (London: Merlin Press, 1974), pp. 205–234.

5 Vincent Mosco, *The Political Economy of Communication: Rethinking and Renewal* (London: Sage Publications, 1996); Robert McChesney, *The Political Economy of the Media* (New York: Monthly Review Press, 2008); Janet Wasko, "The Political Economy of Communications," in *The Sage Handbook of Media Studies*, eds. John D. H. Downing et al. (London: Sage Publications, 2004), pp. 309–329.

6 John Cloud, "The Gurus of YouTube," *Time,* 16 December 2006.

7 Google press release, "Google To Acquire YouTube for $1.65 Billion in Stock," 9 October 2006 – http://investor.google.com/releases/20061009.html [last checked 15 February 2009].

8 For more on Google, see Randall Stross, *Planet Google: One Company's Audacious Plan to Organize Everything We Know* (New York: Free Press, 2008).

9 Google, "Form 10-K Annual Report. Dec. 31, 2007" – http://investor.google.com/pdf/2007_Google_AnnualReport.pdf [last checked 15 February 2009].

10 Ibid.

11 Quentin Hardy & Evan Hessel, "GooTube," *Forbes,* 16 June 2008.

12 Ibid.

13 Nicholas Garnham, *Capitalism and Communication: Global Culture and the Economics of Information* (London: Sage Publications, 1990).

14 Richard Siklos, "News Corporation to Acquire Owner of MySpace.com," *The New York Times,* 18 July 2005.

15 Saul Hansell, "Yahoo Woos a Social Networking Site," *The New York Times* 22 September 2006.

16 Kylie Jarrett, "Beyond Broadcast Yourself: The Future of YouTube," *Media International Australia* no. 126, 2008, pp. 132–145.

17 Richard Koman, "Google CEO: We don't know how to monetize YouTube," Newsfactor.com, 12 June 2008 – www.newsfactor.com/story.xhtml?story_id=60275 [last checked 15 February 2009].

18 Ian Schafer, "We Better Start Monetizing Social Media before It's Too Late," *Advertising Age,* 5 May 2008; Ben Parr, "Who will monetize social media?" *Mashable,* 28 March 2009 – http://mashable.com/2009/03/28/monetize-social-media/ [last checked 29 March 2009].

19 Dawn C. Chmielewski, "The Nation; Warner-YouTube Negotiations Stall; Professional and Fan Videos Using the Music Company's Content begin to Disappear from the Website," *Los Angeles Times,* 21 December 2008.

20 Clive Thompson, "YouTube versus Boob Tube," *New York Magazine,* 2 April 2007.

21 Diane Garrett, "MGM, YouTube Pact for Pics: Select Films to Be Available Online," *Variety,* 9 November 2008.

22 Miguel Helft, "Google Courts Small YouTube Deals, and Very Soon, a Larger One," *The New York Times,* 2 March 2007.

23 Ciar Byrne, "YouTube bows to reality with plan to interrupt clips with adverts," *The Independent,* 23 August 2007.

24 Helft 2007.

25 "International manager of YouTube speaks about YouTube's India plans," *TechShout,* 10 May 2008 www.techshout.com/internet/2008/10/international-manager-of-youtube-speaks-about-youtubes-india-plans/ [last checked 29 March 2009]

26 Abbey Klaassen, "YouTube Ads Bypass User-generated Video," *Advertising Age,* 27 August 2007.

27 Daisy Whitney, "Scripps Share Clips with YouTube; Cable Networks Will Sell Ads against Videos," *Television Week,* 19 May 2008.

28 Daisy Whitney, "Web Talent Tests Ads; Video Creators Seek Bigger Share of Revenue," *Television Week,* 21 January 2008.

29 Ibid.

30 Brian Stelter, "Now Playing on YouTube: Clips with Ads on the Side," *The New York Times,* 16 August 2008.

31 See www.youtube.com/LionsgateLIVE [last checked 15 February 2009].

32 Quentin & Hessel 2008.

33 José van Dijck, "Users like you? Theorizing agency in user-generated content," *Media Culture Society* no. 1, 2009, pp. 41–58.

34 Mike Shields, "Let's (Not) Make a Deal," *Adweek.com,* 11 February 2008.

35 Greg Sandoval, "Could peace be near for YouTube and Hollywood?" *CNET News,* 23 July 2008 – http://news.cnet.com/8301-1023_3-9996905-93.html [last checked 15 February 2009].

36 The MediaVest executive is quoted from Daisy Whitney, "Ads on YouTube: A Portent for Web," *Television Week,* 7 April 2008.

37 *Washington Post,* "Five Months after Its Debut, YouTube Is a Star," May 2006.

38 "YouTube Fact Sheet," 2008 – www.youtube.com/t/fact_sheet [last checked 15 February 2009].

Paul McDonald

Digital Discords in the Online Media Economy: Advertising versus Content versus Copyright

October 2006 was a busy time for YouTube. On October 9, the search engine Google announced it would be buying the video-sharing site. The same day, YouTube also signed licensing deals with two major recorded music companies, the Universal Music Group (UMG) and Sony BMG Music Entertainment, together with the US television network CBS. With these deals UMG, Sony BMG and CBS authorized use of their copyrighted works as content on YouTube. Nearly two weeks later, on October 21, YouTube received notice from the Japanese Society for Rights of Authors, Composers and Publishers ordering the site to remove 29,549 videos that infringed the copyrights of its members.[1]

This cluster of activity summarizes the dilemmas confronting YouTube and its place in the online economy. The site runs on advertising revenues and so needs attractive content to draw the traffic that will persuade advertisers to spend. For this reason YouTube must court major players in the copyright industries as key suppliers of content. Yet users uploading music videos, film clips or television programs owned by those major companies has led to YouTube confronting repeated charges of copyright infringement. This article looks at how YouTube's place in the online economy is defined across tensions between competing demands for advertising revenues, licensed content and copyright compliance. While YouTube can reach an international audience, these digital dilemmas have become most pronounced in engagements between YouTube and advertisers or the copyright industries in the United States.

For this reason, what follows focuses on developments in that territory, although the issues raised apply more broadly to how YouTube is able to address an international community of users.

AdSpace

Established in February 2005, YouTube was still very young when Google acquired the site. Over the year prior to the acquisition, YouTube had only small revenues, yet Google was looking towards the future and opportunities that YouTube offered for new advertising revenues. The exponential growth of YouTube's audience was already suggesting the site held the promise to become prime advertising real estate. Display ads were a regular feature on Google and the company saw in YouTube the potential to expand into online video advertising. As one commentator remarked, the acquisition was "a marriage of two celebrity companies."[2] Acquiring YouTube was part of a program of ad diversification which Google had been pursing: for example, in January 2006 Google bought dMarc Broadcasting, a specialist in radio advertising. On the dMarc and YouTube deals, Google reported to "have broadened the distribution options for our advertisers."[3]

"In the real estate business, it's about location, location, location," notes Sasa Zorovic, analyst at the investment bank Oppenheimer & Co.: "On the Internet, it's about traffic, traffic, traffic. If you have traffic, you will be able to monetize it one way or another."[4] YouTube has plenty of traffic; in early 2009, the site was boasting 200 million unique users each month. With more than 22 separate domain names directed at different international territories YouTube addresses an international audience. Figures from the San Francisco firm Alexa, which tracks Internet traffic through its own toolbar, suggest that although YouTube is capable of reaching a globally dispersed audience, in keeping with other media markets YouTube visitors are largely concentrated in the world's most economically developed nations, with nearly a quarter based in the US. Alexa's system of rankings suggests that in most countries where YouTube draws an audience, it ranks amongst the top two to six of the most visited sites on the Internet.[5]

	Share of total (%)
US	23.7
Japan	7.5
Germany	5.0
UK	3.9
Mexico	3.9
India	3.8
Italy	3.8
Brazil	3.7
France	3.2
Spain	2.7
Canada	2.4
Netherlands	1.4
Poland	1.4
Australia	1.3
Russia	1.3
Saudi Arabia	1.2
China	1.1
Indonesia	1.1
Argentina	1.0
South Korea	0.9

YouTube's International Audience, January 2009
(Source: Alexa, 2009)

According to Hitwise, a New York company specializing in measuring online audiences, in May 2008 YouTube was the top-ranked online video site, attracting over 75 percent of visits by US Internet users to sites in that category.

	Market Share (%)	
	May '08	May '07
YouTube	75.43	59.95
MySpace	9.01	16.06
Google Video	3.73	7.80
Yahoo! Video	1.92	2.77
Veoh	1.13	0.86

Top Five Online Video Sites Visited by US Internet Users, 2008
(Source: Hitwise, 2008)

Based on their research of more than 60 online video sites and a sample of ten million Internet users, Hitwise found that although visits to online video sites had dropped to a little more than one percent of all Internet visits, a significant decline of nine percent compared to the same period the previous year, the amount of time spent on such sites had risen six percent. More than 80 percent of YouTube's traffic came from returning users, i.e. those who had visited the site in the previous thirty days. As Hitwise's director of research, Heather Dougherty, commented, "the majority of searches driving traffic to the website are for the YouTube brand highlighting their prominence and strong brand awareness in the video arena."[6] In August 2008, Hitwise estimated search engines were responsible for directing around 30 percent of all traffic to video sites. Following the acquisition by Google, the amount of traffic from Google to YouTube was estimated to have increased by more than 70 percent over the year.[7] Other data from comScore Video Metrix estimated that during the month of July 2008, Americans viewed 11.4 billion online videos. Over five billion viewings were made through Google sites (i.e. Google Video and YouTube), with YouTube accounting for 98 percent of the Google total.

	Videos (thousands)	Share of Online Video Market (%)
Google Sites (inc. YouTube)	5,044,053	44.1
Fox Interactive Media	445,682	3.9
Microsoft Sites	282,748	2.5
Yahoo! Sites	269,452	2.4
Viacom Digital	246,413	2.2
Disney Online	186,700	1.6
Turner Network	171,065	1.5
Hulu	119,357	1.0
AOL LLC	95,106	0.8
CBS Corporation	69,316	0.6

Top Online Video Properties in the US by Videos Viewed in July 2008 (Source: comScore, 2008)

YouTube "monetizes" this high volume of traffic through advertising. Banner ads appear as static display ads with a click-through function taking the visitor to a destination site hosted by the client advertiser. Rich-media ads have the same click-through functionality but use animation or audio enhancements. Both banner and rich-media ads are commonly found on search sites, but the nature of YouTube has enabled it to carry various forms of video ads. These appear on the homepage or search result pages and use YouTube's Flash media player to present short promotional videos, which are activated by a user-initiated click-to-player button. YouTube makes it a condition of such ads that a companion banner ad be included across the top of the player window or "watch page" as a click-through route to the advertiser's external site. From August 2007, "InVideo" ads were added to the advertising options. The semi-transparent overlays pop-up along the bottom of the watch page; if clicked on they then open up a full advertising pitch for products or services relating to the video which was accessed.

These forms of advertising all depend on clients with deep pockets, but YouTube's cultural significance came from presenting an alternative to big media by providing an outlet for democratizing the mass dissemination of user-generated content. The slogan "Broadcast Yourself" perfectly encapsulates the user-driven ethos that YouTube has self-consciously promoted, and the same spirit has carried over to YouTube's advertising initiatives. With so much content available, individual videos get drowned, and so although user-generated content may be posted and available, will anyone see it? Introduced in November 2008 and currently only available to users in the US, "sponsored videos" were launched as a means for users to promote the videos they posted. Users create their own promotional text to explain their content and self-select targeted keywords that, if searched, direct visitors to their videos. No charge is made for posting a sponsored video; users only pay if visitors click on their video. There is no set fee and users can set their own cost-per-click fee and maximum daily or monthly budget. Matthew Liu, a product manager for YouTube, summarizes the thinking behind this initiative by stating that "YouTube democratized the broadcast experience and now we're democratizing the promotion and advertising experience as well."[8]

Despite all the excitement at the time of the acquisition, so far YouTube has failed to turn into the advertising cash cow Google hoped for. No specific figures have been released, but reports forecast that in 2008, worldwide ad revenues would total only 200 million dollars, far short of Google's expectations, and by the end of the year only three or four percent of all videos on YouTube were estimated to be carrying advertising.[9] There seems to be three reasons for this: firstly, inefficiencies in YouTube's advertising sales systems made the buying of advertising unnecessarily complex. Secondly, although the YouTube concept makes it a popular destination for online traffic, that concept does not necessarily work as a location for advertising. User-generated content may bring in the traffic but frequently does not present the kind of content that advertisers want to be associated with. As one commentator noted, "to date, no one has quite figured out how to make money off of cats playing the piano."[10] To control this situation, YouTube has operated a policy of only selling advertising to accompany content supplied through its program of contracted partners. As Suzie Reider, YouTube's director of ad sales, claimed, the "critical thing to understand is that we only run ads on the content or the videos where we have a direct relationship with a content partner."[11] Ideally this arrangement works by companionability: advertised products or services are linked to relevant videos. In some cases however the marriage between advertiser and partner has not always worked out sweetly. For example, furniture retailer IKEA may not have found the companion video it was hoping for when in spring 2008 the company was advertised alongside the popular video "I'm out of toilet paper." This comedy short featuring a woman sitting on the toilet was supplied by vlogolution, a New York producer and YouTube partner. Finally, the stigma of copyright infringement continues to taint the image of YouTube as a legitimate site for advertising. Through the content partner program, advertisers are unlikely to find their promotions running alongside infringing material, but the issue is whether advertisers want to be associated with a site drawing allegations of infringing activity. Traffic is therefore essential to monetizing the Web but, in YouTube's case, high-volume traffic has not equaled big ad attraction.

BrandSpace

YouTube needs advertising, but to attract advertisers the site also requires inoffensive, non-infringing content. In this respect the content partner program functions as a strategy for legitimizing YouTube as a safe site for advertising. Reciprocally, for producers and owners of content, YouTube can provide a vital means to expand their audience. As the reputation or exposure of videos can rapidly spread through word of mouth, e-mail, blogging, text messages and Instant Messaging, YouTube has become a launch pad for viral video. And it is from this dynamic that YouTube holds the potential to become a platform for viral marketing. If viral video is a statement about the infectious *distribution* potential of video sharing, viral marketing is a statement about the *promotional* opportunities of such exchanges. Catching the viral effects of YouTube allows content owners to extend their audience and promotional reach through electronic word of mouth or "word of mouse."

For producers of media content both large and small, the viral effect of YouTube means their works can enter the global mediasphere and quickly gain exposure. As innovative programming or new networks rapidly build their reputations and audiences, they become YouTube-generated brands, while established names in the media business can also carry their existing brand image into a new media arena.

56 "McNuggets Rap": viral marketing video

To consolidate the presence of these sources, the content partner program creates branded channels, mini-sites within the main YouTube site that are built around the content of partners. For example, visiting the channel for Walt Disney Motion Pictures UK opens up to a page entirely dedicated to and exclusively occupied by Disney content. Video content is limited to trailers of currently available films, which play through the usual watch window. At the top of the page a banner ad acts as a click-through link to the external main website for Disney in the UK. Interactive functions are included to cultivate and nurture their viral potential: visitors can subscribe to a channel for free, and options are provided to share a channel or playlist. Branded channels cover a diverse range of content. On the US site for YouTube, video material uploaded by partners includes content that falls under the categories of how-to (e.g. Expert Village, Make Magazine), music (e.g. Bohemia Visual Music,

EMI), entertainment (e.g. Buck Hollywood, WayoutTV), news and politics (e.g. Forbes, Reuters), style and beauty (e.g. Ford Models, Nylon TV) and sports (e.g. International Fight League, Professional Bull Riders). All content is vetted for adherence to YouTube's terms of use and for copyright compliance.

As a strategy aimed at maximizing the site's legitimacy as a space for effective advertising, YouTube has been particularly keen to recruit content partners from the big media brands. In summer 2006, US television network NBC announced a content licensing deal with YouTube to create an official NBC Channel.[12] This partnership was aimed at forming a conduit for promoting the network's programming through professionally produced previews and user-generated content. Exclusive clips from the comedy series *The Office* were made available, and during July 2006 YouTube users were invited to enter a competition by creating short entertaining videos relating to the series. Shortly afterwards, a deal was concluded with the Warner Music Group (WMG) for distribution of the company's library of music videos, along with artist interviews and behind-the-scenes footage—and a few weeks later the UMG and Sony BMG deals were finalized.

It is worth singling out the importance of this set of deals. With these agreements, YouTube obtained access to content from three of the four major global music companies. Music and music videos represent an ideal form of content for YouTube, which has built its library around a range of short-form video presentations of two to three minutes duration, serving what Jordan Hoffner, YouTube's director of content partnerships, has described as a "clip culture."[13] Not only are professionally produced music videos posted on the site, but also pre-recorded tracks are used in many instances to accompany user-generated material. The agreements with the music majors therefore took the form of two-part licensing deals: record companies became content partners, posting their own videos, but also authorized use of their music libraries by users when creating their own content. Although the terms varied between the deals, each worked on a common revenue-sharing model: income from any advertising accompanying music videos or user-generated content using licensed music would be divided between YouTube and the partner. Completing this trend, in May 2007 YouTube landed a deal with the fourth of the music majors, EMI, and further major content partnerships were agreed with the BBC, PBS, Disney-ABC and MGM.

Date of Deal	Copyright Owner
27 June 2006	NBC
18 Sept. 2006	Warner Music Group
9 Oct. 2006	Sony BMG Music Entertainment
9 Oct. 2006	Universal Music Group
9 Oct. 2006	CBS
2 March 2007	BBC
31 May 2007	EMI Music
16 Jan. 2008	PBS
25 Feb. 2008	HBO
28 Feb. 2008	Disney-ABC Television Group
16 July 2008	Lionsgate Entertainment
10 Nov. 2008	MGM Worldwide Digital Media

Selected Content Deals Between YouTube and Major Copyright Owners, 2006–08

These deals appeared beneficial to the big content partners. In the first month after striking its deal, CBS claimed their channel had not only attracted 29 million views but was also responsible for increasing ratings on the broadcast network. Two years after the original deal, CBS even expanded its licensing. Moving beyond the short-form clips available from other content partners, from October 2008 CBS began to provide full-length episodes from archival television series such as *MacGyver* and the original *Beverly Hills 90210*, along with more recent successes such as *Dexter* and *Californication*. Episodes were accompanied by streamed video advertising from CBS. YouTube had already carried long-form content with a pre-broadcast premiere for the second season of *The Tudors*, co-produced by CBS subsidiary Showtime, but the arrangement with the network saw YouTube make a further step towards becoming a platform for television on demand. UMG also hailed the benefits of partnering with YouTube. Interviewed in December 2008, Rio Caraeff, executive vice president of eLabs, UMG's e-business division, claimed the record company was seeing "tens of millions of dollars" from its deal with YouTube.[14] UMG's music channel had become not only the largest but also the most-viewed channel on YouTube. By the end of 2008, the UMG channel had attracted nearly three billion views, while Sony BMG was in second place with 485 million views. Overall, music-related channels accounted for seven of the top ten channels on the site. Although unconfirmed by the company itself, one industry source speculated UMG was likely to book nearly 100 million dollars in advertising revenue for the year. For UMG, Caraeff affirmed YouTube had become "a revenue stream, a commercial business. It's growing tremendously. It's up almost 80 percent for us year-over-year in the US in terms of our revenue from this category."[15] However, this opinion was not shared by other music majors. Towards the end of 2008 WMG's licensing deal with YouTube was up for re-negotiation, and when terms could not be agreed upon, Warner began to remove its content from the site. WMG was frustrated by the poor return on its revenue-sharing arrangement with YouTube, particularly as competing sites like AOL and MySpace offered better terms.

Protected Space

The reciprocity of these partnerships is clear: content owners can share in the distribution and promotional opportunities presented by YouTube's traffic while the site itself is guaranteed a supply of safe, high-quality, licensed content intended to lure advertisers. Although major media companies now supply licensed content, YouTube's video library has become an arena for disputes over copyright infringement. Shortly after the acquisition of YouTube was completed, Google was said to have reserved over 200 million dollars in stock to cover any potential costs arising from legal actions over alleged infringement, and YouTube's relationship to the copyright industries has been characterized by both concord and conflict.

Speaking in mid-September 2006 at a conference, Doug Morris, chairman and CEO of UMG, leveled criticisms at "companies trying to build businesses using our content without our getting a fair share." Morris mourned how the decision of music companies back in the 1980s to offer music videos to Music Television for free had been a mistake which had seen MTV go on to "buil[d] a multibillion-dollar company on our software." Morris went on to argue that more recently, use of the Internet for video sharing had meant sites such as MySpace and YouTube "owe us tens of millions of dollars." Threats of legal action seemed to hang in the air when Morris warned, "How we deal with these companies will be revealed shortly."[16] It didn't take long for the business world to find out exactly how UMG would tackle YouTube, for instead of entering into litigation, within three weeks UMG had signed its licensing deal to become a content partner. On that occasion, Morris pronounced, "Universal is committed to finding innovative ways to distribute our artists' works and today's agreement with YouTube furthers that strategy by helping transform this new user-generated content culture into a mutually beneficial business opportunity." UMG now regarded YouTube as more friend than foe. Morris further commented, "We pride ourselves in empowering new business models that create new revenue streams for content creators. YouTube is providing a new and exciting opportunity for music lovers around the world to interact with our content, while at the same time recognizing the intrinsic value of the content that is so important to the user experience."[17] Yet UMG's commitment to the potential of video sharing only went so far. Only days after becoming a YouTube partner, Universal filed lawsuits against the video-sharing sites Bolt.com and Grouper.com, the latter owned by Sony. Universal claimed the sites allowed users to illegally exchange copyrighted works, particularly music videos. In a statement coinciding with the filings, UMG said "user-generated sites like Grouper and Bolt that derive so much of their value from the traffic that our videos, recordings and songs generate cannot reasonably expect to build their businesses on the backs of our content and the hard work of songwriters without permission and without in any way compensating the content creators."[18] Backed by the rich coffers of Sony, Grouper survived until it was transformed into Crackle.com, a service stocked with authorized content from the parent company's movie and television program library. Bolt however was less fortunate and, unable to contest the legal action, in March 2007 the company capitulated, reaching an out-of-court settlement with UMG resulting in payment of an undisclosed multi-million dollar sum for damages before its sale to GoFish Corp.

UMG's hate-love-hate relationship with video-sharing encapsulates one of the enduring truths of the media and entertainment business: when it comes to the arrival of new technologies, the copyright industries frequently adopt a contradictory response to innovation. It is this contradiction that has made the battle over copyright one of the main drivers behind the online media economy. "The tension between technological innovation and copyright protection," David Griffith and Bryan McKinney observe, "has often baffled policy makers, particularly in the Internet age. Most agree that innovation should not be stifled; however, most also agree that intellectual property should be respected. When these two vitally important concepts collide, the result can generally be described in one word: litigation."[19] With the copyright industries, the value of technological innovation is always harnessed to commercial opportunism. The copyright industries can only make money if their works reach the public, and technological innovation often brings new opportunities for the public circulation of creative content. At the same time, the very fact media technologies make that content publicly available creates anxiety, as copyrighted works become vulnerable to infringement. It is this contradiction—opportunity in the midst of anxiety—that has characterized the response of the copyright industries to YouTube.

Since the growth of peer-to-peer file sharing in the 1990s, infamously exemplified by Napster, online methods of distribution have raised industry concerns over incidents of copyright infringement. This has been particularly evident in the US, where the copyright industries are recognized as a key contributor to the national economy. In 2005, the core copyright industries in the US were estimated to have contributed some 820 billion dollars in added value, roughly a 6.5 percent share of the nation's total GDP. That same year, piracy was estimated to have resulted in nearly 16 billion in trade losses for the US software, publishing, music, and film and television industries. The value of intellectual property has therefore made the US the prime battleground in the protection of copyright. To modernize intellectual property law in the US, in October 1998 the Digital Millennium Copyright Act (DMCA) was passed, amending Title 17 of the United States Code that outlines copyright law. This legislation served several purposes, but Section 512 limited the liability of online service providers who carry out a range of basic functions necessary for operation of the Internet. These were identified as: transmitting, routing or providing connections for material to pass through a system or network;[20] system caching;[21] the storage of material,[22] and providing information location tools (e.g. directories or indexes) which may link visitors to infringing material.[23] These limitations create a "safe harbor" for online service providers. They are not held liable for infringing material available over their services if the provider has no knowledge the material was available, does not gain any direct financial benefit from the infringing activity, and acts expeditiously to remove or disable access to such material once notification is presented. A designated agent must be appointed by the online service provider to receive and then act on these notices.

These limitations place responsibility on the shoulders of copyright owners to present online service providers with written notification identifying the single work or list of works alleged to be infringed. Under the current legislation the "takedown notice" has therefore become the main instrument for copyright owners to exercise their powers. Consequently, evidence of alleged infringement must be produced and content owners have taken measures to patrol YouTube and other sites for infringing content. In order to file takedown notices, copyright owners have contracted external companies to scan YouTube for infringing material and issue notices on their behalf. Based in Los Gatos, California, BayTSP employs a team of video analysts or "hashers" to log offending clips and e-mail the details to YouTube. In 2007, BayTSP's clients included more than five television or film studios, each prepared to pay as much as 500,000 dollars per month for the company's services. To comply with the legislation but also to win the confidence of valuable content providers, YouTube has taken its own measures to prevent the availability of infringing material. By only carrying advertising with licensed content, YouTube aims to comply with the legislation by not directly profiting from any infringing activity. Furthermore, YouTube has introduced an automated video-recognition system intended to search the site to identify infringing material before takedown notices are received. This service was offered as protection to YouTube's content partners: the software scanned the site for suspected infringing material and checked this against a database of authorized content from partners. From both sides of the fence, YouTube has therefore become a policed space.

It is hard to deny that users post on YouTube content which they have not created or which they do not hold the rights to. Even the most casual browse of the site soon reveals music videos posted in their entirety, or clips from movies and television programs created and distributed by the copyright industries but posted by the user community. By responding to takedown notices, YouTube is acknowledging infringing activity takes place, yet is also complying with the necessary obligations under the safe-harbor provision. Legal action by the media conglomerate Viacom however has directly challenged YouTube's protection from liability. Viacom became a client of BayTSP in fall 2006 and based on information provided, it issued notice to YouTube in October that year informing the site of infringing activity relating to material from its subsidiary network, Comedy Central. Takedown notices were issued and YouTube began removing clips from popular programming, including *The Colbert Report* and *South Park*. Both parties entered into negotiations aimed at finding equitable terms for Viacom content to appear on the site, but when no agreement could be reached, in early February 2007 Viacom issued e-mails demanding the removal of more than 100,000 clips.[24] In a statement, Viacom said, "YouTube and Google retain all of the revenue from this practice, without extending fair compensation to the people who have expended all of the effort and cost to create it."[25] YouTube responded by saying, "It's unfortunate that Viacom will no longer be able to benefit from YouTube's passionate audience, which has helped to promote many of [its] shows." However Mike Fricklas, general counsel for Viacom, countered, "When everyone gets a free pass to the movies, it's no longer promotional."[26] After YouTube removed the clips identified, Viacom claimed that traffic to websites for its own television brands increased significantly: during February 2007, Viacom claimed traffic to MTV.com and ComedyCentral.com went up by almost 50 percent, while Nick.com grew by almost 30 percent, partly as a result of visitors downloading shows. Nielsen/NetRatings however reported weekly traffic to MTV.com remained steady after the removal, while Nick.com showed some signs of an increase. YouTube meanwhile saw its weekly number of unique visitors rise from 17 million to nearly 19 million in the weeks after the Viacom clips were taken down.[27]

57 Sued by UMG: a toddler listening to Prince

Still unconvinced by measures to clean up the site, by mid-March 2007 Viacom filed a lawsuit at the US District Court for the Southern District of New York against YouTube and Google. Citing Section 106 of the US Copyright Act of 1976, Viacom complained that YouTube was directly infringing the company's exclusive rights to reproduce, publicly display and publicly perform its library of copyrighted works. Although users upload videos, clips are converted to YouTube's own software format, creating a copy that may infringe the right to reproduce. Viacom also argued that because searches pull up small thumbnail images of videos, some of which may come from infringing material, YouTube was violating the right to publicly display works. By streaming content in response to requests from users, the plaintiff also complained that YouTube was engaging in unauthorized public performance of copyrighted works. Alongside these charges of direct infringement, Viacom complained that by allowing users to upload unauthorized copies, YouTube was not only liable for inducement but also contributory infringement. Finally, Viacom alleged that as YouTube had the means to supervise and control infringing content but failed to do so for copyright owners who were not licensed partners, the company was vicariously liable.[28]

Viacom claimed YouTube was fully aware of infringing activity but turned a blind eye in order to build traffic drawn by copyrighted content. Furthermore, although content that is not provided by licensed partners is unlikely to be positioned with paid advertising, Viacom claimed that YouTube still profited from using infringing content to build traffic and thereby enhance the site's market share. Viacom claimed YouTube not only had "actual knowledge and clear notice of this massive infringement," but also that "the presence of infringing copyrighted material [...] is fully intended by Defendants as a critical part of their business plan to drive traffic and increase YouTube's network, market share and enterprise value." Consequently, Viacom argued, "YouTube has built an infringement-driven business." In support of these allegations, the plaintiff complained YouTube had the means to identify and remove pornographic videos and so could filter content, yet did not extend the same controls to infringing content.[29] YouTube denied the allegations made by Viacom—and the case has yet to be decided.[30]

What lies behind these arguments is a purely economic evaluation of YouTube's communicative status: will the unauthorized posting of video material undermine the rights of the copyright industries to gain financial compensation from the reproduction, presentation and performance of the works they own? Such arguments inevitably overlook the cultural benefits of YouTube. Whatever the source, the free availability of video content provides millions of users worldwide access to and knowledge of a shared repository of cultural works. Although YouTube does filter certain kinds of content, particularly pornographic and violent material, it still succeeds in providing a relatively open space for the exchange of a wide diversity of material. As that material extends back across time, YouTube acts as a vital cultural archive. Furthermore, by inviting users to comment on the material posted, whether the postings are illuminating or not, the site is still providing a forum for debate and promoting a reflective engagement with a shared culture. These benefits raise issues over whether the dissemination of copyrighted works over YouTube can be defended under the doctrine of "fair use" as specified in the US Copyright Act. Section 107 of the Act places limitations on exclusive rights where copyrighted works are used for the purposes of criticism, comment, news reporting, teaching, scholarship or research. Assessment of fair use is based on considerations relating to the character and purpose of the use, the nature of the copyrighted work, the amount of the work used, and what impact the use may have on the market for or value of the work.[31] Applying this framework, Kurt Hunt argues that user activity on YouTube relating to copyrighted works can be defended as fair use. For this reason, Hunt argues that YouTube is "something other than a community of pirates" and warns that "strict enforcement of copyright threatens to shut down emerging works and important contributions to our culture."[32] Issues of copyright therefore not only position YouTube in the dilemma of technological innovation vs. copyright protection but also between the contradictions of the economic and cultural benefits of online communication as these shape networked societies.

It awaits to be seen what the outcome of the Viacom lawsuit will be. Meanwhile, YouTube continues to comply with current legislation by responding to takedown notices. Yet if Viacom is successful in its action, will the cleansing of YouTube fundamentally undermine its attraction? "The question remains whether YouTube will lose its renegade image if stripped of all its pirated clips. Could cleaning up the site make it boring?"[33] Probably not, as unauthorized clips do not represent the only form of interesting content on YouTube. If the copyright industries continue to look towards YouTube and similar sites as not only a promotional channel but also a revenue stream, it is in their interest to ensure that such spaces do not become boring. They will therefore need to consider how best to balance the interests of both profit and protection. In an era of level or declining movie attendances, falling music sales and the fragmentation of television audiences or loss of viewers to other media options, big old media may need to find how to best fit with rather than fight the communication opportunities provided by a mass audience of viewers migrating to online systems and networks.

Conclusion

YouTube's future rests on how well it can manage and balance the tensions between advertising, content and copyright. Advertising income is necessary for YouTube to survive. User-generated content represents the ethos of self broadcasting but does not present a magnet for advertising. Licensing legitimate content will satisfy copyright owners and may offer the draw to build the advertising value of the site. But what of infringing material? Currently, heavyweight litigation is casting this issue in purely economic terms, while the cultural benefits of YouTube are overlooked. Any defense of YouTube's role as a conduit for cultural criticism and commentary is unlikely to win much of a hearing among the copyright industries. Yet if the economic argument alone is heard, there is a danger that large volumes of audiovisual material will be removed from the arena of public access and debate. These tensions make YouTube equally an arena for paid promotions and publicity, an authorized media revenue channel and a forum for cultural knowledge and debate. While tensions exist between these different perspectives on the site's role and purpose, it is these very contradictions that make YouTube what it is.

Endnotes

1 Verne Kopytoff, "YouTube Reportedly Deletes 30,000 Clips," *San Francisco Chronicle,* 21 October 2006, p. C1.

2 Ibid.

3 Google, *Annual Report 2007* (Mountain View, CA: Google, 2008), p. 8.

4 Sasa Zorovic is quoted from Ellen Lee, "Google Moves YouTube Ahead," *San Francisco Chronicle,* 7 March 2007, p. D1.

5 See Alexa, Youtube.com Daily Traffic Rank Trend, March 2009 – www.alexa.com/data/details/traffic_details/youtube.com [last checked 15 February 2009].

6 See Hitwise press release, "U.S. Visits to YouTube Increased 26 Percent Year-over-Year," 25 June 2008 – www.hitwise.com/press-center/hitwiseHS2004/google-increase-twentysix.php [last checked 15 February 2009].

7 Daisy Whitney, "YouTube Is a Search Engine," *Television Week,* 29 September 2008, p. 16.

8 See "YouTube Sponsored Videos Overview" – http://uk.youtube.com/watch?v=hTffb8OF8_U&feature=channel [last checked 15 February 2009].

9 Kevin J. Delaney, "Google Push to Sell Ads on YouTube Hits Snags," *Wall Street Journal,* 9 July 2008, p. A1; Alan Patrick, "How Does YouTube Make Money?" *Telco 2.0,* 16 December 2008 – www.telco2.net/blog/2008/12/how_does_youtube_make_money.html [last checked 15 February 2009].

10 Thomas Claburn, "Google's YouTube: Finally, a Way to Make Money," *Information Week,* 8 October 2008 – www.informationweek.com/news/internet/ebusiness/showArticle.jhtml?articleID=210800502 [last checked 15 February 2009].

11 See "Welcome to YouTube's Brand Channel" – http://uk.youtube.com/watch?v=894lyciqYmc [last checked 15 February 2009].

12 YouTube press release, "NBC and YouTube Announce Strategic Partnership," 27 June 2006 – http://uk.youtube.com/press_room_entry?entry=c0g5-NsDdJQ [last checked 15 February 2009].

13 Jordan Hoffner is quoted from Jefferson Graham, "YouTube Expands Its Horizons, and Its Video Time Limits," *USA Today,* 22 October 2008, p. 2B.

14 Greg Sandoval, "Universal Music Seeing 'Ten of Millions' from YouTube," *CNET News,* 18 December 2008 – http://news.cnet.com/8301-1023_3-10126439-93.html [last checked 15 February 2009].

15 Ibid.

16 Doug Morris is quoted from Tim Arrango, "YouTube – Universal Music Warns Web Video Swapper," *The New York Post,* 14 September 2006.

17 See YouTube press release, "Universal Music Group and YouTube Forge Strategic Partnership," 9 October 2006 – http://uk.youtube.com/press_room_entry?entry=JrYdNx45e [last checked 15 February 2009].

18 Carl DiOrio, "UMG Sues Sites Over Music Vids," *The Hollywood Reporter,* 18 October 2006.

19 David Griffith & Bryan McKinney, "Can Heather Gillette Save YouTube? Internet Service Providers and Copyright Liability," *Issues in Information* Systems no. 2, 2007, p. 225.

20 *Copyright Law of the United States and Related Laws Contained in Title 17 of the United States Code*, Washington, DC: Library of Congress/Copyright Office, 2007, pp. 153.

21 Ibid., pp. 153–55.

22 Ibid., pp. 155–57.

23 Ibid., p.157.

24 Ellen Lee, "YouTube Removing Viacom TV Shows," *San Francisco Chronicle,* 3 February 2007, p. C1.

25 Viacom statement, 2 February 2007 – www.viacom.com/news/News_Docs/Viacom%20Takedown%20Statement.pdf [last checked 15 February 2009].

26 Ellen Lee, "YouTube Removing Viacom TV Shows," *San Francisco Chronicle,* 3 February 2007, p. C1.

27 Daisy Whitney, "YouTube Undeterred by Takedown Orders," *Television Week,* 12 March 2007.

28 *Viacom vs. YouTube*, "Complaint for Declaratory and Injunctive Relief and Damages," 13 March 2007, 07 CV 02103, Southern District of New York, pp. 10, 11, 21–24, 25.

29 Ibid., pp. 12, 13, 14.

30 *Viacom vs. YouTube*, "Defendant's Answer and Demand for Jury Trial," 30 April 2007, 07 CV 02103, Southern District of New York.

31 *Copyright Law of the United States and Related Laws Contained in Title 17 of the United States Code*, Washington, DC: Library of Congress/Copyright Office, 2007, p.19.

32 Kurt Hunt, "Copyright and YouTube: Pirate's Playground or Fair Use Forum?" *Michigan Telecommunications and Technology Law Review* no. 1, 2007, pp. 221 and 209.

33 Verne Kopytoff, "Copyright Questions Dog YouTube," *San Francisco Chronicle,* 27 October 2006, p. D1.

Mark Andrejevic

Exploiting YouTube: Contradictions of User-Generated Labor

YouTube's vexed status as a commercial entity helps make it a useful object to think through the reluctance of entrenched media industries to concede particular forms of control to users. After going through a period of relative non-profitability, the site's parent company, Google, is intent on "monetizing" YouTube's popularity—finding a way to profit from it. But these efforts are being thwarted, at least in part, by the fact that major media conglomerates are at best wary, and at worst aggressively litigious, toward an enterprise that has built a large audience in part through what they take to be unauthorized use of their content, including everything from music videos to movie clips and even user-generated mashups of copyrighted content. This article argues that the battle over intellectual property rights is a proxy for a broader struggle for control over the interactive media environment and the value generated by YouTube's users. It also argues that YouTube is a contested site in part because it threatens to live up to the hype of the interactive era: the promise that a broader segment of the audience might, thanks to its productive activity, gain a measure of control over the content it consumes.

At stake in efforts by established content providers to adapt to, challenge or compete with the YouTube model is both the attempt to restrict some forms of interactivity and to exploit others. The question of exploitation is—for reasons that will be developed in the following pages—central to the concerns of this article. The goal is to develop a theory of exploitation for the interactive era by drawing on the example of YouTube, and then relate this theory to the promise of greater control over one part of the media environment. In so doing the article attends to the call issued by, among others, Franco Berardi for the development of a "critique of the political economy of connective intelligence."[1] Developing such a theory will entail distinguishing between those forms of interactivity sought out by commercial media enterprises and those that threaten industry control of the media landscape.

Putting YouTube to Work

The accepted industry wisdom about YouTube is that its purchase might be one of the few missteps made by Google on its way to becoming the dominant player in the interactive information economy. Google purchased the popular website despite the fact that, at the time, it was making no profit. But in the hopes that, as one news account put it, the site would eventually "deliver revenue and profits in line with the potential of its huge visitor numbers,"[2] Google's purchase followed the speculative logic of the dotcom boom (whose echoes live on in the phenomenal success of the popular search engine): first acquire a popular site and then figure out how to make money from it. There are obvious affinities between a site like YouTube, which serves largely as a directory for content created by others, and Google, which built its fortune by developing a popular and efficient algorithm for sorting and locating content created by others. However, serving as a directory for a new medium is a very different proposition from drawing upon the content of a more established industry with entrenched interests which is only too willing to come after any entity that seeks to profit from its intellectual property.

In fairness, YouTube represents a hybrid, or perhaps a convergent medium, one in which familiar music videos and copyrighted movie clips rub shoulders with original user-generated content and with content that combines original material with copyrighted material, such as user-created videos that include popular songs as part of their background or soundtrack, or mashups of copyrighted audio and video material. The very fact that much of the popular content on the site is professionally created, copyrighted material is what drew the attention of media conglomerates like Viacom, which, as of this writing, has a one 1 billion dollar lawsuit pending against YouTube for copyright infringement. At the end of 2008, the Warner Music Group pulled its music videos from YouTube following the breakdown of negotiations between the two companies, reportedly over revenue sharing for cover songs uploaded to the site.[3] Both the Viacom suit and the Warner decision represent significant challenges to YouTube and can be read as an aggressive rejection by media companies of the site's revenue-sharing overtures. Viacom claimed that the material it demanded to be pulled from the site, including clips from its MTV, Comedy Central, BET and Nickelodeon channels, amounted to 1.2 billion streams. The popular Comedy Central programs *The Daily Show* and *The Colbert Report* were once YouTube favorites, "consistently on YouTube's top-watched lists."[4] Faced with the assertion that much of the content on YouTube is non-infringing, commentators and media conglomerates are quick to point out that six of the all-time ten most popular videos on YouTube are reportedly music videos.[5]

The lawsuits come in the face of sweeping overtures by YouTube to commercial copyright holders. Early on, YouTube irritated rights holders by placing the onus on them to identify infringing videos and request their removal. When this turned out to be inadequate, it sought to share advertising revenues with copyright holders, arguing that the website served as both an important promotional tool for media outlets and as an alternative source of online revenue. Indeed, the company has struck partnerships with major US networks and other content providers to post authorized clips on the site. Viacom's lawsuit may be an attempt to gain leverage in its negotiations with YouTube, but there is more at stake than copyright protection, as evidenced by the media conglomerate's demand (as part of its lawsuit) that YouTube turn over detailed records of user behavior.[6] As one privacy consultant noted, databases like YouTube's are another of the company's main assets: "These very large databases of transactional information become honey pots for law enforcement or for litigants."[7]

One of the concerns of content producers is that reliance on an intermediate like YouTube relinquishes control over interactively generated user data that is becoming an important resource for targeted advertising campaigns. As one press account put it, the motive behind Viacom's demand "might be that the usage data may come in handy in carving out their own online video market share and in boosting their own advertising revenues."[8]

What appears on its face as one more skirmish in the widening battle for control over intellectual property in the digital era is actually a manifold struggle with at least three elements: the attempt to assert copyright claims and thereby to command the revenues that may eventually flow from them, the attempt to gain control over user-generated data, and the attempt to shape the media environment in accordance with advertising imperatives. The following sections consider each aspect of this struggle in turn, arguing that at its core the contested status of YouTube is tied up with issues of exploitation in an interactive media environment in which every action of users can be captured and put to work by marketers and advertisers. In this regard the struggle over YouTube represents one of the places in which the oft-invoked but under-examined promise of interactive participation is running up against entrenched forms of economic control. If in some contexts interactivity is mobilized as a ruse for channeling and exploiting consumer labor as Bonsu and Darmody have argued,[9] it is possible that there are sites where this control is contested or under threat. Entrenched forms of economic and social power do not reproduce themselves seamlessly, and the struggle over YouTube is, arguably, a site in which some of the seams are splitting. All of which is not to argue that YouTube represents a site of hope or a firm foundation for contesting the replication of the forms of governance, control and exploitation that characterize the emerging interactive economy. It is simply to assert that the contested status of YouTube has something to tell us about the nature of the struggle.

Enclosing Intellectual Property

When Google acquired YouTube, the video site was making scant profit on revenues of around 11 million dollars, and though the company has since upped its revenues to a reported 200 million dollars, this is a tiny fraction of Google's total earnings and reportedly far short of expectations.[10] As one press account put it, "revenue at YouTube has disappointed Google investors since the company bought the start-up in 2006."[11] Google's purchase of the site for more than a billion and a half dollars surely drew the attention of media conglomerates interested in exploring the economic potential of online distribution and thwarting Google's attempts to capture the market—or finding a way to dig into its deep pockets. YouTube has been sued not just by Viacom, but also by France's largest commercial broadcaster, Spain's Telecinco, the Netherlands' Endemol and Italy's Mediaset for half a billion euros.[12]

The broad reach of these lawsuits is evidenced not just by the tremendous value of the damages being sought, but also by the logic of the Mediaset claim, which is based on the assertion that since clips totaling 325 programming hours have been uploaded to YouTube, the companies have lost more than 300,000 days of viewership and the attendant advertising revenues. The suits conveniently overlook the fact that YouTube's 200 million dollars in revenues fall far short of the almost two billion dollars in damages being sought by Viacom and Mediaset (who are clearly looking at the parent company's revenues). The notion that YouTube clips translate directly into a one-to-one measure of lost viewership is absurd on its face, and discounts the promotional power of the site as a means not just for introducing viewers to programming, but for allowing them to share favorite moments with one another and to view highlights from missed shows. The disproportionate size of the lawsuits and the reluctance of Viacom and other broadcasters to come to terms with YouTube on a revenue-sharing agreement suggests an overarching hostility to the YouTube model, and perhaps to its affiliation with an increasingly powerful economic juggernaut of the interactive era.

In the face of YouTube's popularity, media conglomerates are developing their own, alternative sites for online content distribution, the most prominent of which is Hulu, the result of a partnership between News Corp. and NBC. Not all producers are holding out against YouTube, however. The Hollywood studios MGM and Lionsgate have also entered into agreements to make selected clips and full-length movies available via YouTube, complete with advertising. These decisions come in the wake of the site's overtures to the content producers once alienated by its success. As part of its recent reforms, YouTube has developed a system for identifying potentially infringing videos and giving rights holders the option of taking down the videos, tracking them, or receiving revenues for advertising placed in them.

Google is simultaneously developing other strategies for increasing the site's revenues, including adapting its phenomenally successful keyword advertising system (by allowing advertisers to bid on search terms that, when entered on YouTube, would call up links to sponsored videos) and linking videos to relevant retailers (such as Amazon.com or iTunes for music videos of a particular album or track). In short, the company is doing all it can to transform the site from a community of video sharing into a revenue machine. Not surprisingly, it portrays this galloping commodification as a means of enhancing the experience of YouTube's community of users. In their YouTube video announcing the acquisition by Google, YouTube founders Chad Hurley and Steve Chen repeatedly referred to the ways in which the takeover would announce the site's "community" aspect. As Chen put it, "the most compelling part of this is being able to really concentrate on features and functionality for the community."[13] However, the marriage between commerce and community comes across as somewhat forced, as evidenced, for example, by the company's claim that "the addition of retail links will enhance the viewing experience and allow people to engage more deeply with the content they want to consume."[14] In the business world, the shift from a grainy do-it-yourself site to a more tightly organized, controlled and "monetized" site for the distribution of professionally produced content has been greeted as a welcome shift in emphasis: an attempt to enter the fold of the commercial media industry and have its past sins forgotten. As one analyst put it, "YouTube is essentially saying to media companies, 'We are sorry for our past copyright stance; we weren't thinking big enough. Let's see how we can make some money together.' "[15]

58 "A Message from Chad and Steve": "Thanks to all of you!"

Managing the Mediascape

Even if YouTube tries to portray its commercial initiatives as somehow enhancing the site's self-described emphasis on user-generated community, it is far from clear this vision is shared by the industries with which it seeks to partner. One of the obstacles to "monetizing" YouTube—a company that describes itself as "the world's most popular online video community"—is the disparaging attitude advertisers have adopted toward the community's activity. It turns out that YouTube's copyright policy is not the sole sticking point in negotiations with established advertisers and content providers. As one analyst put it, marketers have reservations about the very nature of YouTube's media environment. "Major advertisers don't want to advertise against the user-generated content that dominates on YouTube."[16] Even if user-generated content were to succeed in attracting the proverbial eyeballs prized by advertisers, it would do so in an environment over which they have limited control—and are hence reluctant to participate in. As one commentator disparagingly put it, "advertisers are nervous about placing their brand messages near sophomoric or even vulgar video content, and such user-generated clips make up most of what is available online."[17] Other commentators express concerns over the production quality of user-generated content, claiming that "advertisers have been reluctant to commit major marketing dollars to running brand campaigns alongside grainy, unprofessional home videos."[18] A Google product manager suggested that advertisers are put off by their preconceptions regarding YouTube viewership: "There's the assumption that on YouTube, it's 17-year-old boys watching dogs' skateboarding videos."[19]

Paradoxically, the community-oriented character of the site, promoted in its public-relations material, is seen by some analysts as reducing its commercial viability. Advertisers' apparent concern about sites like YouTube is that commercial messages may not be "well-received," since these "communities were launched without advertising [and users] don't view it as a transactional space. It is a social space."[20] Suggestively, one study has revealed a discrepancy between receptivity to ads on and offline. About half as many people—31 percent as compared to 60 percent—have a "positive impression from mainstream ads. Conversely 21 percent said digital media ads left a negative impression compared with 13 percent of mainstream media ads leaving a negative impression." The study explained the difference by observing, as one account summarized it, "digital media is used by consumers to find specific things and they do not want to be encumbered by advertising."[21]

It is worth parsing the advertiser response to the ostensibly raucous, uncontrolled media landscape of YouTube in a bit more detail. The notion that advertisers are put off by "sophomoric or even vulgar" content can be easily dismissed as empirically false, as is the assertion that advertisers are not interested in gaining the attention of 17-year-old skateboarders. The fact that viewers may be less positively disposed toward ads on social networking or other community-oriented sites may be true, but that doesn't mean advertisers aren't interested in capturing the one-third or so of the audience who respond positively to the ads—especially in the online billing context where advertisers often pay only when an ad is clicked on. The real concern on the part of marketers and commercial content providers seems to be control over the media environment—not whether amateur content can generate revenue, but whether accepting such revenue means ceding the type of control over content to which advertisers have grown accustomed. From a marketing perspective, the potential drawback of a site like YouTube is that "marketers can't control other content on social networks. An ad or other posting by an automaker may share a page with risqué images or user criticism of the company."[22]

Such concerns express the complementary relationship between advertising and content that developed during the era of commercial broadcasting. The concern about YouTube is that the content itself may overflow the bounds of what has come to constitute mainstream commercial culture. Perhaps the most interesting aspect of this claim is what it reveals about the media environment to which advertisers have grown accustomed: it is one in which they can control the environment in which their ad is placed, or, more generally, one in which they can assume unquestioningly that the content they encounter will be conducive to commercial messages. If it is the case that, as one account puts it, "advertisers have found that user-created videos of pet pratfalls and oddball skits are largely incompatible with commercials for cars and other products."[23] We can infer that, by contrast, the content favored by advertisers on mainstream television is already carefully crafted to be compatible with the consumerist messages that support it. Without necessarily celebrating the diversity of content on YouTube, such claims highlight the narrow boundaries of commercially supported media content—boundaries that assure advertisers the shows in which they advertise will neither undermine nor challenge the injunction to consume.

The reluctance of media outlets to embrace YouTube unreservedly, even in the face of the measures it has taken to placate media conglomerates and attract advertisers, becomes clearer against the background of their desire for control over not just advertising, but also content. All of which helps explain why "they also say they are more comfortable with the cleaner, better organized Hulu, which does not have amateur-created videos and which sprang from their own ranks."[24] The concern about YouTube is that user-generated content might not fit the dictates of advertising culture as closely as the forms of mainstream commercial media content that have evolved alongside advertising to meet its needs and reinforce its message. Perhaps unsurprisingly, interactivity in the form of audience participation is welcomed by commercial culture only up to the point that it reinforces, in predictable and familiar ways, the imperatives of marketers. The blueprint laid out for YouTube by advertisers and content providers is clear: focus on becoming a distribution network for commercially produced professional content—this is the content that will generate the revenues necessary to pay for the site and make it profitable. The battle, in other words, is not just one over intellectual property, but over the goal of ensuring that industry-produced content continues to dominate the media landscape.

Exploitation in an Interactive Era

We can start to trace the outlines of the boundary between those forms of interactivity welcomed by commercial content providers and those they reject. Turning control of the media landscape over to audiences threatens a long-established media model in which advertising imperatives have been incorporated into the DNA of commercially produced media content. The hostility of commercial media producers and advertisers toward YouTube is, at least in part, a tacit admission of the complementarity of content and marketing that has become a crucial if publicly downplayed component of commercial broadcasting. By contrast, another type of "user-generated content"—the data generated by users as they view clips online and share them with one another—is emerging as an increasingly important component of target marketing in the digital era. It is a form of data that has been around as long as commercial broadcasting, but digital technology makes it easier and cheaper to collect than ever before.

One of the advantages of an interactive platform for the delivery of commercial content is that it enables the capture of increasingly detailed information about patterns of user behavior and response. Interactive marketers envision not just the ability to target users based on an expanding range of information about their backgrounds, tastes and behavior, but also the ability to conduct ongoing controlled experiments to determine which forms of consumer inducement are most effective in managing and channeling audience behavior. "There's [...] going to be a lot more analytics beneath Internet advertising. In the future, advertisers will come up with 10,100, or 1,000 creative messages for their products and services, then run, test and optimize them in real time," as one analyst put it.[25] In the brave new world of cybernetic marketing, advertisers will also be able to correlate responses with increasingly detailed and complex patterns of taste and behavior in order to optimize campaigns—that is to say, in order to increase the likelihood of influencing consumer behavior and inducing demand.

The media industries understand that such forms of target marketing are being developed by Google, which already has access to large amounts of information about user behavior—and not just from its browser, but also from its growing range of interactive applications. Content providers anticipating the impact of interactivity on the movie and television industry are cognizant of the fact that, as one observer put it, "ultimately, Google's ability to know how a given person uses the web, and match that activity to targeted advertising, has driven this secretive company's business model."[26] Hence, they understand the power they are turning over to Google when they enlist it as a third-party distributor of their content. If they can develop their own interactive delivery platform—via a site like Hulu, or through their own branded websites—they can capture and use this information themselves, without having to rely upon and share revenues with Google. However, it is unlikely they will have as detailed a picture of user behavior or as developed a system for processing it—which may help explain the ambivalence toward Google's model, and the willingness of some broadcasters to experiment with YouTube partnerships.

Either way, the industry's response suggests the importance of distinguishing between two forms of user-generated content—and of considering how the celebration of one underwrites the collection of the other. The interactive marketing model promotes participation as a form of consumer "control" but balks at the prospect of relinquishing control over the relationship between content and advertising. The ideal model pursued by marketers in the interactive era is one in which the same commercially generated, professionally produced content is served up in an environment that allows for the capture of increasingly detailed information about viewer behavior and response.

Free Labor and Exploitation

We might think of the second form of "user-generated" content; the production of information about user behavior, as a form that recent critical literature on the interactive economy calls immaterial labor. Thus, for example, Adam Arvidsson—drawing on the work of Maurizio Lazzarato—describes the work that consumers do in "producing a context of consumption" as a form of compensatory labor to make up for what "a post-modern, highly mediatized lifeworld no longer provides."[27] This formulation is based on Lazzarato's somewhat less abstract claim that one aspect of immaterial labor is comprised of the "activity that produces the 'cultural content' of the commodity, immaterial labor involves a series of activities that are not normally recognized as 'work'—in other words, the kinds of activities involved in defining and fixing cultural and artistic standards, fashions, tastes, consumer norms and, more strategically, public opinion."[28] Such labor corresponds to what Michael Hardt (also following Lazzarato) describes as the "affective" form of immaterial labor. "Finally, a third type of immaterial labor involves the production and manipulation of affects and requires (virtual or actual) human contact and proximity," as Hardt has put it.[29]

In each case, the form of labor in question tends to be "free": both unpaid (outside established labor markets) and freely given, endowed with a sense of autonomy. The logic described by such critiques is one in which the free and spontaneous production of community, sociality, as well as shared contexts and understandings remains in principle both autonomous of capital and captured by it. As Hardt puts it, "in the production and reproduction of affects, in those networks of culture and communication, collective subjectivities are produced and sociality is produced—even if those subjectivities and that sociality are directly exploitable by capital."[30] The notion of exploitation is both a problematic and a crucial one for the development of a critical approach to the productivity of interactive, community-oriented sites like YouTube. In general terms, the notion of immaterial labor as outlined in the work of critical scholars denotes both autonomy from capital and an exploitable surplus. Thus, for example, Arvidsson's analysis, which follows arguments suggested by the critique of immaterial or affective labor, is that the production of community, sociality and subjectivity is, in one important way, analogous to that of the more "material" labor associated with industrial forms of production: it generates the surplus value captured by the mechanism of capitalist exchange. As Arvidsson states in his critical analysis of postmodern branding, the "context of consumption"—the shared meanings associated with particular brands—created by consumers is subject to a process of exploitation.[31] Rather than attempting to directly impose associations that help drive sales, he argues, marketers rely on the productivity of consumers which they then channel for the purposes of increasing sales or profits. He describes this process in a suggestively passive formulation: "It is ensured that the ethical surplus [the set of shared meanings and attachments to a product generated by consumers] evolves in particular directions." That is to say, consumers generate the raw (and "immaterial") material that is used by capital as a means of enhancing brand value and profits: capital appropriates forms of productive free creative activity that nevertheless remain external to it.[32]

However, if the terms "free," "affective" or "immaterial" labor can be used to refer to the user-generated construction of sociality, community and even entertainment on social networking or community-oriented sites like YouTube, the question remains as to whether the capture or appropriation of this activity can be described, critically, as a form of exploitation in the Marxist-inflected sense invoked by the writers cited above. In the most general terms, a Marxist conception of exploitation implies "forced, surplus and unpaid labor, the product of which is not under the producers' control."[33] In capitalism, Marx argues, exploitation takes place in the wage relation, whereby the surplus value generated by labor (not captured by its exchange value) is appropriated by capital.

In other economic systems, surplus product can be captured by more direct forms of force (feudalism, for example); in capitalism the forcible separation of the worker from the means of production is conserved in workers' forced choice to relinquish control over their labor power. However, the potential located in so-called immaterial or affective labor by Arvidsson, Hardt and others lies in the very fact that it is freely or autonomously given. It is by definition not forced. Nor is it clear that this labor is appropriated under the threat of force, which renders the claim of exploitation in need of further explanation.

Perhaps the shortcoming of such approaches is that they fail to make the distinction that emerges from a consideration of the commercial media industry's response to YouTube: that between user-created content and user-generated data. It is the latter category that might be construed as being extracted under terms derived from ownership of the means of ("immaterial") production. It is the fact that the infrastructure for the creation of user-generated content is (at least in the case of YouTube) a privately-owned, commercial one that structures the terms of access to productive resources in ways that compel submission to detailed forms of monitoring and information gathering. Critiquing the economic logic of a site like YouTube means considering how power relations structure the "free" choice, whereby user-generated data is exchanged for access. As suggested by the repeated invocation of an underdeveloped notion of exploitation in accounts of immaterial labor considered in this article, the challenge facing those who would contest the equation of interactive marketing with consumer empowerment lies in developing an adequate and workable conception of the exploitation of the "freely given" consumer labor characteristic of the interactive economy.

Drawing on the example of YouTube, this article invokes Nancy Holmstrom's crucial insight regarding the relationship between exploitation and alienation to suggest how the extraction of user-generated data might be construed as a form of exploitation. For Marx, Holmstrom argues, the appropriation of control over workers' labor represents more than a means of capturing surplus value: it simultaneously reproduces the alienation of workers from the product of their labor. "Being congealed labor, the product is in some sense part of the producers. When it is taken away from them, they are thereby diminished, impoverished, denuded."[34] This is a formulation that draws not from the description of exploitation in *Das Kapital*, but from the 1844 manuscripts, where Marx forcefully elaborates the wages of estranged labor: "The worker places his life in the object; but now it no longer belongs to him, but to the object. [...] What the product of his labor is, he is not. Therefore, the greater this product, the less is he himself."[35] It is worth recalling this overtly humanist formulation if only to note how neatly and systematically it anticipates the promises of the interactive economy: to return to producers control over their creative activity (to overcome the estrangement of the product), to build community (to overcome the estrangement of others), and to facilitate our own self-understanding (to overcome the estrangement of ourselves). If anyone is directly invoking the language of Marx in the current conjuncture, it is not the critical theorists, but the commercial promoters of the interactive revolution. Consider, for example, the triumphant tone of the 2008 ad campaign for TiVo in Australia, which featured a crowd taking to the street as one of its members shouts, "Now the power is in our hands, no one is going to tell us what to do or when to do it, because we're Australian, and we're taking control. Join the revolution!"[36] The TiVo business model, of course, relies in part on the ability to capture detailed information about user behavior thanks to the interactive capability of its digital video recording technology.

Against the background of the appropriation of control over labor power, the promise of interactive participation takes shape: the precondition for the popularity of Web 2.0 is the invocation of forms of estrangement associated with the exploitation of waged labor. In this regard the form of exchange that characterizes interactive sites like YouTube might be understood as a second-order result of forcible appropriation of labor power: users are offered a modicum of control over the product of their creative activity in exchange for the work they do in building up online community and sociality upon privately controlled network infrastructures. As a condition of their "free" acquiescence to engage in this productive exchange, they both construct popular websites and submit to the forms of monitoring and experimentation that are becoming an integral component of the interactive economy. Their free participation is redoubled as a form of productive labor captured by capital—and the offer to overcome estrangement or alienation produces a second-order form of separation between uses and "cybernetic commodities" they generate about their social lives: their behavior; their tastes, preferences, patterns of consumption and response to advertising.

It is in this regard that the frequent invocations of women's historical role in the production of affective or immaterial labor become germane: women's domestic labor in the era of industrial production is also unwaged, and yet provided under conditions shaped by the forcible separation of the means of production from workers. Michael Hardt invokes "feminist analyses" to describe the ways in which (in the information economy) the forms of affective labor formerly associated with the realms of reproduction and consumption become directly exploitable. "What are new [...] are the extent to which the affective immaterial labor is now directly productive of capital and the extent to which it has become generalized through wide sectors of the economy."[37] That is to say, the mode of exploitation specific to women's "affective" or "immaterial" labor is becoming generalized—at least in the realms of consumption. As Antonella Corsani puts it: "This is the sense in which one could agree to analyze the feminization of labor as a situation that extends, 'the mechanisms of subjection applied above all and historically to women.' "[38] One of the unique aspects of this form of exploitation is that it cannot be broken down neatly according to the Marxian formula, whereby a certain amount of labor time can be designated "necessary" (to cover the wages, hence costs, of the laborer) and surplus labor time. As in the case of the form of exploitation associated in this chapter with sites like YouTube, affective labor is redoubled: time spent building social relations is also simultaneously captured by capital insofar as it contributes to the production of labor power. Rather than thinking of productive time in discrete intervals, the exploitation of women's affective labor envisions this work as redoubled: both autonomous (in the sense of relying on shared social and emotional resources) and subject to exploitation at the same time.

Conclusion

A parallel argument to the thoughts above can be made with respect to YouTube. The offer of control over productive activity is redoubled online as a form of exploitation—except in this case, the captured product is rendered in commodity form: that of the data captured by marketers. Labor exchanges entered into freely are dictated by the structure of ownership of the material "means" of immaterial labor (the network, servers, protocols—provided by YouTube). Palpable evidence of exploitation in this instance takes the form, as Holmstrom's analysis suggests, of alienation: the ability to create, view and share user-created video is accompanied by the extraction of user-generated data. This data is captured in order to be returned to its producers in the form of an external influence: the congealed result of their own activity used to channel their behavior and induce their desires. Such is the goal of the "analytics"-based forms of marketing anticipated by the interactive economy. The objective is data-driven control: the channeling of users' own activity to further a goal arrived at neither through shared participation nor conscious deliberation: that of increasingly accelerated consumption. That the offer of a platform for "non-estranged" production might threaten this goal constitutes the contradiction at the heart of YouTube's marketing plan, and helps explain the ambivalence and even hostility of commercial content providers toward "amateur" content. They want the user-generated data without the user-generated content. If sites like Hulu start to gain large and loyal followings, they may well succeed, and in so doing demonstrate that the more appropriate infrastructure for a site like YouTube may not be commercial, but collectively owned and operated.

Endnotes

1 Franco Berardi, "Schizo-Economy," *SubStance* no. 1, 2007, p. 77.

2 Joe Nocera, "Behind the YouTube Suit," *International Herald Tribune*, 17 March 2007.

3 Eliot van Buskirk, "Labels Think They Can Build a Better Mousetrap," *Wired Blog*, 29 December 2008 – http://blog.wired.com/business/2008/12/major-labels-mu.html [last checked 15 February 2009].

4 Ellen Lee, "YouTube removing Viacom TV shows," *San Francisco Chronicle,* 3 February 2007.

5 Brian Stelter, "Warner Hits YouTube," *Canberra Times* 29 December 2008.

6 Miguel Helft, "Google Told to Turn Over User Data of YouTube," *The New York Times,* 4 July 2008, p. 1.

7 Ibid.

8 *Straits Times*, "Online Privacy Vs. Privacy," 21 July 2008.

9 Samuel Bonsu & Aron Darmody, "Co-Creating Second Life: Market Consumer Cooperation in Contemporary Economy," *Journal of Macro-marketing* no. 28, 2008, pp. 355–368.

10 Abbey Klaassen, "YouTube: You Created the Content, Now Sell the Ads," *Advertising Age,* 9 June 2008.

11 Brad Stone & Brooks Barnes, "MGM to Post Full Films on YouTube, as Site Faces New Competition," *The New York Times,* 10 November 2008.

12 *Video Age International*, "YouTube Faces Italy, Turkey (World)," 1 September 2008.

13 Chad Hurley and Steve Chen, "A Message from Chad and Steve," YouTube video, 9 October 2006 – www.youtube.com/watch?v=QCVxQ_3Ejkg. My thanks to Patrick Vonderau for pointing out this connection.

14 *Associated Press Newswires*, "Agreements With iTunes and Amazon.com Provide New Revenue Stream for Content Creators; Platform Enables YouTube Community to Buy Music and Games," 8 October 2008.

15 Stones & Barnes 2008.

16 *PC Magazine*, "YouTube Ads Will Take Years to Boost Google," 16 October 2008 – www.pcmag.com/article2/0,2817,2332703,00.asp [last checked 15 February 2009].

17 *Adweek*, "EMarketer: Web Video Conundrum," 17 September 2008 – www.adweek.com/aw/content_display/news/digital/e3i68343da3c822c82466f1a10015169b3f [last checked 15 February 2009].

18 *PC Magazine*, "YouTube Adds CBS Shows, Including 'Star Trek,' " 13 October 2008 – www.pcmag.com/article2/0,2817,2332369,00.asp [last checked 15 February 2009].

19 Stephanie Clifford, "YouTube to Sell Advertising on Pages of Search Results," *The New York Times,* 13 November 2008.

20 Mary Connelly, "Marketers Tap Social Web Sites: Seeking Face Time Through Facebook," *Automotive News,* 17 November 2008.

21 Neil Shoebridge, "Mainstream Outshines Upstarts," ThinkTV 26 June 2008 – www.thinktv.com.au/media/Articles/BRW_Mainstream_outshines_upstarts_June_26-August_6_2008.pdf [last checked 15 February 2009]. The report is cited from the above article.

22 Connely 2008.

23 Stones & Barnes 2008.

24 Ibid.

25 Calvin Leung, "Q&A: Tim Armstrong," *Canadian Business* 21 July 2008.

26 *Irish Times*, "Google's Birthday," 13 September 2008.

27 Adam Arvidsson, "Creative Class or Administrative Class? On Advertising and the 'Underground,' " *Ephemera* no. 1, 2007, www.ephemeraweb.org [last checked 15 February 2009].

28 Maurizio Lazzarato, "Immaterial Labour," in *Radical Thought in Italy: A Potential Politics*, eds. Paulo Virno & Michael Hardt (Minneapolis: University of Minnesota Press, 1996), p. 137.

29 Michael Hardt, "Affective Labor," *Boundary* no. 2, 1999, pp. 89–100.

30 Ibid.

31 Adam Arvidsson, "Brands: A Critical Perspective," *Journal of Consumer Culture* no. 5, 2005, pp. 235–258.

32 Ibid.

33 Nancy Holmstrom, "Exploitation," in *Exploitation: Key Concepts in Critical Theory* eds. Kai Nielsen & Robert Ware (Atlantic Highlands, NJ: Humanities Press International, 1997), p. 87.

34 Ibid., p. 85.

35 Karl Marx, *The Economic & Philosophic Manuscripts of 1844* – www.marxists.org/archive/marx/works/1844/manuscripts/preface.htm [last checked 15 February 2009].

36 The full ad can be found, unsurprisingly, on YouTube: www.youtube.com/watch?v=I9qDIEfiNVk.

37 Hardt 1999.

38 Antonella Corsani, "Beyond the Myth of Woman: The Becoming-Transfeminist of (Post-)Marxism," *SubStance* no 1, 2007, pp. 164–167.

Toby Miller

Cybertarians of the World Unite: You Have Nothing to Lose but Your Tubes!

Irresistibly enchanted by a seeming grassroots cornucopia, struck by the digital sublime, many "first-world" cybertarian technophiles attribute magical properties to today's communications and cultural technologies—which are said to obliterate geography, sovereignty and hierarchy in an alchemy of truth and beauty. A deregulated, individuated media world supposedly makes consumers into producers, frees the disabled from confinement, encourages new subjectivities, rewards intellect and competitiveness, links people across cultures, and allows billions of flowers to bloom in a post-political Parthenon. In this Marxist/Godardian wet dream, people fish, film, fuck and finance from morning to midnight. The mass scale of the culture industries is overrun by consumer-led production, and wounds caused by the division of labor from the Industrial Age are bathed in the balm of Internet love. Cybertarianism has become holy writ, a celebrated orthodoxy that thinks "everyone is a publisher" thanks to the Internet and its emblematic incarnation in YouTube.[1] These fantasies are fueled and sometimes created by multinational marketers only too keen to stoke the fires of aesthetic and autotelic desire. *Time* exemplified this sovereignty of consumption in choosing "You" as its 2006 "Person of the Year"—"You control the Information Age. Welcome to your world."[2]

This apparent transformation is actually yet another moment in an oscillation we have experienced routinely over the past century. During that period, each media innovation has offered people more of what they never knew they needed commercially, at the same time as it has promised new possibilities democratically. When we consider *Time* magazine's new finding in 2006, if we dig a little deeper we find that, like YouTube's own rhetoric, it's very old: *Candid Camera* was on US TV intermittently for fifty years, pioneering the notion of surveillance as a source of fun, information and narcissism. Host Allen Funt would hail his audience with "You are the star!"[3] Today's touching cybertarian faith that individuals can control their destinies through the Internet, and folksy "prosumers" can overpower big media with their homegrown videos, is the latest version. While we expect coin-operated, corporate-oriented mainstream scholars to buy into such simplistic rhetorical flourishes as they patrol this gleaming new world in search of "new business opportunities,"[4] we also find people with distinguished links to the scholarly left reiterating shopworn Schumpeterian claims about innovation, technology and entrepreneurialism. They disavow decades of research on corporate domination and labor exploitation, discounting such forms of evidence as the detritus of an outmoded era; the putatively revolutionary opportunities provided by YouTube and its brethren make such logics invalid.[5] And their work is now being taken up in business journals.[6] These assertions remind me of the neoliberal arguments I produced when I was a speechwriter for corporations and governments in the 1980s, which attacked progressives and organized labor for questioning the transformative beneficence of new technology.[7] The shift is from an emphasis on workplace technology to domestic technology—otherwise, the same old lines are being trotted out.

Academic cybertarians maintain that the new media provide a populist apparatus that subverts patriarchy, capitalism and other forms of oppression. All this is supposedly evident to scholars and pundits from their perusal of social media, conventions, Web pages and discussion groups, or by watching their children in front of computers. Virginia Postrel wrote a *Wall Street Journal* op-ed in which she welcomed this Panglossian tendency within cultural and media studies as "deeply threatening to traditional leftist views of commerce [...] lending support to the corporate enemy and even training graduate students who wind up doing market research."[8] At such moments, we can say that what Terry Eagleton sardonically named "The Reader's Liberation Movement" is in the house.[9] It can hardly be a surprise, then, to find Robert McChesney lamenting that contemporary media studies is "regarded by the pooh-bahs in history, political science and sociology as having roughly the same intellectual merit as [...] driver education."[10] Or that the *Village Voice* dubs us "the ultimate capitulation to the MTV mind."[11]

Even Stuart Hall recently avowed that "I really cannot read another cultural studies analysis of Madonna or *The Sopranos*."[12]

Cybertarianism dovetails with three utopias: the free-cable, free-video social movements of the 1960s and '70s; the neoclassical, deregulatory intellectual and corporate movements of the 1970s and '80s; and the post-Protestant, anti-accumulative hacker ethos of the 1990s and today. Porta-pak equipment, localism, a disinterested, non-corporate approach to newness, and unrestrained markets supposedly provide an alternative to the numbing nationwide commercialism of mainstream media. Social-movement visions saw this occurring overnight. Technocratic ones imagined it in the "long run." Each claimed it in the name of diversity, and they even merged in the depoliticized "Californian ideology" of community media, which quickly embraced market forms.[13]

True believers in a technological liberation from corporate domination argue that the concept of the cultural industries is outmoded because post-industrial societies have seen an efflorescence of the creative sector via small businesses. But that's inaccurate as a description of a shift in the center of gravity. The western world recognized in the 1980s that its economic future lay in finance capital and ideology rather than agriculture and manufacturing. Changes in the media and associated knowledge technologies since that time have been likened to a new "industrial revolution," touted as routes to economic redevelopment. Between 1980 and 1998, annual world exchange of electronic culture grew from 95 billion to 388 billion dollars. In 2003, these areas accounted for 2.3 percent of gross domestic product across Europe, to the tune of 654 billion euros—more than real estate or food and drink, and equal to chemicals, plastics and rubber. The Intellectual Property Association estimates that copyright and patents are worth 360 billion dollars a year to the US, putting them ahead of aerospace, automobiles and agriculture in monetary value. Global information technology's yearly revenue is 1.3 trillion dollars, and PriceWaterhouseCooper predicts 10 percent annual growth. The cultural and copyright sector employs 12 percent of the US workforce, up from five percent a century ago.[14] This is the underlying reality behind the newer media—their placement in, and impact on, the core of the world economy.

And what about YouTube itself? The site code is kept secret; its viewers' characteristics are only available to corporations; and claims made about "ordinary people's use" of the service are principally derived from personal and press impressions and marketers.[15] Until large-scale questionnaire and ethnographic studies have been undertaken, we should remain cautious in our cybertarian assertions. The best quasi-independent evidence about YouTube comes from well-heeled corporate and business-school research. It suggests that, far from undermining the mainstream media, YouTube videos are the greatest boon imaginable to mainstream US television. Rather than substituting for TV programs, these excerpts and commentaries promote them, promising new business opportunities.[16] While amateur content forms the majority of content on YouTube, it is barely watched by contrast with the vastly more-popular texts that come from the culture industries: fifteen of its top twenty search terms are for US TV programs.[17] Right now, watching YouTube and online video in general appeals to a minority, and a small one, around the world—in the US, less than a fifth of the population.[18] We also know that assertions about the YouTube utopia breaking down geography are overstated. Newly available crawlers disclose the parochial nature of video viewing—most people watch material from their own backyards.[19] That's no crime, but nor is it a triumph of boundary crossing. And we also know this: 87 percent of US YouTube visitors are white, and just 0.2 percent of visits involve posting videos. A tiny fraction of viewers post videos often. The vast majority of YouTube vloggers are men, and women who produce vlogs are sometimes subject to harassment by viewers. Is this new technology producing new social relations—or a rerun of old-style social relations with which we are all too familiar? In this article, I will focus on three aspects of YouTube: its corporate ties and desires; its role in US electoral politics; and its impact on labor. I find that in order to understand the service, we need a mixture of political economy and media and cultural studies to counter the febrile *converso* rhetoric of business boosters and lapsed leftists.

Corporatube

Since its beginning, YouTube has been implicated in corporate life, from almost destroying the servers of a homonym, utube.com, to breaking copyright law and selling advertising. Meanwhile YouTube hides behind provisions of the Digital Millennium Copyright Act that seek to criminalize users rather than distributors in negotiating with big firms.

Needless to say, when gritty "community creators" complain about their work being purloined, YouTube dismisses them as an elephant might a gnat.[20] A year after Google bought YouTube, the site was valued at 4.9 billion dollars. But there is no real revenue stream yet; Google is still monetarizing the property.[21] When it introduced advertising to begin fifteen seconds after each video started and cover a fifth of each screen, who lined up first to advertise? News Corporation, 20th Century Fox, New Line Cinema and Warner Music.[22] During the 2008 Summer Olympics, YouTube/Google laid claim to beneficent corporate social responsibility in making highlights available on line, but hid the same images and sounds from US viewers. Why? The company's main concern was getting on well with General Electric (the massive arms supplier and polluter that owns NBC-Universal), which held exclusive domestic TV rights to the event.[23] There is a sponsored video space, effectively a spot-bidding system for product placement in which advertisers look for materials they like, where YouTube nests their commercials.[24] But YouTube is unpopular with advertisers because the amateurish texts are so variable in quality and theme, and the professional ones are often illegally reproduced.[25]

YouTube is nothing if not obedient to corporate direction. When Universal complained that a video of a toddler dancing to Prince's "Let's Go Crazy" infringed its rights, the people's community, consumer-led movement that supposedly *is* YouTube quietly complied until it was safe to restore the video following a further, related suit. Similar business norms explain why the service fought bitterly to keep its source code a secret in legal struggles. Meanwhile, law enforcement is thrilled at YouTube's surveillance possibilities, both directly observing "crimes" and urging YouTubers to report them.[26] This is part of a growing paradox for the site's cybertarian credentials. Its neoliberal champions love its accessibility—which they actively undermine. The commitment of these advocates to open markets relies, of course, on drawing and policing property lines, because intellectual property is their ultimate deity. This is, paradoxically, especially true for those who fantasize about non-corporate models of capital. What makes YouTube successful is illegal; let's make it legal!

This contradictory set of impulses has a corollary in the different corporate attitudes that flow from it. By early 2007, Viacom claimed that 160,000 illegal clips from its programming were on YouTube, with one and a half billion viewers. Within the ranks of capital, Viacom plays the tough cop, suing YouTube for infringement,[27] and other cultural corporations are the good cops buying advertising.[28] YouTube is a digital distributor, and as such may appear to undermine this crucial part of conventional media power. But it doesn't do anything of the sort. For example, YouTubers receive letters from lawyers on behalf of copyright holders enjoining them to cease and desist from building websites about their favorite musicians—and also receive letters on behalf of advertising agencies representing those same copyright holders, urging them to continue what is seen as free viral marketing.

Steve Chen, YouTube's co-founder, avows that the site represents an "engagement, not an interruption" for the corporate world.[29] That explains the thousands of contracts the firm has signed with mainstream media, and the introduction of Video Identification, a surveillance device for blocking copyrighted materials by tracking each uploaded frame. It spies on users and discloses their Internet protocols, aliases and tastes to corporations, permitting these companies to block or allow reuse depending on their marketing and surveillance needs of the moment. The software was developed with those great alternatives to mainstream-media dominance Disney and Time Warner. Hundreds of companies have signed up in its first year. Sales of Monty Python DVDs on Amazon.com increased by 1000 percent once they became part of the system.[30] This is a triumph of new media over old? This is not corporate capitalism? This is open technology? This is a cybertarian dream? No, this is YouTube becoming Hollywood's valued ally, from tracking intellectual property to realizing the culture industries' dream: permitting corporations to engage in product placement each time their own copyright is infringed on line, and learning more and more about their audiences.[31] In any event, YouTube may soon crumble. It seems that most of what people watch on it comes from the cultural industries, and they are setting up their own, high-resolution video sites such as Hulu (Fox/NBC/Disney) and iPlayer (the BBC)—not to mention TVLand.com, a service that may become a fringe element despite its corporate desires and plans. Hulu, TV.com and Veoh are re-broadcasters of network drama on line. In just twelve months, Hulu became the sixth-most viewed video site in the US, and legal online viewing of TV shows by adults in the US grew by 141 percent in 2008 (streaming is becoming more popular than downloading, as it is generally free, fast, simple and legal). TV.com viewers grew by nearly 1.3 percent in January 2009 over the previous month. Of US Internet users aged 13 to 54, a fifth now use these services, and many do so to get back in touch with favored series prior to the appearance of new episodes on TV. Advertisers flock to Hulu even as they shun YouTube.[32]

Politatube

"This year's campaign [...] has been dubbed the 'YouTube Election' "; "YouTube is to be congratulated on the groundbreaking contributions it has made to the political discourse—McCain-Palin Campaign"; "[The] War on Terror [...] is the first 'YouTube War.' "[33] These three claims regarding YouTube as a utopia opening up access to politics and unlocking journalistic exclusivity as a gateway to the public sphere are illustrative of the site's political potential. Politicians certainly like it. Howard Dean argued that YouTube "basically turned the US Senate over to the Democrats" in 2006, and Tony Blair called it a "shining example of innovation."[34] Each US Presidential candidate in 2008 had a channel. By mid-September, John McCain's had been watched 14.5 million times and Barack Obama's 61.8 million times. In February 2008, will.i.am's "Yes We Can" was launched. Within six months, nine million people had seen it. But far from transcending the asinine trivia of US electioneering, YouTube was encapsulating it. For instance, the McCain people released an advertisement that likened Obama to Britney Spears and Paris Hilton. His celebrity standing was equated with theirs; his depth and seriousness as well. Within two weeks, it had been viewed two million times. Hilton, however, issued a spirited riposte in which she sardonically greeted "the white-haired dude"; the Obama people produced a counter-text via the "Low Road Express" website; and other media over-reported the controversy, even as they under-reported McCain's business dealings, devotion to US imperialism and corporate capital, and disregard for his first wife. And during the election season, by far the most-watched video was an anti-Obama, militaristic rant by a soldier.[35]

Is this somehow desirable as a means of furthering rational, progressive policy debate? It doesn't look like a new age of politics to me. In the 2006 mid-term US elections, 15 percent of voters got their primary electoral information online, down from the 2004 campaign but twice the 2002 mid-terms, and just 25 percent used the Internet for

59 "Totally ready to lead": Paris Hilton thanks the "white-haired dude"

political purposes. Those who did so generally visited not YouTube, but CNN.com and ABCNews.com, i.e. television news sites. For more than 70 percent of voters, television was their principal news source. It was the favored medium for all genres, but its lead was greatest for election programs. Thus, people who saw candidate materials created for YouTube generally watched them on television.[36] It is true that YouTube garnered major media attention in 2006 for screening racist abuse from Republican Senator George Allen to a Democrat staffer and showing Republican Senator Conrad Burns snoozing in Congress. But both instances were recorded and posted by Democrat staffers. Cheap exposure can lead to cheap exposé. Thanks to YouTube, there is less control over messages and their management by contrast with what is achievable with the press corps. But is the outcome "more natural, direct and honest?"[37] New technology is already generating the hyper-discipline of TV, with semi-public moments subject to scrutiny after the fact, and pernicious re-editing done without even quasi-professional journalistic filters. Meanwhile, YouTube is bowing again and again to reactionary forces in cutting off coverage of torture and video eroticism.[38] As YouTube succeeds, it is brought, sometimes noisily and sometimes quietly, within the usual policing norms of public life.

Workertube

The pride with which gullible "MIT-like/lite" subscribers to digital capitalism and the technological sublime welcome the do-it-yourself elements to YouTube is part of the managerialist, neoliberal discourse that requires consumers to undertake more and more tasks for free or at their own cost (like online gamers signing end-user license agreements, and paying to play, but losing all rights to their creativity). This shoves tasks away from corporate responsibility.[39] In YouTube, we have a company culture that relies on unpaid labor for its textuality, and seeks, at the core of its business model, to obfuscate distinctions in viewers' minds between commercials and programs via participatory video ads.

The splenetic anti-amateur and fan of expertise Andrew Keen argues that the anything-goes *ethoi* of YouTube et al. generate a cacophony of loudness and stupidity rather than quality and knowledge, eclipsing "even the blogs in the inanity and absurdity of its content."[40] It's easy to mock Keen as an elitist who fails to appreciate the revolutionary qualities of new technology—but not so easy to prove him wrong. For instance, the mad opposition to infant immunization that has gathered pace among superstitious segments of the US population dominates YouTube videos and responses on the topic. This is just one of countless examples of perilous medical misinformation that circulates irresponsibly on the service.[41] Similarly, as fewer and fewer media outlets become available to them, tobacco companies turn voraciously to the Internet. Medical researchers are concerned at evidence of product placement via "smoking fetish videos" on YouTube. Aimed at underage drug users under the soubriquet of "community engagement," they draw massively positive reactions. Many old TV commercials for cigarettes are also archived there.[42] The paper that won the oleaginously named "Best New Thinking Award at the 2003 Market Research Society Conference" let the hypocrisy of those involved in new-media product placement sing when it acknowledged that effective marketing does not adopt a "view of the consumer as an individual [but rather] part of the herd."[43] Tim Kring, the creator of *Heroes*, refers to people who view his show on network TV rather than through streaming video as "saps and dipshits who can't figure out how to watch it in a superior way."[44] Behind closed doors, the mantra remains the same as it ever was.

Is there a different way of conceptualizing YouTubers? That ugly neologism, the prosumer, is linked to the discourse of casualization, of flexible labor amongst workers who have been segmented through deregulation and new technology. In Western Europe and Japan, this group is renaming itself to fight back. The movement embodies a new style, a new identity, formed from young, female, mobile, international workers within the culture industries, services and the knowledge sector, struggling for security against the impact of neoliberalism. The Euromayday Network organizes Precariat parades across European cities.[45] The Precariat alerts us to an insidious, complex connection between "social-movement slogans reappropriated for neoliberalism." It recognizes that concepts like diversity, culture, access and sustainability create spectacles, manage workers, and enable gentrification. Perhaps cybertarians could look at these joyous but critical activists before they announce a "revolution" that breaks down the barriers between work and play.

Conclusion

I don't hate YouTube. I enjoy it in the same way as I enjoy radio, TV, books and podcasts—YouTube is a pleasant way of spending time, with some informational benefits as well. So what should be the stance of progressive scholars who like YouTube, but beware its rapturous reception by credulous cybertarians? Fortunately, we have some good guides along the way. They can help us maintain post-naïve optimism.[46] It is often alleged that political economists of the media have not accounted for the creativity of audiences and consumers. But they are well aware of this capacity. In the 1950s, Dallas Smythe wrote that "audience members act on the program content. They take it and mold it in the image of their individual needs and values."[47] He saw no necessary contradiction between this perspective and his other principal intellectual innovation, namely that audience attention—presumed or measured—was the commodity being sold in the commercial TV industry, by stations to advertisers. Similarly, in his classic 1960s text *Mass Communications and American Empire*, Herb Schiller stressed the need to build on the creativity of audiences by offering them entertaining and informative media.[48] And at the height of his 1970s policy interventions in revolutionary societies, from Latin America to Africa, Armand Mattelart recognized the relative autonomy of audiences and their capacity and desire to generate cultural meanings.[49] A sadness fills me each time I enter the YouTube scholarly world, because so much academic literature about it either stigmatizes or fails to pay heed to this work—even reinventing the idea of audience labor as something new. Fortunately, the innovations of Smythe, Schiller and Mattelart are constantly being reviewed and renewed by those who admire that tradition of engaged intellectuals.[50]

Media texts and institutions such as YouTube are not just signs to be read; they are not just coefficients of political and economic power; and they are not just innovations. Rather, they are all these things. YouTube is a hybrid monster, coevally subject to text, power and science—all at once, but in contingent ways.[51] I therefore propose a tripartite approach to analyzing it: a reconstruction of "the diversity of older readings from their sparse and multiple traces"; a focus on "the text itself, the object that conveys it, and the act that grasps it"; and an identification of "the strategies by which authors and publishers tried to impose an orthodoxy or a prescribed reading on the text."[52] This materialist history must be evaluated inside consideration of the wider political economy. As Jacques Attali explains, lengthy historical cycles see political-economic power shift between cores. A new "mercantile order forms wherever a creative class masters a key innovation from navigation to accounting or, in our own time, where services are most efficiently mass produced, thus generating enormous wealth."[53] Manuel Castells has coined the term "mass self-communication" to capture this development, which sees affective investments by social movements and individuals matched by financial and policing investments by corporations and states.[54] YouTube is part of the West Coast US heritage of the "mass production of services that enhance the power and pleasure [of people via] nomadic objects."[55] The next step is to consider the types of exploitation that are involved in such changes.

New eras in communication also index homologies and exchanges between militarism, colonialism and class control. The networked computing era has solidified a unipolar world of almost absolute US dominance, with a share taken by other parts of the world economic triad in Japan and Western Europe. None of that has changed or been even mildly imperiled by YouTube or anything else. China and India provide many leading software engineers, but they lack domestic venture capitalists, military underpinnings to computing innovation, and successful histories of global textual power at the mainstream level as per Sony, the BBC, Hollywood, or the Pacific Northwest. When the Precariat declares a new "phenomenology of labor," a "world horizon of production," it is reoccupying and resignifying the space of corporate-driven divisions of labor in ways that cybertarians have simply ignored. Antonio Negri refers to this group as the cognitariat, people with high educational attainment and great facility with cultural and communications technologies and genres. They play key roles in the production and circulation of goods and services through creation and coordination, forming a new proletariat. No longer defined in terms of factories and manufacturers versus middle and ruling classes of force and ideology, this proletariat is formed from those whose forebears, with similar or lesser cultural capital, were the salariat. They operated within secure systems of health care and retirement income. The new group lacks both the organization of the traditional working class and the political entrée of the old middle class. Today's "culturalisation of production" both enables these intellectuals, by placing them at the center of world economies, and *dis*ables them, by doing so under conditions of flexible production and ideologies of "freedom."[56]

We should focus on this group, the precarious cognitariat, in the new era of cultural re-industrialization and economic deregulation. Of course, peer-to-peer downloading has problematized private property in fascinating ways; of course, cybertarianism is right to valorize taking things out of the market; of course, sharing elements gratis is a wonderful counter-capitalist move; but these movements are rapidly being domesticated by processes that are "commodifying people's free relations."[57] In his incisive survey of cybertarianism, Vincent Mosco rightly argues that its "myths are important both for what they reveal (including a genuine desire for community and democracy) and for what they conceal (including the growing concentration of communication power in a handful of transnational media businesses)."[58] Our analysis of YouTube must be bold enough to encompass such wider questions, even as it must be modest and patient until large-scale scholarly surveys of networks and experiences become available. Meanwhile, let's not join an unseemly cybertarian rush to a new day that will turn rapidly into an old night. Remember the faces in the crush of the crowd storming stores to buy Windows 95? Not a pretty sight; not pretty software. Let's not replicate it.

Endnotes

1 Henry Jenkins & John Hartley, "Is YouTube Truly the Future?" *Sydney Morning Herald,* 25 June 2008.
2 Lev Grossman, "*Time*'s Person of the Year: You," *Time,* 13 December 2006.
3 Ron Simon, "The Changing Definition of Reality Television," in *Thinking Outside the Box: A Contemporary Television Genre Reader*, eds. Gary R. Edgerton and Brian G. Rose (Lexington: University Press of Kentucky, 2006), pp. 180–81.
4 Meeyoung Cha et al., "I Tube, You Tube, Everybody Tubes: Analyzing the World's Largest User Generated Content Video System," *Internet Measurement Conference* 2007 – www.imconf.net/imc-2007/papers/imc131.pdf [last checked 15 February 2009].
5 Jason Potts et al., "Consumer Co-Creation and Situated Creativity," *Industry & Innovation* no. 5, 2008, pp. 459–474; Stuart Cunningham, *In the Vernacular: A Generation of Australian Culture and Controversy* (St. Lucia, Australia: University of Queensland Press, 2008); Stuart Cunningham, "Creative Industries as Policy and Discourse Outside the United Kingdom," *Global Media and Communication* no. 3, 2007, pp. 347–352.
6 Adam Arvidsson, "The Ethical Economy of Customer Coproduction," *Journal of Macromarketing* no. 4, 2008, pp. 326–328.
7 You can read my account of this in Toby Miller, *The Well-Tempered Self: Citizenship, Culture, and the Postmodern Subject* (Baltimore: The Johns Hopkins University Press, 1993).
8 Virginia Postrel, "The Pleasures of Persuasion," *Wall Street Journal,* 2 August 1999.
9 Terry Eagleton, "The Revolt of the Reader," *New Literary History* no. 3, 1983, pp. 449–452.
10 Robert W. McChesney, *Communication Revolution: Critical Junctures and the Future of Media* (New York: New Press, 2007), p. 16.
11 Norah Vincent, "Lear, Seinfeld, and the Dumbing Down of the Academy," *Village Voice* ,2–8 February 2000.
12 Colin MacCabe, "An Interview with Stuart Hall, December 2007, " *Critical Quarterly* no. 1–2, 2008, pp. 12–42.
13 Megan Mullen, "The Fall and Rise of Cable Narrowcasting," *Convergence* no. 1, 2002, pp. 62–82.

14 Toby Miller, "Can Natural Luddites Make Things Explode or Travel Faster? The New Humanities, Cultural Policy Studies, and Creative Industries," in *Media Industries: History, Theory, and Method*, eds. Jennifer Holt & Alisa Perren (Malden, MA: Wiley-Blackwell, 2009), pp. 184–198.

15 John C. Paolillo, "Structure and Network in the YouTube Core," in *Proceedings of the 41st Hawaii International Conference on System Sciences 2008* – www2.computer.org/portal/web/csdl/doi/10.1109/HICSS.2008.415 [last checked 15 February 2009].

16 Stefano Pace, "YouTube: An Opportunity for Consumer Narrative Analysis?" *Qualitative Market Research: An International Journal* no. 2, 2008, pp. 1087–1105.

17 Gijs Kruitbosch & Frank Nack, "Broadcast Yourself on YouTube—Really?" *Human Centered Computing '08 – Association for Computing Machinery* – http://portal.acm.org/citation.cfm?id=1462029 [last checked 15 February 2009]; Bill Tancer, "With Hulu, Older Audiences Lead the Way," *Wall Street Journal*, 10 February 2009; *The Economist*, "Hulu Who?" 7 February 2009, p. 59.

18 *World Internet Project Report 2009* – www.worldinternetproject.net/ [last checked 15 February 2009].

19 Fernando Duarte et al., "Geographical Characterization of YouTube: A Latin American View," in *Fifth Latin American Web Congress 2007* – http://ieeexplore.ieee.org/Xplore/ [last checked 15 February 2009].

20 Jacqueline D. Lipton, "A Winning Solution for YouTube and UTube? Corresponding Trademarks and Domain Name Sharing," *Harvard Journal of Law & Technology* no. 21, 2008, pp. 509–545; Andrea Frey, "To Sue or Not to Sue: Video-Sharing Web Sites, Copyright Infringement, and the Inevitability of Corporate Control," *Brooklyn Journal of Corporate, Financial & Commercial Law* no. 2, 2007, pp. 167–195; Michael Driscoll, "Will YouTube Sail Into the DMCA's Safe Harbor or Sink for Internet Piracy?," *John Marshall Law School Review of Intellectual Property Law* no. 6, 2007, pp. 550–569; Kurt Hunt, "Copyright and YouTube: Pirate's Playground or Fair Use Forum?," *Michigan Telecommunications and Technology Law Review* no. 14, 2007, pp. 197–222.

21 Tameka Kee, "YouTube's New Bid to Boost Revenues: Sponsored Videos and a Live Performance," *The Guardian*, 13 November 2008.

22 *BBC News*, "YouTube Introduces Video Adverts," 22 August 2007.

23 *PCMag.com*, "IOC Puts Games on YouTube—But Not Here," 5 August 2008 – www.pcmag.com/article2/0,2817,2327212,00.asp [last checked 15 February 2009].

24 Tameka Kee, "YouTube's New Bid to Boost Revenues: Sponsored Videos and a Live Performance," *The Guardian,* 13 November 2008.

25 Kruitbosch and Nack 2008; Tancer 2009; *The Economist* 2009.

26 Charles Biederman & Danny Andrews, "Applying Copyright Law to User-Generated Content," *Los Angeles Lawyer* no. 31, 2008, pp. 12–17.

27 Its somewhat improbable fellow class-action litigants included the English Premier League, the Scottish Premier League, and Rodgers & Hammerstein. The US District Court's Opinion and Order in Viacom et al. v. YouTube et al. 07 Civ. 2103 is instructive for what it discloses about the real political economy at play.

28 *BBC News*, "Google Must Divulge YouTube Log," 3 July 2008.

29 Quoted in Darren Waters, "Video Service YouTube Grows Up," *BBC News,* 20 June 2007.

30 *BBC News*, "YouTube Rolls Out Filtering Tools," 16 October 2007.

31 In addition, YouTube is also responsible for a huge environmental impact due to server farms' electricity use, communication-tower devastation (millions of birds killed each year in the US alone), radiation, and so on. YouTube expends between fifty and two hundred gigabytes of server bandwidth each day—a monumental contribution to electronic waste that creates an unprecedented carbon footprint. For a discussion, see Richard Maxwell & Toby Miller (2008), "Ecological Ethics and Media Technology," *International Journal of Communication* no 2, 2008, pp. 331–353.

32 Diane Mermigas, "Hulu CEO: More Global Moves Planned for '09," *Media PostNews Online Media Daily,* 29 December 2008; Scott Collins, "Where TV and the Web Converge, There is Hulu," *Los Angeles Times,* 16 June 2008; Jack Loechner, "Downloading TV and Watching Video Online Biggest Gainers in 2008," *Center for Media Research*, 8 January 2009; Wayne Friedman, "Digital Lessons TV Should Learn from Music Companies," *MediaPost's TV Watch,* 26 November 2008; Tancer 2009; *The Economist* 2009; Wayne Friedman, "Net Gains: Nielsen Sizes Up TV Hits Online," *MediaDailyNews,* 12 February 2009; Gavin O'Malley, "CBS' TV.com Sees Rise in Viewership," *MediaDailyNews,* 17 February 2009; Michael Learmonth, "Can Hulu Hold Off TV.com?" *AdvertisingAge,* 17 February 2009.

33 Greg Mitchell, "The 'Online Campaign'—Election 2008—Rolls On," *Editor & Publisher,* 6 September 2008; Trevor Potter, "Letter to Google," 13 October 2008 – www.publicknowledge.org/pdf/mccain-letter-20081013.pdf [last checked 15 February 2009]; Michael A. Cohen & Maria Figueroa Küpçü, "Congress and the 'YouTube War,' " *World Policy Journal* no. 4, 2006/07.

34 Howard Dean quoted in *Mother Jones*, "Politics 2.0: The Big Idea," 1 July 2007 – www.highbeam.com/doc/1P3-1295584311.htmlpp [last checked 15 February 2009]; Tony Blair quoted in Darren Waters, "Video Service YouTube Grows Up," *BBC News,* 20 June 2007.

35 *The Economist*, "Flickring Here, Twittering There," 16 August 2008.

36 Lee Rainie & John Horrigan, "Election 2006 Online," *Pew Internet & American Life Project,* 17 January 2007 – www.pewinternet.org/pdfs/PIP_Politics_2006.pdf [last checked 15 February 2009].

37 Vassia Gueorguieva, "Voters, MySpace, and YouTube: The Impact of Alternative Communication Channels on the 2006 Election Cycle and Beyond," *Social Science Computer Review* no. 3, 2008, pp. 288–300.

38 Consider the twisted treatment of Wael Abbas—see James Orr, "YouTube Pulls Plug on Egypt Activist Over Brutal Videos," *The Guardian,* 27 November 2007.

39 Ellen Goodman, "Our Do-it-Yourself Economy," *Dallas Morning News,* 19 July 2008.

40 Andrew Keen, *The Cult of the Amateur: How Today's Internet is Killing Our Culture and Assaulting Our Economy* (London: Nicholas Brealey Publishing, 2007), p. 12.

41 Jennifer Keelan et al., "YouTube as a Source of Information on Immunization: A Content Analysis," *Journal of the American Medical Association* no. 21, 2007, pp. 2482–2483.

42 Becky Freeman & Simon Chapman, "Is 'You Tube' Telling or Selling You Something? Tobacco Content on the YouTube Video-Sharing Website," *Tobacco Control* no. 16, 2007, pp. 207–210.

43 Mark Earls, "Advertising to the Herd: How Understanding Our True Nature Challenges the Ways We Think About Advertising and Market Research," *International Journal of Market Research* no. 3, 2003, pp. 311–337.

44 Quoted in Michael Hirschorn, "The Future is Cheese," *Atlantic Monthly,* March 2009.

45 Alex Foti, "MAYDAY MAYDAY: Euro Flex Workers, Time to Get a Move On!" *Republicart.net* no. 4, 2005.

46 Dan Schiller, *How to Think About Information* (Urbana: University of Illinois Pres, 2007). For a summary of the issues as applied to media studies more generally, see Toby Miller, " 'Step Away from the Croissant': Media Studies 3.0," *The Media and Social Theory*, eds. David Hesmondhalgh & Jason Toynbee (London: Routledge, 2008), pp. 213–230.

47 Dallas Smythe, "Reality as Presented by Television," *Public Opinion Quarterly* no. 2, 1954, pp. 143–156.

48 Herbert I. Schiller, *Mass Communications and American Empire* (Boulder: Westview Press, 1992).

49 Armand Mattelart, *Mass Media, Ideologies and the Revolutionary Movement* (Brighton, England: Harvester Press, 1980).

50 We summarize the dozens of works in this tradition in Toby Miller et al., *Global Hollywood 2* (London: British Film Institute, 2005).

51 Bruno Latour, *We Have Never Been Modern* (Cambridge, MA: Harvard University Press, 1993).

52 Roger Chartier, "Texts, Printings, Readings," in *The New Cultural History*, ed. Lynn Hunt (Berkeley: University of California Press, 1989), pp. 154–175.

53 Jacques Attali, "This is Not America's Final Crisis," *New Perspectives Quarterly*, 2008, pp. 31–33.

54 Manuel Castells, "Communication, Power and Counter-Power in the Network Society," *International Journal of Communication* no. 1, 2007, pp. 238–266.

55 Attali 2008.

56 Antonio Negri, *goodbye mister socialism* (Paris: Seuil, 2007).

57 Hilary Wainwright, "The Commons, the State and Transformative Politics," *Red Pepper*, 3 January 2008 [last checked 15 February 2009].

58 Vincent Mosco, *The Digital Sublime: Myth, Power, and Cyberspace* (Cambridge, MA: MIT Press, 2004).

Andrei Gornykh

From YouTube to RuTube, or How I Learned to Stop Worrying and Love All Tubes

Changes in communication technology have always been accompanied by both an optimistic anticipation of their potential social uses and fears regarding their possible detrimental effects on society. In this sense, the Internet has prompted reactions similar to those following the alleged technical breakthroughs of radio, cinema and television. From the perspective of liberal technocratic discourse, the Internet is a technoscientific innovation efficiently providing access to information, personal freedom and the public sphere. For others, the Internet seems to irrevocably commodify the micro-texture of communication, infusing advertising into the very last resorts of personal exchange and disinterested pleasure.

YouTube is situated at the very center of these anticipations. By 2009, it has become common to either hype YouTube as the ideal grassroots media platform or condemn it for selling its users to advertisers. My article, however, suggests reconsideration of those claims by comparing YouTube to its little Russian brother, RuTube. By analyzing RuTube's formal organization, this article attempts to provide a measure for understanding what might be YouTube's possible, probable and preferred futures—and what YouTube has already become. Certainly, for many RuTube is just a clone of the "world's leading" website for online video. But is RuTube YouTube's clone? Is it actually an exact copy? Might it not—predominantly as a local version of YouTube—lay bare the latter's cultural logic like an epigone emphasizing the strong or weak sides of the original instead? Traces of local specificity on the surface of YouTube's global format indeed may have important things to tell us.

Although one version of RuTube's history has it that the Russian video distribution platform was contrived even before YouTube itself, RuTube was founded by Oleg Volobuev and Mikhail Paulkin in November 2006. As of March 2008, RuTube was considered the biggest online video-sharing and transmitting service on RUNET (Russia's Internet), with 400,000 daily users and more than 40 million video views a month. In November 2008, TNT – Teleset (TNT-Telenetwork) reported that the media holding company of Russia's gas giant Gazprom, Gazprom-Media, had purchased a majority stake in RuTube, valuing the site at 15 million dollars. While just over the half of Gazprom is owned by the Russian state, Gazprom-Media in turn owns controlling packages in NTV and TNT television channels, NTV-Plus satellite television and five radio stations, including Ekho Moskvy, the Seven Days publishing company, the NTV-Kino film production company, the October movie theater in Moscow and the Crystal Palace in St. Petersburg. The deal to purchase RuTube was announced in June 2007, and it was expected even back then that RuTube would start hosting videos from TNT and other media properties of Gazprom-Media after the acquisition.

According to former co-owner and chief manager Oleg Volobuev, RuTube's purpose was "to create an online multimedia resource for the new generation. We are not just a video website, not just a video-hosting site, not just Internet broadcasting. By combining all these characteristics, we would like to give to our users the broadest possibilities of the Internet by means of video."[1] Volobuev clearly chose a liberal technocratic viewpoint in order to point out the possible future gains of the Russian clone, but he also stated the need to appropriate YouTube's technology to local needs. "Among the interesting features of RuTube that our rivals do not have," Volobuev declared in an interview given in 2007, are "the recording of clips from Webcams, the creation of playlists, automatic postings in blogs, the creation of virtual TV channels, lists of friends' clips, users' ratings, the stimulation to post more interesting clips. [Such features might] at first sight seem [to be] trifles, [but] fast forward and rewind functions during viewing [...] mean that you don't have to wait for a complete download to understand whether you like a clip or not. This is very important for Russian users."[2]

RuTube's promises and its seemingly user-friendly adaptation of the American prototype did of course not remain undisputed. An anonymous user named deuce100 challenged RuTube's merits by pointing out that:

> Using RuTube had been fun for me up until the moment when my clips began to be seen by many people and to be voted for. In the beginning my rating stars started to disappear, then the views of my clips began to be artificially reduced, the numbers were flexible. Not to mention other problems: missing tags, uploading of my clips under other names. [...] Then I started to notice that the best-rated clips of the day and of the week had been posted by the same authors, who proved to be the creators of the site and people from their circle of acquaintance. [...] Dear friends (the creators of the site) if you decide to make "a closed party," then you'd better construct this site for yourselves only and don't advertise it as a new national project. Your idea is the following: the more popular the site, the higher its price on the market, so you can either get money from ads or to sell it later for big money, and we are supposed to help you by means of our clips.[3]

Both the anonymous user's and Volobuev's statements are telling in their opposition and also a rather revealing reflection of the online "Tube" phenomenon in general. While Volobuev underlines the liberating potential of RuTube in his breathless inventory of technological functionalities, deuce100 seems no less naive in his critique of liberal technocratism and the slogans of unlimited self-expression. Furthermore, neither of the two address the new economic raison d'être of amateur aesthetics. Apart from endless opportunities for promotion and advertising, both YouTube and RuTube obviously serve as an indirect way of stimulating sales in the area of mobile video recording devices. The mass production and affordability of such devices at the beginning of the 21st century brings up the question of how to use and to aesthetically legitimate the vast number of videos being produced by amateurs. YouTube and RuTube provide amateurs with a more or less meaningful goal for incessant shooting. When the very process of using a technical novelty loses its freshness, the Tubes will still stimulate consumer pleasure by putting the interest of video devices into the more sublime orbit of public and creative activity.

Categorizing Visual Culture

Raymond Williams once argued that television is not an invention that results from pure scientific and technical research; it was not its inherent properties as an electronic medium that were the cause of external social change, of the transformation of our experience of space and time. Neither was television, from Williams' point of view, a technological cause mediated by economic factors—an invention which changed lifestyles not by itself, having been selected from a range of possibilities as the most effective option for investment. Rather, television arose as the result of the meeting of two social needs. First of all, the need for new forms of social control: television permits centralization of the construction of opinions and lifestyles in a fragmented mass society. Secondly, television is the answer to "passivity, a cultural and psychological inadequacy, which had always been latent in people, but which television now organized and came to represent."[4]

Arguably, this still sounds relevant in relation to YouTube and RuTube, both in terms of the social logic determining a technological "breakthrough" and regarding the Tube's more intimate relation with television. In the same way as its Russian counterpart, YouTube not only is a public video-sharing website, but also a mode of classifying contemporary visual culture. In YouTube's classification, one may find a system of "American" values in a broad sense. First of all, there are some overarching categories like News and Politics, Music and Movies, relating to what a mass audience of users might associate with basic democratic values and "American cultural identity." YouTube also offers a non-hierarchical set of more "global" lifestyle sub-categories, listed in alphabetical order and without ranking: Autos & Vehicle, Comedy, Education, Entertainment, Film & Animation, Gaming, How-to & Style, Nonprofits & Activism, People & Blogs, Pets & Animals, Science & Technology, Sport, and Travel & Events.[5] Categories that struggle to find their place in the mass-media mainstream like Science, Education or Nonprofits appear to be on an equal structural level with genres of mass culture.

RuTube's listings of subjects, on the other hand, consist of two seemingly symmetrical classifications—the creators' classification and that of the users'. The creators' classification is a column of categories (the number of videos is indicated in brackets):

Humor & Entertainment (125,204)
Cinema, TV, TV-show (45,680)
Accidents & Catastrophes, Fights (31,047)
Music & Performances (184,373)
Animation (80,938)
Sport (58,458)
Miscellaneous (46,105)[6]

RuTube's creators do not attempt to reflect cultural identity, seeming instead to reduce such an "identity" to the most primitive clichés of global mass culture.[7] But the listing also contains a hierarchy of numbers indicating something like the specific cultural weight of a category. "Accidents & Catastrophes, Fights" appears to be of huge interest to Russian users, while the "Western" tastes and preferences allegedly represented on YouTube might cling to harmless "German pranks" instead. What is more, the vertical order seems to be an anti-hierarchy or even disorder, as there are no visible criteria to organize the categories. At closer glance, we may notice that all categories are variations of the same meta-category of television entertainment, referring almost without exception to the most popular genres broadcast in Russia. The creator's categories, then, do not of course aim at a universal classification, but rather at delineating a homogenous field of youthful and, to a considerable degree, masculine visual pleasures.

This becomes even more evident if we superimpose the second classification onto the first. The users' classification assumes the form of a tag cloud, and it is through this "hazy" medium that one can grasp the specific structure of the RuTube world—the structure of pure television or television flow. The two main semantic families of tags—animation and music—visually occupy more than half the tag cloud. The rest is made up of a background consisting mostly of names known from Russian TV channels, TV programs and TV genres. There are up to ten keywords designating the very same category, animation, mostly different slang terms for the English or Russian word for "animation." This fact reveals that the multiplied repetition of the same popular genre constitutes the very structure of the RuTube flow.

The cultural space of RuTube is defined by two axes. The vertical axis is that of form—gradations from amateur to high-end professional video. The horizontal axis is that of the values and affects addressed on the content level—from excessively negative subject matter to absolutely positive. All videos are in fact localized within this system of coordinates. Yet, we must also be aware of an absolute domination of both axes' extremes. Both on YouTube and RuTube, it is the most sophisticated products of pop culture (music clips, film trailers, animation) and the formless and senseless scenes of daily life (such as various amateur performances) on the one hand, and extremely dramatic events (bloody tragedies, disasters and violence of all kinds) and episodes of joy and revelry (family celebrations, entertaining scenes, funny occasions) on the other that make up the lion's share of the content in terms of quantity of posts, views and comments.

More to the point, on RuTube all other types of events and genres form thin layers between these extremes. All that is not related to the "ascetic" amateur visual format or pop culture's mainstream—be it the subtle modulation of human feelings and relations represented by the narrative apparatus of modern literature, or an independent expert's opinions, alternative cinema or visual anthropology. In other words, there is a chasm in the center of the RuTube space. There is no system of coordinates, but a building permanently collapsing in upon itself as if after a precisely controlled explosion. The space of RuTube is a spectacle of the professional's and the amateur's flows into each other, the funny and the grievous, the most ordinary and the most dramatic, while television's flow entails some more differentiation between programs and narratives.

RuTube as/and Television

From the very beginning Russian TV was the experimental foundation for the future RuTube, the most obvious evidence being a TV show entitled *Сам себе режиссер* ("You Are the Director"), which pioneered the format in the 1990s. The show presented curious happenings shot by accident and ordinary men demonstrating special abilities like putting their fist into their mouth, wiggling their ears, or producing nonhuman sounds. The audience was invited to vote for specific clips, with the winners being awarded some insignificant prices. More complex forerunners are various reality show formats like *Фабрика Звезд* ("Factory of Stars," the Russian clone of *Star Academy*, the international Endemol brand) that have become immensely popular on Russian television since

2000. "Factory of Stars" systematically blurs the boundary between amateur and superstar, between program and advertisement, engaging viewers to vote for the next instant celebrity.

Within the ongoing convergence of TV and the Internet, RuTube plays a vital part for the conversion of televisual formats. However, RuTube does not do much to advance the passage of television into some post-TV epoch marked by a radical democratization of mass media, but rather embeds television firmly in the fabric of the Web (imagine what the Internet would be if words and not videos had prevailed!). RuTube in fact discloses the immanent potential of TV as a systemic form of consumer coding. It is a "TV 2.0," cost-efficiently eliminating the need to employ an army of specialists (producers, directors, telehosts) who traditionally have been qualified to introduce the values of consumer society into our way of life. In Russian TV YouTubean or RuTubean programs are multiplying. However, the tendency of a "YouTubization" of TV is rather a re-export and re-assimilation of TV content than a reflection of participatory culture feeding back into mainstream media.

60 "Debloid Russians" today on YouTube

On YouTube one can find videos about what first appeared to be a subversive Russian street movement of youngsters called "debloids," which was revealed at a second viewing to be teaser for Russian TV programs. Debloids are teenagers who try to "express themselves" in bizarre and stupid ways, jumping from roofs, falling into water, throwing heavy objects at each other and finding difficulty in replying to questions whether all this is "for no special reason" or "a kind of a protest." Most importantly, debloids record everything they do on video, much of which is posted on RuTube (many videos may be found using the keyword диблои).[8] There is a wonderful irony about these videos,[9] as a television commentator coincidentally "discovered" that the "YouTube generation" responsible for the clips was, in its act of self-expression, reproducing global television clichés, in particular MTV's infamous *Jackass* adventures. In other words, it needed a TV report about the new generation of RuTubers to reveal that television itself had generated a creative generation.

Instead of explaining this phenomenon as another, local example of global mashup culture, one might point to the fact that with online video websites like RuTube, mainstream media merely start imitating their own imitations. Describing this process as original and creative is, then, truly paradoxical. RuTube videos do not feature unique personalities who wish to inform us about their way of life; they compete for ratings, just as TV channels do. What Pierre Bourdieu once said about television might therefore characterize RuTube as well: "People are ready to do almost anything to be the first to see and present something. The result is that everyone copies each other in the attempt to get ahead; everyone ends up doing the same thing."[10]

RuTube reproduces what has been coding the mass audience on television for decades, and what is more, it also legitimates television entertainment as a preexisting reality, veiling the routine and senselessness of dramatic media events, and embellishing the ubiquitous sameness of mass culture with a secondary originality. RuTube therefore cannot be understood outside the context of the Russian media-policy system.[11] The Gazprom-Media subsidiary systematically borrows television's content, turning the idea of participatory culture into just another TV channel where portions of the most popular programs are watched in video-player mode. RuTube works like a video sampler that can be used to compose one's own program from readymade units. Being a selection of "the best of TV," RuTube seems to purify television's biases and disproportions (the dominance of low-brow humor and "news" from different areas, but of the same type) and make a new media standard out of it.

But the form of RuTube can be even more eloquent than its content. Television programs are broken up into a variety of fragments that form television flow. These fragments are multiple and condensed in terms of time and intensity, allowing advertising to be interwoven into the flow organically. Stories narrated on television are interrupted and suspended in many ways; it is, however, still possible to construct a narrative. RuTube, however, tends to be a flow that dissolves any story. In the process of its use, it becomes a mixture of intentional and completely unintentional results. The same of course holds true for YouTube. "A tag like 'slate' could mean all sorts of things, so each page mixes perfect matches with what-the-huh results. A documentary on Scientology links to a South Park episode, which links to comedian Pablo Francisco. A few clicks later I am watching some merry prankster get an unexpected smackdown. In Web 2.0-speak, this is a 'folksonomy.' In English, it means YouTube is a mix of every video genre imaginable."[12] Permanently diverting us from concentrating on one single topic characterizes RuTube to a considerable degree, undermining the narrative form of the organization of our experience.[13]

The RuTube user's constant clicking on different video displays is in fact the very condition of possibility that the format offers. Every user needs to produce her or his own flow, reproducing the codes of television's visual pleasures; he or she is supposed to keep changing windows or channels constantly to see something new, with advertising always present, not only in particular segments of the flow, but contained in every frame as a picture, InVideo ad, banner ad or link. RuTube in itself could, thus, be understood as a form of self-referential advertising, with every video being an announcement of a group of other videos, producing its respective meaning and history by referring to a series of similar isolated moments of new-and-now. Pure postmodernism as described by Fredric Jameson: "The experience and the value of perpetual change thereby comes to govern language and feelings, fully as much as the buildings and the garments of this particular society, to the point at which even the relative meaning allowed by uneven development (or "nonsynchronous synchronicity") is no longer comprehensible, and the supreme value of the New and of innovation, as both modernism and modernization grasped it, fades away against a steady stream of momentum and variation that at some outer limit seems stable and motionless."[14]

Competing for Popularity and Politics

When clicking on the option People (люди) on RuTube's first page, the viewer gets to see an impressive table of user ratings.[15] For academic visitors, this manner of presenting the RuTube community may be evocative of the principle of social taxonomy that Michel Foucault described, with all social "units" occupying their position in the General Table.[16] Positions are assigned to them according to the complex disciplinary index of their activities: the quantity of posted videos, comments made and received, and votes for posted videos. Everyone has a rating. And there are only a few—less than ten—whose rating is incredibly high, almost out-of-reach for the others. The table, then, seems to give evidence to an anti-utopian view of the medialization of social life.

YouTube, on the contrary, lists products according to popularity rather than listing "people." Consider Avril Lavigne's music video "Girlfriend," which outplayed comedian Judson Laipply's performance "Evolution of Dance," the long-time "most viewed" video clip on YouTube. This is not due to the fact that Lavigne herself is more popular, but that her product is (this is even more evident in Laipply's case). A video closely resembling a trailer for a fictitious teen comedy finally proved to attract more viewers than another clip, Laipply's choreographic montage of 50 years of American pop-dance history. RuTube recently adapted this strategy by making the product trailer format dominate the system. On February 6, 2009, it was announced that distributing teasers and trailers would become one of the RuTube project's major lines of media development.[17] As of today, "trailer" has become the primary category in RuTube's classification of videos. It seems as if RuTube itself has turned into a huge and elusive trailer of Russian media history which in the end is supposed to be that of our social life.

Without indulging in the naive pessimism referred to in the beginning of this article, my analysis still suggests that RuTube as a cultural form articulates the vanishing of the narrative or collective dimension of our experience so persistently brought to mind by Fredric Jameson. On RuTube, social life transforms into a non-existent story, a mere pretext for individuals to create their private flows of visual pleasures on the ruins of the public sphere. And all this is a perfect fit for the political state of the art in many post-Soviet states, Russia and Belarus in particular.

One of the most shrewd liberal critics of the present Russian political system, Julija Latynina, recently described the political discourse of the Russian authorities as follows:

> Well, there was war in Georgia. Now it looked like we would struggle incessantly for the recognition of South Ossetia and Abkhazia. Then the problem seems to have been removed. Nicaragua recognized [the new republics] and we are not struggling for it any more. Here is the gas "war" with Ukraine, then it is over. Here is our plan to deploy Iskander missiles [in the Kaliningrad region], then we say: "No, we will not deploy our missiles." In other words, we are fighting with somebody every single moment and we are surrounded by enemies. But if you notice, every day we resume fighting at the moment we stopped the day before.[18]

Latynina's critique translates neatly into the politics of RuTube. Instead of a political strategy, we are presented with a series of extremely similar, striking videos of incoherent fragments of fights with a new enemy, distracting the audience not only from real politics, but from any comprehensible way or even desire to question it. RuTube prompts the viewing of random videos and commenting on them. Compare this activity to a concept of the public sphere, based on "the need of bourgeois private people to create a forum for a critically debating public: to read periodicals and to discuss them, to exchange personal opinions, and to contribute to the formulation of an opinion."[19] Rational, consensus-oriented public debate is perhaps the last thing that comes to one's mind when reading comments in RuTube. Comments normally consist of highly emotional and categorical statements that often contradict each other.[20]

One of the most dramatic examples of this are the polemics exchanged between Russian nationalist channels and posts and those of Caucasians.[21] Russian nationalists describe the Caucasians mostly as savages and new barbarians that are imperceptibly attempting to conquer Russia. The Caucasians, in turn, celebrate the strength and courage of Caucasian men. One can hardly expect to find something like an open dialogue about the history of nations and their problems, although such a political dialogue is badly needed. There is no indication of an attempt at mutual understanding or debate. The accompanying video material boils down to one more selection of street fights—a man of one nationality beats a man of another nationality—and a measure of popularity, the rating of hate or admiration in relation to the same video.

Conclusion

One might argue that RuTube's discourse doesn't know halftones. Its subjects are self-assured in their extreme aesthetic or political judgments about decontextualized fragments of social life. RuTube doesn't advocate one set of values against another (say patriotic versus liberal), but its very format tends to disconnect people from the public sphere or political dimension. It is a kind of state television apparatus that works even more effectively in a cyber form.

This being the current form of RuTube, there are however still strong and positive expectations relating to YouTube. These expectations involve its projected social, economic and political effects. YouTube is supposed to facilitate "socialization among dispersed friends," and to create "new connections and develop social networks."[22] It is believed to strengthen "electoral openness and honesty"[23] by monitoring election practices and to open new prospects for democracy, providing opportunities for potential candidates to get rid of financial restrictions by means of obtaining public visibility at low cost, raising political contributions and recruiting volunteers online.[24] This optimism goes right up to the police's use of YouTube to solve crimes by posting surveillance footage of crimes being committed and encouraging users to identify the perpetrators.[25] As this article has shown, RuTube so far has no firm foundation for such optimistic expectations, but as a cultural form, RuTube and YouTube also have to be understood in light of their given political and industrial contexts.

Endnotes

1 See http://services.bal-con.ru/rutube_ru/comments/ [last checked 15 February 2009].

2 Ibid.

3 Ibid.

4 Raymond Williams, *Television. Technology and Cultural Form* (London: Wesleyan University Press, 1992), p. 6.

5 See www.youtube.com/browse [last checked 15 February 2009]. Recently the fluid YouTube format has changed once again–now we have only a democratic alphabetical classification.

6 See http://rutube.ru/ [last checked 15 February 2009]. Since the end of February 2009 new categories have been added (Technology and Science; Nature, Animals; News and Politics; Art and Creativity; Family, House, Children). In fact, RuTube's first page now looks more like that of YouTube's, though the resemblance is rather superficial. Catastrophes can be redistributed to the category of Politics, Accidents, Family, Violence, Erotic, Art and Creativity, and so forth.

7 Another quite symptomatic element of RuTube are its banners and ads. For instance, the latest banner congratulating Russian men on Defender of the Motherland day (с Днем защитника Отечества). This is one of the most ideologically charged holidays in Russia and closely related to Soviet tradition. Here, RuTube presents a sort of a schizophrenic mixture of Russian and English text, Playboy-type girls and Hollywood military heroes against the background of cinematic special effects.

8 You can also find debloid videos on YouTube; see for instance www.youtube.com/watch?v=bL-MbMylw7I&feature=related [last checked 15 February 2009].

9 See for example the video "Debloids Russian today" at www.youtube.com/watch?v=Qq4jhQz2mIs or the video "Russian Jackass" at www.youtube.com/watch?v=3SOOTJsHLPA&feature=related [last checked 15 February 2009].

10 For a discussion, see Pierre Bourdieu, *On Television* (New York: The New Press, 1999).

11 There is a joke, possibly containing a grain of truth, that contemporary Russia is really controlled by the top managers of two federal television channels.

12 Paul Boutin, "A Grand Unified Theory of YouTube and MySpace," *Slate* 28 April 2006 – www.slate.com/id/2140635/ [last checked 15 February 2009].

13 Andrei Gornykh & Almira Ousmanova, "Aesthetics of Internet and visual consumption. On the RuNet's essence and specificity," in *Control + Shift. Public and private usages of the Russian Internet*, eds. Henrike Schmidt et al. (Nordersted, Germany: Books on Demand, 2006), pp. 23–40. Also available at www.ruhr-uni-bochum.de/russ-cyb/library/texts/en/control_shift/Gornykh_Ousmanova.pdf [last checked 15 February 2009].

14 Frederic Jameson, *The Cultural Turn. Selected Writings on the Postmodern 1983–1998* (London: Verso, 1998), p. 59.

15 See http://rutube.ru/community.html?page=index [last checked 15 February 2009].

16 See Michel Foucault, *Discipline and Punish: The Birth of the Prison* (New York: Random House, 1975).

17 http://newsdesk.pcmag.ru/node/14171 [last checked 20 February 2009].

18 Yuliya Latynina, "Kod dostupa" – www.echo.msk.ru/programs/code/575489-echo/ [last checked 15 February 2009].

19 Jürgen Habermas, *The Structural Transformation of the Public Sphere* (Cambridge, MA: MIT Press, 2006), p. 73.

20 YouTube is formed in another tradition, that of a public sphere with open rationale debates. As a consequence there are more examples of meaningful dialogues and expert opinions on YouTube than on its Russian clone.

21 Try, for instance, entering the following keywords in RuTube: кавказ сила ("the Caucasus is strength") or Славянский Союз (Slavic Union).

22 Patricia Lange, "Publicly private and privately public: Social networking on YouTube," *Journal of Computer-Mediated Communication* no. 1, 2007, pp. 361-380. Others, such as Danah Boyd, stress the fact that YouTube is not used primarily for the creation of social networks. "Yet while sites like YouTube gained tremendous popularity among youth, teens predominantly used them as content-access and distribution tools rather than networked publics." For a discussion, see Boyd's *Taken Out of Context. American Teen Sociality in Networked Publics* (Berkeley: University of California Press, 2008), p. 64.

23 "Consider Video the Vote, a group of citizens armed with video cameras and YouTube accounts. Members shoot videos of polling places and interview disenfranchised voters for immediate Web posting. Someone in Los Angeles can find out about an Ohio voter who faced a faulty voting machine the same day." Michael Kann et al., "The Internet and youth politi-

cal participation," *First Monday* 12, no. 8, 2007 – http://firstmonday.org/htbin/cgiwrap/bin/ojs/index.php/fm/article/view/ 1977/1852 [last checked 15 February 2009].

24 Vassia Gueorguieva, "Voters, MySpace, and YouTube: The Impact of Alternative Communication," *Social Science Computer Review* no. 3, 2008, pp. 288–300.

25 Chris Maxcer, "Cops nab crooks using YouTube," *TechNewsWorld,* 6 March 2007 – www.technewsworld.com/story/56108.html [last checked 15 February 2009].

Curatorship

Giovanna Fossati

YouTube as a Mirror Maze

When the editors of this book asked me to curate a website on YouTube, I accepted before I even had time to realize the implications of such an assignment. In the following days I began to think about the challenges posed by such a task and I felt much less confident. First of all, it would be impossible, for me as for anyone else, to watch the millions (or is it billions?) of clips on YouTube today. A curator is supposed to have a good knowledge of the collection's content as a whole, which I certainly do not have in the case of YouTube. How was I going to select one hundred clips with the claim that they are in some way representative of the whole?

As a curator at a film archive I usually deal with two main kinds of selection: selecting films to be added to the collection (through either acquisition or restoration) and selecting films to be part of a film program. Selecting is always a painful task because you are aware that selecting something means excluding something else. Furthermore, the adopted selection criteria, no matter how "objective" they are, could be challenged by anybody, including yourself, on any other day.[1] However, a selection is also a means of creating interest in the whole by referring to, and partially including, what is not its central focus. For instance, a program on Western films that includes works that fall outside the traditional scope of the genre is a way to promote interest in a lesser known phenomenon (e.g. travelogues shot in the West of the early 1900s or Western films made in the East).[2] Similar examples can be described for the selection process carried out on a daily basis for film archives' collections. Based on an existing collection policy, curators strive, for example, to enrich a particular corpus of film (e.g. documentaries), and at times they run into less familiar subgenres (e.g. advertising films made to be shown in cinemas). Curators can decide to put forward some of these lesser known films with the aim of stimulating interest, which could grow beyond the vaults of a single archive and even become a new subject of research, selection and programming on an international level. This is one of the reassuring thoughts that make it possible for curators to sleep at night.

But then the online archive came about and a whole new set of possibilities emerged. Due to the turn to the digital, film-archival practice is changing very rapidly and, with it, the way we look at the practices of selecting, preserving and presenting films. New forms of digital archives, accessible on the Internet, make use of participatory media and provide a form of open access that traditional film archives never offered before. Film archive curators are now being confronted with a community of users who are taking the selection process upon themselves. Some think that participatory culture is not all good news, and that it is leading to the flattening of culture.[2] From this perspective, the curator still has an important role as someone leading the way to the culturally or aesthetically relevant in the oceanic flow of the online archive.[3]

I am not going to discuss here whether YouTube can be defined as an archive at all.[4] What I would like to address is rather the question of whether YouTube—and similar participatory online repositories—makes the role of the curator obsolete. In a participatory culture, what is the role of a curator? Should the curator become the voice of a collective entity, or even be replaced by the millions of users who together reshape the archive by uploading and tagging? Or should the curator stick out from the online crowd and lead the way through the maze? I think that the traditional curator can coexist with a new collective one, that is, users. As I have argued elsewhere, the chaperoning role of a film archive, and of its curators, can indeed coexist with open and unchaperoned access to content.[5] Furthermore, I argue that in today's media culture, the chaperone mode is no longer the only appropriate way to provide access to audiovisual content, as a community of users is eager to establish an alternative and more open access mode.

By coexisting, the two "curatorial modes" can in fact reinforce each other. Users can choose to be guided to some unexpected aesthetic revelation and then decide to follow their own streams of thought and association for finding new trails and ignore the expert's suggestions. So, reinforced by the thought that there is still a role for me in the online archival business and that, by selecting one hundred clips from the millions on YouTube, I could both assert the novelty of the new participatory form of archives and reassert the role of the curator, I ventured into YouTube. From the perspective of a film archive curator, I started taking note of the differences and similarities between the traditional archive and the new participatory one. In contrast to a traditional archive, YouTube does not select at the gate. Still, it does have other forms of selection which make clips more or less visible. On YouTube there are for instance mechanisms in place for promoting some clips (e.g. most viewed, recommended, featured, spotlight, rising videos) and for censoring other ones. Censorship is mainly related to copyright issues or to the community filtering out pornographic or violent content.[6] In contrast to traditional archives, everything on YouTube is immediately accessible by everyone at any time, as long as one can find it.

Similarly to a traditional archive, YouTube can be used for serving many different aims and by different user groups. From the student to the professional, from the journalist to the artist, anybody can look into the archive. The archive can also be a source of inspiration for creating something new around a specific theme and aimed at specific target groups. All in all, I came to the conclusion that I could start with my selection as I do for a program to be presented on the screen, letting the films, in this case clips, inspire a selection theme and, in turn, evaluating the theme on the basis of a relatively broad selection. So I chose a central theme that would allow some kind of participation on the part of the viewer. Not in the selection of clips, which would be my task, but in the associations that could be made among the selected clips and within YouTube at large.

The Mirror Maze

The theme, or rather concept, I chose is that of the mirror, further complicated in various ways, a metaphor as it were, which reflects the immediate relationship the user can have with the online archive, unknown in the traditional archive with all its institutional filters. This is how I started my curatorial experience within YouTube and its mirror maze. When uploading a video—YouTube is you in front of a mirror. When looking at your computer screen with the webcam on, you are looking at your own reflection. YouTube reflects you and you reflect (on) YouTube. On the other side of the mirror, all YouTubers are watching. For the YouTuber watching, YouTube is hence a mirror maze. Reflections are endless and endlessly reflected into one another. Finding the way out of the mirror maze is as difficult as not clicking the mouse for the next clip, the next mirror.

These thoughts led the way to the conception of www.youtube-reader.com. The website is being realized at the time of this writing by Non Square Pigs, a group of animators, graphic artists and designers based in Berlin who have a highly visual approach to Web design.[7] Confronted with the challenge of selecting one hundred clips that are representative of the millions now online on YouTube, I chose a loose curatorial approach. The mirror should not impose itself as an intruding chaperone, as it works as a visual suggestion in tune with its subject matter. In this perspective, the mirror is meant to be a visual metaphor (what does YouTube look like?) rather than an ontological one (what is YouTube?). YouTube as a mirror, not YouTube is a mirror. YouTube looks like a mirror, behaves like a mirror but is not necessarily a mirror.

YouTube as a mirror reflects all kind of things. The kinds of reflection selected for the website are obviously just a few. Although I tried to choose clips that are representative of many different reflections, my selection could not possibly testify to the richness and the complexity of all the clips online today. Some of the clips that appear on www.youtubereader.com reflect YouTube's (relatively short) life span and some of its milestones. For instance, "Me at the Zoo" is considered the first video ever uploaded to YouTube, on April 23, 2005, while "Evolution of Dance," with its 118,045,248 views (as of April, 19, 2009) is one of the three all-time most viewed clips on the website. However, I did not aim at representing the history of YouTube, as others have done so already in various interesting ways, as is the case of "Internet Memes," a chronology of memes that includes many YouTube milestones.[8] My selection includes both the very popular and the almost unknown, aiming at creating a reflection of the diversity on YouTube, in terms of views also. I cannot deny, however, that I privileged the fairly popular ones.

Within the mirror concept, I have identified four categories into which the clips can be loosely sorted: reflections, global reflections, (meta)reflections and the mirror paradox. They can, of course, be associated in many other ways, for instance by looking at traditional categories, e.g. genre, mise-en-scène, image content and topic. I have selected YouTuber's reflections of and on themselves, life, everyday trivialities and big issues, special personal moments and global events.

Reflections can be monologues, as in the case of "Leave Britney Alone!", "Greg's Vlog" and "First Blog/Dorkiness Prevails," the kinds of reflection celebrated by "Young Girls Talking About Herself." On YouTube, self-reflections often turn into elaborate self-expressions when the message recorded is not merely a monologue for the camera but rather the expression of individual creativity. Playback singing and dance sequences can be one of any form of reflection, in the same way as the classics "Numa Numa," "Chocolate Rain" and "Star Wars Kid" or the collective dance performance of "OK Go—Here It Goes Again." Even a toothbrush or shaving session results in a reflection where my gaze as a viewer is placed literally behind a mirror, as in "Brushing Teeth Song!" and "Straight Razor Shave." The YouTube favorites, babies and puppies, also result in reflections in the YouTube maze of mirrors, as is very literally the case with "Puppy attacks mirror."

Some reflections have spread throughout the community and grown out of YouTube to become material for re-uploading as global reflections. Reflections of single users have spread through the community of YouTubers, leading at times to global expressions like the "Free Hugs Campaign" or the happenings staged by ImprovEverywhere, such as "Human Mirror" or "Frozen Grand Central." YouTubers also reflect on all kinds of other media, and on YouTube itself. These (meta)reflections include the lecture on YouTube given by Michael Wesch at the Library of Congress in 2008 and viewed by a million people, "An anthropological introduction to YouTube," as well as the musical number "The Internet Is For Porn" with its nuance-free analysis of the Internet, whereas "Will It Blend?—iPhone" reflects on Apple's mobile phone in an unexpected way. The beloved puppy is also the object of (meta)reflections in "Spaghetti Cat (I Weep For You)". Next to the phone, the television and the phonograph—see for example "Prince Buster"—movies are another all-time favorite topic of reflection, relating to typographical style ("Pulp Fiction in Motion Graphics") or flipbook animation ("Matrix style flipbook animation"), or by old-school film critics ("Reel Geezers—The Curious Case of Benjamin Button")

Another recurring effect on YouTube, that of the mirror paradox, brings together clips reflecting each other endlessly. A kaleidoscope, if you wish, where all the recycled clips, sequels, responses, remakes, spin-offs, etcetera create those multiplying reflections typical of the YouTube maze. The clip "OK Go" includes remakes as a "wallpaper version" and a Lego version. Of the animation clip "Charlie the Unicorn," there is, among many others, a "high version." The "Algorithm March" has been performed in all kinds of contexts, including that of the Filipino prisoners, as unexpected a presence on YouTube as it is the Chipmunk, recycled and remade in thousand different ways.

As mentioned earlier, there are other ways to associate the clips on www.youtubereader.com, for instance, based on genre, mise-en-scène, image content and topic, categories derived from a more traditional approach to audiovisual archiving. Vlogs (video logs) have the same mise-en-scène, usually a person talking into a camera placed in front of her or him. The same applies to many clips portraying animals, such as "Greg's Vlog" and "Lemur." Also, a vlog, a music video and a clip in typographical style can be linked by topic, for instance Barack Obama, as in the case of "Obama sells his Soul to the Devil," "Yes We Can—Barack Obama Music Video" and "Barack Obama's Election Night Speech: Kinetic Typography." The genre of animation encompasses extremely different clips, such as "Matrix style flipbook animation," an all-analog animation concept, and "Line Rider—Jagged Peak Adventure," an all-digital "internet physics toy," as defined on Wikipedia.[9] In terms of image content "Star Wars Kid—Agent Smith Fight" contains images from the YouTube classic "Star Wars Kid," who replaces Neo in the highly stylized fight against the multiplying Agent Smith in *The Matrix Reloaded*, or the many spin-offs of the *kid scary* clip that all contain the original thing. As for the mirror categories, these ways of associating clips, which crisscross the reflections discussed earlier in other directions and through other dimensions, are also only a few of the many possibilities I identified while selecting the clips for the website.

Finally, the idea of YouTube as a mirror is meant as a suggestive metaphor. By no means an exhaustive one. The mirror, with its derived categories, is rather a productive concept meant to stimulate associations and to formulate more metaphors. And now, to experience your own mirror maze and curate your own reflections on YouTube clips, please visit www.youtubereader.com.

Endnotes

1 The idea of archives as the remains of what has been lost rather than what has been kept relates to Jacques Derrida's discussion of archives in his *Mal d'Archive: une impression freudienne* (Paris: Galilée, 1995). For a discussion, see William Uricchio, "Archives and Absences," *Film History* no. 3, 1995, pp. 256–263.

2 With this respect I would like to refer to Nanna Verhoeff's book on early Western films, *The West in Early Cinema. After the Beginning* (Amsterdam: Amsterdam University Press, 2006) and the film program "100 Years of Westerns" at the Nederlands Filmmuseum in 2002.

3 This perspective has been taken even further by Paolo Cherchi Usai et al. as they normatively state that, "as [an] interpreter of history through the audiovisual collection for the benefit of present and future generations, the curator must ensure that the work is experienced in a form as close as possible to the way it was intended to be seen and/or heard at the time of its creation." See Cherchi Usai et al., eds., *Film Curatorship. Archives, Museums, and the Digital Marketplace,* (Vienna: Synema Publikationen, 2008), p. 153.

4 See Frank Kessler and Mirko Tobias Schäfer's article in this book for an account on the discussion concerning whether YouTube can be considered a proper archive or not.

5 Giovanna Fossati and Nanna Verhoeff, "Beyond Distribution: Some Thoughts on the Future of Archival Films," in *Networks of Entertainment. Early Film Distribution 1895-1915*, eds. Frank Kessler & Nanna Verhoeff (Eastleigh, England: John Libbey Publishing, 2007), pp. 331–339; Giovanna Fossati, *From Grain to Pixel. The Archival Life of Film in Transition* (Amsterdam: Amsterdam University Press, forthcoming in 2009).

6 See www.youtube.com/t/community_guidelines for details on what kind of content YouTube does not allow. Also, see YouTomb (http://youtomb.mit.edu/) for an overview of "dead" clips.

7 See www.non-sqare-pigs.com [last checked 15 May 2009].

8 See for example www.dipity.com/tatercakes/Internet_Memes. For a definition of "meme" see http://en.wikipedia.org/wiki/Memes [last checked 15 May 2009]. Other historical accounts of YouTube can also be found at www.youtubereader.com in the clips "The History of YouTube" and "An anthropological introduction to YouTube."

9 See http://en.wikipedia.org/wiki/Linerider [last checked 15 May 2009].

General Bibliography

Adams, Josh, "White Supremacists, Oppositional Culture and the World Wide Web." *Social Forces* no. 2, 2005, pp. 759–778.

Allen, A., "Battling in the Name of Balance: Evaluating Solutions to Copyright Conflict in Viacom International v. You Tube." *Brigham Young University Law Review* no. 14, 2007, pp. 1023–1054.

Anden-Papadopoulos, Kari, "US Soldiers Imaging the Iraq War on YouTube." *Popular Communication* no. 1, 2009, pp. 17-27.

Anderson, Chris, *The Long Tail* (New York: Hyperion, 2006).

Aoun, Steven, "iPod and Youtube and Everyone we Know." *Metro* no. 152, 2007, pp. 166–175.

Ardito, Stephanie C., "MySpace and YouTube Meet the Copyright Cops." *Searcher* no. 5, 2007, pp. 24–34.

Arseth, Espen, "The Culture and Business of Cross-media Productions." *Popular Communications* no. 3, 2006, pp. 203–211.

Arvidsson, Adam, "Brands: A Critical Perspective." *Journal of Consumer Culture* no. 5, 2005, pp. 235–258.

Arvidsson, Adam, "Creative Class or Administrative Class? On Advertising and the 'Underground.' " *Ephemera* no. 1, 2007, www.ephemeraweb.org.

Arvidsson, Adam, "The Ethical Economy of Customer Coproduction." *Journal of Macromarketing* no. 4, 2008, pp. 326–338.

Atkinson, S. and H. Nixon, "Locating the Subject: Teens online @ ninemsn." *Discourse: Studies in the Cultural Politics of Education* no. 3, 2005, pp. 387–409.

Baker, Wayne E. and Robert F. Faulkner, "Interorganizational Networks." Joel Baum, ed., *The Blackwell Companion to Organizations* (Malden: Blackwell, 2005), pp. 520–540.

Baluja, S., and R. Seth et al., "Video Suggestion and Discovery for YouTube: Taking Random Walks Through the View Graph." *Proceedings of the 17th International Conference on World Wide Web*, Beijing, China, 21–25 April 2008 [retrievable online].

Banerjee, Anirban, and Dhiman Barman, "Characterizing Quality of Content Distribution from YouTube Like Portals." *Proceedings of the 2007 ACM CoNEXT Conference*, New York, NY, 10–13 December 2007 [retrievable online].

Banks, John, and Sal Humphreys, "The Labour of User Co-Creators: Emergent Social Network Markets?" *Convergence: The International Journal of Research into New Media Technologies* no. 4, 2008, pp. 401–418.

Barnes, Susan B., and Neil F. Hair, "From Banners to YouTube: Using the Rear-View Mirror to Look at the Future of Internet Advertising." Working paper, Rochester Institute of Technology, 2007 [retrievable online].

Barnouw, Erik, *Tube of Plenty. The Evolution of American Television* (New York: Oxford University Press, 1975).

Barnouw, Erik, *The Sponsor. Notes on a Modern Potentate* (New York: Oxford University Press, 1978).

Bauwens, Michel, "Class and Capital in Peer Production." *Capital & Class* no 97, 2009, pp. 121–141.

Baym, Nancy K., "The New Shape of Online Community: The Example of Swedish Independent Music Fandom." *First Monday* no. 8, August 2007, www.firstmonday.org.

Beavin Bavelas, Janet, and Linda Coates et al., "Listener Responses as a Collaborative Process: The Role of Gaze." *Journal of Communication* September 2002, pp. 566–580.

Beer, David, "Making Friends with Jarvis Cocker: Music Culture in the Context of Web 2.0." *Cultural Sociology* no. 2, 2008, pp. 222–241.

Benevenuto, Fabricio, and Fernando Duarte et al., "Characterizing Video Responses in Social Networks." ArXiv.org, Cornell University Library, 30 April 2008 [retrievable online].

Benevenuto, Fabricio, and Tiago Rodrigues et al., "Identifying Video Spammers in Online Social Networks." *Proceedings of the 4th International Workshop on Adversarial Information Retrieval on the Web*, Beijing, China, 22 April 2008 [retrievable online].

Benkler, Yochai, *The Wealth of Networks: How Social Production Transforms Markets and Freedom* (New Haven: Yale University Press, 2006).

Biederman, Charles, and Danny Andrews, "Applying Copyright Law to User-Generated Content." *Los Angeles Lawyer* no. 31, 2008, pp. 12–18.

Bilton, Chris, *Management and Creativity: From Creative Industries to Creative Management* (Malden, MA: Blackwell, 2007).

Bolter, Jay David, and Richard Grusin, *Remediation: Understanding New Media* (Cambridge, MA: MIT Press, 1999).

Bortree, D.S., "Presentation of Self on the Web: An Ethnographic Study of Teenage Girls' Weblogs." *Education, Communication & Information* no. 1, 2005, pp. 25–39.

Botello, Chris, and Doug Sahlin, *YouTube for Dummies* (Indianapolis: Wiley Publishing, 2007).

Bromberg, Heather, "Are MUDs Communities? Identity, Belonging and Consciousness in Virtual Worlds." Rob Shields, ed., *Cultures of Internet: Virtual Spaces, Real Histories, Living Bodies* (London: Sage, 1996), pp. 143–152.

Brouwers, Janneke, "YouTube vs. O-Tube: Negotiating a YouTube Identity." *Cultures of Arts, Science and Technology* no. 1, 2008, pp. 106–120.

Brown, Jeffery C., "Copyright Infringement Liability for Video Sharing Networks: Grokster Redux or Breaking New Ground under the Digital Millennium Copyright Act." *The Computer and Internet Lawyer* no. 12, 2006, pp. 10–17.

Burgess, Jean, " 'All Your Chocolate Rain Are Belong to Us?' Viral Video, YouTube, and the Dynamics of Participatory Culture." Geert Lovink & Sabine Niederer, eds., *The Video Vortex Reader: Responses to YouTube* (Amsterdam: Institute of Network Cultures, 2008), pp. 101–109.

Burgess, Jean, *Vernacular Creativity and New Media* (PhD thesis, Creative Industries Faculty, QUT, 2007).

Burgess, Jean, and Joshua Green, "Agency and Controversy in the YouTube Community." Paper presented at Internet Research 9.0: Rethinking Community, Rethinking Place, University of Copenhagen, Denmark, 15 October 2008 [retrievable online].

Burgess, Jean, and Joshua Green, *Online Video and Participatory Culture* (London: Polity Press, 2009).

Burkhalter, B., "Reading Race Online: Discovering Racial Identity In Usenet Discussions." A. Smith & P. Kollock, eds., *Communities in Cyberspace* (London: Routledge, 1999), pp. 60–75.

Burton, A., "YouTube-ing Your Way to Neurological Knowledge." *Lancet Neurology* no. 12, 2008, pp. 1086–1087.

Bush, Vannevar, "As We May Think." *Atlantic Monthly* no. 108, 1945 [retrievable online].

Bush, Vannevar, *Science is Not Enough* (New York: Morrow, 1969).

Bustamante, Enrique, "Cultural Industries in the Digital Age: Some Provisional Conclusions." *Media, Culture, and Society* no. 6, 2004, pp. 803–820.

Butcher, M., *Transnational Television, Cultural Identity and Change* (London: Sage, 2003).

Caldwell, John T., *Production Culture. Industrial Reflexivity and Critical Practice in Film and Television* (Durham, London: Duke University Press, 2008).

Callon, Michel, "Introduction: The Embeddedness of Economic Markets in Economics." Michel Callon, ed., *The Laws of the Market* (London: Blackwell, 1995), pp. 1–57.

Callon, Michel, "Variety and Irreversibility in Networks of Technique Conception and Adoption." D. Foray & C. Freeman, eds., *Technology and the Wealth of Nations. Dynamics of Constructed Advantage* (London: Pinter, 1993), pp. 232–268.

Capra, Robert G., and Christopher A. Lee et al., "Selection and context scoping for digital video collections: an investigation of youtube and blogs." *Proceedings of the 8th ACM/IEEE-CS Joint Conference on Digital Libraries*, Pittsburgh, PA, 2008 [retrievable online].

Carlson, J., and E. Heeschen et al., "Communicating to Generation Y: Dietetic Interns Dissect You Tube Videos to Define What Is Necessary to Use It as a Communication Medium." *Journal of the American Dietetic Association* no. 9, 2008, p. A17.

Carlson, Tom, and Kim Strandberg, "Riding the Web 2.0 Wave: Candidates on YouTube in the 2007 Finnish National Elections." Paper presented at the 4th General Conference of the European Consortium of Political Research, Pisa, Italy, 6–8 September 2007 [retrievable online].

Carr, Nicholas, *The Big Switch: Rewiring the World from Edison to Google* (New York: Norton, 2008).

Carroll, Samantha, "The Practical Politics of Step-Stealing and Textual Poaching: YouTube, Audio-Visual Media and Contemporary Swing Dancers Online." *Convergence* no. 14, 2008, pp. 183–204.

Castells, Manuel "Communication, Power and Counter-Power in the Network Society." *International Journal of Communication* no. 1, 2007, pp. 238–266.

Caves, Richard E., *Creative Industries. Contracts Between Art and Commerce* (Cambridge, MA: Harvard University Press, 2000).

Cha, Meeyoung, and Haewoon Kwak et al., "I Tube, You Tube, Everybody Tubes: Analyzing the World's Largest User Generated Content Video System." *Proceedings of the 7th ACM SIGCOMM Conference on Internet Measurement*, San Diego, CA, 24–26 October 2007 [retrievable online].

Chalfen, Richard, *Snapshots Versions of Life* (Bowling Green, OH: Bowling Green State University Popular Press, 1997).

Chen, Hsinchun, and Sven Thoms et al., "Cyber Extremism in Web 2.0: An Exploratory Study of International Jihadist Groups." Paper presented at the IEEE International Conference on Intelligence and Security Informatics, Taiwan, 17–20 June 2008 [retrievable online].

Cheng, V. J., *Inauthentic: The Anxiety over Culture and Identity* (New Brunswick, NJ: Rutgers University Press, 2004).

Cheng, Xu, and Cameron Dale et al., "Statistics and Social Network of YouTube Videos." *Quality of Service*, 2008, pp. 229–238.

Cheng, Xu, and Cameron Dale et al., "Understanding the Characteristics of Internet Short Video Sharing: YouTube as a Case Study." ArXiv.org, Cornell University Library, 25 July 2007 [retrievable online].

Cherny, Lynn, *Conversation and Community: Chat in a Virtual World* (Stanford: CLSI Publications, 1999).

Cherny, Lynn and E.R. Weise, eds., *Wired Women: Gender and New Realities in Cyberspace* (Seattle: Seal Press, 1996).

Christensen, Christian, "Uploading Dissonance: YouTube and the US Occupation of Iraq." *Media, War & Conflict* no. 2, 2008, pp. 155–175.

Christensen, Christian, "YouTube: The Evolution of Media?" *Screen Education* no. 45, 2007, pp. 36–40.

Christensen, Christian, and Miyase Christensen, "The Afterlife of Eurovision 2003: Turkish and European Social Imaginaries and Ephemeral Communicative Space." *Popular Communication* no. 3, 2009 (forthcoming).

Clark, Jason A., "YouTube University: Using XML, Web Services, and Online Video Services to Serve University and Library Video Content." Laura B. Cohen, ed., *Library 2.0 Initiatives in Academic Libraries* (Chicago: Association of College & Research Libraries, 2007), pp. 156–166.

Clark, Thomas, and Julie Stewart, "Promoting Academic Programs Using Online Videos." *Business Communication Quarterly* no. 70, 2007, pp. 478–482.

Clothier, Ian M., "Created Identities: Hybrid Cultures and the Internet." *Convergence: The Journal of Research into New Media Technologies* no. 4, 2005, pp. 44–59.

Coe, Neil, and Jennifer Johns, "Beyond Production Clusters: Towards A Critical Political Economy of Networks in the Film and Television Industries." Allen J. Scott & D. Power, eds., *The Cultural Industries and the Production of Culture* (London, New York: Routledge, 2004), pp. 188–204.

Cohen, Michael A. and Maria Figueroa Küpçü, "Congress and the 'YouTube War.' " *World Policy Journal* no. 4, 2006/07, pp. 49–54.

Cottle, Simon, ed., *Media Organization and Production* (London: Sage, 2003).

Couldry, Nick, "Liveness, 'Reality,' and the Mediated Habitus from Television to the Mobile Phone." *Communication Review* no. 4, 2004, pp. 353–361.

Crane, R., and D. Sornette, "Viral, Quality, and Junk Videos on YouTube: Separating Content From Noise in an Information-Rich Environment." *Proceedings of AAAI Symposium on Social Information Processing*, 2008 [retrievable online].

Crary, Jonathan, *Suspensions of Perception. Attention, Spectacle and Modern Culture* (Cambridge, MA.: MIT Press, 1999).

Croteau, David, "The Growth of Self-Produced Media Content and the Challenge to Media Studies." *Critical Studies in Media Communication* no. 4, 2006, pp. 340–344.

Cubitt, Sean, "Codecs and Capability." Geert Lovink & Sabine Niederer, eds., *The Video Vortex Reader: Responses to YouTube* (Amsterdam: Institute of Network Cultures, 2008), pp. 45–51.

Cunningham, Stuart, "Creative Industries as Policy and Discourse Outside the United Kingdom." *Global Media and Communication* no. 3, 2007, pp. 347–352.

Cunningham, Stuart, *In the Vernacular: A Generation of Australian Culture and Controversy* (St. Lucia, Australia: University of Queensland Press, 2008).

Deuze, Mark, *Media Work* (Cambridge, MA: Polity Press, 2007).

Dijck, José van, "Homecasting: The end of broadcasting?" *Vodavone Receiver Magazine* no. 18, 2007 [retrievable online].

Dijck, José van, "Television 2.0: YouTube and the Emergence of Homecasting." Paper presented at Creativity, Ownership and Collaboration in the Digital Age, Cambridge, Massachusetts Institute of Technology, 27–29 April 2007 [retrievable online].

Dijck, José van, "Users like you? Theorizing Agency in User-generated Content." *Media, Culture & Society* no. 1, 2009, pp. 41–58.

Dreyfus, Hubert L., *On the Internet* (London: Routledge, 2001).

Driscoll, Michael, "Will YouTube Sail Into the DMCA's Safe Harbor or Sink for Internet Piracy?" *John Marshall Law School Review of Intellectual Property Law* no. 6, 2007 [retrievable online].

Driskell, Robyn Bateman, and Larry Lyon, "Are Virtual Communities True Communities? Examining the Environments and Elements of Community." *City & Community* 1, no. 4, 2002, pp. 373–390.

Duffy, Peter, "Engaging the YouTube Google-Eyed Generation: Strategies for Using Web 2.0 in Teaching and Learning." *Proceedings of the 6th Conference on E-learning*, Copenhagen Business School, Denmark, 4–5 October 2007 [retrievable online].

Duncan, Starkey, and Donald W. Fiske, *Face-to-Face Interaction: Research, Methods, and Theory* (New York/Toronto: John Wiley & Sons, 1977).

Earls, Mark, "Advertising to the Herd: How Understanding Our True Nature Challenges the Ways We Think About Advertising and Market Research." *International Journal of Market Research* no. 3, 2003, pp. 311–336.

Elsaesser, Thomas, " 'Constructive Instability,' or: The Life of Things as the Cinema's Afterlife?" Geert Lovink & Sabine Niederer, eds., *The Video Vortex Reader. Responses to YouTube* (Amsterdam: Institute of Network Cultures, 2008), pp. 13–32.

Ernst, Wolfgang, "The Archive as Metaphor. From Archival Space to Archival Time." *Open* no. 7, 2004, pp. 46–54.

Faris, Robert, and Stephanie Wang et al., "Censorship 2.0." *Innovations* no. 2, 2008, pp. 165–187.

Faulkner, Susan, and Jay Melican, "Getting Noticed, Showing-Off, Being Overheard: Amateurs, Authors and Artists Inventing and Reinventing Themselves in Online Communities." *Ethnographic Praxis in Industry Conference Proceedings*, Colorado, 2007 [retrievable online].

Flew, Terry, "Not Yet the Internet Election: Online Media, Political Commentary and the 2007 Australian Federal Election. Media International Australia Incorporating Culture and Policy." *Media International Australia*, no. 126, 2008 [retrievable online].

Fornäs, Johan et al., eds., *Digital Borderlands: Cultural Studies of Identity and Interactivity on the Internet* (New York: Peter Lang, 2002).

Foucault, Michel, *The Archaeology of Knowledge* (London: Routledge, 2006).

Freeman, Becky, and Simon Chapman, "Is 'You Tube' Telling or Selling You Something? Tobacco Content on the YouTube Video-Sharing Website." *Tobacco Control* no. 16, 2007, pp. 207–210.

Freitas, D., and J. Buckenmeyer et al., "YouTube.com for Teachers: A Useful Resource or Just More Hijinks?" *Proceedings of Society for Information Technology and Teacher Education International Conference*, Chesapeake, VA, 2008 [retrievable online].

Frey, Andrea, "To Sue or Not to Sue: Video-Sharing Web Sites, Copyright Infringement, and the Inevitability of Corporate Control." *Brooklyn Journal of Corporate, Financial & Commercial Law* no. 2, 2007, pp. 23–30.

Fülbier, Ulrich, "Web 2.0: Haftungsprivilegierungen bei MySpace und YouTube." *Computer und Recht* no. 8, 2007, pp. 515–520.

Galloway, Alexander, *Protocol. How Control Exists after Decentralization* (Cambridge, MA: MIT, 2004).

Garnham, Nicholas, *Capitalism and Communication: Global Culture and the Economics of Information* (London: Sage, 1990).

Geisler, G. and Burns, S., "Tagging Video: Conventions and Strategies of the YouTube Community." *Proceedings of the 7th ACM/IEEE-CS Joint Conference on Digital Libraries*, Vancouver, BC, 18–23 June 2007 [retrievable online].

Gershuny, Jonathan, *Changing Times: Work and Leisure in Postindustrial Society* (Oxford: Oxford University Press, 2000).

Gill, P., and M. Arlitt et al., "Characterizing User Sessions on YouTube." *Proceedings of The International Society for Optical Engineering* 6818, 2008 [retrievable online].

Gill, P., and M. Arlitt et al., "Youtube Traffic Characterization: A View From the Edge." *Proceedings of the 7th ACM SIGCOMM Conference on Internet Measurement*, San Diego, CA, 24–26 October 2007 [retrievable online].

Gladwell, Malcolm, *The Tipping Point: How Little Things Can Make a Big Difference* (New York: Little Brown, 2000).

Goldhaber, Michael H., "The Attention Economy and the Net." *First Monday* no. 2, 1997 [retrievable online].

Gomery, Douglas, *A History of Broadcasting in the United States* (Oxford: Blackwell, 2008).

Gonzalez, V.M., and S.H. Kurniawan, "On New Media for Intergenerational Communication: The Case of Geriatric1927." *Proceedings of 2008 IEEE International Symposium on Technology and Society*, Fredericton, NB, 25–28 June 2008 [retrievable online].

Graham, Phil, *Hypercapitalism: New Media, Language, and Social Perceptions of Value* (New York: Peter Lang, 2005).

Granovetter, M., "The Strength of Weak Ties." *The American Journal of Sociology* no. 6, 1973, pp. 1360–1380.

Griffith, David & Bryan McKinney, "Can Heather Gillette Save YouTube? Internet Service Providers and Copyright Liability." *Issues in Information Systems* no. 2, 2007, pp. 225–226.

Griffith, Margaret, "Looking for You: An Analysis of Video Blogs." Presented at the Annual Meeting of the Association for Education in Journalism and Mass Communication, Washington, DC, 8 August 2007 [retrievable online].

Grusin, Richard, "Premediation." *Criticism* no. 1, 2004, pp. 17–39.

Gueorguieva, Vassia, "Voters, MySpace, and YouTube: The Impact of Alternative Communication Channels on the 2006 Election Cycle and Beyond." *Social Science Computer Review* no. 3, 2008, pp. 288–300.

Halvey, Martin J., and Mark T. Keane, "Exploring Social Dynamics in Online Media Sharing." *Proceedings of the 16th International Conference on World Wide Web*, Banff, AB, 2007 [retrievable online].

Hardey, Michael, "Life Beyond the Screen: Embodiment and Identity Through the Internet." *Sociological Review* no. 4, 2002, pp. 570–586.

Hardt, Michael, "Affective Labor." *Boundary* no. 2, 1999, pp. 89–100.

Harley, Ross, "Totally Busted: Do We Need A YouTube For Video Art?" Paper presented at the Video Art Archive Network Forum, Gallery Loop, Yonsei University, Seoul, 8–9 November 2007 [retrievable online].

Hartley, John, "YouTube, Digital Literacy and the Growth of Knowledge." Paper presented at the Media@Lse Fifth Anniversary Conference, London, September 2008 [retrievable online].

Hayles, N.K., *How We Became Posthuman* (Chicago: University of Chicago Press, 1999).

Hilderbrand, Lucas, "YouTube: Where Cultural Memory and Copyright Converge." *Film Quarterly* no. 1, 2007, pp. 48–57.

Hilmes, Michele, ed., *NBC. America's Network* (Berkeley, Los Angeles, London: University of California Press, 2007).

Hossler, Eric W., and Michael P. Conroy, "YouTube as a Source of Information on Tanning Bed Use." *Archives of Dermatology* no. 10, 2008, pp. 1395–1396.

Hunt, Kurt, "Copyright and YouTube: Pirate's Playground or Fair Use Forum?" *Michigan Telecommunications and Technology Law Review* no. 1, 2007, pp. 197–222.

Hunter, Philip, "Pakistan YouTube Block Exposes Fundamental Internet Security Weakness: Concern that Pakistani Action Affected YouTube Access Elsewhere in World." *Computer Fraud & Security*, no. 4, 2008, pp. 10–11.

Illouz, Eva, *Oprah and the Glamour of Misery: An Essay on Popular Culture* (New York: Columbia University Press, 2003).

Jacobs, Katrien, *Netporn: DIY Web Culture and Sexual Politics* (Lanham, MD: Rowman & Littlefield, 2007).

Jarrett, Kylie, "Beyond Broadcast Yourself TM: The Future of YouTube." *Media International Australia* no. 126, 2008, pp. 132–145.

Jenkins, Henry, "Game Design as Narrative Architecture." Noah Wardrip-Fruin & Pat Harrigan, eds., *First Person* (Cambridge, MA: MIT Press, 2004), pp. 118–130.

Jenkins, Henry, *Confronting the Challenges of Participatory Culture: Media Education for the 21st Century* (Chicago: MacArthur Foundation, 2006).

Jenkins, Henry, *Convergence Culture. Where Old and New Media Collide* (New York: New York University Press, 2006).

Jenkins, Henry, "From YouTube to YouNiversity." *Chronicle of Higher Education* no. 24 2007, pp. 9–10.

Jenkins, Henry, "From YouTube to WeTube . . ." *Confessions of an Aca-Fan*, HenryJenkins.org, 2007.

Jenkins, Henry, "Learning from YouTube: An Interview with Alexandra Juhasz." *Confessions of an Aca-Fan*, HenryJenkins.org, 2007.

Jenkins, Henry, "Nine Propositions Towards a Cultural Theory." *Confessions of an Aca-Fan*, HenryJenkins.org, 2008.

Jordan, L. Ashley, "Broadcasting Yourself (and Others): How YouTube and Blogging have Changed the Rules of the Campaign." *Hinckley Journal of Politics*, 2008, pp. 75–84.

Jusasz, Alexandra, "Documentary on YouTube: The Failure of the Direct Cinema of the Slogan." Thomas Austin, ed., *Re-Thinking Documentary* (New York: McGraw Hill, 2008), pp. 13–23.

Jusasz, Alexandra, "The 5 Lessons of YouTube." *Cinema Journal* no. 2, 2008, pp. 145–150.

Jusasz, Alexandra, "Why Not (to) Teach on YouTube." Geert Lovink & Sabine Niederer, eds., *The Video Vortex Reader: Responses to YouTube* (Amsterdam: Institute of Network Cultures, 2008), pp. 133–139.

Kambouri, Nelli, and Pavlos Hatzopoulos, "Making Violent Practices Public." Geert Lovink & Sabine Niederer, eds., *The Video Vortex Reader: Responses to YouTube* (Amsterdam: Institute of Network Cultures, 2008), pp. 125–131.

Kampman, Minke, "Flagging or Fagging: (Self-)Censorship of Gay Content on YouTube." Geert Lovink & Sabine Niederer, eds., *The Video Vortex Reader: Responses to YouTube* (Amsterdam: Institute of Network Cultures, 2008), pp. 153–160.

Karpovich, Angelina I., "Reframing Fan Videos." Jamie Sexton, ed., *Music, Sound and Multimedia: From the Live to the Virtual* (Edinburgh: Edinburgh University Press, 2007), pp. 17–28.

Keelan, Jennifer et al., "YouTube as a Source of Information on Immunization: A Content Analysis." *Journal of the American Medical Association* no. 21, 2007, pp. 1424–1425.

Keen, Andrew, *The Cult of the Amateur: How Today's Internet is Killing Our Culture and Assaulting Our Economy* (London: Nicholas Brealey Publishing, 2007).

Keil, Charlie & Shelley Stamp, "Introduction," Charlie Keil & Shelley Stamp, eds., *American Cinema's Transitional Era: Audiences, Institutions, Practices* (Berkeley: University of California Press, 2004), pp. 1–14.

Kessler, Charles, "Where Were You When YouTube Was Born?" *Journal of Brand Management* no. 3, 2007, pp. 207–210.

Kinder, Marsha, "Hotspots, Avatars and Narrative Fields Forever: Buñuel's Legacy for New Digital Media and Interactive Database Narrative." *Film Quarterly* no. 4, 2002 [retrievable online].

Kirschenbaum, Matthew G., *Mechanisms: New Media and the Forensic Imagination* (Cambridge, MA: MIT Press, 2008).

Kozlowski, Jonathan, "You Tube: Contagious Communications." *Law Enforcement Technology* no. 11, 2007, pp. 22–29.

Kruitbosch, Gijs, and Frank Nack, "Broadcast Yourself on YouTube: Really?" *Proceedings of the 3rd ACM International Workshop on Human-centered Computing*, Vancouver, BC, 31 October 2008 [retrievable online].

Kumar, Parul, "Locating the Boundary between Fair Use and Copyright Infringement: The Viacom – YouTube Dispute." *Journal of Intellectual Property Law & Practice* 184, no. 1, 2008, pp. 775–778.

De Laat, Paul B., "Online Diaries: Eintrag nach Cunninham, Stuart, Reflections on Trust, Privacy, and Exhibitionism." *Ethics and Information Technology* no. 1, 2008, pp. 57–69.

Lamerichs, Nicolle, "It's a Small World After All: Metafictional Fan Videos on YouTube." *Cultures of Arts, Science and Technology* no. 1, 2008, pp. 52–71.

Landry, Brian M., and Mark Guzdial, "Art or Circus? Characterizing User-Created Video on YouTube." *SIC Technical Reports*, Georgia Institute of Technology, 2008 [retrievable online].

Lange, Patricia G., "Commenting on Comments: Investigating Responses to Antagonism on YouTube." Paper presented at the Society for Applied Anthropology Conference, Tampa, FL, 31 March 2007 [retrievable online].

Lange, Patricia G., "Getting to Know You: Using Hostility to Reduce Anonymity in Online Communication." *Proceedings of the Thirteenth Annual Symposium about Language and Society* no. 49, 2006, pp. 95–107.

Lange, Patricia G., "(Mis)conceptions About YouTube." Geert Lovink & Sabine Niederer, eds., *The Video Vortex Reader: Responses to YouTube* (Amsterdam: Institute of Network Cultures, 2008), pp. 87–99.

Lange, Patricia G., "Publicly Private and Privately Public: Social Networking on YouTube" *Journal of Computer-Mediated Communication* no. 1, 2007, pp. 361–380.

Latour, Bruno, *Laboratory Life. The Construction of Scientific Facts* (Princeton, N.J: Princeton University Press, 1986).

Latour, Bruno, *Reassembling the Social. An Introduction to Actor-Network-Theory* (Oxford: Oxford University Press, 2005).

Latour, Bruno, *We Have Never Been Modern* (Cambridge, MA: Harvard University Press, 1993).

Lazzarato, Maurizio, "Immaterial Labour." Paulo Virno & Michael Hardt, eds., *Radical Thought in Italy: A Potential Politics* (Minneapolis: University of Minnesota Press, 1996), pp. 133–150.

Leadbeater, Charlie and Paul Miller, *The Pro-Am Revolution* (London: Demos, 2001).

Lee, Jin, "Locality Aware Peer Assisted Delivery: The Way to Scale Internet Video to the World." Paper presented at Packet Video 2007, Lausanne, Switzerland, 12–13 November 2007 [retrievable online].

Lessig, Lawrence, *Code: Version 2.0* (New York: Basic Books, 2006).

Lessig, Lawrence, *The Future of Ideas: The Fate of the Commons in a Connected World* (New York: Vintage, 2002).

Lessig, Lawrence, *Remix – Making Art and Commerce Strive in the Hybrid Economy* (New York: Penguin Press, 2008).

Liao, Michael, and Randall Young, "YouTube for Ultrasound Education." *Academic Emergency Medicine* no. 1, 2008, p. 226.

Lim, Joon Soo, and Eyun-Jung Ki, "Resistance to Ethically Suspicious Parody Video on YouTube - A Test of Inoculation Theory." *Journalism & Mass Communication Quarterly* no 84, 2007, pp. 713–728.

Lin, Wei-Hao, and Alexander Hauptmann, "Identifying Ideological Perspectives of Web Videos Using Folksonomies." *Association for the Advancement of Artificial Intelligence Fall Symposium Series Papers*, Menlo Park, CA, 2008 [retrievable online].

Lipton, Jacqueline D., "A Winning Solution for YouTube and UTube? Corresponding Trademarks and Domain Name Sharing." *Harvard Journal of Law & Technology* no. 21, 2008, pp. 23–34.

Losh, Elizabeth, "Government YouTube: Bureaucracy, Surveillance, and Legalism in State-Sanctioned Online Video Channels." Geert Lovink & Sabine Niederer, eds. *The Video Vortex Reader: Responses to YouTube* (Amsterdam: Institute of Network Cultures, 2008), pp. 111–123.

Lovink, Geert, "The Art of Watching Databases. Introduction to the Video Vortex Reader." Geert Lovink & Sabine Niederer, eds., *The Video Vortex Reader. Responses to YouTube* (Amsterdam: Institute of Network Cultures, 2008), pp. 9–12.

Lovink, Geert, and Sabine Niederer, eds. *The Video Vortex Reader: Responses to YouTube* (Amsterdam: Institute of Network Cultures, 2008) [retrievable online].

Luttrell, K., and N. Zite et al., "Myths and Misconceptions About Intrauterine Contraception on YouTube." *Contraception* no. 2, 2008, pp. 183–185.

MacKinnon, Catharine A., "Sexuality, Pornography, and Method: 'Pleasure Under Patriarchy.' " Nancy Tuana & Rosemarie Tong, eds., *Feminism and Philosophy: Essential Readings in Theory, Reinterpretation, and Application* (Boulder, CO: Westview Press, 1995), pp. 134–161.

Manovich, Lev, "Database as Symbolic Form." *Convergence* no. 2, 1999, pp. 80–85.

Manovich, Lev, *The Language of New Media* (Cambridge, MA: MIT Press, 2001).

Manovich, Lev, "The Practice of Everyday (Media) Life." Geert Lovink & Sabine Niederer, eds., *The Video Vortex Reader: Responses to YouTube* (Amsterdam: Institute of Network Cultures, 2008), pp. 33–43.

Manovich, Lev, "The Practice of Everyday (Media) Life: From Mass Consumption to Mass Cultural Production?" *Critical Inquiry* no. 2, 2009, pp. 319–331.

Marcus, Aaron, and Angel Perez. "m-YouTube Mobile UI: Video Selection Based on Social Influence." Julie A. Jacko, ed., *Lecture Notes in Computer Science* (Berlin: Springer, 2007), pp. 926–932.

Martin, C.D., "Blogger Ethics and YouTube Common Sense." *SIGCSE Bulletin* no. 4, 2007, pp. 11–12.

Marvin, Carolyn, *When Old Technologies Were New* (Oxford: Oxford University Press, 1988).

Mattelart, Armand, *Mass Media, Ideologies and the Revolutionary Movement* (Brighton: Harvester Press, 1980).

Matthews, Nicole, "Confessions to a New Public: Video Nation Shorts." *Media, Culture & Society* no. 3, 2007, pp. 435–448.

McFall, Liz, "The Culturalization of Work in the 'New Economy': An Historical View." Torben Elgaard Jensen & Ann Westenholz, eds., *Identity in the Age of the New Economy: Life in Temporary and Scattered Work Practices* (London: Sage, 2004), pp. 148–165.

McLuhan, Marshall, *Understanding Media; The Extensions of Man* (London: Abacus, 1973).

McMurria, John, "The YouTube Community." *FlowTV* no. 2, 2006 [retrievable online].

Merewether, Charles, ed., *The Archive* (Cambridge, MA: MIT Press, 2006).

Miller, Michael, *YouTube 4 You* (New York: Que Publishing, 2007).

Miller, Nod, and Rod Allen, *The Post-Broadcasting Age. New Technologies, New Communities* (Luton, England: Luton University Press, 1995).

Miller, Toby, "Can Natural Luddites Make Things Explode or Travel Faster? The New Humanities, Cultural Policy Studies, and Creative Industries." Jennifer Holt & Alisa Perren, eds., *Media Industries: History, Theory, and Method* (Malden, MA: Wiley/Blackwell, 2009, forthcoming.

Miller, Toby, " 'Step Away from the Croissant': Media Studies 3.0." David Hesmondhalgh & Jason Toynbee, eds., *The Media and Social Theory* (London: Routledge, 2008).

Miller, Toby, *The Well-Tempered Self: Citizenship, Culture, and the Postmodern Subject* (Baltimore: The Johns Hopkins University Press, 1993)

Miller, Toby et al., *Global Hollywood 2* (London: British Film Institute, 2005).

Milliken, Mary, and Kerri Gibson et al., "User-generated Online Video and the Atlantic Canadian Public Sphere: A YouTube Study." *Proceedings of the International Communication Association Annual Conference*, Montreal, QC, 22–26 May 2008 [retrievable online].

Molyneaux, Heather, and Susan O'Donnell et al., "Exploring the Gender Divide on YouTube: An Analysis of the Creation and Reception of Vlogs." *American Communication Journal* no. 2, 2008 [retrievable online].

Molyneaux, Heather, and Susan O'Donnell et al., "New Visual Media and Gender: A Content, Visual and Audience Analysis of YouTube Vlogs." *Proceedings of the International Communication Association Annual Conference*, Montreal, QC, 22–26 May 2008 [retrievable online].

Moore, Dinty W., "YouTube Can Be a Published Author." *Creative Nonfiction* no. 31, 2007, pp. 12–15.

Morse, Margaret, "From Medium to Metaphor." *American Art* no. 2, 2008, pp. 21–23.

Mosco, Vincent, *The Digital Sublime: Myth, Power, and Cyberspace* (Cambridge, MA: MIT Press, 2004).

Mullen, Megan, "The Fall and Rise of Cable Narrowcasting." *Convergence* no. 1, 2002, pp. 62-83.

Müller, Eggo, Formatted Spaces of Participation: Interactive Television and the Reshaping of the Relationship between Production and Consumption. Marianne van den Boomen et al., eds., *Digital Material – Tracing New Media in Everyday Life and Technology* (Amsterdam: Amsterdam University Press, 2009, forthcoming).

Nardi, Bonnie A., "Beyond Bandwidth: Dimensions of Connection in Interpersonal Communication." *Computer-Supported Cooperative Work* no. 14, 2005, pp. 28–45.

Negri, Antonio, *goodbye mister socialism* (Paris: Seuil, 2007).

Nelson, Theodor H., "A File Structure for the Complex, the Changing and the Indeterminate." *Proceedings of the 20th National Conference of the Association for Computing Machinery* (New York, 1965), pp. 84–100.

Nightingale, Virginia, "The Cameraphone and Online Image Sharing." *Continuum* no. 2, 2007, pp. 289–301.

Noam, Eli M., and Lorenzo Maria Pupillo, eds., *Peer-to-Peer Video: The Economic, Policy, and Culture of Today's New Mass Medium* (New York: Springer, 2008).

Noam, Eli M., "The Economics of User Generated Content and Peer-to-Peer: The Commons as the Enabler of Commerce." Noam and Lorenzo Maria Pupillo, eds., *Peer-to-Peer Video: The Economic, Policy, and Culture of Today's New Mass Medium* (New York: Springer, 2008), pp. 3–13.

O'Brien, Damian, "Copyright Challenges for User Generated Intermediaries: Viacom v YouTube and Google." Brian Fitzgerald et al., eds., *Copyright Law, Digital Content and the Internet in the Asia-Pacific* (Sydney: Sydney University Press, 2008), pp. 219–233.

O'Brien, Damien, and Brian Fitzgerald, "Digital Copyright Law in a YouTube World." *Internet Law Bulletin* 9, no. 6-7, 2006, pp. 71–74.

Pace, Stefano, "YouTube: An Opportunity for Consumer Narrative Analysis?" *Qualitative Market Research: An International Journal* no. 2, 2008, pp. 213–226.

Paolillo, John C., "Structure and Network in the YouTube Core." *Proceedings of the 41st Annual Hawaii International Conference on System Sciences*, 7 January 2008 [retrievable online].

Parks, Lisa, "Flexible Microcasting: Gender, Generation, and Television-Internet Convergence." Lynn Spigel & Jan Olsson, eds., *Television after TV* (Durham, NC: Duke University Press, 2004), pp. 133–162.

Pauwels, Luc, "A Private Visual Practice Going Public? Social Functions and Sociological Research Opportunities of Web-based Family Photography." *Visual Studies* no. 1, 2008, pp. 34–49.

Peraica, Ana, "Chauvinist and Elitist Obstacles Around YouTube and Porntube: A Case Study of Home-Made Porn Defended as 'Video Art.' " Geert Lovink & Sabine Niederer, eds., *The Video Vortex Reader: Responses to YouTube* (Amsterdam: Institute of Network Cultures, 2008), pp. 189–193.

Pickering, Andrew, *The Mangle of Practice. Time, Agency and Science* (Chicago: Chicago University Press, 1995).

Pink, Sarah, "More Visualising, More Methodologies: On Video, Reflexivity and Qualitative Research." *Sociological Review* no. 4, 2008, pp. 586–599.

Poster, Mark, *What's the Matter with the Internet* (Minneapolis: University of Minnesota Press, 2001).

Potts, Jason, and John Hartley et al., "Consumer Co-Creation and Situated Creativity." *Industry & Innovation* no. 5, 2008, pp. 459–474.

Potts, Jason et al., "Social Network Markets: A New Definition of the Creative Industries." *Journal of Cultural Economy* no. 32, 2008, pp. 167–185.

Rizzo, Teresa, "YouTube: the New Cinema of Attractions." *Scan: Journal of Media Arts Culture* no. 1, 2008 [retrievable online].

Ronell, Avital, *The Test Drive* (Bloomington: University of Illinois Press, 2005).

Rossiter, Ned, *Organized Networks: Media Theory, Creative Labour, New Institutions* (Rotterdam: Nai Publishers, 2006).

Salem, Arab, and Edna Reid et al., "Content Analysis of Jihadi Extremist Groups' Videos." *Proceedings of the Intelligence and Security Informatics*, IEEE International Conference on Intelligence and Security Informatics, San Diego, CA, 23–24 May 2006 [retrievable online].

Schäfer, Mirko Tobias, *Bastard Culture! User Participation and the Extension of Cultural Industries* (PhD diss., Utrecht University, 2008).

Schiller, Dan, *How to Think About Information* (Urbana: University of Illinois Pres, 2007).

Schiller, Herbert I., *Mass Communications and American Empire* (Boulder: Westview Press, 1992).

Schröter, Jens, *Das Netz und die Virtuelle Realität. Zur Selbstprogrammierung der Gesellschaft durch die universelle Maschine* (Bielefeld, Germany: Transcript, 2004).

Sconce, Jeffrey, *Haunted Media. Electronic Presence from Telegraphy to Television* (Durham, NC: Duke University Press, 2000).

Sedgwick, John, and Michael Pokorrny, eds., *An Economic History of Film* (New York, London: Routledge, 2005).

Seijdel, Jorinde, and Liesbeth Melis, eds., *Open 13: The Rise of Informal Media. How Phenomena Such as Weblogs, Videologs and -podcasts Change the Public Domain* (Rotterdam: Nai Publishers, 2008).

Seiter, Ellen, *Television and New Media Audiences* (New York: Oxford University Press, 1999).

Sekula, Allan, "Reading an Archive – Photography Between Labour and Capital." Liz Wells, ed., *The Photography Reader* (London: Routledge, 2003), pp. 109–130.

Silva, Paula Alexandra, and Alan Dix, "Usability – Not as we know it!" *Proceedings of HCI. The 21st British HCI Group Annual Conference*, University of Lancaster, UK, 3–7 September 2007 [retrievable online].

Simpson, B., "Identity Manipulation in Cyberspace as a Leisure Option: Play and the Exploration of Self." *Information & Communications Technology Law* no. 2, 2005, pp. 115–131.

Slabbert, Nicholas J., "Orwell's Ghost: How Teletechnology is Reshaping Civil Society." *CommLaw Conspectus: Journal of Communications Law and Policy* no. 2, 2008, pp. 349–359.

Smith, Linda, "Memex as an Image of Potentiality Revisited." James M. Nyce & Paul Kahn, eds., *From Memex to Hypertext: Vannevar Bush and the Mind's Machine* (Cambridge, MA: MIT Press, 1991), pp. 261–286.

Snelson, Chareen, "YouTube and Beyond: Integrating Web-Based Video into Online Education." *Proceedings of Society for Information Technology and Teacher Education International Conference*, 2008 [retrievable online].

Spigel, Lynn, "My TV Studies . . . Now Playing on a YouTube Site Near You." *Television and New Media* no. 1, 2009, pp. 149–153.

Spigel, Lynn, and Jan Olsson, eds., *Television after TV. Essays On A Medium In Transition* (Durham, London: Duke University Press, 2004).

Spurgeon, Christina, *Advertising and New Media* (London: Routledge, 2008).

Stiegler, Bernard, *La technique et le temps 3. Le temps du cinéma et la question du mal-être* (Paris: Galilée, 2001).

Suhr, Hiesun Cecilia, "The Role of Participatory Media in Aesthetic Taste Formation: How do Amateurs Critique Musical Performances and Videos on Youtube.com?" *International Journal of Technology, Knowledge and Society* no 2, 2008, pp. 213–222.

Tanner, Jeremy, ed., *The Sociology of Art. A Reader* (London, New York: Routledge, 2003).

Terranova, Tiziana, "Free Labour. Producing Culture for the Digital Economy." *Social Text* no. 2, 2000, pp. 33–58.

Trier, James, " 'Cool' Engagements With YouTube: Part 1." *Journal of Adolescent & Adult Literacy* no. 5, 2007, pp. 408–412

Ulges, Adrian, and Christian Schulze et al., "A System That Learns to Tag Videos by Watching Youtube." Julie A. Jacko, ed., *Lecture Notes in Computer Science* (Berlin: Springer, 2008), pp. 415–424.

Varnelis, Kazys, "Simultaneous Environments – Social Connection and Mew Media." *Receiver Magazine* no. 21, 2009 [retrievable online].

Virno, Paolo, *A Grammar of the Multitude* (New York: Semiotexte, 2004).

Waldfogel, Joel, "Lost in the Web: Does Web Distribution Stimulate or Depress Television Viewing?" *NBER Working Paper* no. W13497, October 2007 [retrievable online].

Wallsten, Kevin, " 'Yes We Can': How Online Viewership, Blog Discussion and Mainstream Media Coverage Produced a Viral Video Phenomenon." Presented at the Annual Meeting of the American Political Science Association, Boston, MA, 2008 [retrievable online].

Walters, Ben, "Cyberpicketing." *Film Quarterly* no. 3, 2008, pp. 66–67.

Walters, Ben, "The Online Stump." *Film Quarterly* no. 1, 2007, pp. 60–61.

Warmbrodt, John, and Hong Sheng et al., "Social Network Analysis of Video Bloggers' Community." *Proceedings of the 41st Annual Hawaii International Conference on System Sciences*, Waikoloa, HI, January 2008 [retrievable online].

Webb, Michael, "Music Analysis Down the (You) Tube? Exploring the Potential of Cross-media Listening for the Music Classroom." *British Journal of Music Education* no. 24, 2007, pp. 147–164.

Weber, Samuel, *Mass Mediauras. Form, Technics, Media* (Stanford: Stanford University Press, 1996).

Winograd, Morley, and Michael D. Hais, *Millennial Makeover: MySpace, YouTube and the Future of American Politics* (New York: Rutgers University Press, 2008).

Young, Jeffrey R., "An Anthropologist Explores the Culture of Video Blogging." *Chronicle of Higher Education* no. 36, 2007, p. A42.

Young, Jeffrey R., "YouTube Professors: Scholars as Online Video Stars." *Chronicle of Higher Education* no. 20, 2008, p. 19.

Zink, Michael, and Kyoungwon Suh et al., "Watch Global, Cache Local: YouTube Network Traffic at a Campus Network – Measurements and Implications." *Proceedings of the SPIE, Vol. 6818, Multimedia Computing and Networking*, 2008 [retrievable online].

Contributors

Mark Andrejevic is an associate professor at the University of Iowa's Department of Communication Studies. He is also a postdoctoral research fellow at the University of Queensland's Centre for Critical and Cultural Studies. He is the author of *iSpy: Surveillance and Power in the Digital Era* (2007) and *Reality TV: The Work of Being Watched* (2003), as well as numerous articles and book chapters on surveillance and digital media.

Joost Broeren has studied Theater, Film and Television Studies, and Media Studies at Utrecht University. He was the founding editor of the student journal *BLIK* and regularly contributes as a film journalist and editor to *Filmkrant*—www.filmkrant.nl—the biggest film publication in the Netherlands. Broeren's work focuses on the recurrence of old media in new media as well as on issues of media translation.

Jean Burgess is a research fellow at the Australian Research Council Centre of Excellence for Creative Industries & Innovation, Queensland University of Technology. She has published several journal articles and book chapters in the areas of cultural studies and Internet research, focusing particularly on user-created content. She is the author (with Joshua Green) of *YouTube: Online Video and Participatory Culture* (2009), and Review Editor of the *International Journal of Cultural Studies*.

Christian Christensen is an associate professor of Media and Communication Studies at Karlstad University in Sweden. He is the editor of a forthcoming volume entitled *Human IT: Technology in Social Context* and guest editor of a special issue of *Studies in Documentary Film* (2009) examining documentary film after 9/11. Christensen has published in journals such as the *International Journal of Press/Politics; Global Media and Communication; Media, War & Conflict; Studies in Documentary Film*; and the *British Journalism Review*.

Thomas Elsaesser is an emeritus professor, Department of Media & Culture at the University of Amsterdam, and since 2005 a visiting professor at Yale University. A former research fellow at UC Berkeley, IFK

Vienna, Sackler Institute Tel Aviv, Stockholm University and Churchill College, Cambridge, his most recent books include *Studying Contemporary American Film* (2002, with Warren Buckland); *European Cinema: Face to Face with Hollywood* (2005); *Terror und Trauma* (2007, English edition 2010); *Filmtheorie: zur Einführung* (2007, with Malte Hagener; English edition 2009) and *Hollywood heute* (2009).

Mary Erickson is a PhD candidate at the School of Journalism and Communication, University of Oregon. She is the co-editor (with Janet Wasko) of *Cross-Border Cultural Production: Economic Runaway or Globalization?* (2008). Erickson has also published articles in *The Business of Entertainment: Movies* and is currently working on her dissertation, which focuses on the commercialization of independent film.

Joëlle Farchy is a professor of Information and Communication Sciences at the Centre d'économie de la Sorbonne, University of Paris 1, Panthéon Sorbonne. She has published numerous books and articles on the economics of the audiovisual, culture, and intellectual property and the Internet.

Giovanna Fossati is curator at the Nederlands Filmmuseum in Amsterdam. She has published several articles on colour in early film, digital film restoration and curated an educational website on film restoration (http://filmmuseum.newstream.nl/filmrestauratie/index.html). Her most recent book is *From Grain to Pixel. The Archival Life of Film in Transition* (2009).

Andrei Gornykh is a professor at the Faculty of Social Sciences, European Humanities University in Vilnius, Lithuania. He is the author of *Formalism: From the Structure to the Text and Beyond* (2002) as well as articles on modern visual culture, critical theory and psychoanalysis (in Russian and English). Gornykh has also created a number of media products such as the CD-ROM *Lines of Difference in the History of Art* (2006), the DVD-ROM *History, Society, Cinema* (2008) and various educational films for television.

Joshua Green is a postdoctoral research fellow in the Comparative Media Studies Program at MIT and a researcher for the Convergence Culture Consortium. He has published articles and book chapters on new forms of television, online video and participatory culture. He is the author (with Jean Burgess) of *YouTube: Online Video and Participatory Culture* (2009).

Richard Grusin is a professor of English at Wayne State University. He has published numerous essays and articles and three books. With Jay David Bolter he co-authored *Remediation: Understanding New Media* (MIT, 1999), one of the first works to set forth a general theory of new media. Grusin has just completed a fourth book, *Premediation: Affect and Mediality after 9/11* (forthcoming).

Vinzenz Hediger is a professor of Film and Media Studies at Ruhr University Bochum. He is the author of numerous articles, anthologies and books. Forthcoming in 2010 is his new book, *Nostalgia for the Coming Attraction. American Movie Trailers and the Culture of Film Consumption* (New York: Columbia University Press).

Gunnar Iversen is a professor of Film Studies at the Department of Art and Media Studies, Norwegian University of Science and Technology, in Trondheim. He has published a number of books and articles on Norwegian film history, documentaries, early cinema, television aesthetics and visual culture.

Frank Kessler is a professor of Media History at Utrecht University. He is a former president of DOMITOR, an international association dedicated to the study of early cinema and a co-founder and co-editor of *KINtop. Jahrbuch zur Erforschung des frühen Films.* He has published widely on various issues of film history and film theory. Together with Nanna Verhoeff, he edited *Networks of Entertainment. Early Film Distribution 1895–1915* (2007).

Patricia G. Lange is an anthropologist conducting research at the Institute for Multimedia Media Literacy, University of Southern California. She has published in a variety of edited volumes, such as *The Video Vortex Reader: Responses to YouTube* (2008) and journals including

Discourse Studies, The Scholar & Feminist Online and *The Journal of Computer-Mediated Communication.* As a scholar of online media, she has been invited to the International Film Festival, Rotterdam, as well as Pixelodeon, the first independent video-blogging festival, held at the American Film Institute.

Trond Lundemo is associate professor at the Department of Cinema Studies at Stockholm University. He has published on questions of technology, intermediality and the theory of the archive in various journals and anthologies and edited two volumes of theoretical writings on cinema's relations to the other arts. He has also been a visiting professor at Seijo University of Tokyo on several occasions.

Paul McDonald is a professor of Film and Television at the University of Portsmouth, UK. He is the author of *The Star System: Hollywood's Production of Popular Identities* (2000) and *Video and DVD Industries* (2007). Recently, he co-edited *The Contemporary Hollywood Film Industry* (2008). McDonald is currently completing a study of stardom in modern Hollywood and co-editing the British Film Institute's International Screen Industries series.

Toby Miller is a professor and the Chair of Media & Cultural Studies at the University of California, Riverside. He is the author and editor of over 30 books and hundreds of journal articles and book chapters. He edits the journals *Television & New Media* and *Social Identities* and his latest book is *Makeover Nation: The United States of Reinvention* (2008).

Eggo Müller is an associate professor of Film and Television at the Department of Media and Culture Studies, Utrecht University. He has published extensively on television entertainment and the transformation of television in the context of commercialization, globalization and digitalization, using dating shows as examples. His latest book is *Not Only Entertainment. Studies on the Pragmatics and Aesthetics of Popular Television* (2009).

Kathrin Peters is an art historian and cultural scientist. Currently, she teaches European Media Studies at the University of Potsdam. Peters is the editor of a number of German anthologies and has published widely on the aesthetics of photography, contemporary art, and gender and media studies.

Rick Prelinger's collection of 60,000 advertising, educational, industrial and amateur films was acquired by the Library of Congress in 2002, 20 years after it was established. Prelinger has partnered with the Internet Archive to make 2,500 films from Prelinger Archives available online for free viewing, downloading and reuse, and is co-founder of the Prelinger Library (www.prelingerlibrary.org), an appropriation-friendly private research library in San Francisco.

Mirko Tobias Schäfer is an assistant professor at the Department for Media and Culture Studies, University of Utrecht. Schäfer has organized and co-curated [d]vision - Vienna Festival for Digital Culture and has written a dissertation on participatory culture. Schäfer runs the site www.mtschaefer.net and has published on modified electronic consumer goods, software development and the sociopolitical debates concerning information and communication technology.

Jens Schröter is a professor of the Theory and Practice of Multimedia Systems at the University of Siegen. For assignments and recent publications, see www.multimediale-systeme.de and www.theorie-der-medien.de. Schröter's research interests are the history and theory of digital media, the history and theory of photography, intermediality, and the history of science in relation to media history, Marxism and media theory.

Andrea Seier is a guest professor for Film Studies at the Department for Media Studies, Ruhr University Bochum. From 2007 to 2009 she was a guest professor at the Department of Theatre, Film and Media Studies, University of Vienna. She has published on film and television, gender and media theory. Her current research project discusses developments of reality television and the relationships between technologies of the self and those of media.

Pelle Snickars is an associate professor and Head of Research at the Swedish National Library. He is the editor of numerous books on Swedish media history, for example *1897: Mediehistorier om Stockholmsutställningen* (2005, Media Histories around the Stockholm Exhibition), *Berättande i olika medier* (2007, Narrative in Different Media) and *Mediernas kulturhistoria* (2008, A Cultural History of Media). Internationally, Snickars has published extensively on both early cinema and new media.

Markus Stauff is an associate professor and teaches Media Studies at the University Amsterdam. His main research interests are television and digital media, media and governmentality, and media sports. Stauff recently co-edited the German-language anthology *Mediensport. Strategien der Grenzziehung* (2009, Media Sports – Strategies of Containment).

Bernard Stiegler is a professor, head of the Department of Cultural Development at Centre Pompidou in Paris and co-founder of the political group Ars Industrialis. He is the author of numerous books, among them *Technics and Time, 1: The Fault of Epimetheus* (1998), *Echographies of Television: Filmed Interviews* (2002, with Jacques Derrida) and *Technics and Time, 2: Disorientation* (2008). His latest book is *Pour en finir avec la mécroissance – Quelques réflexions d'Ars Industrialis* (2009, with Alain Giffard & Christian Faure).

Bjørn Sørenssen is a professor of Film and Media at the Department of Art and Media Studies, Norwegian University of Science and Technology (NTNU) in Trondheim. His main research interests are documentary film and new media technology. He has published on these and other film-related subjects in numerous international journals and anthologies. He has also published books in Norwegian, most recently *Å fange virkeligheten. Dokumentarfilmens århundre* (2007, Catching Reality: A Century of Documentary).

William Uricchio is a professor and the director of Comparative Media Studies at the Massachusetts Institute of Technology and a professor of Comparative Media History at Utrecht University. Uricchio works on old media—when they were new. His most recent books include *Media Cultures* (2006) and *We Europeans? Media, Representations, Identities* (2008).

Patrick Vonderau is an assistant professor at the Department for Media Studies, Ruhr University Bochum. He has published widely on media history and theory. His most recent book publications include a case study on the cultural history of film distribution, *Bilder vom Norden. Schwedisch-deutsche Filmbeziehungen, 1914–1939* (Marburg, 2008), an anthology on industrial films, *Films that Work. Industrial Film and the Productivity of Media* (Amsterdam: Amsterdam University Press, 2009, with Vinzenz Hediger) and a book on the aesthetics of production (forthcoming 2010).

Malin Wahlberg is a research fellow at the Department of Cinema Studies, Stockholm University. She is the author of *Documentary Time. Film and Phenomenology* (2008), and has published several articles on related issues in the field of classical film theory, amateur film, experimental film, video, and new media. Recently Wahlberg co-edited an anthology on Swedish television, *TV pioneers and Free Filmmakers* (2008).

Janet Wasko is the Knight Chair for Communication Research at the University of Oregon. She is the author of *Hollywood in the Information Age: Beyond the Silver Screen* (1994), *Understanding Disney: The Manufacture of Fantasy* (2001) and *How Hollywood Works* (2003). She has edited a number of books on the political economy of communication and democratic media, as for example *Dazzled by Disney?* (2001) and *A Companion to Television* (2005). Recently she co-edited (together with Paul McDonald) *The Contemporary Hollywood Film Industry* (2008).

List of Illustrations

Index

Index of Names

Index of Subjects

Index of Films, Blogs, Clips